THIRD EDITION

CLINICAL SUPERVISION in the Helping Professions

A PRACTICAL GUIDE

Gerald Corey
Robert Haynes
Patrice Moulton
Michelle Muratori

AMERICAN COUNSELING
ASSOCIATION

6101 Stevenson Avenue, Suite 600
Alexandria, VA 22304
www.counseling.org

THIRD EDITION
CLINICAL SUPERVISION
in the
Helping Professions

AMERICAN COUNSELING ASSOCIATION
6101 Stevenson Avenue, Suite 600, Alexandria, VA 22304

ASSOCIATE PUBLISHER
Carolyn C. Baker

DIGITAL AND PRINT DEVELOPMENT EDITOR
Nancy Driver

SENIOR PRODUCTION MANAGER
Bonny E. Gaston

COPY EDITOR
Kay Mikel

Text and cover design by Bonny E. Gaston.

LIBRARY OF CONGRESS CATALOGING-IN-PUBLICATION DATA
Names: Corey, Gerald, author.
Title: Clinical supervision in the helping professions : a practical guide / Gerald Corey,
    California State University, Fullerton, Robert Haynes, Borderline Productions, Patrice
    Moulton, Northwestern State University, Natchitoches, Louisiana, Michelle Muratori,
    Johns Hopkins University.
Description: Third edition. | Alexandria, VA : American Counseling Association, [2021] |
    Includes bibliographical references and index. |
Identifiers: LCCN 2020016109 | ISBN 9781556204036 (paperback)
Subjects: LCSH: Clinical psychologists—Supervision of. | Counselors—Supervision of. |
    Psychotherapists—Supervision of. | Health services administration.
Classification: LCC RC480.5 .C58 2021 | DDC 616.89/14—dc23
LC record available at https://lccn.loc.gov/2020016109

DEDICATION

To our supervisees and students,
who have taught us many lessons
about how to supervise.

CONTENTS

PREFACE

The field of supervision has rapidly emerged as a specialty area in the helping professions. In the past, supervisors often learned how to supervise based on their own, and often limited, experiences when they were supervisees. Few professional standards specifically addressed supervision practices, and separate courses in supervision were rare. Today the trend is toward including a course in supervision in graduate programs in the helping professions, especially in doctoral programs. If there is not a separate course, topics of supervision are frequently incorporated into one or more courses. Higher education accreditation boards, such as CACREP, provide specific requirements for supervision of entry-level professional practice in practicum and internship. They also outline required supervisor qualifications. In addition, state licensing and certification boards are increasingly requiring formal training in supervision as a part of the licensing and certification process. To practice as a supervisor, it is now mandatory to complete coursework or to take continuing education workshops in supervision and show evidence of competence not only in skills and techniques but also in supervisory processes and procedures.

This book is a practical guide to becoming a supervisor that is informative, interesting, personal, encouraging, and challenging. We address topics essential to becoming an effective supervisor, emphasizing the knowledge and skills new supervisors need to supervise others in a variety of settings. We believe one of the best ways to learn how to supervise is for new supervisors to reflect on what they have learned from their own supervision.

The information provided and our suggestions for becoming a supervisor are based on both the supervision literature and our collective professional experience in supervision. Throughout this book we discuss the ethics and professional codes and the relevant literature, but we also state our own position on these topics and offer commentary on how we might approach various cases. Each of us presents a detailed personal perspective on our journey to becoming a supervisor (see Chapter 1), and Personal Perspectives are featured throughout the chapters to enhance many of the topics. We balance theory with personal beliefs, attitudes, and relevant experiences regarding supervision. A unique feature of this book, Voices From the Field, provides a glimpse into the experiences of other practicing supervisors on key issues in the practice of supervision. Forty-nine separate essays provide diverse perspectives on a wide range of topics in clinical supervision.

We do not present a single best approach to supervisory practice. Instead, we encourage reflective practice and ask supervisors and supervisees to integrate their own thoughts and experiences with our presentation of the material in each chapter. Most of all, we recommend that readers continually reflect on what supervision has been like for them at various stages of their professional development. It is important to have both a solid foundation of the theories and methods of supervision and an understanding of what has been learned from their own experiences as a supervisee and as a supervisor.

This book has a practical emphasis, including tips for practical application, case examples, sample forms, interactive questions, and activities that can be done in small groups. It is designed as a practical guide for new and practicing supervisors, but it can also be a primary or supplementary text in a variety of doctoral and master's-level courses.

Clinical Supervision in the Helping Professions: A Practical Guide (Third Edition) is appropriate for use in counselor education, counseling psychology, clinical psychology, marriage and family therapy, human services, social work, school counseling, mental health counseling, rehabilitation counseling, addiction counseling, psychiatric nursing, and other mental health specializations. It is an ideal resource for practicum, fieldwork, and internship seminars in these disciplines and for advanced undergraduate courses in human services and social work programs. In addition, this book can be used as a resource for both prelicensed professionals and practicing supervisors.

Getting the Most From This Book

This book is different from traditional textbooks in supervision; it is an interactive tool that will assist you in formulating your own perspective on supervisory practice. The many questions and exercises interspersed throughout the text are intended to stimulate you to become an active learner. If you take the time to think about the chapter focus questions and do the suggested activities at the end of each chapter, your learning will be more meaningful and personal. Supervision is not a topic that can be mastered solely by reading about theory and research. Supervision is best learned by integrating the theoretical material with your own supervision experiences.

Overview of the Book

Each chapter focuses on a specific aspect or dimension of supervision that is vital to effective supervision. Here is what you can expect in each chapter:

- Chapter 1 lays the groundwork by defining supervision and discussing the goals and objectives of supervision. In line with the personal focus of the book, each author offers her or his unique perspective on supervision and highlights some of the experiences that have shaped their views.
- Describing the multiplicity of roles that supervisors may need to adopt, ranging from teacher and coach to administrator and empowerer, Chapter 2 focuses on the supervisor's roles and responsibilities. The chapter also explores how supervisees can get the most from their supervision and fieldwork experiences.
- The quality of the supervisory relationship is of paramount importance, and Chapter 3 focuses on factors, issues, and characteristics of supervisors and supervisees that facilitate or hinder the supervision process. Conflict in the relationship and other challenging situations are addressed as well.
- Chapter 4 describes several current models of supervision. Therapeutic approaches as well as models developed specifically for clinical supervision such as developmental and integrative approaches are examined.
- Chapter 5 focuses on the practical methods used in supervision and explains how various methods can be implemented in an integrated supervision model.
- Chapter 6 addresses the importance of developing multicultural competence as a supervisor as well as preparing trainees to be competent in serving diverse client

populations. Supervisors have a responsibility to model social advocacy for their trainees and to encourage trainees to carry out this important function in their work with clients.

- Ethical issues and multiple relationships are the focus of Chapter 7. This discussion addresses what every supervisor needs to know about ethical supervisory practice and teaching supervisees to practice ethically. Important issues dealing with impairment and incompetence and recognizing ethical violations are also discussed.
- Chapter 8 is devoted to legal and risk management issues. Given today's litigious climate, supervisors need to have a basic understanding of the legal issues they might encounter. This legal primer includes an extensive list of risk management strategies relative to supervision.
- Most trainees are ill equipped to handle crisis incidents. Chapter 9 explores the responsibilities of supervisors in guiding supervisees through crisis situations. Preparing supervisees to competently navigate through client crises and the special role supervisors may fulfill to support supervisees in the aftermath of crises are important components of crisis management.
- Chapter 10 explores evaluation, a critical component of ethical supervision that sets supervision apart from counseling and psychotherapy. The evaluation process tends to cause both supervisees and supervisors a great deal of anxiety. Understanding the process and methods of evaluation will help supervisors approach this task with a clearly defined plan and, consequently, with less anxiety.
- Chapter 11 paints a picture of the effective supervisor and encourages you to continue your journey down the path toward your own style of supervision.

The Suggested Activities at the end of each chapter are designed to augment your professional development. These activities will aid you in thinking about and reflecting on what you have just read. For students and supervisees, this can be a way to bring more thought to your supervision sessions. For supervisors, this may give you some ideas for topics to discuss with supervisees. These activities can be adapted for individual work or group discussion.

What's New in the Third Edition of
Clinical Supervision in the Helping Professions: A Practical Guide

The Third Edition has been reviewed and updated with current research, concepts, and practice in clinical supervision. The following chapter-by-chapter list highlights material that has been added, updated, expanded, and revised for this new edition.

Overall Changes

- Voices From the Field features 45 contributors who share their perspectives on key topics in each chapter. These contributors represent a broad cross-section of clinicians with a range of professional experience, and many of them are considered leading experts in their specialty field.
- All citations have been reviewed and updated to provide the most current literature and reasearch.
- Recent disasters, crises, and social changes in the United States have altered the social landscape, affecting clients, supervisees, and the practice of supervision. The text in this edition reflects the changing roles of those in the helping professions.
- The relevant codes and regulations pertaining to supervision have been updated.
- The role of technology in supervision (and in counseling more generally) has expanded in recent years, and the global coronavirus pandemic is forcing an even

more expansive use of online supervision methods. The pros and cons and a cautionary tale regarding distance counseling and supervision are explored throughout the book.

Chapter 1: Introduction to Supervision

- The authors' Personal Perspectives are updated to reflect their current professional activities.
- Key goals of supervision are defined and discussed.
- Increased attention is given to the differences between administrative and clinical supervision.

Chapter 2: Roles and Responsibilites of Supervisors

- New supervisor roles include the supervisor as role model, crisis manager, and technology consultant. These roles are identified and discussed in detail.
- A contributor captures the essence of how supervisors often serve in the role of a mentor.
- The ethical and professional standards regarding roles and responsibilities of a supervisor have been updated.
- A completely revised Supervision Contract is included in Appendix 2A.

Chapter 3: The Supervisory Relationship

- Recent research indicating that a functional supervisory relationship is essential to facilitating supervisee self-disclosure is provided.
- New information is provided to aid supervisors in managing their countertransference with supervisees.
- Multicultural diversity competence is presented as an ethical imperative in supervision.
- A new Voices From the Field offers suggestions for ways a supervisor can manage parallel process with a supervisee.
- An updated discussion of "ethical bracketing" is presented as a means for supervisees to become aware of value conflicts they may have with clients.
- A new Voices From the Field reveals the doubts and fears that most novice supervisees experience.

Chapter 4: Models of Supervision

- Discussion of second-generation models of supervision and neuro-informed constructs in supervision have been added.
- A new Voices From the Field describes neuro-informed clinical supervision.
- Psychotherapy-based supervision models have been revised.
- A new section describes the common factors discrimination model.
- A comprehensive description of the new team-based supervision model developed by one of the authors provides a practical approach that enriches supervisees' learning.

Chapter 5: Methods of Supervision

- An updated and expanded treatment of individual supervision, triadic supervision, and group supervision is provided.
- Eight contributors share their expertise in Voices From the Field on various aspects of methods of supervision.
- A revised discussion of peer supervision groups highlights the value of this approach to supervision.
- New discussions on the cotherapy method in supervision and using technology in supervision are featured.

- Contributors address training counselors to provide online supervision, ethical considerations for online supervision, and teaching supervision online.
- A new section describes developing communication skills.
- A discussion of deliberate practice for clinical supervision and training has been added.

Chapter 6: Becoming a Multiculturally Competent Supervisor

- Nine contributors share their expertise in Voices From the Field.
- The *Multicultural and Social Justice Counseling Competencies* are described.
- A new section is devoted to embracing multiple identities and intersectionality in supervision.
- Several new Voices From the Field shed light on what is involved in becoming a multiculturally skilled supervisor, and a new section highlights the implications of failing to practice multicultural supervision.
- Practicing multicultural counseling and supervision competently is given increased attention.
- Ethics codes and standards regarding multicultural supervision have been revised.
- The concept of broaching behavior in clinical supervision is explained, and a contributor shares her perspective on training counselors and supervisors to broach effectively.
- Multicultural and social justice competencies are provided as a guide to supervisory practice.
- The concept of modeling social advocacy is explained, and a clinical supervisor shares her thoughts on a social justice and advocacy approach to clinical supervision.
- Practicing affirmative supervision is defined and explained.
- A new section describes supervising international trainees in counselor education programs, and another new section supports trainees serving clients with disabilities.
- The discussion of spirituality as a facet of multicultural supervision has been revised and expanded, and contributors share their views on addressing spirituality and religion in supervisory relationships.
- Using technology effectively to create inclusion is addressed.

Chapter 7: Ethical Issues and Multiple Relationships in Supervision

- The discussion of how ethical standards provide a framework for understanding multiple roles and relationships has been updated.
- Revised sections deal with problematic behavioral characteristics of trainees, monitoring trainee competence, and professional competence problems of supervisees.
- A revised and expanded discussion of the codes of ethics and supervisors' ethical responsibilities deals with supervisee incompetence and reasons for dismissal of students from a training program.
- A counselor educator discusses a host of issues in the remediation in clinical supervisees.
- The section on managing multiple roles and relationships in the supervisory process has been revised and expanded.
- A counselor educator shares her views on managing boundaries in supervision.
- A new section on managing boundaries in social media explores the ethical implications for clinical supervision, and a contributor explains how she establishes boundaries with clients using technology.
- The discussion on sexual intimacies in the supervisory relationship has been updated.

Chapter 8: Legal and Risk Management Issues in Supervision

- Three counselor educators and attorneys reviewed this chapter and contributed Voices From the Field on various aspects of legal and risk management.

- Risk management strategies in clinical supervision are presented, including designing a supervision contract to limit legal liability.
- A new section explains the unique challenges supervisors face when working with school counselor interns.
- Revised and updated ethical standards regarding legal issues are presented.
- A contributor explains the complications and the pitfalls of dealing with child custody cases in supervision.
- A contributor offers advice for supervisees on measures to take to avoid legal problems and problems in applying for licensure.
- There is a new discussion on disciplinary supervision.
- A new section highlights ethical standards and legal perspectives when counseling minors.
- Expanded coverage has been devoted to supervising trainees in school counseling.

Chapter 9: Crisis Management in Supervision

- Revised ethics codes and standards for managing crisis situations in supervision are described.
- Updated research findings are presented on the high levels of stress and burnout for crisis workers.
- The role of supervisors in helping supervisees manage complex situations during crises is expanded, and information about emergency preparedness has been added.
- A new section on the CARE model of crisis-based clinical supervision brings a practical perspective to clinical supervision.
- A contributor shares his thoughts on the challenges of coping with a pandemic, such as COVID-19.
- A section has been added on mass trauma counseling guidelines, and there is a new section on psychological first aid.
- Updated information is given on suicide and suicide attempts.
- Five new contributors of Voices From the Field address various aspects of crisis management.
- The need to care for the caregiver and an emphasis on self-care for supervisors and supervisees is expanded.

Chapter 10: Evaluation in Supervision

- Increased emphasis is given to the importance of evidence-based supervision techniques.
- Revised ethics codes and standards regarding evaluation in supervision are presented.
- A section on gatekeeping and evaluation has been added, and a contributor shares her experience of gatekeeping in supervision.
- A contributor explores the balance between evaluative aspects of supervision and creating a safe climate conducive to effective supervision.
- A new section deals with diversity and evaluation.
- A new section describes team feedback as a way for supervisees to develop skills.

Chapter 11: Becoming an Effective Supervisor

- Four new contributors add their Voices From the Field regarding effective supervisors.
- Increased emphasis is given to the supervisory relationship as being central in effective supervision.
- There is a revised and expanded discussion of the characteristics of an effective supervisor.

Sharing our personal perspectives and hearing directly from practicing supervisors and counselor educators brings the practice of clinical supervision to life. We hope this book empowers you to find your own voice and inspires you to seek your own style as a supervisor. In Voices From the Field, supervisors from different professional backgrounds and with varying levels of experience candidly describe some of the challenges they have faced as well as the joys of supervising. The 45 contributors, most of whom are new to this Third Edition, add rich diversity to our discussions. If this book engages you in a personal as well as an academic way, and if it raises questions for your reflection, our purpose will have been achieved.

ACKNOWLEDGMENTS

We would like to thank the 45 contributors who shared their expertise in Voices From the Field. These contributors added practical advice and provided readers with ideas for reflection. Thanks goes to Bonny Gaston for her creative work on the interior design and the cover of this book. We want to express our gratitude to Carolyn Baker, associate publisher at ACA, for her dedication and support for this project. Carolyn reviewed the entire manuscript and provided feedback that was incorporated in the final manuscript. We very much appreciate the talents of our manuscript editor, Kay Mikel, who made sure this book was reader-friendly. It has been delightful working with both Carolyn and Kay on the third edition of this book.

ABOUT THE AUTHORS

GERALD COREY, EdD, ABPP, is professor emeritus of Human Services and Counseling at California State University at Fullerton. He received his doctorate in counseling from the University of Southern California. He was awarded an honorary doctorate in Humane Letters in 1992 from National Louis University. He is a Diplomate in Counseling Psychology, American Board of Professional Psychology; a licensed psychologist in California; and a National Certified Counselor. He is a Fellow of the American Psychological Association (Division 17, Counseling Psychology; and Division 49, Group Psychotherapy); a Fellow of the American Counseling Association; and a Fellow of the Association for Specialists in Group Work. He also holds memberships in the American Group Psychotherapy Association, the Association for Counselor Education and Supervision; and the Western Association of Counselor Education and Supervision. He received the Lifetime Achievement Award from the American Mental Health Counselors Association in 2011, the Eminent Career Award from ASGW in 2001, and the Outstanding Professor of the Year Award from California State University at Fullerton in 1991. He is the author or coauthor of 16 textbooks in counseling currently in print, along with more than 70 journal articles and numerous book chapters. His book, *Theory and Practice of Counseling and Psychotherapy*, has been translated into Arabic, Indonesian, Portuguese, Turkish, Korean, and Chinese. *Theory and Practice of Group Counseling* has been translated into Korean, Chinese, Spanish, and Russian. *Issues and Ethics in the Helping Professions* has been translated into Korean, Japanese, and Chinese. With his colleagues, he has conducted workshops in the United States, Germany, Ireland, Belgium, Scotland, Mexico, Canada, China, and Korea—with a special focus on training in group counseling.

The following seven books are published by the American Counseling Association:

- *Clinical Supervision in the Helping Professions: A Practical Guide,* Third Edition (2021, with Robert Haynes, Patrice Moulton, and Michelle Muratori)
- *Personal Reflections on Counseling* (2020)
- *The Art of Integrative Counseling,* Fourth Edition (2019)
- *Counselor Self-Care* (2018, with Michelle Muratori, Jude T. Austin, and Julius A. Austin II)
- *ACA Ethical Standards Casebook,* Seventh Edition (2015, with Barbara Herlihy)
- *Boundary Issues in Counseling: Multiple Roles and Relationships,* Third Edition (2015, with Barbara Herlihy)
- *Creating Your Professional Path: Lessons from My Journey* (2010)

Recent publications by Gerald Corey and colleagues with Cengage Learning include:

- *Theory and Practice of Counseling and Psychotherapy,* Enhanced Tenth Edition (2021)
- *Becoming a Helper,* Seventh Edition (2021, with Marianne Schneider Corey)
- *Issues and Ethics in the Helping Professions,* Tenth Edition (2019, with Marianne Schneider Corey and Cindy Corey)
- *Groups: Process and Practice,* Tenth Edition (2018, with Marianne Schneider Corey and Cindy Corey)
- *I Never Knew I Had a Choice,* Eleventh Edition (2018, with Marianne Schneider Corey and Michelle Muratori)
- *Theory and Practice of Group Counseling,* Ninth Edition (and *Student Manual*) (2016)
- *Group Techniques,* Fourth Edition (2015, with Marianne Schneider Corey, Patrick Callanan, and J. Michael Russell)
- *Case Approach to Counseling and Psychotherapy,* Eighth Edition (2013)

Gerald Corey and his colleagues have made several educational DVD programs on various aspects of counseling practice, all of which are available through Cengage Learning: (1) video to accompany *Counseling Gwen From Various Perspectives* (2021); (2) group video to accompany *Theory and Practice of Group Counseling* (2019); (3) *Ethics in Action* (2015); (4) *Groups in Action: Evolution and Challenges DVD and Workbook* (2014, with Marianne Schneider Corey and Robert Haynes); and (5) DVD for *Theory and Practice of Counseling and Psychotherapy: The Case of Stan and Lecturettes* (2013).

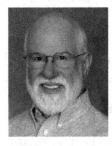 **ROBERT HAYNES, PhD,** is a clinical psychologist, author, and producer of psychology video programs for Borderline Productions. Bob received his doctorate in clinical psychology from Fuller Graduate School of Psychology and is a member of the American Counseling Association and the Association for Counselor Education and Supervision. He has been actively involved in professional psychology through private practice as well as consulting, leading workshops, and writing on a variety of topics. In addition, Bob taught psychology, criminology, team building, and management courses at the University of California at Santa Barbara, California Polytechnic State University, San Luis Obispo, and California State University, Sacramento. He also served as chair of Site Visiting Teams for the Committee on Accreditation of the American Psychological Association. Bob retired after 27 years as training director of the accredited clinical psychology internship program at Atascadero State Hospital in California.

Bob served for 35 years in the capacity of both administrative and clinical supervisor in a variety of academic and clinical settings. He also provided consultation and training in clinical supervision, criminology, disaster mental health, psychotherapy methods, team building, conflict resolution, stress management and burnout, suicide assessment and intervention, and theoretical approaches in psychotherapy.

Bob's publications include the following:

- *Clinical Supervision in the Helping Professions: A Practical Guide,* Third Edition (2021, with Gerald Corey, Patrice Moulton, and Michelle Muratori)
- *Coping Skills for a Stressful World: A Workbook for Counselors and Clients.* (2020, with Michelle Muratori). American Counseling Association
- *Managing Crisis: Personally and Professionally.* (2021, Chapter 14 with Marianne Schneider Corey and Gerald Corey). *Becoming a Helper,* Eighth Edition. Cengage Learning
- *Take Control of Life's Crises Today! A Practical Guide.* (2014). Aventine Press

Bob has produced a number of psychology training videos in collaboration with Marianne Schneider Corey and Gerald Corey, including *Groups in Action: Evolution and Challenges DVD and Workbook* (2014); *Ethics in Action* (2015); and *The Art of Integrative Counseling* (2001).

PATRICE MOULTON, PhD, serves as full professor of psychology at Northwestern State University in the master's program for clinical psychology. She lives in Natchitoches, Louisiana, with husband Michael Moulton, a graduate professor in sports administration. Their son, Bryce, is completing his sophomore year at Tulane University. She has worked as an educator, administrator, practitioner, supervisor, and consultant for over 30 years.

Patrice is the author of multiple self-help and higher education textbooks and journal articles on topics including addiction counseling, supervision, online teaching, and crisis counseling. Recent publications include:

- *Clinical Supervision in the Helping Professions: A Practical Guide,* Third Edition (2021, with Gerald Corey, Robert Haynes, and Michelle Muratori)
- *Helping Others.* (2019). Ekta Publishing.
- The Status of Mental Health in Nepal. *ICMS Journal, 1,* 12–15. (2018).
- Unspoken, Unanswered, Unaddressed: Issues of Young Women in Nepal. *ICMS Journal, 1,* 1–4. (2018, with B. Gurung).
- Distress. *Kathmandu Post.* (2018).
- How Are We Doing? Making Service-Learning Assessment Simple. *Journal of Service-Learning in Higher Education, 2,* 37–46. (2013, with Michael Moulton).
- *This Is Not a Fire Drill: Crisis Intervention and Prevention on College Campuses.* (2011, with R. A. Myer and R. K. James). John Wiley & Sons.
- How to Tackle an Excessive Force Complaint. *National Journal of Criminal Justice,* 7(1), 13–18. (2011, with J. Logan, R. Myer, and R. James).
- Conflict Negotiation: Is Control the Goal? *NSU National Journal of Criminal Justice,* 5(6), 15–16. (2010, with R. Myer and D. James).
- *Triage Assessment System Training Manual: Higher Education.* (2007, with R. A. Myer, N. D. Rice, R. K. James, P. Cogdal, and S. Allen). CIP-Solutions, Inc.

Patrice is a licensed professional counselor, a licensed substance abuse counselor, a clinical member of the American Association of Marriage and Family Therapy, and a licensed psychologist. She is a member of the American Counseling Association and the American Association of Marriage and Family Therapy. She is active in supervision at the graduate level of training in the United States where she supervises graduate students on practicum and intern experiences. She also serves as an active visiting international faculty member through her work with the Fulbright Association. She served as a Fulbright Specialist to Nepal in 2017 and continues her work in Nepal, collaborating in higher education and advocating for human rights. She is a board member for Empower Nepali Girls Organization, which provides educational opportunities to girls at high risk for slavery. Patrice loves traveling, adventure, trekking (climbed to Everest base camp 2019), advocacy, volunteering, and community involvement.

MICHELLE MURATORI, PhD, is a senior counselor at the Center for Talented Youth at Johns Hopkins University, in Baltimore, Maryland, where she works with highly gifted middle school and high school students who participate in the Study of Exceptional Talent and their families. After earning her MA in counseling psychology from Northwestern University in Evanston, Illinois, Michelle received her PhD in counselor education from the University of Iowa where she developed her research and clinical interests in gifted education. Her graduate research on the academic, social, and emotional adjustment of young college entrants earned her recognition from the Iowa Talented and Gifted Association, the National Association for Gifted Children, and the Mensa Education and Research Foundation and Mensa International, Ltd. At the University of Iowa, Michelle also earned the Howard R. Jones Achievement Award, the Albert Hood Promising Scholar Award, and the First in the Nation in Education (FINE) Scholar Award.

Since 2005, Michelle has been a faculty associate in the Johns Hopkins School of Education in the master's of science counseling program. She has taught a variety of courses but has a passion for group counseling and loves training students in the art of group facilitation. In 2014, she was honored with the Johns Hopkins University Alumni Association Excellence in Teaching Award. Michelle regularly presents at national conferences in counseling and gifted education and is a member of the American Counseling Association, the Association for Counselor Education and Supervision, the Association for Specialists in Group Work, the Maryland Counseling Association, and the National Association for Gifted Children. When she is not engaged in these professional activities, Michelle enjoys writing, attending concerts, and spending time with her family and friends.

In addition to scholarly articles and book chapters, Michelle has authored/coauthored the following publications:

- *Clinical Supervision in the Helping Professions: A Practical Guide,* Third Edition (2021, with Gerald Corey, Robert Haynes, and Patrice Moulton)
- *Coping Skills for a Stressful World: A Workbook for Counselors and Clients.* (2020, with Robert Haynes). American Counseling Association.
- *Counselor Self-Care.* (2018, with Gerald Corey, Jude T. Austin, and Julius A. Austin II). American Counseling Association.
- *I Never Knew I Had a Choice: Explorations in Personal Growth,* Eleventh Edition. (2018, with Gerald Corey and Marianne Schneider Corey). Cengage Learning.
- *Entrance to College: A Guide to Success.* (2007). Prufrock Press.

ABOUT THE CONTRIBUTORS
Voices From the Field

We are especially indebted to the students and practicing supervisors who gave generously of their time to share their thoughts and experiences with supervision. You will find their thoughts in their own words in the Voices From the Field feature throughout the book.

Rachel Alvarez, MS, is a clinical psychology graduate student at Northwestern State University of Louisiana.

Jude T. Austin II, PhD, LPC, LMFT-Associate, NCC, CCMHC, is an assistant professor and clinical coordinator in the professional counseling program at the University of Mary Hardin-Baylor. A recent coauthored book is *Surviving and Thriving in Your Counseling Program.*

Julius A. Austin, PhD, LPC, is a clinical therapist and the coordinator for the Office of Substance Abuse and Recovery at Tulane University. A recent coauthored book is *Surviving and Thriving in Your Counseling Program.*

Elie Axelroth, PsyD, retired as the director of Counseling Services at California Polytechnic State University, San Luis Obispo.

Jeffrey E. Barnett, PsyD, ABPP, is professor of psychology at Loyola University Maryland. He is a licensed psychologist and is board certified in clinical psychology and clinical child and adolescent psychology.

Burt Bertram, EdD, is in private practice in Orlando, Florida, and is an adjunct faculty member at Rollins College in Winter Park, Florida. He is coauthor of *The Counselor and the Law.*

Jamie Bludworth, PhD, is a licensed psychologist, director of Masters Training, director of the Counselor Training Center, and clinical assistant professor in the Counseling and Counseling Psychology Department at Arizona State University. His areas of expertise are crisis intervention, clinical supervision, and clinical administration.

Erik Braun, PhD, NCC, is an associate professor of counseling at Northwestern State University of Louisiana and a mental health counselor at the NSULA mental health clinic.

Leah Brew, PhD, CCMHC, NCC, LPCC, is professor and chair of the Department of Counseling at California State University, Fullerton.

Craig S. Cashwell, PhD, is professor in the Department of School Psychology and Counselor Education at The College of William & Mary. He is coeditor of *Integrating Spirituality and Religion Into Counseling: A Guide to Competent Practice.*

Theodore J. Chapin, PhD, is president of the Neurotherapy Institute of Central Illinois. He is coauthor of *Integrating Neurocounseling in Clinical Supervision: Strategies for Success.*

Amanda Connell, MS, graduated from California State University, Fullerton, where she currently teaches part-time for the Department of Human Services. She also works as an associate marriage and family therapist and associate professional clinical counselor for a community mental health agency.

Marianne Schneider Corey, MA, MFT, NCC, received her master's degree in marriage, family, and child counseling from Chapman University. She has coauthored five books with Cengage Learning, one being *Issues and Ethics in the Helping Professions* (10th edition).

Wendy Logan Cuellar, MAEd, LCMHCS, is a school counselor at Enka Intermediate School and an adjunct professor at Lenoir Rhyne University. She is a licensed supervisor who provides clinical supervision to graduate students from Western Carolina University and East Tennessee State University as well as to clinicians pursuing licensure.

Norma L. Day-Vines, PhD, is a professor and associate dean for Faculty Development at the Johns Hopkins School of Education in Baltimore, Maryland.

Perry C. Francis, EdD, NCC, ACS, LPC, is professor and counseling training clinic coordinator at Eastern Michigan University and has been a long-standing member of the ACA Ethics Committee.

Janee Both Gragg, PhD, LMFT, LPCC, CDAC, is associate professor of counseling at the University of Redlands.

Matt Gragg, MS, LMFT, LPCC, is the director of the Counseling Center at the University of Redlands.

Barbara Herlihy, PhD, LPC-S, NCC, is professor in practice, doctoral program director, in the Department of Counseling, at the University of Texas at San Antonio. She is coauthor of *Ethical, Legal, and Professional Issues in Counseling* (6th edition); *ACA Ethical Standards Casebook*; and *Boundary Issues in Counseling.*

Mary Hermann, JD, PhD, is associate professor in the Department of Counseling and Special Education at Virginia Commonwealth University.

Alicia M. Homrich, PhD, LPY, LMFT, is professor emeritus in the graduate studies in counseling program at Rollins College in Winter Park, Florida. She is the coeditor of *Gatekeeping in the Mental Health Professions.*

Abigail Hunter, MS, is a clinical psychology graduate student at Northwestern State University of Louisiana and is currently pursuing doctoral studies.

Marty Jencius, PhD, is an associate professor of Counselor Education and Supervision at Kent State University. He received a PhD in counselor education from the University of South Carolina.

W. Brad Johnson, PhD, is a clinical psychologist and a professor in the Department of Leadership, Ethics & Law at the U. S. Naval Academy and a faculty associate in the Graduate School of Education at Johns Hopkins University.

Kellie Kirksey, PhD, is a holistic psychotherapist; she earned her doctorate in counselor education and psychology at The Ohio State University.

Staci Maddox, MS, is a graduate student at Northwestern State University.

Manpreet Mann, MSW, is a graduate of the University of Nevada, Reno School of Social Work.

Gretchen McLain, MA, CSC, is a certified school counselor and a doctoral student in the counseling program at the University of Texas at San Antonio. She has served as a school counselor for 11 years and as a public school teacher for 9 years.

Rick Myer, PhD, is the department chair, Educational Psychology and Special Services, at the University of Texas, El Paso. He received his doctorate in counseling psychology from the University of Memphis.

Benjamin Noah, PhD, NCC, LPC, is on the adjunct faculty, School of Counseling and Human Services at Capella University.

Mary M. Read, PhD, LMFT, is director of clinical training in the Department of Counseling at California State University at Fullerton.

Theodore P. Remley Jr., JD, PhD, LPC, NCC, is both a counselor educator and an attorney. He is professor of counseling at the University of Holy Cross in New Orleans, Louisiana. He is coauthor of *Ethical, Legal, and Professional Issues in Counseling* (6th edition). Each February or March he coordinates the Law and Ethics in Counseling Conference in New Orleans.

Tony Rousmaniere, PsyD, is on the clinical faculty at the University of Washington and is in private practice in Seattle. He is the author of *Deliberate Practice for Psychotherapists, The Cycle of Excellence, Master the Inner Skills of Psychotherapy,* and coeditor of *Using Technology to Enhance Clinical Supervision.*

Valerie Russell, PhD, is a forensic psychologist for the Board of Parole Hearings in California. She also works with graduate students in her private practice.

Lori A. Russell-Chapin, PhD, is a professor of counselor education at Bradley University and codirector of the Center for Collaborative Brain Research in Peoria, Illinois. She is coauthor of *Integrating Neurocounseling in Clinical Supervision: Strategies for Success.*

Janna Scarborough, PhD, is a professor of counseling and the dean (in the interim) of Clemmer College at East Tennessee State University; she earned her doctorate in counselor education at the University of Virginia in Charlottesville.

David Shepard, PhD, is professor in the Department of Counseling at California State University Fullerton, where he teaches trainees in both beginning and advanced practicum courses. He also is a private practitioner in Los Angeles. He received his doctorate in counseling psychology from the University of Southern California.

Mark A. Stebnicki, PhD, LCMHC, DCMHS, CRC, CMCC, is professor emeritus in the Department of Addictions and Rehabilitation, East Carolina University. One of his many books is *Empathy Fatigue: Healing the Mind, Body, and Spirt of Professional Counselors.*

Naomi Tapia, MS, is a graduate student in the counseling program at California State University, Fullerton.

Logan Turner, BS, is a first-year clinical psychology master's student at Northwestern State University of Louisiana.

Judy Van Der Wende, PhD, is a licensed psychologist who has a private practice in Southern California; she earned her doctorate at Pacific Graduate School in Palo Alto, California, and was a postdoctoral fellow at the Mental Illness Research, Education, and Clinical Center in Baltimore, Maryland.

Michelle E. Wade, EdD, LCPC, LPC, NCC, is an assistant professor at the University of New Orleans, and her main area of research is in the use of technology in counseling.

Anne Marie "Nancy" Wheeler, JD, is an attorney who gives workshops on risk management strategies and is the coauthor of *The Counselor and the Law.*

Robert Wubbolding, EdD, is professor emeritus of counseling at Xavier University, Cincinnati, Ohio; he is the director of the Center for Reality Therapy in Cincinnati, Ohio. He has written numerous journal articles and books on choice theory/reality therapy. A recent book is *Reality Therapy and Self-Evaluation: The Key to Client Change.*

J. Scott Young, PhD, NCC, LPC, is professor in the Department of Counseling and Educational Development at the University of North Carolina at Greensboro. He is coeditor of *Integrating Spirituality and Religion Into Counseling: A Guide to Competent Practice.*

CHAPTER 1

Introduction to Supervision

FOCUS QUESTIONS

1. What do you think of when you hear the term "supervision"?
2. Think about your own personality and learning style. What learning strategies would assist you in becoming a competent supervisor?
3. What concerns or fears do you have about becoming a supervisor? What do you look forward to in becoming a supervisor?
4. What is the primary purpose of supervision?
5. How would you explain the primary responsibilities of a supervisor? To what degree is protecting the welfare of the client the supervisor's responsibility?
6. What multiple roles do you think a supervisor might be expected to fulfill? How much of the role of the supervisor should focus on advancing the supervisee's self-learning and self-development?
7. Is the supervisor a gatekeeper for the profession? What role, if any, should the supervisor play as a gatekeeper?
8. Think of times you have felt empowered when learning and taking on new roles. What steps or actions might you take to use those experiences to empower your supervisees?
9. What qualities and characteristics are most important for you in an effective supervisor?
10. What critical issues in clinical supervision would you most like to explore in depth?

Supervision has been practiced in the helping professions from the beginning, but it is only in recent decades that supervision has come to be seen as a separate and distinct field with its own set of skills and tools. Supervision is used in virtually all of the helping professions to assist counselors-in-training in developing their clinical and professional skills. All students will be supervised over the course of their training, and the majority of students will find themselves becoming supervisors at some point in their career. Most new supervisors are anxious about performing the tasks and responsibilities of supervision, and supervisees typically are anxious about being supervised and evaluated.

Our goal is to provide you with the knowledge and skills you need to become a competent, ethical, and effective supervisor. We hope this will reduce your anxiety about assuming the role of supervisor. Whether you are a beginning student in the helping professions, an experienced supervisor, or at some stage in between, you will be involved in the process of supervision, either as a supervisee or as a supervisor.

As the field of supervision has evolved, so have the issues surrounding the practice of supervision. We have followed the major developments in clinical supervision since the second edition of this book and have found there is an increasing focus on the following topics:

- Competence for both supervisors and supervisees
- Legal and ethical issues in supervision
- Accountability and documentation
- Technology and online resources and methods
- Crisis supervision
- Multicultural and social justice issues in supervision
- Addressing spirituality and religion in supervision

These trends and developments are discussed in depth in the chapters that follow.

In this chapter we define supervision, discuss the evolution and current status of clinical supervision, and outline the goals of supervision and the objectives for the supervisee. We share our personal experiences and struggles in becoming supervisors to give you insight into the personal aspects of becoming a supervisor.

Supervision Defined

Supervision has become a specialty field with unique competencies (knowledge and skills), theories, methods, evaluations, and legal and ethical duties and obligations. Many counselors are poorly prepared for the supervision experience, and the challenge of supervising competently, as well as ethically and legally, can be daunting. Our goal is to provide a practical and complete guide to becoming a competent, ethical, and effective supervisor, including the skills needed to handle challenging supervisory situations.

Supervision is a unique professional relationship between a supervisor, a supervisee, and the clients served. Bernard and Goodyear (2019, pp. 72–73) referred to the broadest view of this relationship as a "triadic system." This relationship changes over time and with experience. As supervisees become increasingly competent in practicing the skills of their profession, they require less direction from the supervisor. Competent supervision requires a fine balance on the supervisor's part between providing professional development opportunities for supervisees and protecting clients' welfare. While assisting supervisees as they learn the art and craft of therapeutic practice, supervisors also are expected to monitor the quality of care clients are receiving and serve as gatekeepers for the profession. A primary aim of supervision is to create a context in which the supervisee can acquire the experience needed to become an independent professional. In most cases, the supervisor-supervisee relationship is not equal; rather, it is hierarchical, having an evaluation component as its cornerstone. It seems somewhat contradictory to place the terms "relationship" and "evaluation" in the same sentence, but both are important components of supervision. Even though the supervisor has a monitoring and evaluating function, a productive supervisory relationship must be established with supervisees.

Some call supervision an art, and successful supervision certainly is artful, but it is also a formal arrangement with specific expectations, roles, responsibilities, and skills. Supervision in the broadest sense involves teaching, consultation, and evaluation, and the supervisory relationship extends over time (Bernard & Goodyear, 2019, pp. 9–12). Other supervisory functions include counseling, advising, coaching, and mentoring.

There are two general categories of supervision: clinical and administrative. *Clinical supervision* focuses on the work of the supervisee in providing services to clients. In our view, clinical supervision is best defined as a process whereby consistent observation and evaluation of the counseling process is provided by a trained and experienced professional who recognizes and is competent in the unique body of knowledge and skill required for professional development. Supervision also is defined by many external forces, including governing bodies, licensing agencies, and the settings in which we work. For example, supervisors have very different roles and responsibilities when supervising students in a training program than when supervising prelicensed professionals in a mental health agency, especially if the clinical supervisor is not an employee and is not affiliated with the mental health agency. Supervisory practice, roles, and responsibilities vary depending on the setting and other requirements.

Administrative supervision focuses on the issues surrounding the supervisee's role and responsibilities in the organization as an employee. It involves directions given by direct line administrators to their employees. The purpose of administrative supervision is to see that counselors who are employed are doing their jobs competently. Administrative supervisors generally have direct control and authority over those they supervise (Remley & Herlihy, 2020).

Many of the principles and methods discussed throughout this book apply to both clinical and administrative supervision. It is not unusual for counselors to be supervised by someone who is required to function in both clinical and administrative roles, a situation that can lead to some common challenges.

The Evolution of Supervision

Clinical supervision, as a distinct specialty area within the helping professions, has seen vast changes in the past 30 years. Clinical supervision derived from the practice of psychotherapy, and a commonly held belief for many years was that if you had some clinical experience and good counseling skills you were qualified to supervise. Guidelines were minimal and focused primarily on the number of supervision hours required for trainees. Many supervisory relationships were relatively informal, and "good" counseling skills were thought to be sufficient to assist trainees in becoming productive therapists. We are not implying that effective supervision did not occur prior to the formalization of supervisor training, nor are we minimizing the importance of having sound counseling skills as a supervisor. However, the role of the supervisor today bears little resemblance to the informal mentoring/therapeutic relationship of the past.

Counselors must be prepared to assist their supervisees in today's challenging times. We are seeing more divisiveness and hatred, discrimination of marginalized groups, and tribalism, as well as fears about climate change and international disasters such as the COVID-19 public health crisis. Human-caused disasters such as mass shootings are also on the rise. Clients seeking counseling are reporting a heightened level of stress and anxiety, and counselors, supervisors, and supervisees are also affected by these dramatic shifts in our world. Supervisors must be prepared to help supervisees examine how these changes affect both them and their families and their counseling work with clients.

Little attention was given to competency issues or formal documentation procedures in the past, and most supervisors did not have formal training in supervision. In recent years, however, supervision has become an area of specialized training in academic programs, postgraduate training, and professional development workshops. This emphasis has evolved from the growing need to conduct supervision in a professional and accountable manner, under increased liability, and to adhere to the regulations of various governing bodies.

Within the past four decades, the governing bodies of many helping disciplines have developed specific criteria for the practice of supervision and have provided standards and guidelines. The American Association of Marriage and Family Therapy (AAMFT) was one of the first to develop standards for supervisor training, and they established a designation of Approved Supervisor in 1983. The American Counseling Association (ACA) adopted the Association for Counselor Education and Supervision (ACES) standards for supervisors in 1989. ACES developed the *Best Practices in Clinical Supervision* in 2011. The National Association of Social Workers (NASW) published *Guidelines for Clinical Social Work Supervision* in 1994, and the National Board for Certified Counselors (NBCC) published *Standards for the Ethical Practice of Supervision* in 1999. The American Psychological Association (APA) published *Guidelines for Clinical Supervision in Health Service Psychology*, in 2015.

Today, clinical supervisors typically are responsible for maintaining a professional supervisory relationship with each supervisee and each client that the supervisee counsels. One caveat is when a supervisor is sought out privately to consult on a particular case. In that circumstance, the supervisor might be exempt from responsibility for *every* client that a supervisee counsels. In such an instance, agreement would be reached in advance that the supervisor could be held responsible only for clients and cases on which there had been supervision rather than consultation.

Accountability requires a more formal arrangement, consisting of professional disclosure statements and contracts that outline the model to be used in supervision, the goals of supervision, and the assessment and evaluation methods. State-of-the-art supervision today requires supervisors to have a multitude of skills and procedural knowledge including the following:

- Formalized training in supervision
- Knowledge of formal contracts and agreements
- The ability to initiate and maintain a positive supervisory relationship
- The ability to assess both supervisees and the clients they serve
- Multiple modes of direct observation of the supervisee's work
- Policies and procedures for practice
- Knowledge of proper documentation methods
- Specific feedback and evaluation plans
- Effective risk management practices
- Knowledge of relevant ethics codes and standards
- Thorough knowledge of legal topics and issues and relevant state licensure requirements and processes

The body of knowledge needed to practice supervision now includes, but certainly is not limited to, roles and responsibilities, relationship dynamics, counseling skills, instructional skills, legal and ethical decision-making knowledge and skills, technology skills, multicultural competencies, and evaluative skills.

The Goals of Supervision

Many authors have addressed the issue of supervision goals, and there is considerable agreement regarding the goals of supervision. Although some professional standards do not address the goals of supervision directly, the goals often can be inferred from the discussion of related topics. For example, in *Best Practices in Clinical Supervision* (ACES, 2011), goals for best practices for supervisors can be seen in the description of tasks for initiating supervision (see Box 1.1).

Our Views on Goals of Supervision

In our view, the goals of supervision are fourfold: (1) promote supervisee growth and development, (2) protect the welfare of the client, (3) monitor supervisee performance and

---

Box 1.1
BEST PRACTICES IN SUPERVISION

Association for Counselor Education and Supervision (2011)

Best Practices in Clinical Supervision

1. The supervisor facilitates a discussion about the supervision process to foster the supervisory working alliance.
2. The supervisor establishes the beginning of a supervisory working alliance that is collaborative and egalitarian to assist in lessening supervisee anxiety about the supervision process.
3. The supervisor describes his/her role as supervisor, including teacher, counselor, consultant, mentor, and evaluator.
4. The supervisor describes the structure, process, and content of all relevant formats of supervision sessions (e.g., individual, triadic, peer, group supervision).
5. The supervisor and supervisee discuss the supervisee's past experiences with supervision as well as preferred supervision styles and supervision interventions.
6. The supervisor initiates a conversation about multicultural considerations and how they may affect both counseling and supervision relationships, indicating that such multicultural considerations will be an expected part of supervision conversations.

---

act as gatekeeper for the profession, and (4) empower the supervisee to self-supervise and carry out these goals as an independent professional. Let's examine each of these goals in more detail.

Promote Supervisee Growth and Development

Many supervisors view teaching supervisees how to effectively counsel clients as the primary task of supervision. This is an essential component of the supervision function because supervisors must ensure the welfare of both current and future clients of the supervisee. It is not enough simply to teach about the specifics of each case; supervisees must learn how these issues may translate into their independent practice in the future. The broader definition of this goal of supervision is promotion of supervisee growth and development as a competent clinician and professional, which may involve teaching or assuming any number of other supervisory roles (see Chapter 2). Promoting supervisee development is clearly a major goal of supervision, but it must be balanced with a focus on the welfare of the client.

Protect the Welfare of the Client

The supervisor is charged with protecting the welfare of the supervisee's clients. State requirements for the supervision of unlicensed mental health professionals are designed to protect the consumers of those mental health services. The supervisor must ensure that both current and future clients receive competent and professional services from the supervisee, and the supervisor can intervene in whatever way is necessary if the client is not receiving competent services. Protection of the welfare of the supervisee's clients requires that supervisors have knowledge of those clients and the goals of counseling.

Monitor Supervisee Performance and Act as Gatekeeper for the Profession

Another function of the supervisor is to serve as gatekeeper for the profession (Baldwin, 2018). Given the increased awareness of possible damage caused by mental health professionals who lack the personal qualities and skills necessary for effective practice, it is reasonable that there is an ethical imperative for supervisors and training faculty to serve as gatekeepers for the profession. This gatekeeping function involves monitoring and evaluating the supervisee's competence to become licensed in fields such as counseling, social work, marriage and family therapy, or psychology. Obviously, gatekeeping is an important function when training and supervising students in graduate programs. The gatekeeping function of the supervisor will vary depending on the setting in which supervision takes place and the level of education and training of the supervisee. Licensing and professional standards outline the requirements for supervisors when overseeing the clinical work of supervisees. Supervision has a pivotal role in the evaluation of competence of the supervisee to practice within the profession. We discuss evaluation and gatekeeping in more detail in Chapter 10.

Empower the Supervisee to Self-Supervise

Another important function is to assist the supervisee in developing the ability to self-supervise (Bernard & Goodyear, 2019, pp. 234–236). In addition to teaching the supervisee, protecting the client's welfare, and serving as gatekeeper for the profession, a basic goal is to assist the supervisee to develop the skills, awareness, and resources necessary for self-evaluation. This is accomplished by providing the opportunity for supervisees to learn problem-solving and decision-making skills and to practice self-evaluation and self-supervision. These practices in supervision help supervisees learn to trust their clinical judgment. Personal and professional development is certainly a desired outcome of the supervisee's empowerment. Our conviction is that if supervisees become empowered personally and professionally, and if they are competent practitioners, they will place the client's welfare first and will not bring harm to clients. Competent professionals will be able to monitor their own performance, be aware of the limits of their competence, be able to identify how personal issues affect professional practice, and know when and how to seek consultation and additional supervision.

Although the aforementioned goals are equally important, particular situations will determine which takes priority at any given moment. If a conflict exists between teaching the supervisee and protecting the welfare of the client, professional ethics codes require that protecting the welfare of the client be first and foremost. For example, when a supervisee reports that a client has expressed suicidal ideation, the goals of supervision quickly change from teaching the supervisee to a focus on the immediate need to protect the welfare of the client. Teaching is not abandoned but is temporarily suspended until the crisis is resolved. It is essential to return to teaching the supervisee about suicide assessment and intervention once the needs of the client have been met. It might help to think of the goals of supervision as occurring simultaneously rather than hierarchically. Effective supervision depends on the supervisor having a clear understanding of the goals of supervision and being able to communicate those goals to the supervisee.

Establishing Goals With the Supervisee

In addition to the four overall goals previously stated, the supervisor and supervisee work together to establish a specific plan of action in a collaborative manner. This collaborative design and agreement regarding the requirements and expected outcomes of supervision is given priority in the supervisory relationship. On this point, ACES (2011) *Best Practices in Clinical Supervision* are as follows:

> b. To the extent possible, the supervisor co-develops specific goals for supervision with the supervisee.
>> vii. The supervisor and supervisee renegotiate the supervisory contract and supervisee's goals as needed over the course of supervision.
>> viii. The supervisor helps the supervisee develop goals that are realistic, measurable, and attainable within the context of the particular academic, field placement, or post-degree practice setting.

Becoming a Competent Counselor and Supervisor

Becoming a competent supervisor is an ongoing journey very much like that of becoming a competent clinician. Both involve coursework, continuing education, and consultation. Following are some requirements for achieving competence, both as a counselor and as a supervisor:

- Become knowledgeable about counseling theories, methods, and practice.
- Have a broad understanding of diagnosis and treatment methods.
- Know the limits of personal competence, including how and when to seek consultation and supervision.
- Show evidence in practice of the basic helping skills of empathy, acceptance, respect, and genuineness.
- Be aware of how personal issues affect clinical work and what impact these issues may have on clients.
- Identify which clients are easy to work with and which are more difficult, and explore the reasons for this.
- Know how to recognize and work with resistance, reluctance, and ambivalence in clients.
- Know and apply the relevant ethics codes of the profession and the laws that apply to clinical practice and supervision.
- Have sound judgment and a clear decision-making model regarding clinical and ethical issues.
- Develop an awareness of how multicultural issues affect the counseling process and how to work with multicultural differences with clients, colleagues, and supervisees.
- Acquire self-confidence, and show evidence of competence with increased practice.
- Develop the ability to examine one's role as a counselor or as a supervisor.
- Be willing to expand skills even though there is a risk of making mistakes, and talk about this in supervision.
- Strive to create one's own personal style of doing supervision.
- Develop the practice of self-evaluation.

It is incumbent upon supervisors to have a clear picture of the goals of supervision and to introduce this topic for discussion throughout the supervision process. Although being a counselor and a supervisor have quite a bit in common, those striving to become competent supervisors must have additional special knowledge and skills. Supervisors need to be current on a diverse range of supervision methods, be up-to-date on legal and ethical aspects of supervision, have knowledge of the areas in which they are supervising (such as working with clients who have been traumatized), and have supervision when they are learning how to supervise.

Perspectives on Supervision

We want to introduce ourselves to you by sharing our background and experiences with supervision. Each of us describes our work setting, our philosophy of supervision, experiences we have had as both supervisees and supervisors, and what we have learned from those experiences. By reading about our experiences, you will come to understand our point of reference in writing about the supervision process. Throughout the book we often talk about our reactions, thoughts, and experiences regarding a particular topic, and we hope you will examine your own experiences and learning in the same way.

JERRY COREY'S PERSONAL PERSPECTIVE

My Work Setting

Since the early 1970s I have worked in a university program in which I provide group supervision for group facilitators. Almost all of my professional experience as a supervisor has been with group supervision. From my vantage point, one of the best ways to teach and to supervise trainees who want to become group practitioners is to conduct this supervision in a group context. In addition to working with trainees, my colleagues and I have done a considerable amount of group supervision in agency settings and through professional workshops. This supervision is aimed at helping trainees acquire knowledge about how groups function and refine group leadership by being part of a training and supervision group.

My Philosophy of Supervision

I credit both humanistic and systemic thought on influencing my current views and philosophy of supervision. I see my role as a supervisor as being a guide in a process of self-discovery. In much the same way as in counseling, I believe in the value of establishing collaborative relationships in supervision. Clients get the most from therapy when they are educated about how therapy works and when they collaboratively design personal goals for the therapeutic work. Likewise, I think supervisees profit the most from supervision when they become partners in this endeavor. For myself, I do not subscribe to a supervision style that is directed largely by the supervisor, telling supervisees what they did wrong and what they should try next. Empowerment is one of the aims of personal therapy with clients, and in many ways supervisees need to feel a sense of empowerment if they are to grow personally and professionally.

When I am doing group supervision, I ask the trainee coleaders to talk about their own perceptions about the efficacy of their interventions in the group. By beginning with trainees' thoughts, reactions, intuitions, and perceptions, the stage is set for learning by self-discovery as opposed to listening to the expert who observed their work. I am not diminishing the expertise of a supervisor; rather, my goal is to guide trainees in the process of learning to monitor what they are doing in a training group, to raise their own questions, and to discover the answers to some of these questions.

My Struggles as a Supervisor

I tend to have the most difficulty supervising professionals and trainees who are closed about themselves, who are defensive, and who are not willing to engage in self-examination. I can certainly appreciate a beginner's anxieties as a group counselor and the resulting lack of therapeutic responsiveness in a group. I am willing to help trainees explore their fears, self-doubts, and insecurities in the context of group supervision, and I find that many opportunities open up for significant learning in this context. However, trainees who are judgmental and closed to new learning do pose a challenge for me. Included in this list of supervisees I perceive as "difficult" are individuals who limit most of their interactions with others to giving advice or asking questions.

I do not have the expectation that supervisees will engage in highly personal self-disclosure pertaining to their outside lives in group sessions; the training and supervision group is not a therapy group. I do, however, expect trainees to talk about their reactions to the here and now of the supervision and training group as well as bring up for exploration any difficulties they are having in fully participating in the supervision process. Supervisees in a group training setting are asked to identify personal concerns or characteristics that are likely to get in the way of effectively counseling others. I must admit that I struggle with trainees who obviously are having many reactions to being part of the supervision group yet hold back from becoming active participants in the group. For example, trainees often have difficulty feeling competent and struggle with imposter syndrome, and they may want to withdraw. At the very least, I hope that they disclose this and are willing to work on these struggles in group supervision.

Some supervisees experience transference toward me, and this can be explored effectively within the group training situation. Likewise, my own countertransference reactions are sometimes triggered, and these can be discussed as well in working with supervisees. Although I need to be mindful about how I explore any possible countertransference I may have, I realize that I can provide valuable modeling if I am willing to be open in certain situations. Exploring both transference and countertransference reactions is one of the values of doing supervision in a group setting. My intention is to give honest feedback to trainees in a way that is helpful to them. To accomplish this, it is often necessary to talk about what is going on within the here-and-now context of the supervision group itself.

Fortunately, the vast majority of trainees I supervise in various group counseling courses are a sheer delight to work with, are eager to learn, are open to exploring how they are being affected through their work as a group facilitator, and are willing to be vulnerable. They do not view their personal vulnerability as weakness. I find that these trainees are best able to acquire the skills to facilitate groups by being willing to deal with potential barriers in themselves during the group supervision meetings.

What I Have Learned About Supervision

In almost 50 years of doing group supervision with trainees in group counseling courses, it has become evident to me that the best supervision is to encourage trainees to develop a sense of educated intuition. So often my colleagues and I discover that group workers we train and supervise have a wealth of insights and sensitive intuition, yet all too often they do not trust their knowledge and intuition. As a supervisor, my goal is to encourage trainees to be themselves in their role as group facilitators and to follow through on some of their clinical intuitions.

Here are some of the lessons that continue to become manifest in the context of group supervision with group counselor trainees:

- It is essential to prepare supervisees both academically and personally for the experience of being group counselor trainees.
- Supervisees do not need to have all the right answers to every situation they might encounter in a group counseling setting.
- It is not necessary for supervisees to worry about making mistakes. There are many ways to creatively intervene in any counseling situation, and it is limiting to operate under the assumption that there is one best way to deal with a problem. We can learn by reflecting on what we consider to be mistakes, and we can recognize that reflecting on mistakes can be an opportunity for learning.

- Supervisees learn best in a climate of support and challenge.
- Trainees can best learn how to facilitate a group from the experience of being a group member and reflecting on what they find most useful for them personally.
- It is desirable that members of a supervision group function as teachers for one another. The source of wisdom is not exclusively with the supervisor.
- One of the best ways to teach and to supervise is by modeling. How a supervisor behaves in the group supervision context is often a more powerful source of influence to trainees than simply telling them what to do.
- Before giving trainees my thoughts, it is often more productive to ask trainees to share their perspective on that situation. More often than not, if trainees are given a chance to explore how they might function more effectively, they will come up with their own insights and suggestions.

BOB HAYNES'S PERSONAL PERSPECTIVE

My Work Setting

Most of the clinical supervision I have provided occurred during my 27 years as director of an accredited clinical psychology internship program at Atascadero State Hospital in California. This maximum-security forensic hospital provided care and treatment for sex offenders and mentally ill offenders. I provided individual and group supervision to interns, postdoctoral fellows, prelicensed psychologists, and those providing clinical supervision to interns—including psychologists, social workers, psychiatrists, and marriage and family therapists. In the private practice settings where I worked part time for more than 10 years, I participated in peer supervision with colleagues in a group practice.

Two issues stand out for me from my work with supervisors and supervisees. First, nearly all supervisors express that they initially felt ill prepared to become supervisors and were unclear in their understanding of the nature and purpose of supervision. It often took some time for them to develop confidence and clarity regarding their supervisory role. Formal training in supervision did expedite their development, but experience in supervision was also a major factor. Second, nearly all supervisees are anxious about their performance and are very concerned about the evaluation component. They expend considerable time and energy trying to determine what to say and do in supervision. Often, pleasing a supervisor seems as important as learning from the training experience for which they are being supervised.

My Philosophy of Supervision

I learned about supervision solely from supervisors. Courses in supervision were not offered in my undergraduate or graduate years in psychology in the 1960s and 1970s. There was no consideration that it was a field in itself or that specific skills were involved. At that time, supervision was seen as a subset of therapy skills. Once you had mastered therapy skills, it was assumed that you were ready to supervise others. Over the course of my career, I have been fortunate to be able to participate in formal training in supervision practices.

I view supervision as a process whereby the supervisor helps the supervisee learn and grow in knowledge, clinical skills, ethics, legal concerns, professional issues, and the personal development of judgment and maturity. From my perspective, the primary purpose of supervision is the development and empowerment of the supervisee. While pursuing this goal, it is equally important that the supervisor protect the welfare of clients and act as a gatekeeper for the profession. My greatest hope is that supervisees will move from relying on me as the supervisor to feeling empowered to provide their own self-supervision, to effectively problem solve clinical situations, and to know how and when to seek help, consultation, and supervision from others.

Supervision is a collaborative process and is most effective in a healthy relationship of transparency, genuineness, trust, honesty, and mutual respect. I believe it is the responsibility of the supervisor to foster the collaborative process by involving the supervisee in the development of supervision goals, methods, and evaluation procedures. Trust, honesty, and respect take time to develop and can be modeled and encouraged by the supervisor. Being available for the supervisee when needed, being honest about my observations and thoughts, and respecting the beliefs and training needs of the supervisee go a long way toward developing a healthy supervisory relationship.

I employ a developmental model of supervision wherein the supervisee is seen as being somewhere on a continuum of development, and supervision begins at the supervisee's current level. Consideration must also be given to the context in which supervision occurs. That includes the purpose of supervision, my own models of therapy and supervision, the developmental level of the supervisee, the setting in which the supervision occurs, and the ethical and legal obligations that apply.

My Struggles as a Supervisor

I feel comfortable in the role of supervisor, but I still struggle with the task of working with supervisees who possess significant personal issues that affect clinical performance. I have encountered supervisees with personality traits that seem contrary to those necessary for becoming an effective helping professional. I work to maintain a proper balance between supervision and counseling, and between helping the supervisee and protecting the client, the profession, and myself. In recent years, supervisees have become more likely to threaten and to take legal action against supervisors for any number of reasons. We have become an increasingly more litigious society, and the practice of supervision has not escaped that trend. Supervision has increasingly become a factor in complaints to licensing boards and in issues of liability. My actions as a supervisor have been challenged with threats of legal action on behalf of a trainee. I learned firsthand the legal responsibilities and liabilities for supervisors and for training programs. This experience forced me to more clearly define the purpose of supervision, the legal and ethical responsibilities of the supervisor and the supervisee, and the importance of detailed and accurate documentation especially when working with any problem situation. Problems such as threats of legal action often lead to improvements in various aspects of program policies and procedures.

Supervising those not responsive to supervision has been another hurdle for me. I know from my own experience that competent professionals need to be open to feedback and must be aware of their personal and professional limitations and strengths. It troubles me to see new clinicians who are unwilling to look at their work and reluctant to grow and develop.

A distinction must be made between performance anxiety and not being responsive to supervision. The novice clinician often lacks confidence, and performance anxiety leads to wanting to please the supervisor. This individual can become unresponsive to supervision due to fear and anxiety, but with time and a supportive supervisor the supervisee will begin to open up. Many interns begin the training year eager to impress the training staff, but they become defensive when they hear the first feedback that includes the need for improvement. Supporting and encouraging these interns is usually very effective, as is the supervisor's assurance that most new clinicians find it difficult to hear negative feedback from supervisors. It helps to remind supervisees that they are in our training program to develop both personally and professionally and that we do not expect novice clinicians to be fully competent.

Supervising colleagues can be challenging because experienced clinicians are often more set in their opinions, beliefs, and practices than novice clinicians. They often know more than I do about certain topics, and I can see that either as threatening or as an opportunity for my own learning. I have to remind myself in these situations that I am not expected to know everything as a supervisor, and a supervisee may well have more expertise on any given topic. Experienced clinicians may be given more freedom than is warranted, thus creating a potential hazard for clients. In these situations, I focus more of my supervisory effort on encouraging and modeling openness to feedback and learning as a hallmark of a competent clinician. I try to enlist the supervisee in a collaborative effort in which we examine how we can learn together about a variety of clinical topics.

I am concerned about supervising those with backgrounds different from my own, with gender and ethnicity being the major areas of difference. I find myself wondering if I am understanding their world and whether I know enough about what their world is like. In the forensic setting, for example, I know that women have unique experiences and concerns when working with an all-male population. Although I may know about those experiences and concerns, I am not certain I fully understand what it must be like for them. I usually share my perspective with supervisees and encourage them to talk about their experiences and what I need to know to provide useful supervision.

What I Have Learned About Supervision

- Every situation and supervisee is a new experience with new twists and turns that provide a new learning experience for me.
- It is essential to do those things as a supervisor that will protect my license and professional standing.
- A written supervisory contract is best developed early in supervision and with the collaboration of the supervisee.
- Documentation of supervisory sessions is essential.
- Demonstrating support, encouragement, and respect toward the supervisee is important, but I must also be willing to challenge the supervisee to learn.
- It is important to maintain a healthy sense of humor with supervisees; however, there is no place in supervision for the use of sarcasm.
- Work collaboratively with the supervisee to establish ground rules regarding supervision, and use those rules to resolve conflicts in the supervisory relationship.
- It is essential to establish clear and consistent boundaries with supervisees.

In recent years, I have realized that now, more than ever, all supervisees need training in working with clients in crisis situations. Crises are occurring more frequently and on a larger scale, and anyone in the counseling and helping professions may be called upon to assist individuals and communities in crisis.

 ## PATRICE MOULTON'S PERSONAL PERSPECTIVE

My Work Setting

I presently serve as full professor in the Department of Psychology at Northwestern State University. My current job responsibilities include teaching, supervising, and conducting research in the graduate level clinical psychology program. I have experience in supervision at the program level, supervision of faculty, and the direct supervision of graduate students during practicum and externship experiences. I also serve as a Fulbright Specialist in the field of psychology and have the honor of working collaboratively as visiting faculty internationally to assist in the development of training programs for mental health professionals around the world.

My Philosophy of Supervision

I view supervision as a collaborative process with a developmental emphasis. I have developed and practice a TEAM model of supervision, which is described in Chapter 4. I believe in mutual respect, and this includes respecting supervisees' knowledge and life experiences as they approach the therapeutic process. Supervision is the balance of providing both opportunities and challenges while maintaining a positive and safe professional relationship. This balance requires a firm foundation of appropriate boundaries and information sharing about the process of supervision. I believe trust is established when I am forthright with supervisees about the supervisory process, including my expectations and my range of responsibilities. Honest and ethical communication is the key to providing a safe environment for supervisees.

Moreover, I see managerial responsibility and crisis intervention as components of supervision but not as acceptable foundational models. True supervision is about much more than putting out fires, maintaining units of service (such as the number of hours counselors spend in direct service), and documentation. In my view, supervision entails personal and professional development gained through experience and the supervisory relationship. I am a strong promoter of mentoring through modeling and of empowering supervisees to learn to view cases through multiple lenses. It is a wonderful challenge and opportunity to teach supervisees about clients and presenting issues through various perspectives (theory, ethnicity, culture, socioeconomic status, and sexual orientation) in developing case conceptualizations that will direct their work.

Supervision requires ongoing personal and professional monitoring. I do not think personal counseling is an appropriate component in direct supervision. However, personal exploration, as it applies to the supervisee's ability to function as a therapist, is essential. It is appropriate to discuss the background and personal reactions of supervisees and to seek insight into how these reactions may affect their ability to practice therapy. The issues identified in supervision can become strengths for the evolving professional. If not identified and not addressed, however, these personal issues may become barriers to working effectively with clients.

There is no substitute for experience in the field, but experience alone is not sufficient to provide quality supervision. A specific set of skills and knowledge is required to provide competent supervision. Personal and professional integrity are of primary importance in maintaining a positive supervisory relationship. In addition, a sense of humor is an asset when used appropriately in supervision.

I value the early stages of teaching and watching ideas form with my supervisees. I appreciate supervisees who are willing to question my point of view. It is meaningful when supervisees begin coming to me in supervision, not to seek answers and direction but to discuss alternatives and inform me of the path they will be taking with a particular client.

My Struggles as a Supervisor

I still struggle personally with the logistics of supervision and the time that must be dedicated to quality supervision, and I must admit, I spend more time these days pondering the liabilities involved. Supervision is a tremendous commitment that requires a great deal of time and many resources. It is inaccurate to view supervision with each supervisee as a one-hour per week commitment. It takes much more to maintain responsibility to both supervisees and the clients for whom they provide therapy. My favorite part of supervision is the relationship that is built while teaching and mentoring. I am happy to provide the hard feedback, the reality moments, and the challenges if it leads to a trainee becoming a competent colleague. My least favorite part is maintaining updated documentation including contracts, progress notes, and feedback sheets. However, I value this component and would never consider supervising without it.

What I Have Learned About Supervision

- To value the process of the supervisory relationship and the transitions as I share the stages of professional development with supervisees
- To seek out the differing opinions of my supervisees
- To be willing to share vulnerabilities about not having all the answers
- To challenge supervisees by setting high expectations and then providing the support they need to reach them
- To require evidence-based practice of basic skills from supervisees
- To appreciate the need to explore case conceptualization through various lenses and theories before determining either diagnosis or treatment
- To acknowledge and rely on consultative relationships with other professionals regarding supervisory issues
- To provide the necessary structure, though difficult at times, to protect myself, my supervisees, and our clients
- To encourage appropriate risks, expect mistakes (they are part of the learning process), and use them as windows of opportunity
- To provide opportunities to supervisees by modeling through practice, role play, and coleading to build confidence and competence in skill
- To remember to set high expectations and celebrate small successful moments

 ## MICHELLE MURATORI'S PERSONAL PERSPECTIVE

My Work Setting

Since 2005, I have worked as a faculty associate in the Master of Science in Counseling program at Johns Hopkins University in Baltimore, Maryland. Most of the courses I have taught have included an intensive "laboratory" component, in which the students (all master's level) practice their counseling or group facilitation skills/techniques. All of the courses, without exception, have placed a heavy emphasis on experiential learning, personal growth, and professional development.

In contrast to the other authors, I did receive formal supervisory training in my doctoral program at the University of Iowa. There, I was fortunate to take a supervision course taught by Ursula Delworth, one of the developers of the integrated developmental model (IDM), shortly before her death. As part of my training, I also completed a supervision practicum in which I was supervised by a faculty member (who also embraced a developmental perspective) in providing supervision to master's students in Iowa's counseling program.

My Philosophy of Supervision

I view supervision as a developmental process. Although my perspective undoubtedly has been shaped by the developmental emphasis of my supervisory training, I attribute my point of view to other experiences as well. Long before entering graduate school, I realized that learning experiences were more meaningful when I started to value the process and not become overly fixated on outcomes. Outcomes are important (and, in the context of counselor preparation, certain competencies are critical to achieve), but it seems that trainees stand a better chance of achieving competence if they are encouraged to learn from the process and from their mistakes. As cliché as this may seem, I do "trust the process," not only in terms of counselor trainees' development but also with regard to my own professional growth as a counselor.

One of my goals when supervising students in experiential courses is to create a safe and trusting environment in which trainees can take interpersonal risks and experiment with new behaviors, try out different techniques without fear of being judged harshly, and engage in a level of self-exploration that is needed to become competent clinicians. I work with students in the early part of their training program before they start counseling clients, and it is imperative that they receive a solid foundation in ethics, counseling theories, group work, and other core subject areas. But as you well know, content knowledge alone is insufficient to prepare a person to be an adept counselor. For many students who have little or no prior experience with personal therapy or who have not engaged in some form of personal growth, there is a rather steep learning curve during this period. I've heard repeatedly from students at the end of each semester that they were not surprised by the demands of the coursework, but they were not expecting to be required to engage in such deep self-examination. Many have been surprised to discover that counseling is such a complex process.

Faced with various types of challenges during their training (educational, emotional, and interpersonal), counseling students may feel overwhelmed at times. This has always been true; however, today's trainees and tomorrow's clinicians will have the additional burden of helping their clients navigate an increasingly stressful world plagued by divisiveness, tribalism, and hate; the catastrophic effects of climate change and serious public health crises such as COVID-19; and problems that are by-products of social media and technology (such as cyberbullying, vulnerability to disinformation campaigns, and cybersecurity threats). Trainees can expect to see increasing rates of depression, anxiety, and trauma in their caseloads as disturbing trends in society continue to unfold, and they may need support in strengthening their own resilience as they prepare to enter the counseling field and take on the helping role. Supervisors and counselor educators can play a vital role in preparing their graduate students for this challenge.

I believe it is very important for clinical faculty and supervisors to balance their obligation to function as gatekeepers of the profession and monitor competence with a commitment to empower trainees to follow their intuition, take appropriate risks, and develop their clinical judgment. Realistically, growth does not occur without risks being taken, and when risks are taken, the odds are good that mistakes will be made. It can be useful to talk about these mistakes and what can be learned from them in supervision.

Although I had a couple of less-than-optimal supervisory experiences as a trainee, I consider myself fortunate to have received excellent supervision for the most part. In retrospect, one of the most powerful learning tools my supervisors had to offer was effective modeling. Now that I am in a position to supervise students in an experiential group course that I frequently teach, I constantly keep this in mind. For instance, I remind students with perfectionist tendencies that they are expected to model being self-aware human beings, not perfect beings, for their clients, and my credibility would be diminished if they observed me being hypercritical of my own shortcomings. Of course, I tell my trainees not to go out of their way to be imperfect, but if mistakes do happen, I stress the importance of addressing them and learning from them. In the classes I teach, I tend to do a lot of processing out loud to model for my students the internal process I experience. When I make mistakes, I use these opportunities as teachable moments. Many trainees suffer from self-doubts and fears of not being able to handle difficult client issues, and I find that I often try to help them get out of their own way and gently use humor to accomplish this.

My Struggles as a Supervisor

I value each trainee as a unique individual, so my assumption is that each trainee will have a unique developmental process. As mentioned, I believe in giving beginning trainees space and time to develop their skills without the looming threat that their every move will make or break their careers as counselors. The last thing I want to do is exacerbate trainees' performance anxiety. Some students blossom later than others, and it would be a shame to prematurely deem a student as unsuitable for the counseling profession simply because the student is on a slightly different trajectory or because the student's initial performance anxiety masked the ability to demonstrate competence. The main issue I struggle with is determining when certain students are not making sufficient progress to warrant them remaining in a training program. Although I am not currently in a position to make such decisions, I am cognizant that my feedback on lab performance forms and grades does factor into the decisions that are made by the department head.

What I Have Learned About Supervision

I have learned a lot about supervision from many different sources. My supervisory training in my doctoral program was very helpful, and my experiences as a supervisee in several different clinical settings gave me many valuable insights about the process. I have also learned a great deal about supervision through informal conversations with colleagues and in my interactions with graduate students. Here are a few lessons I would like to share with you:

- I have learned to trust the process, and I have become much more comfortable with not knowing.
- I find it helpful to view supervision and counseling as parallel processes. As we have noted, they certainly are not identical processes; however, knowing the ways in which they are similar enriches the experience.
- Contrary to the naïve assumption I held when I first started working with counselor trainees, I have learned that some trainees are not naturally empathic, and they don't all have keen insights and instincts.
- I have learned that there are limits to the amount of responsibility I should take when a trainee is not performing up to par or working hard enough.
- I have learned to deliver constructive feedback without feeling apologetic, and I sense that my increased comfort with this puts the trainee at ease.
- I have experienced several different supervision formats that have worked very well. This has reinforced my belief that there are often multiple ways to accomplish tasks, and that using a variety of methods only increases my learning.

We have each learned about supervision from different experiences and, with the exception of Michelle, who received some coursework in supervision, the common theme is that in our beginnings as supervisors we had little to guide us except learning from trial and error. We hope we can assist you in learning about supervision from the theory, literature, and personal experiences we present in this book.

Summary

As a supervisor, it is essential that you have a clear understanding of the four goals of the supervisory process and that you communicate them to your supervisees. The four major goals of supervision are to (1) promote supervisee growth and development, (2) protect the welfare of the client, (3) monitor supervisee performance and act as a gatekeeper for the profession, and (4) empower the supervisee to self-supervise and carry out these goals as an independent professional. To carry out these goals, it is essential to have a clear picture of the specific objectives you hope your supervisees will accomplish.

SUGGESTED ACTIVITIES

1. Write about or discuss in small groups in class your reactions to the thoughts and experiences of each of the authors. What stands out for you in what each of them said? What are the commonalities and differences among the authors? Are there specific ideas that resonate with you?

2. Arrange a meeting with a former supervisor and ask the same questions that were addressed by the authors: (a) In what settings have you been a supervisor? (b) What is your philosophy of supervision? (c) What are some ways in which you struggle as a supervisor? (d) What have you learned about supervision? (e) What is your favorite part of supervision? Summarize your findings from this interview with your small group.

3. On a 1–10 scale, with 1 = little or none and 10 = all that I need, how would you rate yourself in terms of having knowledge and skills in supervision? In small groups, discuss what you think you need to learn to become an effective supervisor. How will you go about doing that?

4. What would you most want to say you have learned and accomplished at the conclusion of reading this book (or of taking this course)? How can this text (and course) help you accomplish that? Discuss in groups what you hope to learn and how you can benefit most from the reading materials. What kind of class activities would facilitate your learning experience?

5. In seeking a supervisor, what qualities would you like to see? What qualities would you hope to avoid?

6. What personal attributes do you bring to the supervisory process that you believe will enhance your role as a supervisor? What personal attributes of your own might interfere with your supervision and need to be addressed?

CHAPTER 2

Roles and Responsibilities
of Supervisors

FOCUS QUESTIONS

1. What would you consider the most important role of the supervisor? What are other roles of the supervisor?
2. Think about those who have served as your supervisors. In what roles did they function? What did you learn from your experience with them about becoming a supervisor?
3. How would you handle a supervisee who is in a personal crisis? Would you attempt to do therapy with this supervisee? Are there any conditions under which providing personal counseling to a supervisee is appropriate? Why or why not?
4. What importance do you place on the role of the supervisor as an evaluator and monitor of the supervisee's clinical work?
5. How might supervisees prepare for their work with a supervisor?
6. How might supervisees gain the maximum benefit from fieldwork, internship, or their clinical practice?

Supervision is a complex process that entails a multitude of roles and responsibilities. *Roles* are the functional relationships between supervisors and those they supervise; *responsibilities* include the clinical, ethical, and legal duties of the supervisor. Supervisors are responsible for being informed and knowledgeable about what their roles entail. In this chapter, we discuss the roles and responsibilities of supervisors and provide several case studies to clarify this process. One important aspect of supervision is to assist supervisees in deriving the maximum benefit from their supervision experience and from their internship, field placement, or clinical practice. In this chapter, we also discuss how supervisees can take an active role to achieve their own goals during supervision. The suggested activities at the end of the chapter will help you focus on the key concepts from this chapter.

Roles of the Supervisor

The role of the clinical supervisor in the helping professions is distinct from any other role we assume as clinicians, but it has elements in common with other roles, such as teaching, therapy, and consultation. Supervisors may serve many different functions—often simultaneously. In a single supervisory session, a supervisor might teach a clinical approach, act as a consultant on how to intervene with a culturally diverse client, act as a recorder in documenting the supervisory session, and provide evaluative feedback to supervisees regarding their progress as clinicians.

The role of the supervisor is a composite of many roles, and these roles change as the focus of supervision changes. Competent supervisors have a clear idea of their role in any given situation, why they are serving in that role, and what they hope to accomplish with the supervisee. Case Studies 2.1 and 2.2 illustrate how the roles of supervisors may differ due to the setting and the supervisee. It is important to assess each supervision situation to be sure that appropriate supervision is provided.

CASE STUDY 2.1: RYAN

Ryan is a licensed counseling psychologist supervising Myra, who has a doctorate in counseling but is not yet licensed. In their private practice setting, they work primarily with clients with serious mental illness and with the families of those clients. Ryan is confident in Myra's abilities and judgment and provides supervision as needed.

CASE STUDY 2.2: TONY

Tony is a licensed social worker who is supervising a bachelor's-level counseling trainee in a community college counseling center. Students come to the center for counseling on relationship difficulties, academic performance anxiety, and personal issues such as depression. In his role as supervisor, Tony is the expert, with many years of experience and getting close to retirement, but he must provide opportunities for his supervisees to grow in knowledge and skills through hands-on training as well.

In reflecting on the cases of Ryan and Tony, ask yourself these questions: Which supervisory roles might be most appropriate for these situations? Which supervisory role would be more comfortable for you?

A skilled supervisor is able to sort out the supervisory needs in various situations and assist supervisees with their work in a manner consistent with client needs and agency policy. Ethical supervisors do not relax their supervision duties in frequency or content even though the supervisee appears to be clinically competent based on education or experience.

Bernard and Goodyear (2019) summarized the supervisory roles suggested by several authors whose work has been most influential. A supervisor's role is often identified as that of teacher, counselor, and consultant. Less frequently mentioned roles are evaluator and administrator. It should be noted that providing counseling is not a typical function of a supervisor. It is not appropriate for a supervisor to assume a primary role as a counselor. However, on occasion, the supervisor may address the supervisee's personal issues as they affect the supervisee's counseling work.

There are many commonalties among the various descriptions of the supervisor's role, and no one role is correct for all situations. Much depends on the supervisor, the supervisee, the setting, the client, and the professional and ethical standards that apply to the role of the supervisor in that setting (see Box 2.1).

Box 2.1
ETHICAL AND PROFESSIONAL STANDARDS
REGARDING THE ROLES AND RESPONSIBILITIES
OF THE SUPERVISOR

American Counseling Association (2014)

ACA Code of Ethics

A primary obligation of counseling supervisors is to monitor the services provided by supervisees. Counseling supervisors monitor client welfare and supervisee performance and professional development. To fulfill these obligations, supervisors meet regularly with supervisees to review the supervisees' work and help them become prepared to serve a range of diverse clients. Supervisees have a responsibility to understand and follow the *ACA Code of Ethics* (F.1.a.).

Association for Counselor Education and Supervision (2011)

Best Practices in Clinical Supervision

1.a. Initiating Supervision: The supervisor engages in sound informed consent practices.
2.a. Goal-Setting: To the extent possible, the supervisor co-develops specific goals for supervision with the supervisee.
3.a. Giving Feedback: The supervisor provides regular and ongoing feedback.
4.a. Conducting Supervision: The supervisor adheres to appropriate professional standards (e.g., accreditation, certification, and licensure regulations) in establishing the frequency and modality of supervision sessions.
5.a. The Supervisory Relationship: The supervisor operates with an awareness that the supervisory relationship is key to the effectiveness of supervision as well as the growth and development of the supervisee.
6.a. Diversity and Advocacy Considerations: The supervisor recognizes that all supervision is multicultural supervision and infuses multicultural considerations into his/her approach to supervision.
7.a. Ethical Considerations: The supervisor conveys to the supervisee that both the supervisor and supervisee are expected to adhere to the ethical codes and guidelines endorsed by the American Counseling Association, the Association for Counselor Education and Supervision and other ACA divisions, relevant credentialing bodies, and models of ethical behavior.
8.a. Documentation: The supervisor maintains documentation that provides a system of supervisor accountability.
9.a. Evaluation: The supervisor understands that evaluation is fundamental to supervision and accepts his/her evaluation responsibilities.
10.a. Supervision Format: The supervisor employs various supervision formats (e.g., individual, triadic, peer/colleague review, group supervision) in ways that adhere to accreditation standards and regulations of credentialing bodies (e.g., frequency of individual and group supervision) *and* that meet the needs of the supervisee, is appropriate to the site, and adequately addresses the needs of clients.
11.a. The Supervisor: The supervisor is competent in providing clinical supervision.
12.a. Supervisor Preparation: Supervision Training and Supervision of Supervision: The supervisor has received didactic instruction and experiential training in clinical supervision (concurrent and/or sequential).

(Continued)

Box 2.1 *(Continued)*

American Psychological Association (2015)

Guidelines for Clinical Supervision in Health Service Psychology

Assumptions of the Guidelines on Supervision

- is a distinct professional competency that requires formal education and training
- prioritizes the care of the client/patient and the protection of the public
- focuses on the acquisition of competence by and the professional development of the supervisee
- requires supervisor competence in the foundational and functional competency domains being supervised
- is anchored in the current evidence base related to supervision and the competencies being supervised
- occurs within a respectful and collaborative supervisory relationship, that includes facilitative and evaluative components and which is established, maintained, and repaired as necessary
- entails responsibilities on the part of the supervisor and supervisee
- intentionally infuses and integrates the dimensions of diversity in all aspects of professional practice
- is influenced by both professional and personal factors including values, attitudes, beliefs, and interpersonal biases
- is conducted in adherence to ethical and legal standards
- uses a developmental and strength-based approach
- requires reflective practice and self-assessment by the supervisor and supervisee
- incorporates bi-directional feedback between the supervisor and supervisee
- includes evaluation of the acquisition of expected competencies by the supervisee
- serves a gatekeeping function for the profession
- is distinct from consultation, personal psychotherapy, and mentoring (p. 5).

To the roles described in the literature, we have added "empowerer." We believe this role describes the essence of supervision in the long run. This concept is implicit in much of the literature, but it is important to make this role explicit. Here is our complete list of supervisor roles in the helping professions:

Teacher/Coach
Mentor
Consultant
Counselor
Sounding Board
Adviser
Administrator
Role Model
Crisis Manager
Technology Consultant
Evaluator
Recorder and Documenter
Advocate
Empowerer

Teacher/Coach

The supervisor instructs supervisees on assessment, diagnosis, counseling approaches and skills, ethics, legal issues, and a host of other topics that arise in supervision. The teaching may include assigning readings, suggesting a literature search on a specific topic, offering suggestions for attending workshops, and discussing with the supervisee any number of related topics. Teaching can be done experientially and often entails demonstrating a technique. An important function of the supervisor as teacher is to provide information to supervisees regarding how supervision works and how they can maximize their supervision experience. For example, supervisors might provide written guidelines to their supervisees on how they can assume an active role in their field placement.

When supervisors act as a *coach,* they function in many ways. Coaching consists of a combination of providing instruction, demonstration, modeling, guidelines, and positive and negative feedback. The level of coaching needed is often commensurate with the level of knowledge and skill that the supervisee possesses. The higher the level of the supervisee's knowledge and skill, the lower the level of coaching that is necessary.

Mentor

The supervisor is the trusted guide for the supervisee. The mentor role includes providing direction and guidance for supervisees and assisting them with assessing their current abilities and desired goals as clinicians. Johnson and Ridley (2018) summarized the characteristics of mentors, stating that they are typically kind, healthy, and competent and demonstrate empathy, compassion, understanding, humility, and authenticity. They often make themselves available at a deeper level of communication and use their history and experience in the field to help mentees succeed in ways that may not have occurred to them without the wisdom and generosity of their mentor. Mentors share opportunities for personal and professional growth and at times even integrate the supervisee into a shared professional network, often resulting in an identity transformation in the supervisee. Examples of mentoring may include actions such as introducing a supervisee to professional colleagues to enhance the supervisee's professional network; providing opportunities for professional development by asking a qualified supervisee to assist in giving a presentation; offering a supervisee the opportunity to coauthor a paper; or something as simple as keeping track of the supervisee's own successes in the field and offering acknowledgment and congratulations along the way. One of our colleagues, Brad Johnson, has written several books on mentoring, and this Voices From the Field captures how supervisors often function as valued mentors.

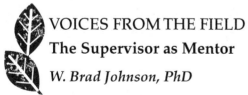

VOICES FROM THE FIELD
The Supervisor as Mentor
W. Brad Johnson, PhD

Mentoring relationships are dynamic, reciprocal, personal relationships in which a more experienced member of a profession (mentor) acts as a guide, role model, teacher, and sponsor of a less experienced person (mentee). In the best scenario, some of our supervisory relationships will take on the characteristics of mentorship. In fact, nearly any assigned training relationship (e.g., academic adviser, teacher, research sponsor, or clinical supervisor) may move across the developmental relationship continuum and begin to embody elements of mentoring.

As a formal supervision pairing grows in the direction of mentorship, three simultaneous processes tend to unfold. First, a sense of mutual trust emerges. A supervisee begins to trust a supervisor who is calm, consistent, affirming, and who clearly has both the client's and the supervisee's best interests at heart. In turn, a supervisor begins to trust a supervisee who is responsive to supervision, nondefensive, and eager to use the supervisory connection to grow, both personally and professionally. Second, the inevitable structure, hierarchy, and formality present at the start of any training assignment slowly becomes more fluid, reciprocal, and collegial. Although supervisors never lose sight of their professional responsibility and relative relational power, as trust emerges, so too does a palpable sense of mutual friendship. Research with mentees reveals that this growing collegiality with a mentor ushers in feeling welcomed into the professional guild; a supervisor's trust and friendship is a powerful endorsement that a neophyte is increasingly regarded as a junior colleague by an admired role model.

The third process indicative of a growing mentoring connection in supervision is increasing social support and broader career guidance on the part of the supervisor. Decades of research on high-quality mentoring relationships reveals two broad categories of mentoring functions. *Psychosocial functions* include affirmation, encouragement, personal counsel, and friendship. *Career functions* encompass direct teaching, coaching, challenge, networking, and sponsorship for the next training opportunities or employment. These functions often increase in frequency and intensity as a supervision relationship moves farther along the mentoring continuum.

Many undergraduate and graduate students have no experience with mentorship with their academic advisers or other faculty, so it is often a delightful and positive experience for both clinical supervisors and trainees when a mentoring connection grows from a supervisory assignment. Even if a supervisee has an academic mentor, we know that junior professionals with a constellation or network of mentors are often better equipped for success both personally and professionally.

Although not every supervision experience is likely to evolve into an enduring mentorship, I encourage supervisors to be open to offering an increasing variety of mentoring functions—both career and psychosocial—to supervisees, especially those who are clearly mature enough and prepared for greater reciprocity and collegiality. Although the supervisor is always responsible to ensure appropriate boundaries, to render honest and accurate competency evaluations, and to balance the best interests of clients and trainees, I predict that some of your most rewarding and enduring mentoring experiences in the helping professions will begin with a formal supervisory pairing.

To learn more about mentoring, see *The Elements of Mentoring* (Johnson & Ridley, 2018).

Consultant

The supervisor may consult with the supervisee to resolve a problem or to help the supervisee make a decision, such as choosing the best treatment approach for a client. The issues addressed can be clinical or administrative in nature. Consultants assist consultees with immediate problems and offer solutions for similar problems that may occur in the future. It is not uncommon for supervisors to require that supervisees seek consultation in emergency situations. The consultation process is aimed at helping people work more effectively on the individual, group, organizational, or community level.

Counselor

There has been much discussion about whether it is appropriate for a supervisor to function in the role of counselor to the supervisee. Corey, Corey, and Corey (2019) state that there seems to be basic agreement in the literature that the proper focus of the supervision process is on the supervisee's *professional* development rather than on *personal* concerns. They add that there is a lack of consensus and clarity about the degree to which supervisors can work ethically with the supervisee's personal problems.

We need to keep in mind that supervision may have therapy-like qualities, but it is not therapy. Becoming the supervisee's therapist creates a conflict of interest, but there are times when the supervisor serves the supervisee well by functioning as a counselor. Clear boundaries must define this relationship, and an appropriate referral should be made if warranted. The supervisor can help the supervisee deal with issues of personal strengths and weaknesses as they relate to the supervisee's practice as a clinician, explore countertransference issues, and cope with stress and burnout. In most cases, the supervisor's role as a counselor is occasional and brief; any need for intensive psychotherapy on the part of the supervisee should be referred to another therapist. Supervisors are ethically obligated to encourage supervisees to identify and work through personal problems that could inhibit their potential as helpers. Although supervision is a process distinct from psychotherapy, the supervisory process can be therapeutic and growth producing. Supervisees can gain significant insights into their personal dynamics through their supervision sessions.

Sounding Board

One of the most important services a supervisor can provide is that of being a sounding board for the supervisee. Supervision should provide a safe place where the supervisee can discuss ideas with the supervisor, get feedback, and seek an objective perspective. As occurs so often in therapy, talking aloud in supervision about clinical issues helps supervisees clarify their thinking process and make sound decisions. Supervision is also an appropriate place for supervisees to discuss fears, hopes, and frustrations with their work and training.

Adviser

Although the primary approach in supervision is to empower supervisees to learn how to make their own decisions, occasions do arise in which giving advice about a situation is in order. Issues surrounding suicide, dangerousness, duty to warn, court appearances, crisis management and intervention, and treating minors may require direct intervention by the supervisor with the supervisee. In these instances, there may not be time to process the matter (although this should be done at some point for the learning of the supervisee), and immediate action may be necessary to provide for the safety of the client and others.

Administrator

Administrative functions are a necessary part of the supervisory relationship. In the administrative role, supervisors are responsible not only to and for their supervisees and their supervisees' clients but also to their team in their work setting. Supervisors must attend to policies and procedures of the organization or setting, licensing body, or professional association. This could include dealing with legal and ethical matters, supervising client documentation, attending to billing matters, assisting the supervisee in learning ways to cope with bureaucracies, ensuring adherence of the supervisee to licensing regulations, and reviewing with the supervisee the legal requirements involved in reporting potential violence or suspected abuse.

Role Model

Our supervisees look to us for knowledge, comfort, guidance, and skill. It is easy to underestimate how much they want to do well, want our approval, and follow our lead. Significant responsibility comes with mentoring and supervising. What we *do* as supervisors is as important as what we say. Our supervisees watch intensely during moments of tension, conflict, or inappropriateness to see how we react, what words we use, and if we actually use the techniques we teach them. They need to see us model compassion, kindness, tolerance, and inclusion. Our responses determine the level of trust and respect they have for us personally, and for the role we play in the field. As clinical supervisors, how we conduct ourselves in supervision sessions will have a significant impact on how our supervisees function as professionals (Barnett & Molzon, 2014). Our demonstrations of professionalism, gatekeeping, appropriate boundaries, and conflict management along with how we deal with frustration, vulnerability, and assertiveness are significant in their development. How we talk about other faculty, supervisees, and clients models what it means to be a professional. It is our job to show our supervisees how to interact using the skill sets we teach. We need to keep in mind that they are learning by watching us closely, and what we model is often what our supervisees learn.

Crisis Manager

The role of crisis manager has become a necessity in today's environment. Historically, serious critical incidents happened on occasion in our practices, but they have become a part of daily life today. Abassary and Goodrich (2014) point out that on a day-to-day basis professional counselors encounter a variety of crises, disasters, and trauma-based situations when listening to clients' stories. The scholarly literature has shown that helping professionals have a variety of reactions to these stories, including stress, anxiety, and trauma. Clinical supervisors must be prepared to help their supervisees navigate these intense and often complex situations. In addition to attending to supervisees' stress and vicarious trauma, supervisors operating as crisis managers must consider the needs of the supervisees' clients.

We must be aware of the vicarious liability we hold as supervisors. We are responsible for the work of our supervisees. This means that our assessment of their training, skills, ethics, and emergency management skills (particularly lethality assessments) are demanding. Developing and clearly communicating a risk management plan is imperative. This plan should provide clear steps for a supervisee to take in seeking assistance in times of emergency. Contact information, backup plans, and emergency resources need to be readily available. A positive supervisory relationship and clear expectations regarding notification of concern increases the chance of early intervention in critical incidents.

Technology Consultant

If you choose to use technology-assisted supervision, competency issues must be addressed for both supervisors and supervisees. Many of us may have some level of technological anxiety, but we have a responsibility to understand and use these new tools when they can provide enhanced experiences and learning for our supervisees. Supervisees will look to us to orient, guide, and assist them when there are technology breakdowns in the process. Simply leaving them on their own to figure it out is not appropriate. We are not expected to be information technology specialists, but we must consult with supervisees to be sure they know how to use the technological devices we require for their education.

Evaluator

Evaluation of the supervisee is a primary responsibility in supervision. Supervisors are ethically required to provide the supervisee with regular and systematic feedback and evaluation (ACA, 2014; ACES, 2011; APA, 2015; NASW, 2017). Frequently, supervisors are requested to provide information to licensing boards, professional associations, universities and graduate programs, and prospective employers regarding the performance and personal characteristics of supervisees. When supervisees apply to security-oriented agencies such as correctional and law enforcement agencies, extensive background checks regarding professional activities as well as character references may be required.

In the role of evaluator, supervisors typically serve as gatekeepers for their profession. As Falender (2018) points out, "supervisors are at the forefront of the process because of their roles as evaluators and gatekeepers. Supervisors engage in ongoing assessment, monitoring, evaluation, and feedback, but with the added purpose of ensuring supervisees are aware of their competence development and are planfully accruing greater competence" (p. 1244). Many of the ethical and legal dilemmas that arise in supervision occur as a result of our gatekeeping function (see Homrich & Henderson, 2018). In addition to evaluating supervisees' clinical competence, Falender and Shafranske (2017) note that supervisors must be able to evaluate their own competence in providing supervision. Aside from guiding supervisees' skill development, supervisors must be able to accurately assess the ability of supervisees to competently oversee the specific services to be provided to clients. Supervisors have responsibilities to supervisees' current clients and to their future clients as well and have the responsibility to monitor and evaluate each supervisee's conduct.

In academic programs, faculty members need to be apprised of the progress of their trainees. Although personal information that supervisees share in supervision generally remains confidential, supervisees have a right to be informed about what will and will not be shared with other faculty members. One of the best ways for supervisors to model professional behavior for supervisees is to deal appropriately with confidentiality issues pertaining to supervisees. For more detailed information about evaluation in supervision and the role of gatekeeping, see Chapter 10.

Recorder and Documenter

Another role of the supervisor is that of recorder of supervisory sessions. This is essential for the protection of the supervisee and the supervisor. It is good practice for a supervisor to keep track of what the supervisee is bringing to supervision. Professional practice entails maintaining records of every session, including any major issues that arise in the discussion. The confidentiality of those records should be maintained as well.

Advocate

Social justice and advocacy are areas of increasing concern for all counselors (Lee, 2018; Lee et al., 2018; Lee & Zalkalne, 2019). Ideally, all counselors will make a commitment to promoting change on both individual and community levels; however, they do not all have the same areas of interest and expertise. Because marginalized clients are often oppressed to some degree by the dominant society, counselors can do a great deal to further the welfare of their clients by both speaking on their behalf and teaching them skills to become advocates for themselves. One role of a supervisor is to address with supervisees how they can begin thinking in terms of speaking out for their clients. We discuss advocacy in more detail in Chapter 6.

Empowerer

The best way to sum up the many roles of the supervisor is as an empowerer of the supervisee. The supervisor empowers a supervisee by gradually and over time transferring the tasks and the power of supervision to the supervisee. As the supervisee becomes more able to self-supervise, the focus of supervision and consultation is adjusted to enhance the supervisee's growth. Our goal is to help the supervisee become self-sufficient in overseeing the clinical work using the skills and abilities learned through the process of supervision. In our view, empowerment is a process, not a one-time event.

Supervisors serve in many roles, often simultaneously. The role chosen should be a good fit with the purpose of the supervisory context. As long as you practice within accepted professional and ethical standards, supervisors have some latitude in their approach in working with supervisees and, at the same time, serving the best interests of the client. Self-monitoring is essential as you develop your approach to supervision (Falender & Shafranske, 2017). Now that you have an understanding of the roles supervisors play, read Case Study 2.3 and see if you agree with Victor's advice to Jennifer.

CASE STUDY 2.3: JENNIFER

Jennifer is a newly licensed marriage and family counselor who works at a community mental health center with children who have severe behavioral problems. She has been assigned two counseling students to supervise. Having completed one theory-based course on clinical supervision in graduate school, Jennifer is nervous about her new role and finally putting her knowledge into practice. Her senior colleague, Victor, who has supervised hundreds of counseling students and will supervise her supervision, encourages Jennifer to relax and just let the supervision happen. He says that all she really needs to do is practice good listening skills and let the supervisee do the rest. According to Victor, if you are a good therapist, you will be a good supervisor.

What is problematic about Victor's approach? Although Victor's intention may be to help Jennifer feel at ease and trust her instincts, his advice does not take into account that Jennifer may need more specific suggestions at this early point in her development as a supervisor. Moreover, Victor's perception of the role of the supervisor and the purpose of supervision may have been acceptable in years past, but it is not today. Supervision is similar to therapy in that many of the same relationship and problem-solving skills are used, but the main goal of supervision is to protect clients while teaching, monitoring, and evaluating the supervisee. Jennifer can probably rely on Victor as a consultant but not as someone who can help her define her role as a supervisor. Our advice to Jennifer is to first consider speaking directly with Victor about her concerns. Next, she might examine the agency and relevant professional standards in determining the roles and responsibilities of the supervisor. She might also consider seeking a different supervisor with whom she can be clear about her supervision needs.

Responsibilities of Clinical and Administrative Supervisors

Clinical supervisors' teaching, training, mentoring, and monitoring roles ensure that trainees develop and maintain competence. According to Campbell (2006), "administrative supervisors and clinical supervisors function under two separate models with different purposes, different missions, and different rule books" (p. 4). Utilizing a business management model, *administrative supervisors* focus on maintaining a well-functioning organization and are concerned with productivity, workload management, and accountability. A study by Tromski-Klingshirn and Davis (2007) found that supervisees who received both clinical and administrative supervision from the same supervisor reported overall satisfaction with their supervisors and did not view this dual role as problematic.

These functions do not conflict and can be carried out ethically and competently by the same supervisor. The ultimate goal of supervision is to ensure that current and future clients will receive the best services available from the supervisee.

The scope of legal and ethical responsibility in supervision is far-reaching. Generally, the supervisor is legally and ethically responsible for all of the professional activities of the supervisee as well as his or her own actions as a supervisor. Practically, this means that supervisors must have some knowledge of all the clinical activities and cases of the supervisee and be available to provide supervision as needed (ACA, 2014). Legal responsibilities are discussed further in Chapter 8. Supervisors can provide effective supervision to supervisees in a practical and reasonable fashion within their normal workload.

The major responsibilities of supervisors are summarized in the following pages, and most are discussed in greater detail in subsequent chapters.

1. *Recognize that the supervisor is ultimately responsible, both legally and ethically, for the actions of the supervisee.*

The clinical supervisor shares responsibility for the services provided to the client (ACA, 2014; Herlihy & Corey, 2015b). Liability of supervisors has been determined by the courts and includes direct liability related to negligent or inadequate supervision and vicarious liability related to negligent conduct by the supervisee.

From both a legal and ethical standpoint, trainees are not expected to assume final responsibility for clients; rather, their supervisors are legally expected to carry the decision-making responsibility and liability. Bernard and Goodyear (2019, pp. 274–276) state that supervisors bear both direct and vicarious liability. *Direct liability* is incurred when the actions of supervisors are the cause of harm; for example, giving tasks to trainees that exceed their competence. *Vicarious liability* pertains to the responsibilities supervisors have for the actions of their supervisees because the supervisee is legally regarded as an extension of the supervisor. Liability for the actions of supervisees is based on supervisors' professional relationships with supervisees. (This topic is discussed in greater detail in Chapter 8 dealing with legal and risk management issues.) In Case Study 2.4, a supervisee places the supervisor in a difficult situation. Do you think Ayesha should be held responsible for something her supervisee did of which she was unaware?

CASE STUDY 2.4: AYESHA

Ayesha, a well-respected, licensed counselor, was supervising an unlicensed counseling assistant who, unbeknownst to Ayesha, began providing counseling services to clients for a fee at another office in town. These counseling services were not supervised by any licensed professional. A complaint was filed with the licensing board against the counseling assistant for practicing (out of the second office) without a license and without proper supervision.

With the assistance of legal counsel, Ayesha submitted in writing to the board a complete description of her understanding of these events and how they had occurred. Because the board has jurisdiction only over licensed counselors, it was Ayesha rather than the counseling assistant who was disciplined. The board ruled that Ayesha, as the supervisor, was responsible for all the professional activities of the counseling assistant, and she was disciplined for the unauthorized practice of the supervisee. She was placed on probation as a licensed counselor for one year, restricted from supervising counseling assistants during the probationary period, and required to attend a course on supervision. Following the successful completion of these requirements, Ayesha will have her license fully restored by the board.

- Do you think it is justified for a supervisor to be responsible for all of the professional activities of the supervisee?
- Considering the legal responsibilities of supervisors, how would this influence your decision to become a supervisor?

2. *Have knowledge of every case or client with whom the supervisee is working.*

Supervision is a broad and comprehensive responsibility that encompasses everything supervisees do in their professional capacity. It is the supervisor's responsibility to monitor all professional actions of supervisees. When problems occur, licensing boards look to the supervisor to understand the extent of guidance and direction provided to the supervisee.

To fulfill their ethical and legal responsibilities, supervisors must check on their supervisees' progress and be familiar with each case of every supervisee. Supervisors may not be cognizant of all the details of every case, but they should at least know the direction in which the cases are being taken. Supervisors should consider meeting at least briefly with every client with whom the supervisee is working. Many supervisors consider this to be unrealistic because of time and caseload constraints, but legal liability does attach responsibility to the supervisor. An alternative might be watching video recordings of every client so the supervisor has some direct experience with those clients. As daunting as this may seem to those who plan to supervise, it should be reassuring to know that risk management strategies do exist to minimize liability in such situations. For example, one way to minimize risk is to create a clear supervision contract that explains the supervisee's responsibility to discuss any high-risk clients about whom there are concerns. An extensive list of risk-management strategies is presented in Chapter 8.

3. *Provide feedback and evaluation to supervisee regarding performance.*

Supervisors are expected to provide feedback and evaluation to supervisees on a regular basis (ACA, 2014; ACES, 2011; APA, 2017; NASW, 2017; NBCC, 2016). Supervisors are expected to tell supervisees how they are doing, how they see their strengths and weaknesses as they relate to their clinical work, how they are proceeding in terms of their goals for supervision, and the expectations for remediating any deficits. This evaluative function enhances supervisee self-awareness and skill development. Feedback from supervisors ranges from informal verbal discussions to a structured and standardized process. In our experience, using standardized forms and scheduling systematic times for feedback helps to objectify the process and provides a framework for constructive feedback to the supervisee. Relying on informal verbal feedback is more subjective and may only occur in response to a specific problem brought to the attention of the supervisor. Chapter 10 is devoted to a comprehensive discussion of evaluation in supervision.

4. *Monitor the actions and decisions of the supervisee.*

Monitoring the actions and decisions of supervisees is an integral part of supervision because supervisors are ultimately responsible for the actions of their trainees. The *ACA Code of Ethics* (ACA, 2014) states that monitoring client care is the paramount responsibility of the clinical supervisor. It is essential to monitor and evaluate the diagnosis and treatment decisions of supervisees. Monitoring is done in supervision sessions by being vigilant about what supervisees are reporting, how they are making decisions, their openness to and utilization of feedback, and the self-awareness supervisees demonstrate regarding the limits of their clinical competence. One of the best ways to monitor the actions and decisions of supervisees is to observe clinical sessions or request that the supervisee bring video recordings of clinical sessions to supervision. This firsthand look at the actions and decisions of the supervisee is often more reliable than the supervisee's self-report. The second part of monitoring involves intervening as necessary to help supervisees modify their actions and decision-making process. Interventions depend on the nature of the situation and the degree to which clients may be put at risk by the actions of the supervisee.

5. *Document the supervisory sessions.*

Record keeping has gained in importance for helping professionals of all disciplines in this increasingly litigious era (Bernard & Goodyear, 2019, p. 157). Documenting supervisory sessions serves multiple purposes, all of which are important. Careful documentation allows for tracking clients and issues of our supervisees; supports documentation requirements for licensing boards, professional associations, and prospective employers; and serves as a risk management strategy. From an ethical, legal, and clinical perspective, an important responsibility of supervisors is to keep adequate records. From a *clinical* perspective, record keeping provides a history that a supervisor can use in reviewing the course of the supervisory relationship; it also provides reminders of topics to follow up in subsequent supervision sessions. From an *ethical* perspective, records can assist supervisors in providing their supervisees with assistance in delivering quality care to their clients. From a *legal* perspective, state or federal law may require keeping a record, and accurate and detailed documentation of the supervision process provides an excellent defense against possible malpractice claims. From a *risk management* perspective, record keeping may be the standard of care for both counselors and supervisors (Wheeler & Bertram, 2019).

Writing progress notes can be a simple and straightforward process that takes little time. The complexity, length, and content will vary according to what happens in a particular session, and most sessions can be adequately documented in a brief way. We think this general advice also fits well with documentation pertaining to the supervisory process. It is important to document specific instructions or directives provided to supervisees (Wheeler & Bertram, 2019).

6. *Supervise only within the scope of your expertise and refer out for additional supervision/consultation as necessary.*

Supervisors are expected to have in-depth knowledge of the specialty area in which they provide supervision (ACES, 2011). When issues, topics, and diagnoses arise that are outside the supervisor's areas of expertise, the supervisor will have to decide how to provide adequate supervision. This can be done in any number of ways: reading on the topic, seeking consultation from another supervisor competent in the area, referring the supervisee to another supervisor for adjunctive supervision, or addressing the issue as a collaborative effort between supervisor and supervisee.

When an issue is clear cut, determining competence is not difficult. For example, if a client may have a neurological dysfunction and the supervisor has had no training or experience in that area, it is prudent to seek consultation from a supervisor with such expertise. The consultant might meet with the supervisor and the supervisee, thus providing both with the opportunity to expand their knowledge on the topic. Determining competence is more complex when the supervisor has some knowledge of the topic but perhaps little experience. How much knowledge and experience is enough to render the supervisor qualified to supervise on the topic? It is a judgment call on the part of the supervisor, and the "standard of care," or what other similarly trained clinicians would consider to be the necessary knowledge and experience, is a good measure for how to proceed. When unsure, supervisors should consult with colleagues regarding their ability to supervise certain aspects of practice.

7. *Provide supervisees with due process information.*

Due process is a legal term often described as "notice," and a "hearing" must be provided before a right can be removed (CACREP, 2016). In supervision, due process includes providing supervisees with clear expectations for performance, outlining the procedure for handling adverse actions and disciplinary action, and explaining supervisees' rights to appeal such actions when performance expectations are not met. The procedures vary tremendously between academic and nonacademic settings and between public and private settings, but all supervisees, regardless of setting, have the right to be given this information. Timely feedback should be provided to supervisees so that they have ample opportunity to correct their mistakes or demonstrate improvement. Information about due process can be provided in a written contract, which both supervisee and supervisor review and sign to show that a clear understanding of this process has been established. This is best done at the beginning of the supervisory relationship and long before any problematic situation arises and should be reviewed periodically.

8. *Have a written contract between the supervisor and supervisee regarding the scope and expectations in supervision.*

The use of a simple, clear, comprehensive contract can clarify the many facets of the supervisory relationship and provide a framework for problem resolution. A supervision contract that addresses both rights of and expectations for supervisees is provided in Appendix 2A at the end of this chapter. A written contract details the framework for a successful supervisory experience for both supervisor and supervisee. As such, it protects the supervisor, the supervisee, the agency, and, most important, the client. In addition to informed consent in the supervisory process, it is the responsibility of supervisors to ensure that supervisees carry out an informed consent process with their clients prior to beginning a counseling relationship. This informed consent must address the purpose of supervision and the communication of sensitive information during supervision sessions, especially if the supervisee is involved in group supervision.

Thomas (2007) contends that it is considered the standard of practice to give clear informed consent material to supervisees, both orally and in writing. The goal of informed consent is to enhance the quality of the supervision experience. It is beneficial to discuss the rights of supervisees from the beginning of the supervisory relationship, in much the same way as the rights of clients are addressed early in the therapy process. If this is done, the supervisee is empowered to express expectations, make decisions, and become an active participant in the supervisory process. When supervisees know what they can expect in all aspects of their supervision and what they need to do to achieve success, both supervisee and supervisor benefit. Misunderstandings are minimized and both parties are more likely to experience satisfaction in their respective roles. Thomas suggests topics such as the following be included in a supervision contract: supervisor's background, methods to be used in supervision, the responsibilities and requirements of supervisors, supervisee's responsibilities, policies pertaining to confidentiality and privacy, documentations of supervision, risks and benefits, evaluation of job performance, complaint procedures and due process, professional development goals, and duration and termination of the supervision contract. More detailed information regarding contracts can be found in Chapter 8 and in the appendix at the end of this chapter.

9. *Monitor the personal development of the supervisee as it affects the practice of counseling.*

Too often, developing self-care practices is seen as the responsibility of the supervisee rather than as the duty of the counselor educator and supervisor. According to Stebnicki

(2008), it is incumbent upon a clinical supervisor to address issues of supervisees' personal growth and self-care needs. Examining the thoughts and feelings of supervisees during a supervision session is appropriate because supervision addresses personal issues that affect supervisees' work with clients. It is important for the supervisor to keep a watchful eye on issues that affect the supervisee's counseling practice and to recommend action as needed. Policies and procedures for intervening with impaired professionals should be established as well. These topics are addressed in detail in Chapter 7.

10. *Model effective problem-solving skills and help supervisees develop problem-solving capabilities.*

Modeling and assisting supervisees in developing their own problem-solving capabilities are primary roles and responsibilities of the supervisor. Bernard and Goodyear (2019) clearly state that the primary responsibility of supervisors "is to model what they aspire to teach" (p. 280). A developmental accomplishment in supervision is to assist supervisees in creating their own system of problem solving, both for themselves and to assist clients in their problem solving.

It is easy to slide into feeling responsible for supervisees and to cover bases for them when they are just getting started. It is important to gauge the amount of guiding, reminding, and answering you take on as a supervisor. Early in the process there will be more of these verbalizations and actions, but these should progressively slow down as supervisees take on more of the responsibility for themselves. If this progressive independence in responsibility and behavior does not occur, it can create dependence, which is not a healthy dynamic for the supervisor, the supervisee, or clients of the supervisee.

11. *Promote the supervisee's ethical knowledge and behavior.*

Another major responsibility for the supervisor is to assist the supervisee in becoming a competent and ethical professional and to provide services in compliance with ethical standards of practice. This is supported explicitly or implicitly by the major professional standards and codes of practice (see APA, 2017). The main purposes of ethical standards for clinical supervision are to provide behavioral guidelines to supervisors, to protect supervisees from undue harm or neglect, and to ensure quality client care (Bernard & Goodyear, 2019). The supervisor assists the supervisee in understanding specific ethical standards and codes and how they apply to the supervisee's work with clients. Assisting the supervisee's development of ethical knowledge and behavior requires teaching, consulting, and providing feedback about the ethical responsibilities in counseling. Modeling appropriate ethical behavior is another tool that supervisors can use to promote their supervisees' professional development.

12. *Promote the knowledge and skills required to understand and work effectively with clients' individual and cultural differences.*

The supervisor is both a model and a teacher when helping supervisees understand and work with clients' individual and cultural similarities and differences. These topics can be included in the discussion of every case to help the supervisee bring into focus how similarities and differences play a role in the counseling process and how the supervisee can best work with them. One of the major messages supervisors can communicate to supervisees is the need to learn from clients what cultures they most closely identify with and how this might affect the counseling relationship. The supervisor introduces issues of culture, diversity, and power early in the supervisory relationship, indicating the importance these topics have for supervisees' counseling relationships (ACES, 2011). The *ACA Code of*

Ethics (ACA, 2014) states that "counseling supervisors are aware of and address the role of multiculturalism/diversity in the supervisory relationship" (F.2.b.). Chapter 6 provides a detailed discussion of multicultural and social justice issues in supervision.

13. *Educate supervisees about underlying critical ethics issues when working within a managed care system.*

Many supervisees will work in a managed care setting, and they should understand the ethical issues unique to this work environment. Ethical dilemmas most commonly surface in a managed care system in these five areas: informed consent, confidentiality, abandonment, utilization review, and competence (Acuff et al., 1999; Cooper & Gottlieb, 2000; Davis & Meier, 2001; Younggren, 2000).

Informed Consent

Supervisees need to know that informed consent is an ongoing process. If they expect to work within a managed care setting, they need to provide full, complete, and accurate information to their clients. Supervisees should not assume that clients will have complete information regarding how the managed care system affects their treatment. Clients have a right to know that other forms of treatment are being denied to them solely for cost-containment reasons. They have a right to know whether the therapist is versed in brief therapy, that an outside person is likely to judge what kind of treatment will be given and how many sessions will be allowed, the specific limitations of the plan in which clients are participating, and who decides the time of termination of therapy.

Confidentiality

Although confidentiality is considered an ethical and legal duty imposed on therapists to protect client disclosures, confidentiality is seriously compromised in a managed care context. Because of the restrictions on confidentiality, counselors have an obligation to inform clients from the outset of the professional relationship about the relevant limits of confidentiality under their managed care policy.

Abandonment

The codes of ethics of the various professional organizations state that mental health practitioners do not abandon clients, but clients in a managed care system are likely to feel abandoned if their treatment ends abruptly, which might well happen. Under managed care programs, termination is not often a collaborative process between counselor and client; rather, termination is generally decided by the managed care provider. For that reason, the clinician should determine the limits of each client's insurance coverage and make realistic treatment plans with that in mind.

Utilization Review

Managed care programs monitor all treatment. Utilization review refers to the use of predefined criteria to evaluate treatment necessity, appropriateness of therapeutic intervention, and therapy effectiveness. Although the needs of the client should be given primary consideration, managed care focuses on ways to contain costs.

Competence

Many managed care companies require the use of brief treatments or group treatment. Clinicians who work in a managed care system need to have special knowledge, skills, and competencies to deliver a variety of brief services in a flexible and holistic manner with a diverse range of client populations and client problems. Treatment plans need to be formulated rapidly, goals must be limited in scope, and the emphasis must be on attaining results.

14. *Recognize the importance of self-care and educate the supervisee in developing self-care strategies.*

Supervisors have a responsibility to recognize the signs of stress and to take good care of themselves. If supervisors are not practicing self-care habits, they are most likely not going to be able to carry out most of the responsibilities we have discussed. If supervisors are coping with stress effectively, both personally and professionally, they can influence their supervisees in a positive way. The work of counselors can lead to significantly increased levels of stress, which is often manifested in physical, mental, emotional, occupational, and spiritual fatigue (Stebnicki, 2008).

Counselors are called upon to listen for hours to stories laden with pain and sadness. They hear stories revolving around themes of loss and despair, oppression and powerlessness, and hopelessness. Being present and working with the stressful stories of clients subject counselors and trainees to their own stress on a daily basis, and this can be especially troubling if they are not practicing self-care. Supervisees may be particularly vulnerable to the effects of this stress, which can result in diminished professional competence if supervisors do not address it.

In addition to many professional stressors, counselors are subject to pressures and stresses in their personal life. Counselors may experience the death of loved ones, interpersonal conflicts with family members and others, divorce and custody battles, financial problems, physical and mental health issues, various forms of discrimination, and struggles finding a healthy work-life balance. Counselors cannot escape the constant bombardment of stressful news about local, national, and international events. Attached to our smartphones, in seconds we learn about crises occurring locally and throughout the nation and the world as they unfold in real time. Counselors often find it extremely taxing to process their own reactions to major stressful events occurring in the world and then spend so much time each week helping their clients process their reactions to the same events. If trainees and counselors do not engage in self-care practices, they are at risk of not being able to carry out their professional duties (Corey, Muratori, et al., 2018). Unmanaged stress is a major cause of burnout and eventual impairment. Supervisees should have opportunities to discuss ways that stress is influencing their work with clients, and they should explore ways to maintain their vitality. For more on the topic of how stress influences the work of counselors, see Stebnicki (2008); for recommended resources for self-care for mental health practitioners, see Norcross and VandenBos (2018), Corey, Muratori, Austin, and Austin (2018), and Corey (2020).

In the Personal Perspective, Michelle Muratori describes how she addressed self-care practices with her graduate students.

MICHELLE MURATORI'S PERSONAL PERSPECTIVE

I formerly taught an introductory counseling course for master's-level students and would require each of them to design a self-care project that they would implement over the course of the semester. I explained to them that to remain energetic and effective as practitioners and to prevent burnout, self-care is a necessity. I emphasized that self-care needs to be incorporated into their daily lives, and there is no time like the present to get started on it. I asked them to come up with a self-care goal and a plan for achieving it. They would be assisting their clients in formulating personal goals and monitoring the attainment of their goals, and this project gave trainees an experience with goal setting.

I received a range of reactions to this assignment. Invariably, a few students found it to be extremely difficult. The project was intended to enhance their lives and reduce their stress, but the concept of self-care seemed so foreign to them that initially it raised their stress level. In other cases, students approached the project with gusto. I recall one student who said that he had always wanted to climb a mountain and that he wanted to do that for his project. I helped him to modify his goal so that it was attainable within the time frame of the course. He ended up working on physical training to build up his endurance. Others chose to learn practical skills such as cooking, becoming more organized at home, or learning to manage their finances, and some experimented with new hobbies that they always wanted to try such as knitting or hip-hop dancing. Students kept a journal to document their progress toward their goal and wrote about their setbacks and struggles as well as their successes. At the end of the course, students shared their projects with the class, and many of them reported that it was their most fulfilling and meaningful assignment. I reminded them of the importance of continuing their self-care projects even after the class ended and to come up with new ones.

The roles of the supervisor are numerous and varied, ranging from providing support to evaluating the supervisee, from teaching to monitoring, and from empowering to advocating. The supervisor must be knowledgeable about the various roles; about which roles apply in which situations; and how any given role will best serve the supervisee, the setting, the client, and the supervisor. A great deal of knowledge, flexibility, and judgment are necessary to carry out the roles and responsibilities of the supervisor.

Teaching Supervisees How to Use Supervision Effectively

Beginning trainees may not have established a strong enough foundation to know what their needs are and what questions to ask. Supervisees may believe that an experienced professional will provide answers that help supervisees make sense of their work with clients. A critical role of supervisors is to teach supervisees how to involve themselves in the supervisory process so they gain the maximum benefit from supervision. Unfortunately, some supervisors only briefly mention how supervision works, what trainees can expect from them, and what roles they will play. More responsibility then falls on supervisees to take an active role by asking questions and expressing what they need from their supervisor.

In the first session with your supervisees, provide an orientation to the process of supervision and begin a discussion of informed consent, which will continue until the termination of the supervisory relationship. This process should include a discussion of topics such as your role as a supervisor, expectations for both supervisor and supervisee, the process of evaluation and feedback, and ethical and legal standards. Encourage supervisees to assume an active stance in supervision by asking what they hope to accomplish.

Supervisees will want to know how supervision works, including the respective responsibilities of both supervisee and supervisor. What supervision models and methods will be used? Will supervision address both personal and professional concerns, or will the supervisor direct the sessions? Will there be opportunities to discuss the supervisory relationship itself? What does the supervisee need to do to be successful in this placement? How and when will evaluation occur?

Supervisees can assume responsibility for deriving maximum benefits from supervision by being prepared for this experience. Here are some suggestions that can help you get the most from your supervision:

- Know the general purpose of supervision.
- Recognize that supervisors are individuals who may enact their role in a variety of ways.
- Accept that a certain level of anxiety is to be expected in the supervision process.

- Clarify any aspects of your contract with your supervisor regarding the content of the supervision sessions.
- Ask how supervision will work.
- Ask how and when evaluation will occur.
- Strive to be as honest and open as possible during your supervision sessions, and ask your supervisor for what you need.
- Spend time preparing before meeting with your supervisor. One way to prepare is to write summaries of your cases and identify questions in advance that you would like to explore with your supervisor.
- Engage in the supervision process in a way that is meaningful to you. Be willing to ask difficult questions of your supervisor and also of yourself.
- Do your best to work within the framework of your supervisor's style.

Perhaps one of the best ways to assist supervisees in learning how to use supervision effectively is for supervisors to take the initiative and prepare a written statement that clarifies supervisees' rights and responsibilities in the supervisory process. It is a good practice to explain that supervisees will be asked to evaluate their supervision experience near the end of their work assignment. Providing this opportunity for supervisees to look over specific dimensions of their experience that they will be asked to evaluate at a later point can help supervisees focus their attention on what they can expect from supervision.

Assisting Student Supervisees in Taking an Active Role in Fieldwork Experiences

For those of you who supervise students in fieldwork and internship settings, we encourage you to discuss practical strategies with your supervisees that will increase their chances of deriving the maximum benefit from their fieldwork and internship experiences. Students will benefit from learning the following strategies for getting the most out of their placements, and supervisors can lead these discussions. Many of these tips have been adapted from material in *Becoming a Helper* (Corey & Corey, 2021, chap. 10).

- *Seek a variety of placements with a diverse range of client populations.* If you think you want a career working with older people, for example, consider an internship with troubled adolescents. By working with diverse populations, you can deepen your experience and develop new interests. If you focus solely on a narrow population or problem area, you are likely to limit your possibilities of finding a job. Stretch your boundaries and discover where your talents lie.
- *Realize that you can be of assistance to clients who are different from you.* Some supervisees believe that to help a person they must have had the same life experience. A young male counselor may doubt his capacity to effectively counsel an elderly woman who has lost her husband and is struggling to find meaning in her life. A trainee may doubt that she can work with a client of a different race. Or a trainee who has not experienced trauma may wonder about her ability to empathize with clients who have had intense pain in their lives. There is value in drawing on your own life experiences when working with clients who differ from you. Your experiences can help you to identify with the feelings and concerns of your clients, even if your circumstances differed dramatically from theirs. It is more important to be able to understand the client's world than to have had a similar problem.
- *Fit into the agency rather than trying to get the agency to fit you.* Be open to learning from the staff and the clients who come to the agency. You can learn a good deal about an agency by being attentive and by talking with coworkers. Ask about

agency policies, about the way programs are administered, and about management of the staff. At some point, you may be involved in the administrative aspects of a program.

- *Recognize the limits of your training, and practice only within those boundaries.* Put yourself in situations where you will be able to obtain supervised experience. Regardless of your educational level, there is always more to learn. It is essential to find a balance between being overly confident and being plagued by self-doubt.

- *Be flexible in applying techniques and interventions to diverse client populations.* Avoid falling into the trap of fitting your clients into one particular theory. Use theory as a means of helping you understand the behavior of your clients. Discuss your ideas in supervision sessions, and clarify your goals and rationale for interventions.

- *Learn how to use community resources and community support systems.* Draw on support systems by making connections within the community. You can do this by talking to other professionals in the field, by asking fellow students about their connections in the community, and by developing a network of contacts. This kind of networking can lead to a range of job opportunities.

- *Keep a journal and record your observations and personal reactions to your work.* Rather than focusing on the problems of your clients, strive to write about how you are being personally affected by your relationships with different clients and what lessons you are learning.

- *Look for ways to apply your academic learning to your fieldwork.* Academic content comes to life when you are able to put it into action. Find ways to work cooperatively with others at your placement site and to combine your talents, interests, and ideas with theirs.

- *Be prepared to adjust your expectations.* Do not expect the agency staff to give you responsibility for providing services to clients before they have a chance to know you. You will probably start your fieldwork in an observing role. Later you may sit in on a counseling group and function as a coleader. Over time, you will be given greater responsibility.

- *Treat your field placement like a job.* Approach fieldwork in much the same way as you would if you were employed by the agency. Think and act in a self-directed way. Look for opportunities to propose your ideas and offer your assistance. Unpaid internships often turn into paid positions. At the very least, you will be looking to your site supervisors for letters of recommendation for employment, so leave a good impression.

- *Do not allow your idealism to be eroded by others' negative attitudes.* If you find yourself in an environment in which your supervisor, peers, and colleagues have negative attitudes, recognize that you do not have to "go along to get along." Although you may experience feelings of discouragement at times, find a safe place where you can talk about your disillusionment and look for what you *can* do rather than focusing on what you cannot do. A practicum seminar may offer the ideal setting to discuss your concerns.

- *Recognize that learning is never finished.* You need to develop a certain level of competence before launching your career as a counselor, but be aware that learning never ends. Be open to acquiring new information and developing new skills. As part of your fieldwork or internship placement, you will usually receive on-the-job training and supervision. Learn from coworkers and supervisors and apply that learning in working with clients.

- *Be aware of the emotional and physical toll your work may have on you.* Unfinished business may surface as you get involved with clients. If you want to work with people who have a range of human problems, be ready to deal with personal issues that might surface for you. Recognize that you may be anxious about performing well. As a student or intern, you are in the placement to learn and are not expected to know everything. Do not be afraid to say, "I don't know." Talk with your supervisor for guidance, and if your anxiety level becomes immobilizing, seek counseling.

- *Consider seeking therapy to explore personal issues that surface as you begin working with clients.* Not only can your experience in therapy be a source of personal growth, but you can learn much about how counseling works by being a participant in this process. In your supervision sessions, you may identify some unresolved personal issues or areas of countertransference that need to be explored beyond the scope of supervision. Personal therapy can be an excellent supplement to your supervision. As a therapy client, you can explore your self-doubts, perfectionist tendencies, feelings that are triggered by working with certain clients, anxieties pertaining to being a trainee, and other personal issues.

There are many different ways to maximize your fieldwork experiences. In Voices From the Field, Jamie Bludworth, a counseling psychologist licensed as a psychologist in the state of Arizona, reflects on his own training experiences and shares his thoughts on how to get the most benefit from supervised fieldwork experiences. Jamie Bludworth's account emphasizes the importance of taking an active role in preparing for supervision sessions.

 VOICES FROM THE FIELD

Taking an Active Role in Supervision

Jamie Bludworth, PhD

Even though I learned a great deal through the difficulties I experienced in my first supervision group, I believe I could have been better prepared by my instructors to utilize supervision effectively. When supervision was discussed in class, it seemed to me like a mysterious process in which an experienced practitioner would provide answers and guidance for trainees who were struggling to make sense of their clients. It was described in generalities and then only briefly.

The various roles that a supervisor might assume were never revealed to me. I think it is important for the supervisee to be aware of the many and varied roles a supervisor may be required to assume. Is my supervisor interacting with me as a teacher, a consultant, a counselor, or an advocate? How will that role influence the choice of material I bring to our sessions? An awareness of the many supervisory roles is paramount to trainees taking a more collaborative stance toward their supervision, allowing them to better assist supervisors in the creation of an experience that is satisfying for all concerned.

Beyond a cursory knowledge of supervision as a concept, I have found it helpful to ask my supervisors at our first meeting to describe the ways in which they see their role as a supervisor. What will be our focus? Will we primarily examine client issues from a clinical perspective? Or will we primarily explore the ways in which the counseling process is affecting me as a person and a professional? Do they prefer a particular theoretical perspective? Over the course of my training, it was important for me to continually define what I wanted from supervision (not only at the outset but also on a session-by-session basis). It has been crucial for me to prepare for each supervision session beforehand, coming in with examples of my work and clear questions relating to those examples. It was also very helpful to ask my supervisors the rationale behind the suggestions and answers that they provided.

Being prepared for supervision comprises understanding what the process might demand of both you and your supervisor. Being prepared also means being willing to engage the process in a way that is meaningful. Sometimes that means asking difficult questions of yourself as well as of your supervisor.

Summary

Teacher/coach, adviser, mentor, administrator, consultant, role model, evaluator, crisis manager, technology consultant, counselor, recorder and documenter, sounding board, advocate, and empowerer—these are the roles of the supervisor. Although they vary depending on the specific context and clinical setting in which one practices, the supervisor focuses not only on helping the supervisee grow and learn but also on protecting clients and the profession. Clinical supervisors typically function in multiple roles with their supervisees, and self-monitoring of those roles and boundaries is essential.

Supervisors are legally and ethically responsible for the actions of their trainees and are expected to have some knowledge of every case with which their supervisees are working under their supervision. Documentation of supervision is essential. Supervisors must practice within the limits of their expertise, and they have an obligation to provide trainees with timely feedback; monitor trainees' actions and decisions; teach trainees about due process and their rights; guide their personal development as it pertains to their clinical competence; and model and teach effective problem-solving skills, ethical behavior, and multicultural competence. By providing this information in the supervision contract, supervisees can establish realistic expectations about the process of supervision.

In this chapter, we have emphasized the importance of the supervisor providing adequate information about the supervision process so that supervisees can assume a role in establishing goals and the means to achieve these goals in supervision. Informed consent in supervision is as important as informed consent in the client-therapist relationship. Supervisees will profit more from supervision if supervisors make a concerted effort to teach them specific ways to involve themselves as active participants in the supervisory relationship.

SUGGESTED ACTIVITIES

1. Three styles of supervision are described in the following examples. After reading each case, respond to these questions:
    - What roles are emphasized in each case?
    - What are the legal and ethical ramifications as they apply to roles and responsibilities?
    - How would you respond to the different styles of supervision? Which style most closely fits with your own?
    - What are the elements of the supervisory relationship in each situation, and how does the relationship help or hinder the supervision?

CASE STUDY A

Dr. Snyder, a licensed clinical social worker, believes her role as supervisor is to provide a great deal of monitoring and direction for her supervisees. She believes a social work trainee should have few independent clinical responsibilities and should have direct clinical supervision at all times. She devotes a great deal of time and energy to her supervisees and has them follow her and observe her leading groups, participating in team meetings, and conducting case conferences. Her trainees benefit from seeing her at work but do not develop clinical competencies as a result of doing the work on their own. Many of the social work trainees under Dr. Snyder's supervision come away from the training experience feeling no more confident in their clinical abilities than when they began the training.

CASE STUDY B

Ms. Li meets weekly with her supervisees and has clearly defined goals for the supervisory relationship. She gives her supervisees her cell phone number so they can contact her whenever needed. She gives feedback to her supervisees on a regular basis and has a reputation for being direct if not somewhat critical of her supervisees' work. Ms. Li is a very competent clinician. She typically tells her supervisees how to work with their clients, and her supervisees usually find her advice very helpful. Some of her supervisees think Ms. Li could show more warmth and concern for her supervisees; however, most trainees feel that they benefit greatly from being under her supervision.

CASE STUDY C

Mr. Adams is a marriage and family therapist and supervisor who sees the supervisee as a junior colleague who should be able to function rather independently. Mr. Adams learned through the old "sink or swim" method, and he believes in this method of supervision because that model worked out quite well for him as a trainee. His method of supervision is to allow the marriage and family therapist trainee to do the work and to seek his consultation only when the trainee needs assistance. Most trainees under Mr. Adams's supervision like him a great deal, but many feel they would like more structure and direction in their work experience.

2. Consider the following questions and explore them in small groups:
   - In which supervisory roles would you feel most comfortable?
   - Which roles would you least like to assume?
   - Which roles would be the most challenging for you, and in what ways?
   - Is there some other style of supervision you might prefer? If so, describe it and explain why you prefer it.

Appendix 2A

SUPERVISION CONTRACT

This contract is for practicum in which faculty serve in both clinical and administrative capacities. If the supervisor is supervising the counselor for licensure purposes and the counselor has an administration supervisor in his or her work setting, the terms of the contract should look different from what it would if the supervisor is also the supervisee's direct supervisor at work.

I, _____ *(print name)*, as the supervisor, offer this agreement to you, _____ *(print name)*, as the supervisee, and consent to the following conditions set forth for this supervisory relationship. Please read the agreement and sign your name if you fully understand and consent to the conditions.

Professional disclosure of supervisor: This includes but is not limited to the supervisor providing professional credentials, licensures, certifications, etc.

_____
_____
_____

Supervision Model of Supervisor

Example: I follow the developmental model of supervision in which I provide fairly intense supervision early in the relationship, including direct observation of therapy sessions, frequent homework assignments and role playing, providing more guidance, etc. Then as you progress in skills, knowledge, and competency, you will be given more responsibility and the supervision will be less intense. This is not to imply you will ever work independently as we will always share 100% of the responsibility. It simply means that, as you develop professionally, I will encourage you to exercise more judgment and confidence in your skills and decision-making abilities.

As the supervisor, I agree to the following:

- I will provide a minimum of one hour of individual supervision weekly for the patients you are providing services to as part of the requirements of the university practicum.
- I will provide a clear plan of action to you for steps to take should there be an emergency.
- I will adhere to APA's *Ethical Principles of Psychologists and Code of Conduct* (2017) and help you with the awareness of and application of the ethical principles and standards. As part of my ethical responsibilities, I will disclose any factors that might influence your consent to participate in a supervisory relationship with me.
- During supervisory sessions, I will focus on two primary areas: your personal development as a professional and the development of your clinical skills. As part of this concentration, I will help you with developing skills in the areas of theory identification and application, case conceptualization, crisis management, becoming more culturally sensitive, selecting and applying empirically supported techniques, and identifying processes, types of clients, or skills with which you may have difficulty.
- I will not allow you to accept a case that is outside the limits of my competence or too complicated for your level of skill. Therefore, I will observe your intake session of each prospective client, and you and I will discuss each case to determine if it is appropriate for your level of skill and my areas of competency.

(Continued)

Appendix 2A *(Continued)*

- In addition to weekly informal feedback, I will evaluate your performance and provide you with written, formal feedback two times during the semester. The areas of the evaluation will include your professional development, clinical skills, and performance/behavior in supervision and with your peers in practicum. The semester will include a midterm and final evaluation. At that time, I will review the evaluation with you and ask that you sign it to indicate your receipt of the evaluation. You will receive a copy of the evaluation form so you will know from the outset what the criteria are for evaluation. Please be aware that the original evaluation will be entered into your student file and will be discussed with other members of the graduate faculty who participate in your training. Such practice is usual and customary for training programs in clinical psychology.

  Also, be aware that a negative evaluation from me can serve as a full or partial basis for your retention in or dismissal from the program. If such a situation should occur and depending on the reason(s) for the evaluation, you may have the remainder of the semester to make improvements, you may have to repeat the practicum, or you may be dismissed from the program. If you disagree with the evaluation that you receive, you may follow the appeals process described in the Student Review & Retention Policy located in your student handbook.

From you, the supervisee, I expect the following:

- You are to have knowledge of and adhere to the APA's (2017) *Ethical Principles of Psychologists and Code of Conduct.*
- You are to act in accord with the practicum policies and procedures.
- Confidentiality for your client is expected to be a priority. All information and documentation regarding your client must always remain in the graduate clinic/lab. Legal client files must not be removed from the allotted secure area. Only computers and printers on secure servers in the graduate lab are to be used for client documentation, and USB drives with video must not be taken from the area. Your USB must be security encrypted, and you should only have your client information on the drive.
- You are to be prompt and prepared for each of the supervisory sessions. Being prepared means you are to provide the case files with completed progress notes and forms for review (preferably prior to our session) and my signature and the video recordings for that week's session(s). It also means you are to have identified on video any areas during the therapy session that are of particular concern to you and that you want to discuss.
- At the outset of treatment with each prospective client, you are to present him/her with the informed consent form, read it aloud, and explain each of the components verbally, specifically including the limits of confidentiality. This explanation is to include your status as a student-in-training and that you are being supervised by me. You are also to explain that as your supervisor I will often be observing the sessions behind the one-way mirror and/or on video. This explanation should also include any other individuals who might observe your work, such as other graduate students or faculty members who will be observing your work as part of peer-observation and group supervision. Please provide the client with my name and university phone number. I want to view your video of this session, and I want your progress notes to indicate what you told the potential client regarding the elements of informed consent, limits of confidentiality, and your status as a student-in-training. The notes should also reflect the response of the client that indicated his or her understanding.

(Continued)

Appendix 2A *(Continued)*

- You are expected to maintain healthy boundaries with your clients. Sexual contact with your clients is **ABSOLUTELY FORBIDDEN**. However, it is not uncommon for clients or therapists to experience feelings of sexual attraction for one another; therefore, I must be informed of any sexual attraction between you and your client so we may discuss the experience and the best manner with which to handle the situation if deemed necessary.
- You and I share 100% of the responsibility for your client's welfare, and I expect you to **immediately** inform me of any problems. Such problems include but are not limited to suspected child, elder, or dependent abuse; domestic violence; report of danger to self or others; or use of any nontraditional treatment methods.

_____	_____
Signature of Supervisee	*Date*
_____	_____
Signature of Supervisor	*Date*

Source: Adapted from Northwestern State University, Natchitoches, LA, Department of Psychology, and designed by Cynthia Lindsey and Patrice Moulton, 2020. Reprinted with permission.

CHAPTER 3

The Supervisory Relationship

FOCUS QUESTIONS

1. As a supervisee, what kind of relationship would you want with your supervisor? As a supervisor, how will you develop the relationship into one of mutual trust and respect?
2. What are the connections between a close interpersonal relationship and effective supervision?
3. As a supervisee, what are some ways you may have displayed reluctance in bringing your concerns into your supervision session? As a supervisor, what can you learn from this and apply to helping your supervisees challenge their reluctance to being open during supervision?
4. Have you ever experienced a serious conflict with a supervisor? What actions did you take? How did your supervisor react? As a supervisor, how would you like to handle conflicts with supervisees?
5. What would you see as being a failure on a supervisee's part in working with a client? If your supervisee experiences client failures in therapy, how will you assist your supervisee in dealing with this in supervision?

Authentically connecting with others in a meaningful way is central to effective counseling, and the supervisory relationship can serve as a model for the relationships supervisees develop with clients. Regardless of the specific roles and functions supervisors serve, the relationship created between supervisor and trainee is critical to the supervisee's success.

In this chapter, we look at several segments of the supervisory relationship. The importance of the supervisory relationship resonates throughout the literature on clinical supervision (Norcross & Wampold, 2019). The effectiveness of the supervisory relationship is a key element in the growth and development of the supervisee (Borders et al., 2014). Personal and interpersonal issues in supervision include power and authority in the supervisory relationship, the role of a supervisee's and a supervisor's values, issues of trust between supervisee and supervisor, and conflicts between supervisor and supervisee (ACES, 2011). We also explore how supervisors might teach supervisees to effectively deal with a range of challenges, such as coping with doubts and fears, determining when it is appropriate for trainees to self-disclose to their clients, recognizing personal needs, recognizing and managing countertransference, and understanding diverse value systems of clients. Challenges for supervisors are examined, including helping supervisees deal with their anxiety and assisting supervisees in understanding the meaning of failures with their clients.

Abundant research has demonstrated that the quality of the client-therapist relationship makes substantial and consistent contributions in determining therapeutic outcomes, probably more than the particular treatment method (Norcross & Lambert, 2019; Norcross & Wampold, 2019). In much the same way, the quality of the supervisory relationship is a key component for the successful outcome of the supervisory process.

Personal and Interpersonal Issues in Supervision

Considerable research has analyzed the supervisory relationship and the process of supervision. From an empirical base and practical knowledge, Holloway (1999) identified three essential components of the supervisory relationship: (a) the interpersonal structure of the relationship, including the dimensions of power and involvement; (b) the phases of the relationship; and (c) the supervisory contract, establishing a set of expectations for the tasks and functions of supervision.

Holloway (1995) looks at the supervisory relationship from a contextual perspective and separates the supervisory tasks into three distinct phases. During the *early phase* of the relationship, the tasks are clarifying the nature of the relationship, developing ways to work collaboratively and effectively in supervision, designing a supervision contract, selecting supportive teaching interventions, developing competencies, and designing treatment plans. At the *mature phase*, the emphasis is on increasing the individual nature of the relationship and promoting social bonding. As the roles of supervisor and supervisee become less distinct, trainees develop skills of case conceptualization, increase their level of self-confidence, and are willing to explore personal issues as they relate to professional performance. The *termination phase* reflects a greater collaborative working structure. Trainees understand the linkage between theory and practice in greater depth, and there is less need for direction from the supervisor. This is the time for a summative evaluation process, including a discussion of the meaning of termination and the feelings and thoughts associated with it. Time is also allocated for discussion of future professional development and goals.

In this section, we address elements of the supervisory relationship and its importance to the outcomes of the supervisory process.

Supervisor-Supervisee Relationship

One of the most important elements in the supervisory process is the kind of person the supervisor is and his or her ability to establish and maintain a good connection with the supervisee. The quality of the supervisor-supervisee relationship is primary, with techniques and methods being secondary. The methods and techniques supervisors use are more likely to be helpful if an effective and collaborative working relationship with supervisees has been established. Norcross and Popple (2017) concur that "supervision occurs within, by, and through the relationship; maps and methods can facilitate the journey, but ultimately success depends largely upon the supervisory alliance" (p. 48). For best outcomes in therapy and in supervision, practitioners concurrently use evidence-based relationships and evidence-based treatments (Norcross & Wampold, 2019). Efforts to implement evidence-based treatments without including the relationship are incomplete and potentially misleading (Norcross & Lambert, 2019). Essential elements of the supervisor-supervisee relationship include establishing trust and a safe environment, encouraging self-disclosure, identifying transference and countertransference, examining diversity issues, and establishing appropriate boundaries (ACES, 2011).

Trust

Trust is best defined as being able to rely on another with a certain sense of predictability. In everyday relationships, trust takes time to develop. People must learn that they can rely on how others will act and react. In the supervisory relationship, trust is essential because both supervisor and supervisee need to be honest with each other. Supervisors would do well to discuss with supervisees what they both can do to create a trusting supervisory relationship. Supervisors might encourage their supervisees to bring up any concerns they have about trust during the supervisory sessions. Of course, how a supervisor responds when supervisees disclose their anxieties pertaining to trust will affect supervisees' openness to such discussions in the future and may lead them to play it safe if the supervisor conveys a judgmental or defensive tone.

Self-Disclosure

Self-disclosure refers to the willingness of both supervisor and supervisee to be open to and discuss all issues that may arise in the supervisory relationship. Self-disclosure of personal issues and experiences by the supervisor should occur only if it provides something constructive for the supervisee regarding the topic at hand. The supervisory session is not meant to provide an arena for supervisors to resolve personal issues or to vent complaints about their job. When a supervisor engages in self-disclosure, the focus should be on the supervisee rather than satisfying the supervisor's needs (Hill et al., 2019). Generally, the freer supervisees are to self-disclose thoughts, fears, hopes, and expectations regarding the work they are doing, the more valuable the supervisory sessions will be. This level of openness is built on a foundation of trust. Hutman and Ellis (2019) point out that "supervisors depend on supervisees' willingness to disclose accurately and fully in supervision. Most supervision models implicitly assume that supervisees willingly disclose information about themselves, clients, therapy, and supervision" (p. 1). They argue that this is not always the case and conducted research to learn more about the reasons supervisees withhold information from their supervisors. They discovered that the supervisory working alliance emerged as the dominant predictor of supervisee nondisclosure and that "when supervisors are not sensitive to culture in supervision, supervisees withhold information to protect themselves and their clients" (p. 6).

Self-disclosure by the supervisor can be beneficial if done in a skillful, tactful, intentional, timely, and appropriate manner. Supervisors' appropriate and timely self-disclosure often results in supervisees' self-disclosure, especially when supervisors are willing to share their own struggles as counselors. Perhaps the most important kind of self-disclosure in the supervisory relationship is for the supervisor to initiate a discussion pertaining to the quality of their relationship. Immediacy is as important in the supervisor-supervisee relationship as it is in the counselor-client relationship. Immediacy involves talking about what is going on within the therapeutic and supervisory relationship. If supervisors expect their supervisees to disclose their reactions to their experience in supervision, it is important that supervisors create a safe climate that encourages honest supervisee disclosure and that they model facilitative disclosure to their supervisees. As Hutman and Ellis (2019) suggest, "a supportive supervisory alliance involves supervisors creating a climate where supervisees can openly discuss (a) the relationship, (b) the power differential in supervision, (c) their reactions to the supervisor and supervision, and (d) the supervisor's, supervisee's, and client's multiple intersecting identities" (p. 6). When supervisors broach these issues, an atmosphere of transparency is created that increases the willingness of diverse supervisees to self-disclose in supervision sessions. Thus, greater attention to the relationship dynamics is warranted in the supervisory process.

Hill, Knox, and Pinto-Coelho (2019) conducted an original qualitative meta-analysis of the empirical literature to determine what is known about the clinical consequences of therapist self-disclosure. Although their research was focused on psychotherapy, we think there are significant implications for both supervisors and supervisees. Hill and colleagues offered the following practice recommendations for therapist self-disclosure, many of which may apply to disclosure in the supervisory relationship:

- Therapist (supervisor) self-disclosure needs to be thoughtful and delivered with skill.
- Disclosure should be client-focused (supervisee-focused).
- It is important to evaluate the impact disclosure is having on the client or the supervisee.
- Attend to the quality of the therapeutic (supervisory) relationship in determining when to self-disclose.
- Use disclosure sparingly, and keep it brief with few details.
- Make disclosure relevant to what is going on with the client (supervisee).
- Focus on similarities between therapist and client (between supervisor and supervisee).
- Turn the focus back to the client (supervisee) after making a disclosure.

Based on many years of experience training and supervising novice therapists, Hill and colleagues (2019) have found that self-disclosure and immediacy are among the most difficult skills to learn to use effectively. They note that it is difficult for beginning therapists to set boundaries pertaining to appropriate self-disclosure with clients and to determine when to talk about problems that may arise in the immediate relationship. They suggest that trainees can learn these skills by bringing to supervision specific situations in which they have concerns about disclosure with clients. Role playing and deliberate practice are useful ways to acquire and hone disclosure skills. Practicing disclosure and immediacy skills with supervisor feedback provides a model for trainees to use in effective interventions with clients. Clevinger, Albert, and Ralche (2019) recommend that future research examine the impacts of supervisor self-disclosure on supervisee development. They suggest that training on supervisor self-disclosure be more readily available and integrated into existing supervision training opportunities.

In the following Personal Perspectives, Michelle Muratori and Patrice Moulton share their views and experiences regarding the use of self-disclosure to assist in building a relationship of trust and to lessen the anxiety experienced by supervisees.

 MICHELLE MURATORI'S PERSONAL PERSPECTIVE

I attempt to normalize trainees' anxieties by sharing some of the concerns that I once held when I was in training. When it seems appropriate, I also talk about mistakes I made as a new counselor, with an emphasis on how I used these situations as opportunities to move the counseling forward. For instance, I have told trainees about the time I could not contain my laughter when an anxious client told me about an odd experience she had that week. It was important for me to explain to my trainees that I very much liked the client and that we had established good rapport and trust, so we were able to process what happened in a productive way. Beginning counseling students often feel immobilized by the notion that they might make mistakes. They seem to be comforted when they hear that they are not expected to be perfect beings but rather human beings who are willing to grow and learn from their errors. When I teach a course and make a mistake, such as saying something that could be construed in a way that was not intended, or if I have a strong reaction to something that occurred in class, I make it a point to model transparency and appropriate self-disclosure and to avoid getting defensive. By doing this in my teaching and supervision, I find that I am able to create a trusting relationship with trainees.

PATRICE MOULTON'S PERSONAL PERSPECTIVE

I often share with my supervisees my earliest counseling session experiences. I share experiences of success, surprise, humor, and, yes, failure while developing as a therapist. I remember when I was first in training under supervision and realized that I had a 50-minute session with a one-way mirror and bug-in-the-ear technology. I remember being excited, anxious, sick at my stomach, and the whole situation feeling a bit surreal. Within 15 minutes into the intake session, I had adapted to hearing my supervisor's voice and found it comforting to know he was there should I need him. I tell my supervisees about my early experiences as a trainee so they will know that I do not expect them to have all the answers when they are in training and first beginning to see clients. I let them know that I would be more concerned if they had no anxiety about their performance. My hope is that trainees will trust my care for them and their development and that they will be open to hearing and considering the constructive feedback I provide.

In Voices From the Field, Staci Maddox underscores the point that a supervisor's respect for a supervisee is largely responsible for creating a safe and productive climate, which encourages the supervisee to be open and to initiate an exploration of genuine concerns in supervision.

VOICES FROM THE FIELD
Respectful Intervention With Supervisees

Staci Maddox, MS

During my practicum experience it was apparent, to both my supervisor and me, that I was experiencing issues practicing therapy. We had a short conversation in which she inquired about my difficulties, and I was honest in saying that my client reminded me of myself. However, I also told her that I had been taking steps to deal with these issues by myself for a while. However, the stress of the semester continued to build, and I realized I was expending more energy in my struggles to keep my mental state stable than I liked.

Coming from a small town in the southern part of the United States, where the importance of mental health issues can be undermined or even stigmatized, I was nervous about many things. Who can I talk to? I'm on my parent's insurance, so what if they don't approve? Isn't it strange that someone in a psychology master's program needs psychological help? If I do find someone to talk to, am I just going to hear all the same things I've been learning about in my classes? If so, then what is the point?

I approached my supervisor asking for her opinion on my situation and if she had any suggestions on how to move forward. From the beginning of our classes, my supervisor had said that "we can't serve from an empty vessel." This was a big factor in my decision to go to her for advice. I think it's important to stress to all students that their mental health is just as important as that of their client. This touches on the relevant issue of professional liability as well as the sense of care supervisors have toward their supervisees.

As a supervisor, it's important to remember that supervisees are not your clients and that you are in a position of power over your supervisees. Even with the best intentions, it is easy for a supervisor's concerned inquiry to feel like a lecture or scolding, especially if the student is feeling fragile. My supervisor was able to ease my mind during our conversation. When I explained my situation and my diagnostic assumptions, she did not ask me "Are you sure?" or "Why do you think that?" She simply asked if I had taken the *DSM-5* criteria into account in my self-reflection, and she reassured me that I could discuss those points with her if I was comfortable doing so. This gave me confirmation that she cared about my mental health just as much as my professional performance. Despite my vulnerability, she acknowledged and respected my experience and education in psychology and did not discount my strengths as she encouraged me to seek help.

Transference and Countertransference

Transference is a psychodynamic term defined as the client's unconscious shifting to the therapist of feelings and fantasies, both positive and negative, that are displacements from reactions to significant others from the client's past (Corey, 2019). In the supervisory relationship, a supervisee may transfer those feelings and fantasies to the supervisor. It is not uncommon for supervisees to begin to idealize their supervisor as a result of the support they receive and because of their own feelings of insecurity. However, if supervisees have unresolved authority issues, these may play out in the supervisory relationship in the form of resistance. The role of the supervisor in such instances is to be aware of transference reactions and to assist supervisees in developing their own sense of competence and problem-solving ability. It would be a mistake, in our opinion, to challenge supervisees forcefully about their transference issues.

A trusting climate and encouragement by the supervisor will enable supervisees to discuss any of their reactions that may affect their ability to be open during supervisory sessions. For example, a supervisee may be anxious about "doing well" for the supervisor, and this anxiety can result in the supervisee carefully monitoring and silently rehearsing what is said during supervision sessions. If this supervisee takes the risk of disclosing his or her need to be seen in a positive light by the supervisor, the supervisee has already taken a significant step toward becoming more authentic in the supervisor's presence.

Countertransference refers to the reactions therapists have toward their clients that are likely to interfere with their objectivity (Corey, 2019). Some mental health professionals prefer a narrower definition, limiting this concept to reactions that stem from a therapist's unresolved personal problems (Hayes et al., 2019). Countertransference on the part of the supervisor is not uncommon. Unresolved personal issues, and sometimes even problem areas that have been worked through, can be triggered through interactions with supervisees. It is critical for the supervisor to be self-aware and identify any countertransference that may arise and understand how it is affecting the supervisory relationship. Ethically, supervisors are expected to identify and deal with their reactions through their own supervision, consultation, or personal therapy and to protect supervisees from any negative effects in the supervisory relationship. Through their awareness of their countertransference reactions, competent supervisors are more able to prevent their feelings from influencing their behavior with supervisees. Examples of countertransference reactions include the arousal of guilt or anxiety from unresolved personal problems, experiencing an impasse with a supervisee and frustration over not making progress, and impatience with a supervisee. Other common countertransference reactions include an intense need to help and rescue the supervisee or a dislike of the supervisee. What is most important is for therapists and supervisors to learn how to manage their countertransference. This requires a commitment and willingness to examine one's psychological health, one's reactions to clients and supervisees, one's current motivations for doing supervision, and the effect of doing supervision on one's life (Hayes et al., 2019).

If the supervisor needs to discuss these countertransference reactions, we recommend consulting with colleagues rather than with the supervisee as a first step. Talking about the supervisor's countertransference issues directly with the supervisee may be overwhelming for the person, just as a client might be surprised by a therapist's disclosures pertaining to countertransference. The supervisee has enough to deal with in learning to become a competent clinician. After discussing countertransference reactions with a colleague, however, it may be appropriate and useful for the supervisor to share and explore some aspects of this reaction with the supervisee. The developmental level of the supervisee should be considered when deciding whether or not to address transference and countertransference reactions directly with the supervisee.

Diversity Issues

A discussion of the differences between a supervisor and the supervisee should be incorporated into supervision sessions. Most codes of ethics call for supervisors to demonstrate knowledge of individual differences with respect to age, gender, race, ethnicity, culture, spiritual values, sexual orientation, and disability. Furthermore, supervisors need to understand how these contextual factors influence supervisory relationships. Writers in multicultural supervision emphasize the supervisor's responsibility for introducing cultural variables into the supervisory dialogue throughout the supervisory relationship.

Multicultural and diversity competence is an ethical imperative in clinical supervision. Individual and contextual differences must be addressed and incorporated throughout professional practice (Falender & Shafranske, 2017). Diversity competence is an inseparable and basic component of supervision and involves relevant knowledge, skills, and values/attitudes (APA, 2015). Supervisors should include cultural and advocacy competencies in the supervisory contract and intentionally address these topics throughout the supervisory process. Supervisors recognize that all supervision is multicultural supervision, and they infuse multicultural, diversity, and advocacy considerations into their approach to supervision (ACES, 2011).

Supervisors can teach their supervisees to respect the role diversity plays in the counseling relationship by making supervision a multicultural experience in which race, ethnicity, socioeconomic status, sexual orientation, religion, spirituality, gender, and age are discussed. Because of the power dynamics inherent in the supervisory relationship, it is the supervisor's responsibility to serve as the catalyst for facilitating discussions about diversity issues. Too often supervisors emphasize client similarities and minimize racial and cultural differences. If supervisees do not understand the cultural context in which their clients live, they will not be able to effectively work with their clients. There is a price to be paid for ignoring racial and ethnic factors in supervision. If supervisors do not address these factors as they become relevant, this will certainly weaken the trust level on the part of supervisees.

Supervisors can do a great deal to create an open climate that fosters honesty in the supervisory relationship. Supervisors can model curiosity about the supervisee's differences and be eager to learn from the supervisee as well. To do so, however, it is essential that supervisors possess specific multicultural competencies. Regardless of the specific aspect of diversity that is characteristic of a supervisory relationship, any factor that influences the interpersonal relationship should be a topic of discussion. Multicultural and advocacy competencies are dealt with in considerable detail in Chapter 6.

Appropriate Boundaries

It is not uncommon to enjoy the collegiality of the supervisory relationship, to become friendly with a supervisee, and to extend the relationship beyond the sessions, especially as the supervisee matures professionally. How far can the boundary be extended while the relationship remains ethical and professional? Supervisors need to think about the ramifications whenever they consider extending the boundaries of the supervisory relationship. Supervisors must take full responsibility for determining the limits of the relationship and take action when they believe the boundaries are becoming less clear or when expanding the boundaries is adversely affecting the supervisory task. Supervisors are responsible for defining the boundaries of the supervisory relationship and avoiding multiple roles or relationships with supervisees that are likely to negatively influence supervisees or the supervisory relationship (ACES, 2011).

When boundaries are crossed or extended, there should be a good rationale for doing so. However, there is a difference between a *boundary crossing* and a *boundary violation*, with the latter being a serious violation of legal or ethical standards. A boundary crossing should have little potential to harm to the supervisee; in fact, extending the boundaries should have a good chance of benefiting the supervisee or the supervisory relationship. For instance, suppose Nancy invites Shelly, her supervisee, to attend a local conference on PTSD. It is likely that in addition to professional activities at the conference, Shelly will participate in social activities with her supervisor. They might go to dinner or receptions together, and Nancy may introduce Shelly to other professionals and colleagues in an informal setting. Extending boundaries in this particular instance may have a positive impact on Shelly's professional identity and sense of belonging in the profession. Managing boundaries is a topic covered in more detail in Chapter 7.

Ethical Practice

Effective and ethical supervisors provide constructive feedback to their supervisees in a supportive and nonjudgmental environment. They regularly include a discussion of ethics in their feedback to supervisees. They are well trained, knowledgeable, and skilled in the practice of clinical supervision. They limit their supervision to those areas in which they are competent, and they delegate portions of supervision when necessary to make sure that supervisees receive the best quality of supervision possible.

Power and Authority

The supervisory relationship by definition has a built-in power differential—the supervisor is the authority figure in the relationship. Supervisors are aware of the power differential inherent in the supervisory relationship, and they discuss this with supervisees (ACES, 2011). Even though person-centered and feminist models of supervision are based on the assumption that supervisors will do what they can to minimize the power differential and to establish a collaborative relationship, there is still an inherent difference in power. Supervisors continually evaluate the work of the supervisee and provide that evaluative information to licensing boards, prospective employers, and other requestors long after the supervisory relationship has ended. Because the supervisee has relatively less power in the supervisory relationship, supervisors are responsible to clearly inform their supervisees of the evaluative structure of the relationship, the expectancies and goals for supervision, the criteria for evaluation, and the limits of confidentiality in supervision.

We want to underscore the importance of self-monitoring so that power and authority, which are an inherent part of the supervisory role, are used in an ethical and constructive manner. In contrast to supervisors who have a strong need to be in control at all times and impress their trainees with their vast knowledge and wisdom, supervisors who use their power and authority appropriately may empower their trainees to take necessary risks and to develop professional autonomy without feeling threatened.

There is a range of differences among supervisors with respect to how they use their power and authority. Outstanding supervisors pride themselves on self-awareness, are open to feedback from colleagues and supervisees, and show a sense of humility, recognizing that there is always something to be learned from a situation and from their supervisees. Their supervisees are active members of the problem-solving team and usually exude a sense of confidence and calmness that they have developed through supervision.

Less effective supervisors tend to be rigid, focused on their authority and professional role, and closed to feedback; act as if they have all the answers; and use supervision as a forum to display their knowledge. These less effective supervisors tend to emphasize what they have to offer rather than assisting their supervisees in learning how to deal effectively with a range of problems they may encounter with a variety of clients. This often plants the seeds for conflict between supervisees and their supervisors.

Parallel Process

Interactions between supervisor and supervisee may offer insights into the way the supervisee relates to clients. This idea, called *parallel process*, has its conceptual roots in psychoanalytic supervision (Borders & Brown, 2005). Because certain aspects of the relationship between the supervisee and his or her client may be paralleled in the supervisory relationship, it is useful for supervisors and supervisees to pay attention to and explore the various manifestations of parallel process in supervision. For example, a supervisor might observe that her trainee, who is typically very confident and self-assured, becomes unsure of herself and appears helpless as she processes the case of a needy and childlike client. Sharing this observation with her could lead the trainee to gain valuable insights about the dynamics of the counseling process with that particular client.

Although parallel process in the psychodynamic sense may not always occur, a number of parallels between counseling and supervision are readily observable. A supervisee who recognizes the similarities between the roles of and processes of the supervisory relationship and the relationship experienced by counselor trainees and clients is noticing parallel processes. For instance, just as trainees must increase their self-awareness to enhance their counseling skills and competence, clients are encouraged to increase their self-awareness to improve the quality of their life and resolve issues. In addition, counseling students may find the process of training to be emotionally intense at times, and they must remember that clients are likely to find the process of counseling to be emotionally intense at times too. The similarities do not end there. Both trainees and clients must take interpersonal risks if they wish to grow, and both must invest a lot of hard work and effort into their respective undertakings to make progress. Clients must be motivated to change to achieve their treatment goals, just as trainees must be motivated to learn what it takes to achieve competence. Trainees are expected to develop strong personal and professional boundaries with their supervisors throughout the training process, and learning to set healthier boundaries in the counseling process may be an important goal for clients.

In Voices From the Field, Jude Austin and Julius Austin describe some of the similar dynamics between the therapeutic process and the supervisory process.

 VOICES FROM THE FIELD

The Butterfly Effect of Supervision

Jude T. Austin II, PhD, and Julius A. Austin, PhD

Supervision is a critical component of the therapeutic process. Clients may go through the entire therapeutic experience without ever meeting their therapist's supervisor. Despite never meeting, the supervisor influences that client's life and the lives of the client's family members. We think about this interaction as a butterfly effect between supervision and client outcomes. One suggestion or event in supervision can push a client toward healing or derail a client's therapeutic journey. Supervisors who do not own this responsibility are doing their supervisees and the clients they work with a disservice.

To better appreciate the connection between supervision and client treatment outcomes, the counseling process needs to be understood. Many studies support the idea that counseling is most effective when counselor and client build a strong therapeutic alliance. Regardless of the theoretical orientation counselors hold, it is their ability to facilitate this connection that makes them effective counselors. The success of evidence-based treatments also is dependent on a strong therapeutic relationship, and counselors are trained to develop strong therapeutic relationships with clients. In that training, students undergo clinical supervision to build their skills, knowledge, and demeanor to be effective counselors.

Supervisors influence their supervisees both consciously and unconsciously. Supervisors make a conscious effort to ensure the supervisee's and the client's safety and growth. Unconsciously, supervisors influence their supervisees in countless ways. There is an old saying in counseling that "you get the clients that you need." This generally means that trainees get the experience they need to grow. We would expand that saying to include supervisors also getting the supervisees they need to grow. The limitations of a supervisee often trickle down into the client's life. We have had several personal experiences in which struggles in our personal lives paralleled struggles in our supervisees' clinical experiences as well as in their client's therapeutic experience. We can recall telling supervisees things that we should listen to in our own lives. Calling out this parallel process can unstick supervisees, who can then unstick their clients.

The butterfly effect in supervision is not a negative element of the process. However, without awareness of its influence, it may erode the supervisory relationship and have a negative influence on the client's progress in session. We have found a number of processes helpful when managing the butterfly effect in supervision.

- Acknowledge the power we have as supervisors over the supervision and therapeutic process.
- Find our own support system outside of supervision to ensure that we are providing the best services for our supervisees.
- Process the supervision relationship with our supervisees.
- Follow a self-care plan that involves doing something active outside of the office.
- Seek our own therapy to process our lives and reflect on the parallel processes we see in our supervisees and their clients.
- Openly discuss how the client's experience with the supervisee relates to the supervisee's experience during supervision.

Following these guidelines have helped us prepare to manage the privilege and responsibility of supervision. Supervisors have an impact on supervisees, and supervisors also have an impact on clients. Within this process is the potential for supervisors to have a profound effect on the lives of others.

Personal Variables Affecting the Supervisory Relationship

We have explained the importance of exploring diversity issues to strengthen the supervisory relationship. These include values, attitudes, beliefs, age, gender, ethnicity, and spirituality, to name a few. It is important for supervisors to be aware of the many personal variables that may affect the supervisory relationship. In Case Study 3.1, personal values become entangled in the supervision provided to Michaela.

CASE STUDY 3.1: CAROL

Carol, a licensed marriage and family counselor, is supervising Michaela, a marriage and family counselor-in-training. Michaela is talking with Carol about a case in which the parents feel their 2- and 4-year-old children are out of control, yet the parents seem unable to set limits or to enforce discipline in the household. Carol forcefully lectures Michaela on the need for parents to be firm disciplinarians in this era as kids are developing a sense of entitlement at an early age.

Following the supervision session, Michaela has another counseling session with the parents. Michaela emphasizes the need for the parents to regain control of their children. She begins brainstorming with them how they might go about setting clearer limits, being more consistent in following through to enforce those limits, and providing more reinforcement when the children do act appropriately. The parents are appreciative of the direction provided but are puzzled about whether the new approach will work. Michaela was pleased that she was able to take direction from her supervisor and adapt these suggestions to fit her own counseling style and the needs of the parents.

Our values and attitudes affect the supervision that we provide. Even though we may believe we are objective and will not impose our personal values on supervisees, our values influence us in many subtle ways.

- What do you think of Carol's method of providing supervision?
- If you believe something strongly, should you make that belief known to your supervisee?
- How would you respond if you were Michaela?
- If you were Carol and suddenly realized you were imposing your values, how would you proceed from there?

Respecting Diverse Value Systems

A problematic trait of some counselors-in-training is their tendency to impose their values on clients. Even if trainees do not directly impose their values on clients, they may influence clients in subtle ways to embrace their views. It may be difficult to avoid communicating your values to your clients, even if you do not explicitly reveal them. Your nonverbal behavior and body language give clients indications of how you are being affected. Clients who feel they need to have your approval may respond to these cues by acting in ways they imagine will meet with your favor. For example, an unhappily married man who believed you thought he was wasting good years of his life in his marriage may initiate a divorce mostly because of his perceptions of your beliefs. Although we may not actively coerce clients into acting in ways that agree with our own values, we must be sensitive to the subtle messages we project because they can be powerful influences on clients' behavior. For instance, if a school counselor subtly communicates her disapproval of a teacher who has frequent classroom management issues, a student coming for counseling may get the impression that the counselor is taking the student's side in a conflict with the teacher.

Through modeling, supervisors can teach supervisees ways to monitor how values operate in the counseling process. Supervisors are expected to avoid imposing their own meanings, interpretations, values, and beliefs on their supervisees (ACES, 2011), and supervisees must honestly assess whether their values are likely to interfere with the objectivity needed to be useful to clients. Supervisees can explore barriers that prevent them from working objectively with clients during supervisory sessions. Diversity in supervision is explored in greater depth in Chapter 6.

Dealing With Value Conflicts in the Supervisory Process

Some values that may affect the supervisory process are rooted in personal beliefs about religion, abortion, marriage, divorce, sexual orientation, parenting, spirituality, the change process, suicide, and end-of-life decisions. The key for supervisors is to be aware of their own values and attitudes and how they affect their ability to supervise. It is not necessary for the supervisor and supervisee to have similar values and beliefs for supervision to be effective, but it is a good idea for supervisors to initiate discussions about similarities and differences as they emerge. Modeling the exploration of values helps supervisees learn how to do the same with their clients.

How should value conflicts between the supervisor and the supervisee be resolved? Some supervisors think they can work with any supervisee regardless of value differences that might occur. Others are too quick to suggest discontinuing supervision when differences occur and to refer the supervisee to another supervisor. Most value differences can be worked on effectively within the supervisory relationship. Assuming the supervisor is cognizant of the clash of values, differences can be discussed openly and frankly. When it comes to the practice of counseling, clinicians are expected to develop the ability to manage their personal values so they do not unduly influence the counseling process. Kocet and Herlihy (2014) describe this process as *ethical bracketing*, which they define as the "intentional setting aside of the counselor's personal values in order to provide ethical and appropriate counseling to all clients, especially those whose worldviews, values, belief systems, and decisions differ significantly from those of the counselor" (p. 182). Setting aside the personal values of counselors does not mean that they are expected to give up or change their values. Counselors do not have to like or agree with their clients' choices to fulfill their ethical obligation to help those seeking their assistance. Merely disagreeing with a client's value system is not ethical grounds for a referral. It is possible to work through value conflicts successfully. From an ethical perspective, a referral should be considered only when a counselor clearly lacks the necessary skills to deal with the issues presented by the client. It is unethical to refer clients because of a counselor's lack of agreement with their values. This model of value conflicts in therapeutic situations also has relevance to a lack of agreement on values between supervisor and supervisee. This is an opportunity for supervisors to model ethical behavior in working through value conflicts and realizing that the supervisor and supervisee do not have to have the same values in all areas to work together effectively.

In Voices From the Field, Perry Francis addresses how supervisors can assist supervisees in learning to manage their value differences with clients. He also discusses how he attempts to deal with his own value differences with a supervisee.

VOICES FROM THE FIELD

Managing Personal Values

Perry C. Francis, EdD

One area that seems to cause confusion for counselors-in-training centers around the difference between a values conflict with a client and being competent to provide counseling to the client. This uncertainty usually indicates that the supervisee has not yet integrated the values of the profession, is struggling with some countertransference issues, or is honestly concerned about causing harm to the client because of this values conflict. In these cases, I ensure that the supervisee understands the difference between competence and the ability to provide quality services in the midst of a values conflict. I have often said, "if you can counsel Adam and Eve on communication issues, you can counsel Adam and Steve for the same thing." To accomplish this, the supervisee has to learn how to manage his or her personal values.

Please note that I did not say *change* your personal values. This concern is often voiced to me by supervisees—Will I be required to change or bury my values if I continue to work in this field? I reinforce the concept that a counselor's most effective tool in session is the ability to be genuine and at the same time to manage personal values when entering the client's world. This is a learned skill, and it requires some work on my part as a supervisor and on the part of the supervisee. I begin with a conversation about the personal values of the supervisee, the values and expectations of the profession as presented in the Preamble of the 2014 *ACA Code of Ethics*, and where these values may converge or differ. In many cases, the values of the profession and those of the supervisee are very close, and it is important to explore how both sets of values affect the person as a counselor and as an individual. Helping a supervisee create a list of personal values and exploring their meanings and their impact on the supervisee's development helps me understand more about this person as an individual and highlights areas that may give root to countertransference, personal rigidity, and the ability to conceptualize a client. Having the supervisee explore the values and expectations of the profession reinforces the developing professional identity of the supervisee as a counselor.

Next, the supervisee's ability to conceptualize the client's presenting issues is expanded to include managing the supervisee's values within the values of the profession. So often in a values conflict the supervisee can only see the differences between the supervisee's values and those of the client. When this happens, the supervisee misses the opportunity to gain a better insight into the client's issues and to match those to the supervisee's skills and abilities to help (i.e., competence). Why is the client seeking help? How are the client's thoughts, feelings, or behaviors affecting the client's desire to live a healthy life? What treatment plans and goals can the supervisee create, in consultation with the client, to help the client achieve a better life? Helping the supervisee focus on the issues at hand rather than on the differences that divide them helps the supervisee move into the client's world without judgment (or with less judgment) and see the client as a human in need of help.

During my exchange with the supervisee, I also have to be aware of and manage my own values, reactions, and judgments. Can I keep my own frustrations in check if my supervisee struggles with bracketing values or rigidly adheres to a point of view that is different from my own? A first step in my own process is to be aware of what triggers me, just like I ask supervisees to be aware of what triggers them. This is where my own self-awareness is key in working with supervisees and clients who present with value-related issues that are in contrast to my own. I have to bracket my values to hear what the supervisee is asking, which, in the vast majority of cases, is How do I hear and help my clients without harming them due to my own internal conflicts? The answer is often the same for both of us, consult with a trusted colleague, seek further education, or seek supervision.

Tips for Effective Supervision

Supervision can be effective even if the supervisory relationship is not ideal, but both the supervisor and the supervisee may need to work harder to ensure that the goals of supervision are accomplished. Let's look at some practical tips for establishing a good working relationship.

Establishing a Healthy, Productive Relationship With Supervisees

- Treat supervisees with respect; be open and honest about what you do and do not know.
- Work at developing a spirit of mutual trust and collaboration.
- Listen diligently to what supervisees are both saying and not saying, and try to tune into their fears, struggles, and hopes.
- Have a clear understanding of the purpose and the limits of the supervisory relationship.
- Be available, especially by being fully present during the supervisory session and by making sure this is "protected time," free from interruptions.
- Be willing to seek consultation when you are unfamiliar with the topic under discussion.
- Be clear on the boundaries of the relationship.

Guarding Against Imposition of Your Values

- Work on having a clear understanding of your values, beliefs, and attitudes regarding the range of typical issues that come up in supervision.
- Discuss with your supervisees their values and beliefs, and share yours as well.
- Talk openly about how values and beliefs affect the supervisory relationship and supervisees' work.
- Initiate discussions with supervisees regarding their values about marriage and divorce, cultural diversity, sexual orientation, religion and spirituality, end-of-life decisions, and child rearing. Share your ideas if you believe it will help supervisees and the supervisory relationship.

Characteristics That Facilitate or Hinder the Supervision Process

A variety of characteristics associated with the supervisor-supervisee relationship can influence the outcomes of the supervision process. Lowry (2001) conducted a study of the characteristics of supervisors and supervisees that both facilitate and hinder successful supervision, gathering information from practicing psychologists who are or have been supervisors regarding their own supervisory experiences (positive and negative). Lowry also questioned supervisors about trainee characteristics they believed facilitated or hindered the supervisory process. The discussion that follows summarizes these characteristics.

Supervisor Characteristics

Participants in Lowry's (2001) study perceived the following supervisor characteristics and factors as most important to foster a positive supervisory experience (in descending order): good clinical skills/knowledge, an accepting supervisory climate, a desire to train/investment in supervision, matching the supervisee's level of development, providing constructive feedback, being empathetic, being flexible and available, possessing good relationship skills, and being an experienced clinician.

Conversely, some supervisor characteristics and factors were thought to have an adverse impact on the supervisory relationship (in descending order): being judgmental or overly critical, being personally or theoretically rigid, not being committed to the supervisory process, being unavailable to the supervisee, having limited clinical knowledge and skills, being unethical or demonstrating poor boundaries, and being too self-focused. Other factors mentioned included a supervisor's lack of compassion, arrogance, the inability to provide helpful feedback, lack of preparation for supervision, and lack of supervisory experience.

Supervisee Characteristics

Lowry (2001) found that characteristics of supervisees or factors that were rated as helpful in promoting a positive supervisory experience included (in descending order) a desire to learn and improve, being nondefensive and open to feedback, general openness and flexibility, possessing knowledge and good clinical skills, intelligence, being responsible and prepared for supervision, and a willingness to take initiative and risks. Other factors rated as promoting effective supervision were good interpersonal and communication skills on the part of the supervisee, the ability to be empathetic, self-acceptance, insight, genuineness, the ability to ask questions, a focus on the client, and maturity.

Characteristics of supervisees or factors that were rated as impediments to successful supervision included a lack of openness and fear of evaluation, personal rigidity, defensiveness, arrogance and a perception that they are all-knowing, lack of motivation or interest in supervision or clinical work, lack of intelligence, psychopathology, and immaturity. Other supervisee factors perceived to hinder supervision included a poor knowledge and skill base, poor interpersonal skills and boundaries, being unprepared or disorganized, a lack of personal insight, and passivity or dependency.

Conflicts Between Supervisor and Supervisee

Conflicts are a natural part of all relationships. ACES (2011) reminds us that supervisors have a responsibility to recognize that conflict may arise in the supervisory relationship and that they need to assist the supervisee in dealing effectively with such conflicts. In most cases, conflicts can be resolved by listening, understanding, and working to clarify the ground rules about the relationship. When either or both parties in a conflict act as if they are right, the other is wrong, and the only solution is for the other party to change, the relationship usually takes a turn for the worse. Some supervisory relationships are characterized by unacknowledged conflict, discontent, and strife; however, if conflicts are recognized and openly discussed in a respectful manner, both supervisors and supervisees can learn a great deal.

It is important to set the tone for working with conflict early in the supervisory relationship before problems emerge. A supervisor could explain to supervisees that the supervisory session is a place where they can express any of their concerns or raise any questions pertaining to their relationship. This kind of climate is likely to make it easier for supervisees to express their complaints, which can be dealt with in an open manner in supervision. A good relationship allows for this kind of honest discussion of what is going on in the supervisory process.

We would like to think that, in most cases, filing formal complaints can be avoided. To reiterate, if both parties are willing to work through a conflict in a respectful and constructive manner, the quality of the supervisory relationship is likely to improve considerably. Case Study 3.2 describes a supervisee who openly expresses her discontent with her supervisor.

CASE STUDY 3.2: RACHEL

Dr. Allen has been supervising Rachel, a master's-level social work intern working part-time in a university counseling center. Dr. Allen, a professor in the social work program, teaches the Clinical Interventions Seminar in which Rachel is a student. In today's supervision session, Rachel expresses dissatisfaction with the direction of the supervision of her work in the counseling center. Rachel explains that she feels as though Dr. Allen simply tells her how to work with her clients without any discussion or input from her. To Rachel, it seems like a one-way street. Rachel believes she learns best through discussion and collaboration with a supervisor. Dr. Allen listens attentively but views Rachel's dissatisfaction as "resistance to supervision" and sees Rachel as not being open to supervision. Dr. Allen decides not to change his approach with Rachel.

If you were the supervisor, how might you receive and respond to Rachel's expression of dissatisfaction? What would you most want to say to Rachel? As the supervisor, how would you proceed to resolve this situation? How could you do so in a manner that would be a learning experience for Rachel?

It took courage for Rachel to offer critical feedback to her supervisor. Many supervisees are not as forthcoming about conflict with a supervisor because they do not want to challenge the supervisor, and they know that a supervisor has the ability, through evaluations and recommendations, to greatly affect their career. They find themselves suffering through supervision until it is over and they can move on to another placement. Rachel thinks she may have to make this decision too, but she wants to get the most out of her internship. She decides to try to think of another way to engage Dr. Allen and benefit from her internship under his supervision.

Conflict in supervision is not uncommon, but it can be difficult to resolve because the problem may be due to different perceptions of the supervisory interaction. It is difficult to convince either person that his or her perception may be incorrect or distorted. Nevertheless, it is the task of the supervisor to attempt to resolve the differences. The first task is to delineate a clear understanding of the specific plan of action when there are sharp differences between supervisee and supervisor. The supervisor can then return to the original contract that defines the nature of the supervisory relationship, the methods of supervision to be used, and the ground rules that define how they are going to work together. If clear ground rules are in place early in the supervisory relationship, the solution to their differences may be resolved by reviewing them. For example, the contract may state that the supervision methods are largely teaching and evaluation of the clinical work of the supervisee. If this is the case, then Dr. Allen's approach (see Case Study 3.2) may be quite appropriate. If the methods are not clearly defined, then it is time to collaborate to develop a clearer definition regarding how they are going to work together. What appear to be personality conflicts often turn out to be a lack of clarity about the nature of the working relationship. Clarification should lead to a more productive work environment.

Another task is to ask how the supervisor and supervisee can work together to make their relationship more satisfactory. When there is a conflict in a supervisory relationship, too often the tendency is to attribute blame to the other party. Our approach would be to ask each party to describe what the relationship would "look like" if it were working satisfactorily and to identify what would be needed to move it to that point. An open dialogue may lead to a discovery that both supervisor and supervisee have similar goals for supervision, yet each has a different idea about how to accomplish these goals. It might well be that the supervisor and the supervisee have never openly discussed their hopes and expectations for supervision and how to accomplish these goals.

Supervisors can take steps to enhance the supervisory relationship by demonstrating an understanding of the many challenges supervisees face. If supervisors recognize, appreciate, and understand the phenomenological world of supervisees, they are in a position to encourage supervisees to explore their struggles in working with clients and in maximizing the benefits of supervision. Openness on the supervisor's part and a willingness to engage in frank discussions about the concerns of supervisees can deepen the supervisory relationship.

Preparing Supervisees for Challenges

Ask yourself this question: How might I prepare supervisees to best deal with the difficulties they are likely to encounter? In this section, we present several challenges for supervisees: dealing with doubts and fears, identifying unresolved personal problems, avoiding the role of problem solver, identifying countertransference, and committing to personal growth. We also describe some problematic behavioral patterns of supervisees. If you apply this section to your own experiences as a supervisee, you will have a better sense of how you can assist supervisees in addressing challenges they encounter. You might even consider having your supervisees read this section and use this information as a topic of discussion.

Take a few minutes to reflect on your own experience when you first began seeing clients and began working with a supervisor. What experiences do you most remember when you initially began to counsel others? What did you learn from these experiences? What was it like for you to be in supervision? What self-doubts did you have as a trainee? How did you deal with these self-doubts or concerns? Will these experiences help you to identify with the concerns supervisees may bring to supervision sessions? One supervisee shared her experience as a trainee working on a pediatric unit. She was so anxious about meeting with her supervisor that she would unknowingly sit in one of the children's chairs during supervision. Through the use of humor, the supervisor was able to bring this situation to the supervisee's awareness, which then opened a dialogue regarding their power differential.

Dealing With Doubts and Fears

We want to shift our focus and speak directly to the supervisee in the following list, but keep in mind that many of these doubts and fears fit equally well for supervisors at various levels of development. Here are a few statements that supervisees often say to themselves:

- I am fully responsible for my clients' outcomes, and negative outcomes mean that I am not competent.
- I must be successful with every client and should be able to help my clients solve all of their problems quickly.
- I must be available at all times.
- I am afraid I won't know enough to help my clients and may actually make matters worse for them due to my lack of experience.
- Too often I compare my performance with others and tell myself that I do not measure up.
- Sometimes I worry that a client will not like me and will confront me in an angry way.
- It is very difficult for me to be fully present with clients because I am so concerned about what I will say or do next.
- Whenever my supervisor is in the room, I get anxious because I am sure she will discover that I am not competent.
- I worry about not being able to understand a client's pain if I have not had a similar kind of life experience.
- I must please my supervisor at all times. My supervisor should agree with and approve of everything I do.
- I feel intimidated by my supervisor and fear sharing this with her.

Most of these examples of supervisees' self-talk involve feelings of inadequacy, a fear of failing as a counselor, a nagging belief that one should be more, and a chronic sense of self-doubt. When counselors assume the lion's share of responsibility for their clients, they are relieving their clients of the responsibility to direct their own lives, in addition to creating stress for themselves.

As a supervisee, rather than pretending that you do not have any self-doubts or anxieties about being effective in your fieldwork assignment, strive to identify the ways your fears might get in your way. Bring these fears into the supervision session and explore them. Realize that many of your peers share your anxiety. By verbally expressing how you experience your anxiety, you move in the direction of diminishing the power of this anxiety. Once you have given voice to your fears surrounding your performance and others' evaluation of you, these anxieties will consume less energy.

Many trainees keep good reactions, insights, and intuitions to themselves, but we encourage you to put words to them rather than engaging in an internal monologue. It is not necessary to express all of your thoughts, feelings, and reactions to your clients, but in supervision meetings it is wise to verbally express the self-talk that often remains silent within you. Challenge yourself to change an internal rehearsal into verbal expressions during your supervision sessions.

Acknowledging your fears is the first major step in constructively dealing with them. Courage is not the absence of any performance anxiety; rather, courage entails identifying and challenging these fears. It takes honesty and courage to admit your perceived imperfections and to avoid becoming frozen out of fear of making mistakes. Some degree of performance anxiety is to be expected, and what you do about this anxiety is important. Recognize errors you might make, avoid punishing yourself if you do make them, and talk openly with your supervisor about them. If you are not willing to acknowledge when you make a mistake, you probably will not be willing to try anything new. If you are not open to making less than ideal interventions with clients, you seriously limit the scope of your creativity. The problem is not in making mistakes but in how you deal with mistakes. You will be overly conscious about what you are doing and whether you are doing it "right." You must, of course, assess the willingness of your supervisor to be open to such discussions, but in most cases, you can take full advantage of your role as a trainee. In this role, you are certainly not expected to know everything; allow yourself the freedom to be a learner. If you can free yourself from the shackles of trying to live up to the unrealistic ideal of perfection, you will be taking significant steps toward curbing your performance anxiety.

A quality supervisory relationship is the foundation upon which trainees can learn to challenge their inner critic, acquire a sense of trust in their abilities, and find a voice to express themselves. Trainees often need to identify and learn to challenge their inner critic in supervision. In Voices From the Field, Naomi Tapia, a graduate student in a counseling program, shows how she made strides in moving from self-doubt to trusting herself, largely because she had a solid working alliance with her supervisor.

 ## VOICES FROM THE FIELD

Learning to Trust Myself Through Supervision

Naomi Tapia, MS

Competent supervision is critical during the beginning stages of your counseling career. A great supervisor can be instrumental in establishing the foundation of who you want to be as a therapist. Before beginning my journey, I heard many stories about supervision styles. As a beginning marriage and family therapist trainee, I was unsure of what exactly I needed from a supervisor. All I knew was that I was a new intern who was anxious and who was struggling tremendously with the imposter syndrome.

Starting off, I was terrified of doing anything wrong. I was constantly overthinking, wondering if I was really capable of being a therapist. What if I hurt someone? What if I did too much? What if I did not do enough? What if I got stuck? I was doubting my intuition and found myself starting to reconsider the career I had chosen. I was not sure I was meant to be here. I did not believe that I had the ability to be effective with anyone. After all, who did I think I was? What made me capable of helping people cope with their problems? I did not know what I needed to hear, but my supervisor did. Whenever I doubted myself, or was unsure of my capabilities, he reminded me of what got me here in the first place. He directly, and indirectly, addressed all of my concerns. He reminded me that simply being myself contributed to my ability to become a more effective counselor. My life experiences and my ability to be present with people during the roughest moments of their lives was more beneficial than I realized. His strengths-based approach helped me acknowledge my positive attributes instead of focusing on the loop of insecurities that kept replaying in my mind.

Once, after a therapy session, I felt extremely discouraged and could not stop thinking about all of the things I did "wrong." My inner critic was eating me alive. The following day, I was not as present during sessions. I kept thinking of all the things I "should not do," and I found myself criticizing everything I said or did after each session. When I finally talked to my supervisor about feeling discouraged, he listened to my concerns and helped me process my feelings. He allowed me to vent about everything I did "wrong" and complain until I had nothing left to say. I expected him to give me tips on how to "fix" my "errors." I wanted him to give me answers. To my surprise, he did not pay any mind to my "errors." On the contrary, he asked me to repeat everything I had just shared and then identify things I did well. Every time I mentioned a strength, he reinforced it by giving me an example of how it enhanced the therapeutic alliance I had with my clients. He noted that many of the qualities I possessed did not come from school, but from my experiences and heart. His words went a long way toward developing trust in myself. It was the proudest I had felt in years. He helped ground me and reminded me of what brought me to this career in the first place.

The sessions following this conversation were incredible. I finally felt connected to myself, my intuition, and my heart. I was able to connect and more accurately empathize with my clients. I had found my footing as well as my own voice and had learned to accurately use it with my clients. I learned a great deal from his perspective, presence, and personality.

Most professionals have feelings of self-doubt and question their competence at certain times and in certain situations. Most of us experience self-doubt, especially when we first begin counseling others. Learning to challenge self-doubts can be a pathway to acquiring self-confidence. Your supervised fieldwork or internship is a place where you can acquire specific knowledge and where you can develop the skills to translate the theory you have learned into practice. It is part of the supervisor's responsibilities to assist you in addressing these insecurities and feelings of anxiety. In the following Personal Perspectives, you will learn how Michelle Muratori and Jerry Corey dealt with their self-doubts as supervisees.

 ## MICHELLE MURATORI'S PERSONAL PERSPECTIVE

Dealing with self-doubt and low confidence was a real battle for me during my undergraduate experience as a human services major. I constantly monitored my words and criticized myself for not being as skillful as I wanted to be, which compounded the problem. In the beginning of my training, my perfectionist tendencies really sabotaged my ability to be fully present. Fortunately, my discomfort with being such a perfectionist was so great that it motivated me to address the problem in a proactive way. Although I admit this sounds compulsive, I took an experiential group leadership course four times (not because I failed the first, second, or third time—just for the record). The practice component of this particular course was so amazing that it gave me and others an opportunity to facilitate a semester-long self-exploration group and to participate in group supervision. So I addressed my fear and feelings of inadequacy by forcing myself to do what scared me the most. I practiced, and practiced, and practiced. And over the course of four semesters, the experience of cofacilitating groups in conjunction with group supervision every week transformed me into someone who was more confident and comfortable in the role of counselor. (It also fueled my passion for group work, which is now my favorite course to teach.) In group supervision, I was able to work through my self-doubts, and I learned to realistically appraise my skills and professional development. Some people say that "practice makes perfect"; I'd rather say that "practice makes imperfection tolerable." I still have very high standards, but I am a much more effective counselor and counselor educator today because I let go of being a perfectionist. I guess you can say that I take being an "imperfectionist" very seriously! I am beginning to see that the more experienced I become, the more realistic I am about not having to be perfect.

 ## JERRY COREY'S PERSONAL PERSPECTIVE

What stands out the most for me in my own supervision was how inadequate I felt as a counselor trainee. I did not have much confidence in my ability to tune into what a client was saying and know how to respond therapeutically. As I recall, my supervisors did not devote a great deal of time or attention to talking with me about my self-doubts and unresolved personal issues that restricted my ability to be present with a client. Most of the supervision sessions were case focused, with some discussion of possible interventions to employ with different types of client problems.

During my supervised postdoctoral year, I gathered most of my hours by doing individual counseling with college students and by coleading therapy groups. I often felt lost, and I did not know how best to proceed in sessions with individual clients. If clients did not "get well quickly," I was convinced that this was evidence of my lack of competence as a counselor. My early attempts at providing individual counseling were characterized by what seemed like the slow progress of my clients and my desire for positive feedback from them. I compared myself to my supervisors and wondered how they would intervene with my clients.

Coleading intensive group therapy sessions with my supervisor proved to be the most helpful of all my supervised experiences. After the therapy sessions, we spent time processing my interventions as a facilitator and what the group brought out in me personally. The actual coleading with this supervisor was painful for me, however, because I constantly compared myself to this person who had many years of experience. I convinced myself that I was not measuring up and that I had little to offer anyone in the group. My supervisor's insight and clinical skills intimidated me, which heightened my own sense of insecurity and inadequacy. I felt totally inept during these early experiences with supervised work. I seemed very mechanical and rehearsed in my responses. Rather than creating my own style, I tried to figure out how my supervisor might respond and imitated that. In essence, I lost my own unique direction by striving to become like my supervisor.

The most important thing I learned during this experience was how critical it is to be willing to take an honest look at myself. I recognized that I had an exaggerated need for approval and acceptance from both my clients and my supervisor. This need often got in my way of being present with my clients and in bringing up material to explore in sessions with my supervisor. I recognized that a parallel process was operating and that my need for being accepted inhibited my ability to express myself as fully as I might. These experiences and insights as a supervisee taught me that I cannot help clients on their journey if I have not been willing to engage in my own self-exploration.

The professional development process is called a "process" for a good reason. Although one might wish to transform into a fine clinician with the wave of a magic wand, in truth, it takes time, courage, and practice to develop into a competent counselor or therapist. When addressed in supervision, the discomfort of having self-doubt can be the impetus for a professional growth spurt and can deepen your capacity to have compassion for clients who struggle with self-doubt and feelings of inadequacy.

Therapeutic goals can suffer if we have a strong need for approval and focus on trying to win the acceptance of our clients. To the degree to which we are unaware of our needs and personal dynamics, we become vulnerable to using our work primarily to satisfy our own unmet needs.

Recognizing Unresolved Personal Problems

Although trainees may think they have effectively dealt with their personal problems, they are often surprised when they recognize in themselves some of the struggles their clients bring to them. Trainees may see themselves in their clients, and painful memories are frequently unleashed. These issues should be explored in personal therapy. If we are unaware of these conflicts, our unresolved personal problems can interfere with the therapeutic process to the detriment of the client. This is not to say that you must resolve all personal difficulties before you begin to counsel others. Just be *aware* of your biases, your areas of denial, and the issues you find particularly difficult to deal with in your life. Struggling with anger in one's personal life, for example, might translate into avoiding any hint of anger in counseling and supervisory relationships.

To illustrate this point, suppose that you experience serious difficulties in a significant relationship in your life. You may be wrestling with some pivotal decisions about what you want to do about the relationship. You may be caught between fear of loneliness and a desire to be on your own, or between your fear of and need for close relationships. How might a personal problem such as this affect your ability to counsel others effectively?

If you have difficulty staying with a client in an area that you are reluctant or fearful to address, consider what present unfinished business in your own life might be affecting you as a counselor. The critical point is not *whether* you happen to be struggling with personal questions but *how* you are struggling with them. Do you recognize and try to deal with your problems, or do you invest a lot of energy in denying their existence? Are you willing to consult with a therapist, or do you tell yourself that you can handle it, even when it becomes obvious that you are not doing so? Is there consistency between your personal life and professional life? In short, are you willing to do in your own life what you expect your clients to do? Bring these concerns into your supervision, not for the purpose of getting therapy but to more clearly see how your conflicts might be blocking your progress with clients.

Identifying and Managing Countertransference

As mentioned earlier in this chapter, although it is not necessarily problematic to identify with your clients in some respects, it is possible to lose a sense of yourself by overidentifying with clients. In a broad sense, countertransference can be viewed as any projections, from your past or the present, that can potentially get in the way of helping a client. Performance anxiety, perfectionistic strivings, or a need to solve a client's problems might all be manifestations of countertransference. When you become aware of such reactions to clients, discuss what is going on in your supervision or with a trusted colleague.

Effective counselors use their own life experiences and personal reactions to help them understand their clients and as a method of working with them. When drawing on your personal experiences, it is important that you be able to establish clear boundaries so you do not get lost in your client's world. The process of working therapeutically with people is bound to open up personal themes in your life. As a partner in your client's therapeutic journey, you can be deeply affected by a client's pain. The activation of painful memories might resonate with your own life experiences, stirring up unfinished business and opening old wounds. If your countertransference reactions are not recognized, and if you do not manage your countertransference, these dynamics can result in a great deal of pain and stress in your life. Training and supervision can ideally incorporate identifying, analyzing, and strategically using countertransference as a tool for self-understanding and as a valuable tool in both supervisory and therapeutic work.

Avoiding the Role of Problem Solver

Trainees sometimes have a tendency to focus too quickly on solving clients' presenting problems before clients have had a chance to identify and explore these concerns. Ask yourself how patient you are in allowing clients to get to the essence of their problem areas and to struggle with finding their own answers. Do you tend to delve quickly into problem solving? Or do you have a tendency to give a great deal of advice? Clients who seek immediate answers to ease their suffering can easily encourage you to give advice. However, the opportunity to give advice places you in a superior, all-knowing position, and you may convince yourself that you do have answers for your clients. Another aspect of this pattern might be a tendency to engage in excessive self-disclosure, especially by telling your clients how you solved a particular problem in your own life. In doing so, the focus of therapy shifts from the client's struggle to your situation. Even if a client asks you for advice, it is a good idea to reflect on whether you might be helping or hindering the person by providing it. How might you respond to advice-seeking clients in a way that will empower them to explore for themselves?

Committing to Personal Growth

The person you are is perhaps the most critical element of your ability to successfully reach clients. If you are willing to recognize some ways that your personal characteristics could get in your way as a counselor and a supervisee, you are in a good position to do something about the situation. Your life experiences, attitudes, and caring are crucial factors in establishing an effective therapeutic relationship. If you are unwilling to engage in self-exploration, it is likely that your fears, resistances, and personal conflicts will interfere with your ability to be present for clients. Honest self-appraisal is essential if you are committed to being as effective as you can be in your roles as counselor, supervisee, and ultimately, as a supervisor.

In Voices From the Field, Jamie Bludworth shares his first encounters with supervision as a trainee. Can you identify with his experience? Are there any lessons to be learned from his account? Have you wanted to express your thoughts and reactions to your supervisor yet found yourself holding back?

VOICES FROM THE FIELD
Learning to Be True to Myself in Supervision
Jamie Bludworth, PhD

I came to my first supervision group with bright-eyed idealism. Each of us was cofacilitating a personal growth group, and we were required to attend 1.5 hours of group supervision per week. I imagined that we were going to enrich the lives of our clients while learning the finer distinctions of counseling practice from our esteemed supervisor. I envisioned us growing individually and professionally through the process of serious self-reflection and compassionate inquiry. I was quickly disillusioned.

In group supervision meetings, I found myself disagreeing with the manner in which my peers and supervisor were discussing clinical issues relating to group practice. Instead of expressing my disagreement, I grew more and more silent. I eventually recognized that my continued silence in supervision was counterproductive. Nevertheless, I also recognized that to voice my dissatisfaction with supervision could prove to be a risky endeavor.

Certainly, I had great respect for my supervisor's clinical judgment. Yet I strongly disagreed with the atmosphere of our supervision group. My disappointment was turning to resentment. I had to voice my concern if I was to receive any benefit from supervision. When I finally gathered enough courage to speak out to my supervision group, my colleagues expressed strong reactions toward me. My supervisor, however, responded graciously to my concerns. It was clear that I was alone in my sentiments, but it was also clear that my supervisor was willing to hear me.

In retrospect, I see now that I made many mistakes in the use of my first supervision experience. I was much too slow in the disclosure of my personal values. I could have displayed the kind of authenticity and congruence that I secretly demanded of the supervisor. In keeping my most powerful reactions hidden, I helped to foster an environment that I found most distasteful. What's more, I missed many of the valuable insights and suggestions offered by our supervisor in my resistance to the developing norms of the supervision group.

Although this initial experience was difficult for me, I learned volumes about myself and the ways in which I can more effectively use supervision to expand my knowledge and skill sets and, most important, better serve my clients. I learned that it is contingent upon me, and me alone, to determine how satisfying my supervision experience will be. I learned to take responsibility for my perceptions of the process. Above all, I learned the value of being true to myself in supervision, allowing my voice to be heard, authentically and respectfully.

Challenges for Supervisors

One of the things we often hear from supervisees is how anxious and overwhelmed they feel regarding their clinical performance and their ability to help others. Supervisors need to understand and appreciate this anxiety and be willing to work with supervisees in supportive and constructive ways. This section addresses the supervisor's role in assisting supervisees in dealing with anxiety and with supervisees' reactions to client failures, whether perceived or real.

Supervisee Anxiety

A large number of supervisees are anxious about the supervision experience and their ability to perform well. Some supervisees experience more anxiety than others, but nearly all experience some anxiety, whether in a bachelor's-level social work program or a doctoral-level clinical psychology program. They are worried about performing up to standard and about the whole process of being evaluated by supervisors. Most have done well in their academic programs, but the anxiety escalates when they begin to put their knowledge into practice. As supervisors, we should be aware of how common, and maybe even healthy, it is for supervisees to have anxiety and focus on what can be done to help supervisees manage anxiety effectively. ACES (2011) encourages supervisors to seek ways to lessen supervisee anxiety that is detrimental to supervision but to recognize that some anxiety is normal, inevitable, and basic to supervisee growth. You can see how one supervisor dealt with his supervisee's anxiety in Case Study 3.3.

CASE STUDY 3.3: ALEXANDER

Alexander has a bachelor's degree in psychology and has begun the master's counseling psychology program. He has gone straight through school without any time off to gain work experience except for seasonal summer jobs. He started his first semester of practicum training under the supervision of Dr. Moore at Veterans' Hospital, where he works as a psychologist. Alexander is bright, young, enthusiastic, and motivated to learn. He is, however, extremely anxious about doing everything correctly, and it is clear that he is eager to please his supervisor. Dr. Moore has just observed Alexander in a counseling session with a client, and it is clear that his need for the client to like him is getting in the way of his counseling. He frequently asked the client how the session was going, whether he was getting anything out of their discussion, and how the client liked working with him. He concluded the session by asking if the client thought he had done a good job in counseling him.

Alexander is an intense, young student who is a first-generation graduate from an immigrant family, and he feels pressure to succeed. He is eager to please and do a good job. Dr. Moore does not want to dampen his spirit, motivation, and enthusiasm, but he needs to provide Alexander with honest, constructive feedback and supervision without him unraveling. Support and understanding are essential with a trainee like Alexander. Dr. Moore approaches Alexander in this way: "You seemed like you were eager to have the client like you in that you asked him in several ways how he thought you as the counselor were doing. Being anxious to do well as a counselor is something that most of us experience, especially when we are beginning. What is crucial, however, is how you cope with your anxiety about 'doing well.' It is important that your anxiety doesn't get in the way of the counseling you are doing and obstruct your perception of the client's needs and goals. I would certainly be open to exploring ways that you might manage your anxiety effectively."

If you were supervising Alexander, how would you guide him in thinking through his need for approval and how it affects his counseling relationships? What challenges is Alexander facing, and how do you think he will do over the course of his supervision? What specific supervision strategies might you use to support Alexander in his development?

Most new trainees feel some degree of performance anxiety, which should decrease over time. Sharing some of the struggles you experienced as a trainee will go a long way toward putting your supervisees at ease. Let them know that counseling is not an exact science and that we make mistakes as we work and learn. Get supervisees into activities where they can develop a sense of mastery of some tasks and skills. Supervisees have potential to grow and learn under your supervision, and you are in a position to be of tremendous benefit to them as both supervisor and mentor. One useful intervention is to treat supervisees as colleagues when appropriate and encourage them to believe in their ability to learn and function creatively as clinicians. It may be tempting to figure things out for your supervisees and provide them with answers, but as with the client in therapy, supervisees have the ultimate task of discovering their own answers.

Supervisee Reactions to Client Failures

One of the most difficult situations for a counselor to deal with is the failure of clients to benefit from therapy. This is difficult even for the seasoned clinician, and it is especially difficult for trainees and prelicensed clinicians who want to be successful in their work. The job of the supervisor is to help the supervisee do everything possible to bring about a positive outcome in therapy and counseling and to assist the supervisee in putting it in perspective when the outcome is not so positive.

There are many opportunities for client failures in counseling, just as there are many opportunities to experience success in the therapeutic venture. Clients often attribute their success to something other than the work of the therapist. When there are failures, however, the therapist may be identified as the cause. This may come from the client or the client's spouse or family. All too often, this identification of the cause of a therapy failure comes from the therapist, and this can be very disconcerting. Seasoned clinicians learn how to assess the factors contributing to a therapy failure, but new clinicians often lack the experience and self-confidence to self-assess. As with Roberto in Case Study 3.4, they quickly turn to themselves as the reason therapy failed and become discouraged.

CASE STUDY 3.4: ROBERTO

Roberto has been working with a married couple in therapy at the family service center. The couple seem to love each other and want to be together, but as soon as they begin to talk, they fight. Roberto has been working with them on communication skills, and they seem to be making some progress. Hours before their next scheduled session, Roberto gets a call from the wife indicating that they have had another fight, have decided to seek a divorce, and would like to cancel future counseling sessions with him. Roberto asks, "What happened that led to this decision so quickly? How are you doing with this? How is your husband doing with this? What led you to want to cancel the counseling sessions? Would either or both of you be willing to come in one more time to discuss your decision?" Roberto has strong religious beliefs and personal values regarding the sanctity of marriage, and these beliefs were a large influence in his desire to practice with couples and families. Roberto comes to the next supervision session feeling discouraged and frustrated about this case and about his future work with couples and relationship issues.

How would you respond to Roberto's thoughts, feelings, and concerns about this case? Would you help Roberto decide what further action he could take regarding counseling this couple? What do you need to teach Roberto to help him cope with these kinds of therapy failures in the future?

It is important to remember that change is a complicated process. When clients are provided with the tools for change, they frequently do not implement them. Even though they have come to therapy to change something, the change may be risky or frightening. Clients often say they want to change a certain behavior, yet their actions indicate they are not yet ready or willing to do what is needed to bring about this change. Clients often know why they *should* change a behavior and probably spend many hours thinking about how life would be better if they were to change.

Your role as the supervisor is to help the supervisee disengage from the successes and failures of the client. Actually, learning this detachment is a very difficult process because we like to see the fruits of our work. The key to long-term survival in this field is to have a delicate and healthy balance between caring and objective disengagement. Some helping professionals are successful in achieving this balance, and some are not. Supervisors would do well to help their supervisees examine their cognitive processing of what they are saying to themselves about their clinical competence and their client failures. A cognitive restructuring approach in supervision may be in order to help supervisees develop a more realistic set of expectations about their own role and the client's role in the therapeutic process.

Summary

The quality of the supervisory relationship is just as important as the methods a supervisor chooses. The essential elements of the supervisor-supervisee relationship include trust, self-disclosure, understanding transference and countertransference, acknowledging diversity, and establishing appropriate boundaries. The supervisory relationship has a built-in power differential, which can be mediated by a collaborative relationship style. Parallel processes can be seen between supervisory relationships and the client's relationship with the supervisee. It is important for supervisors to be aware of their personal values and beliefs and those of supervisees that may affect the supervisory relationship.

Because the supervisory relationship is unequal, conflicts can easily occur. Working through a conflict can enhance the quality of the supervisory relationship. Supervisees face many challenges as they begin their clinical practice. Supervisors can help supervisees deal with feelings of self-doubt and anxiety and provide a context for talking about client failures.

The time and effort supervisors devote to establishing and maintaining a collaborative relationship with supervisees will pay dividends in terms of the quality of their learning. The relationship is the foundation upon which therapeutic knowledge and skills are acquired. Reflecting on what you valued in your own relationships with your supervisors may be a good way for you to design your approach to supervising others.

SUGGESTED ACTIVITIES

1. In small groups, discuss the elements of the supervisory relationship you believe are essential for supervision to be effective. Discuss what you have learned about this from your own experience with supervision. How might your experiences as a supervisee assist you in getting a clearer picture of what you will want to bring to your work as a supervisor? Have each group share the common themes with the larger group.

2. Reflect on your own supervision and write in your journal about some of the fears and concerns you had when you first began seeing clients. How did these fears affect your ability to work with clients? How did you deal with your fears and concerns? How can you use this insight to improve as a supervisor?

3. In small groups, identify a few strategies you can use to address your supervisee's reactions to a client's therapy failure. How do you view failure in your clients? How might you determine the degree to which you are responsible for client failures? As a group, explore supervisory strategies for coping with both real and perceived mistakes your supervisees might make with clients.

4. As a small-group discussion topic, identify and share your main concerns about becoming a supervisor. What are some of the most challenging things you might face?

5. In a discussion group, identify some ways a supervisee's countertransference might best be addressed. There is a fine line between supervision and therapy, and dealing with countertransference issues takes courage on the part of the supervisee and wisdom on the part of the supervisor.

6. Hold a debate with classmates regarding the effect of the "Me Too" movement on the supervisory relationship.

CHAPTER 4

Models of Supervision

FOCUS QUESTIONS

1. What supervision models did each of your supervisors use? If they discussed their approaches with you, how were they described?
2. What model are you most inclined to follow in your supervision practice at this time? How might this approach influence what you expect from supervisees?
3. What are the benefits of a team-based approach in supervision?
4. What aspects from various theories might you most want to incorporate into your own integrative supervision model?
5. If you were asked in a job interview to describe your model of supervision, what would you say?
6. Why is having a model of supervision important? How does a model influence supervision?
7. What value would your supervisees and their clients gain from your practice of neuro-informed supervision?

In this chapter, we focus on the theoretical foundations of supervision. Supervisors must be able to articulate, for example, why they use a psychodynamic approach and believe in exploring transference and countertransference, why they base supervision on a trainee's level of professional development and provide more structure during early training experiences, why they utilize peers in the supervision process, or why they integrate theories and draw from a variety of approaches. We examine several developmental, psychotherapy-based, and integrative models of supervision. In addition, we introduce a new team-based process model for supervision developed by Moulton (2019b). By providing a range of models that can be used in clinical supervision, we hope to inspire you to consider how you might approach developing a framework that works best for you, your trainees, and their clients. This broad view of theoretical frameworks of supervision is fundamental to the discussion of applied topics in later chapters.

Some models of supervision are based on established psychotherapy approaches, and others have been developed specifically for the process of supervision. Many of these models are relatively new, and some expand or build on elements of existing models.

The way these models address supervision and the methods for application are uneven, making it difficult to compare and contrast models. To give you a basis for comparison, we provide our perspective regarding the components of the various models.

You can support your supervisees in getting the most from supervision by demystifying the process and explaining the supervision approach or model on which your supervision is based, including the policies, goals, and theoretical orientations toward counseling and training. The *AMHCA Standards for the Practice of Clinical Mental Health Counseling* (American Mental Health Counselors Association [AMHCA], 2016) state that clinical supervisors should "understand and have a working knowledge of current supervision models and their application to the supervisory process" (III.B.1.c.). To aid you in this process, we examine each of these models in detail and discuss how it can be applied in the practice of supervision.

Understanding Models of Supervision

A *model* of supervision is a theoretical description of what supervision is and how a supervisee's learning and professional development occur. Some models describe the process of learning and development as a whole; others describe the specifics of what occurs in supervision to bring about learning and development. A complete model addresses both how learning occurs and what supervisors and supervisees do to bring about that learning. Effective supervisors have a clearly articulated model of supervision. They know where they are going with their supervisees and what they need to do to get there.

Early models of supervision relied heavily on psychotherapeutic processes. This was consistent with the notion that clinicians skilled in conducting therapy would also be skilled in supervision. As the body of information regarding supervision has advanced, models designed specifically for supervision have been developed. These models are still evolving and may look different in the future.

Bernard and Goodyear (2019) classify supervision models into four groups: developmental models, psychotherapy-based models, process models, and second-generation models. Second-generation models have emerged in the past 20 years, and they include *combined models*, which integrate two established supervision models; *target issue models*, which focus on specific critical issues such as multiculturalism and include constructs from one or more existing models; and *common factors models*, which focus on the common characteristics of a number of supervision models (p. 56). To assist you in developing your own personalized model of supervision, we discuss the characteristics and differences of supervision models sorted into three groups: developmental models, psychotherapy-based models, and integrative models of supervision.

A supervision model serves as a theoretical road map for developing supervision techniques. Understanding how you view the supervisee, the task of supervision, and the roles of the supervisor will help determine which of the many intervention strategies you will choose. As you begin to outline your theoretical model of supervision, keep in mind that your model will evolve as you gain clinical and supervisory experience and as you develop the wisdom that comes with life as well as professional experience.

Developmental Models

Developmental models view supervision as an evolutionary process, and each stage of development has defined characteristics and skills. The novice clinician is characterized by a lack of confidence and limited basic skills. The more advanced supervisee has developed confidence and skill with experience and supervision and is becoming a self-sufficient clinician. In developmental models, supervision methods are adjusted to fit the confidence and skill level of supervisees as they grow professionally. Supervisors need to be flexible because various styles may be needed, even with the same supervisee. Case Study 4.1 shows how one supervisor responded to two supervisees with very different levels of skill.

CASE STUDY 4.1: JASPER AND SANDRA

Jasper and Sandra are students in a master's-level counseling program, and both are beginning their internship training at a community mental health center. Jasper is new to the counseling profession, whereas Sandra has considerable coursework in marriage and family counseling and has worked in community mental health settings for many years. They have both been assigned to the family treatment unit.

Dr. Raman is supervising both students at the center, and he performs an initial assessment of the current level of clinical competence of each trainee. He determines that Sandra is very knowledgeable and skilled in her work with families, whereas Jasper is a novice in his clinical experience with this population. Within a matter of weeks, Dr. Raman is primarily using the case consultation method in his supervision of Sandra. Together they brainstorm various approaches and discuss the research supporting these approaches. Sandra catches on quickly, responds to feedback, and takes initiative in her learning. Dr. Raman asks, "How can we learn together about the newest methods in family work?" Both he and Sandra read journal articles on a variety of topics, and supervision sessions are used to discuss what they have learned.

In supervising Jasper, Dr. Raman takes a different approach. He notices that Jasper appears uncertain, has difficulty focusing on details, procrastinates on assignments, and is easily frustrated when receiving constructive criticism. Jasper shares that he struggles with ADD and that the pressure of performing under supervision is difficult for him. Dr. Raman takes extra time to sit with Jasper and review information regarding approaches, strategies, and steps for therapy with his clients. Jasper observes Dr. Raman conducting family therapy sessions, and the two of them discuss the methods used and why they are appropriate in working with the family. After some time, Dr. Raman has Jasper participate as a cotherapist with him so he can directly observe Jasper in his clinical work. Over the course of the training, he will use direct observation and video recording as he gives Jasper more autonomy in working with families.

With Sandra, Dr. Raman's role is more of a coach and a consultant, whereas with Jasper, he is a model and a teacher of clinical methods. Dr. Raman chose a supervision approach based on the competence level of each supervisee.

- What types of supervision goals are appropriate for each of these students?
- What challenges might you face in working with a student like Sandra?
- What are the rewards of working with a student at the professional developmental level of Jasper?
- Which of these students would you relate to more easily, and how might that affect your supervision role?

Integrated Developmental Model

One of the most useful developmental models is the integrated developmental model (IDM) created by Stoltenberg and colleagues (McNeill & Stoltenberg, 2016; Stoltenberg et al., 1998; Stoltenberg & McNeill, 2010). This model describes three levels of supervisee development and the corresponding role of the supervisor for each developmental level. "The hallmark of this model . . . is that supervisees develop along a continuum, have different generic needs at different points on the continuum, and need different interventions at various points on the continuum" (Westefeld, 2009, p. 300). Stoltenberg and colleagues (1998) emphasized that, similar to human developmental stages, the supervisee does not pass cleanly through the three levels. A supervisee may be highly skilled in individual therapy but be a novice when it comes to leading group therapy. Level 1 supervisees are entry-level therapists and generally lack confidence and skill. They need more structure and direction from the supervisor. Level 2 supervisees are more confident and begin to rely on their own abilities and decision-making processes. The supervisor may occasionally provide direction but focuses more on process issues, examining how the supervisee's own personal reactions and issues affect his or her functioning as a therapist. In Level 3, the supervisee provides most of the structure in supervision. Confidence levels are growing rapidly, and the supervision is more informal and collegial, with the supervisor acting as a consultant. Stoltenberg and colleagues identified eight domains of clinical practice in which to assess the developmental level: intervention skills competencies, assessment techniques, interpersonal assessment, client conceptualization, individual differences, theoretical orientation, treatment plans and goals, and professional ethics.

The IDM is a well-conceived and versatile developmental model of supervision that can be used in a variety of contexts and settings, including in schools (Gallo, 2013), treating eating-disordered clients in mental health clinics (Boie & Lopez, 2011), and with international counseling students (Yee, 2018; Zhou et al., 2019), just to name a few. Supervisors must understand the developmental stages of their supervisees and be able to match their skills and approach to each stage of development. A wide range of supervision methods and techniques can be employed to help the supervisee move through the stages in becoming a competent clinician. Michelle Muratori thinks the IDM is a useful framework for guiding trainees' professional development, and she has found it helpful for understanding her own development as a supervisor as well, which she explains in this Personal Perspective.

MICHELLE MURATORI'S PERSONAL PERSPECTIVE

Supervision is a complex enterprise, so having some sort of framework to make sense of what is happening is a necessity. On a number of occasions, beginning trainees have commented to me on how surprised they were to learn that counseling is far more complex than they initially thought. Shortly after beginning the developmental process of becoming counselors, trainees realize that what appears to be a natural conversation between counselor and client actually requires a great deal of skill, knowledge, self-reflection, and practice. They are drawn to the field of counseling because they consider themselves to be good conversationalists and compassionate listeners, but at a critical point early in their development, trainees see that effective conversations with clients, unlike those with friends and family members, must be grounded in a theoretical framework and have a sound rationale. Knowing enough about something to realize that one has a vast amount to learn is overwhelming but can be the impetus for growth. Although trainees invariably find this developmental stage (Level 1) uncomfortable, I consider it exciting and hopeful because those who have a strong desire to be counselors are going to invest in the process and move out of their discomfort zone and in the direction of becoming more autonomous (Level 2).

I am a believer in parallel process, and it makes sense to me that just as counselors experience a developmental process, so do supervisors. Having strong counseling skills certainly helps supervisors perform their job with greater competence, but these skills alone are not sufficient for successful supervision. Although I may have been a Level 3 counselor when I was enrolled in my supervision practicum as a doctoral student, my skills as a supervisor had not yet been developed. I had never been in a position to evaluate a trainee's competence, and the responsibility of being a gatekeeper for the profession made me anxious. Using the IDM helped me to have more patience with myself because it normalized my reactions and helped me anticipate some of the concerns and issues my supervisees might have based on their developmental level.

The IDM also helps to make sense of certain dynamics that occur in supervision. A new supervisor may feel the need to do everything "right" and to cover every conceivable point with trainees. If a Level 1 trainee is matched with this inexperienced (Level 1) supervisor, things may work out well because the trainee is looking for guidance and is eager to acquire knowledge about therapy. On the other hand, a Level 3 supervisee who has had years of clinical experience may not benefit from or have a lot of tolerance for this Level 1 supervisor's approach. A Level 2 trainee, who has mastered the basics and wants more autonomy, may also resist this Level 1 supervisor's direction. The inexperienced supervisor might interpret the trainee's resistance as a sign of disrespect, whereas a more experienced (Level 3) supervisor, who has more confidence in his or her own supervisory skills, may view the trainee's behavior in a developmental context and not take it personally. Of course, we must also consider the influence of factors such as personality, temperament, age, gender, race, ethnicity, sexual orientation, abilities/disabilities, and experiences with oppression and social injustice. Add those factors to the equation, and supervision becomes exponentially more complex.

Life-Span Model

An expanded developmental model has been proposed by Skovholt and Ronnestad (1992, 1995, 2012). They described the developmental process of counselors as occurring over a long period of time and not being limited to the graduate school years. As Purswell and her colleagues (2019) point out, "understanding counselor identity development over the professional life span is especially important for leaders in counseling so they can be intentional in facilitating identity development of pre- and post-master's degree counselors as well as in how they work to influence the profession" (p. 129). Qualitative and quantitative research has shown that shifts in counselor-in-training and professional counselor identity can be observed over time (Purswell et al., 2019). Skovholt and Ronnestad (1992) interviewed clinicians from graduate students to those with years of experience and identified eight themes that characterize counselor development: competence, transition to professional training, imitation of experts, conditional autonomy, exploration, integration, individuation, and integrity. As their ideas evolved, Skovholt and Ronnestad (1995) conceptualized counselor development as including six phases. These phases were "one pretraining phase (Lay/Conventional Helper), followed by two student phases (Beginning Student, Advanced Student), and three postgraduation phases (Novice Professional, Experienced Professional, and Senior Professional)" (Purswell et al., 2019, p. 131). This model is useful in helping the supervisor conceptualize the developmental process that clinicians experience. Supervisors can then adjust their supervision methods to fit the needs of their supervisees.

For a more detailed treatment of the developmental models, see McNeill and Stoltenberg (2016), Skovholt and Ronnestad (1992), Stoltenberg and McNeill (2010), and Stoltenberg, McNeill, and Delworth (1998).

Incorporating Neuro-Informed Constructs Into Developmental Supervision

In today's rapidly changing world, advances in neuroscience are leading clinicians to focus on the importance of the physiological and biological underpinnings of mental health issues. At the same time, rates of anxiety, stress, depression, and other mental health issues are increasing. Helpers have long spoken about the mind-body connection, and we now have a greater appreciation for the role of neuroscience in uncovering the mysteries of mental illness and mental health. Russell-Chapin and Chapin (2016, 2020) have been leading voices in promoting neuro-informed counseling and supervision, and they describe how neurocounseling constructs can be implemented within a developmental supervision framework to enhance the process (Russell-Chapin & Chapin, 2020). In Voices From the Field, they describe how neurological concepts and processes operate in supervision and have an impact on supervisees' skills, ranging from the use of immediacy to emotional self-regulation.

 VOICES FROM THE FIELD

Neuro-Informed Clinical Supervision

Lori A. Russell-Chapin, PhD, and Theodore J. Chapin, PhD

Although we know from functional magnetic resonance imaging (fMRI) research that counseling changes brain neuroplasticity in a positive direction, there are no studies demonstrating the neural benefits of clinical supervision. Considering the parallel process in counseling and supervision, it makes sense that the same positive neuroplasticity occurs in supervision. Therefore, it's imperative that clinical supervisors and supervisees become neuro-informed and understand the basic concepts of neurocounseling and its implication for clinical supervision. Briefly stated, neurocounseling provides a unifying model, based on the physiological underpinnings of behavior, to connect the brain and body to emotional and behavioral health.

Every component of the supervision process and each supervision model has important neuroscience complements that enhance the intentional selection of best fit supervision skills and models. Understanding the basics of neuroanatomy and neuronal networks helps supervisors and supervisees more deliberately select techniques that capitalize on key brain functions. For example, we know that the use of summarization helps clients internally reflect, activate social working memory, and create a better understanding of their world. When doing so, they have engaged their brain's default mode network (DMN). In the same way, when a supervisor asks a supervisee to reflect on a supervision question, explain the rationale for a particular skill choice, or simply engage in a moment of mutual silence, the DMN is also activated, lending more depth and understanding of one's experience. Supervision quality and outcome can be greatly improved by understanding how neurological processing influences clinical supervision.

A second example involves the use of immediacy. Focusing on the "here and now" allows us to pause and engage several possible neuronal networks. These may include the prefrontal cortex for executive functioning (planning, organizing, or impulse control) and the limbic system for emotional and memory processing. Through the reciprocal process of supervision, both supervisor and supervisee can reflect on each other's reactions, note their similarities, appreciate their differences, and benefit from this neurologically enriched response.

Although there are many specific examples, one general but central neurological construct applied to clinical supervision is the practice of physiological and emotional self-regulation. Skills such as diaphragmatic breathing, heart rate variability, and skin temperature control (basic biofeedback skills) can help a supervisee remain calm and access optimal cognitive efficiency. This improves the supervisee's use of supervision, benefits the supervisee's personal life, and enables transfer of the same skills to the supervisee's work with clients.

Skillful talk therapy and supervision become more effective when neuro-counseling self-regulation skills are taught to supervisees and clients as a first-level intervention. Once established, supervisees can better maintain their sense of personal safety and become more engaged and receptive to supervision feedback. Learning theory's concept of negative bias suggests that supervisees may shut down when feeling threatened. Critical and even constructive feedback may elicit a defensive reaction causing the limbic system to take control. Under such conditions, only the negative feedback will be remembered; any positive feedback will be minimized or forgotten because it is not needed for survival. Supervisors who employ interpersonal skills to establish rapport, teach neurologically based self-regulation to ensure a safe supervisory environment, and repeat positive feedback two or three times will enhance supervisee learning.

Without understanding the brain and body connection, supervisors will be less effective. How can we fully engage supervisees and clients without looking at the core physiology that drives all of us? Empowering supervisees with neurocounseling-informed education offers knowledge and skills that benefit them and their clients. When our clients and supervisees begin practicing improved self-regulation, they consistently exclaim, "If I can control my breath and skin temperature, surely I can control the problems in my life." This renewed sense of internal control holds great promise for the future of our students, their clients, and our profession.

For a more in-depth discussion of this topic, see *Integrating Neurocounseling in Clinical Supervision: Strategies for Success* (Russell-Chapin & Chapin, 2020).

Psychotherapy-Based Models

Psychotherapy-based models apply the concepts developed for psychotherapy to the supervision setting. Depending on your therapy orientation, you may find that one or more of these models resonate with your own style.

Psychodynamic Model

Norberg and colleagues (2016) have noted that "there has been a longstanding historic controversy in psychoanalytic thinking on supervision concerning 'patient-centered' supervision that focused on the supervisee's understanding of the client and technical problems in the encounter, and 'therapist-centered' supervision that focused on the therapist's emotional reactions and countertransference" (p. 268). Today, according to these scholars, the supervisory relationship is more egalitarian, and supervisors have moved away from pathologizing their supervisees, which they may have done in the past. This more contemporary form of psychodynamic supervision (a relational model) has put the supervisory relationship at the center of supervision.

Within a safe environment in which a strong learning or working alliance has been established, the primary focus of supervision is on the supervisee's development of self-awareness of intrapersonal and interpersonal dynamics and on development of the skills necessary to use a psychodynamic approach in counseling. The supervisor is concerned with the supervisee's personal issues to the extent that these issues are influencing the course of therapy.

This model emphasizes the dynamics of supervisees, such as resistance, their way of reacting to clients, and the client's reactions (transference) to the therapist. Because transference is common in the therapeutic process, it is important to conceptualize the meaning of a client's reactions to a counselor and for the counselor to understand his or her own reactions to the client's transference. The psychoanalytic model offers the richest perspective for grasping the implications of both transference and countertransference. In psychodynamic approaches, transference and countertransference are viewed as central to the therapy process. With this model of supervision, emphasis is given to understanding how client-counselor reactions influence the course of therapy.

As noted in Chapter 3, parallel process is often discussed in conjunction with psychodynamic approaches (Borders & Brown, 2005). It refers to the supervisee's interaction with the supervisor that parallels the client's behavior with the supervisee as the therapist. The supervisor's task is to explore these parallel relationships with the supervisee to help the supervisee learn how to become a better therapist. For example, a counselor may experience difficulty terminating with clients. Her ambivalence about ending a therapy relationship may mirror the client's resistance to talking about ending the professional relationship. The counselor may have unresolved personal conflicts pertaining to losses and ending relationships in her own life, and this may surface when concluding the supervisory relationship. The parallel process provides a lens through which to view and understand ways that therapy may stall because of the therapist's unresolved personal problems.

Here are some questions and statements typically made by supervisors with a psychodynamic orientation:

- What similarities do you see between our supervisory work and the relationship you share with your client?
- We've talked about your wanting my approval as a supervisor. Could it be that you are hesitant to challenge your client lest she not approve of you?
- Think out loud for a bit about what purpose your client's resistance might be serving.
- You appear to be having a very strong emotional response to your client; where and with whom else in your life might you experience this emotion?

Person-Centered Model

In the person-centered approach to supervision, the supervisor assumes that the supervisee has immense resources for both personal and professional development. The supervisor is not viewed as the expert who does all the teaching; rather, the supervisee assumes an active role in this process. Learning that occurs in the supervisory process results from a collaborative venture between supervisor and supervisee. Rather than relying on providing supervisees with directives or advice, supervisors encourage supervisees to think about how they might best proceed with their cases. Just as therapy outcomes are greatly influenced by the quality of the therapeutic relationship, in supervision the outcomes of the process hinge on the quality of the supervisory relationship.

In this model, the supervisor's empathy, warmth, and genuineness facilitate a trusting relationship in which the supervisee can grow and develop. It is the job of the supervisor to provide an atmosphere in which growth can flourish. When supervisees feel understood, they are more likely to take an active role in bringing their concerns to supervision sessions.

Supervision from the person-centered perspective downplays the evaluative role of the supervisor and questions the role of the supervisor as gatekeeper of the profession.

This may present possible ethical or legal dilemmas for the supervisor because the responsibilities of the supervisor typically include evaluation and gatekeeping.

Here are some statements and questions typically made by the person-centered supervisor:

- I'd like to hear you talk more about how it was for you to be with the client for that session.
- I encourage you to begin to place more trust in your own internal direction.
- You are saying that you really don't know how to proceed, but if you did know, what actions might you take?
- What did you find to be important in the experience you shared with your client today?
- I'd like to hear you talk more about the climate you are creating with your client.
- To what degree do you feel you understand the world of your client?
- What are your expectations for what we might do in today's session?

An approach closely aligned with the humanistic and person-centered approaches to counseling and supervision is motivational interviewing (MI). Wahesh (2016) has written about the value of using MI techniques in supervision when encountering supervisee resistance, which can manifest in a variety of ways, including as evaluation and performance anxiety. According to Wahesh, "supervisees might resist supervision because they are ambivalent about changing a specific behavior or coping strategy recognized by their supervisor. This anxiety to change represents an internal struggle within the supervisee between sustaining the status quo and changing" (p. 49). If a supervisee's resistance is conceptualized as ambivalence to change, the supervisor can explore the supervisee's internal conflict and promote change talk through listening, questioning, and reflecting. In the process of doing so, it is imperative that the supervisor instill a sense of hope in the trainee that change is possible.

Embracing the MI spirit, a person-centered supervisor might use the following statements or questions to elicit change talk from supervisees:

- What changes do you think you can make to help you follow through with what we've discussed so far?
- Let's outline some steps we can take together to help you move forward and meet the goals you described in our last supervision session.
- Discussing what's uncomfortable for you is an important part of the supervision process, and I look forward to having those conversations. Are there other ways I can support you?

Cognitive Behavior Model

Cummings, Ballantyne, and Scallion (2015) state that clinical supervision "should be a proactive and considered endeavor, not a reactive one. To that end, supervisors should choose supervision processes that are driven by theory, best available research, and clinical experience" (p. 158). A key task in cognitive behavioral supervision is teaching techniques and correcting misconceptions about this approach with clients. These sessions are structured, focused, and educational, and both supervisor and supervisee are responsible for the structure and content of the sessions. In supervision, the focus is on how the cognitive picture of the supervisee's skills affects his or her ability as a therapist. By focusing on this, the supervisee also learns how to apply these cognitive behavioral methods with clients.

Liese and Beck (1997) outlined nine steps that typically occur in cognitive therapy supervision. These steps provide an example of the content of a session.

1. *Check-in*: Asking "How are you doing?" to break the ice.
2. *Agenda setting*: The supervisor teaches the supervisee to carefully prepare for the supervision session and asks,"What would you like to work on today?"
3. *Bridge from previous supervision session*: The work of the previous supervisory session is reviewed by asking, "What did you learn last time?"
4. *Inquiry about previously supervised therapy cases*: Progress or particular difficulties with previously discussed cases are reviewed.
5. *Review of homework since previous supervision session*: Homework might include readings, writing about cases, or trying new techniques with a client.
6. *Prioritization and discussion of agenda items*: A review of the supervisee's audio recordings of therapy sessions is a major focus for the supervisory session. Teaching and role playing are common supervision methods.
7. *Assignment of new homework*: As a result of the session, new assignments are given that will help the supervisee develop knowledge and skills in cognitive behavior therapy.
8. *Supervisor's capsule summaries*: The supervisor's reflections of what has been covered in the session keep the session focused and emphasize important points.
9. *Elicit feedback from supervisee*: The supervisor asks for feedback throughout the session and ends the session with questions such as, "What have you learned today?"

These steps closely parallel the steps that occur in a cognitive behavior therapy (CBT) session with a client. In the process of supervision, the supervisee learns both from the content of the supervision and from the supervisor modeling how to conduct a cognitive behavior session. James, Milne, and Morse (2008) emphasized the importance of using microskills when conducting supervision and describe 14 activities in which CBT supervisors generally engage. These include listening, gathering information, supporting, managing, giving feedback, summarizing, checking theoretical knowledge, challenging, educating, using experiential learning, self-disclosing, disagreeing, using video observation, and other activities. Cummings, Ballantyne, and Scallion (2015) emphasize agenda setting, encourage trainee problem solving, and provide formative feedback as essential processes in cognitive behavioral clinical supervision.

Reality Therapy/Choice Theory Model

Reality therapy is based on choice theory, which postulates that people strive to gain control of their life to fulfill their needs. Like the cognitive behavior models, reality therapy is active, directive, structured, and psychoeducational. It puts primary emphasis on actions but includes discussions of cognition and feelings such as attitudes, insight, transference, exploring one's past, and unconscious motivations. Reality therapy focuses on helping clients gain a sense of inner control regardless of their external circumstances, no matter how uncomfortable or threatening they might be. Clients learn to cope with the demands of reality by making more effective choices. People can improve the quality of their life through honestly examining their wants, needs, and perceptions. Clients are challenged to evaluate their current behaviors (actions, cognitions, and feelings), formulate a plan for change, commit themselves to their plan, and follow through with their commitment.

The WDEP system, formulated by Robert Wubbolding, outlines the procedures used in reality therapy. Specifically, the strategies help clients identify their *wants*, determine the *direction* their behavior is taking them, and *evaluate* the effectiveness of their behaviors and the realistic attainability of their wants in order to design and commit to a *plan* for change. Wubbolding's model can also be applied to the supervisory context. In Voices From the Field, Robert Wubbolding describes the process of supervision using the framework of reality therapy. He identifies some mistakes beginning trainees make in applying reality therapy in counseling practice and emphasizes the importance of establishing an accepting therapeutic relationship.

VOICES FROM THE FIELD

Supervision From a Reality Therapy Perspective

Robert Wubbolding, EdD

Supervision of trainees who wish to use the principles of reality therapy focuses on helping them expand their knowledge and skill and increasing their confidence in implementing the theory and practice. The supervisor helps supervisees use the principles of reality therapy in an increasingly spontaneous manner. Neophyte practitioners often employ the procedures in an overly structured and rigid manner, sometimes using an authoritative tone. The supervisor acknowledges that the system can lend itself to the perception that reality therapy is practiced in an overly directive or mechanical manner. The supervisor helps learners to identify this perception, and alter it if necessary, as well as incorporate specific nonthreatening ways to improve their counseling relationships.

The supervisor's responsibility is to encourage supervisees to realize that no one practices reality therapy perfectly. When they come to believe this principle, they relax and are less afraid of making mistakes. At the same time, the supervisor is aware of miscalculations commonly made by beginners, including underestimating the necessary establishment of a compassionate relationship. The procedures of reality therapy are tools for achieving a connection with clients and can be applied in a wide variety of ways. Supervisees learn that using reality therapy is more than following a recipe. It is a *skillful art* developed by trial and error, by practice, and by self-evaluation. Another miscalculation is to proceed too quickly, rushing into treatment planning. The supervisee needs to help clients identify their goals and wants; examine their actions, thinking, and feelings; and conduct a searching self-evaluation. Self-evaluation precedes making an action plan, and supervisees learn that these plans are more efficacious and need-satisfying to the client. The role of the supervisor is to facilitate this process in a compassionate manner without communicating in a critical manner. Reality therapy interventions used by the supervisor are very useful and begin with "What do you want to accomplish from this supervisory process?" Throughout the process, supervisors use interventions such as "When you said such and such, did that help as much as you had hoped?" If there is a solid professional relationship between supervisor and supervisee, the latter arrives at a higher level of competence. Skilled supervisors assist supervisees to realize that reality therapy itself is a complete system and yet an open one in which they can incorporate techniques derived from other counseling systems.

For an in-depth treatment of reality therapy, see *Reality Therapy and Self-Evaluation: The Key to Client Change* (Wubbolding, 2017).

Family Therapy Model

Family therapy typically involves working with the family as a system, examining the various relationships and dynamics. Family therapy supervision, much like family therapy, is active, directive, and collaborative. According to MacKay and Brown (2014), "for over 20 years the family therapy field has championed collaborative approaches to training and supervision where the hierarchy between the expert teacher and the 'not knowing' supervisee has been replaced by a model aiming for equality and mutual learning in the supervisory relationship" (p. 325). "Live supervision," which involves immediate direction and intervention during the therapy session, appears to be the most widely used method in family therapy training programs (Taylor & Gonzales, 2005). The supervisor encourages supervisees to examine their own intergenerational dynamics, values, and culture to further their awareness and growth and to learn about becoming a family therapist. Gutierrez (2018) urges marriage and family therapy supervisors to address intersectionality in supervision sessions and proposes a framework for doing so. The family therapy supervisor works with the supervisory relationship as a system and with the supervisee and his or her clients as a system.

Some family therapists place primary emphasis on the therapist as a person, which has implications for supervisors working within the family therapy model. They view exploring the personal characteristics of supervisees as being of major importance. Bitter (2021) identified the following personal characteristics and orientations of effective family practitioners: presence; acceptance, interest, and caring; assertiveness and confidence; courage and risk; openness to change; paying attention to goals and purposes of a family; working in patterns; appreciating the influence of diversity; being sincerely interested in the welfare of others; tending to the spirit of the family and its members; and involvement, engagement, and satisfaction in working with families.

The family therapy approach to supervision is based on the assumption that a trainee's mental health—defined by relationships within the supervisee's family of origin—has implications for professional training and supervision. Supervisees can benefit from exploring the dynamics of their family of origin because this significant knowledge enables them to relate more effectively to the families they will meet in their clinical practice. If supervisees lack awareness of ways that particular members of their own family of origin may trigger strong emotional reactions in them, it is likely that they will react too quickly or inappropriately to client families. Supervisors of family therapist trainees generally assume that it is inevitable that trainees will encounter similar dynamics between the family members whom they are counseling and the members of their own family of origin. Such supervisees are then likely to project feelings they had toward their own family onto their clients. Supervision addresses how supervisees' clinical work is influenced by their experiences with their own families of origin.

Most family therapy training programs encourage students to explore their own family-of-origin issues. The family therapy supervisor assists the supervisee in exploring these family dynamics using techniques such as genograms, family history, and family sculpting. The supervisee is encouraged to identify patterns such as enmeshment, detachment, and triangulation. The purpose of this exploration is to determine ways in which one's own family of origin will affect the supervisee's ability to function as a family therapist.

Feminist Model

The underlying philosophy of the feminist model is being gender-fair, flexible, interactional, and life-span oriented. This approach emphasizes that gender-role expectations profoundly influence our identity from birth onward. Feminist therapy encompasses both individual change and social change. The overall aim is to replace the current patriarchy with a feminist consciousness, creating a society in which relationships are interdependent, cooperative, and mutually supportive (Corey & Corey, 2021).

The basic concepts of feminist therapy can be applied to the process of clinical supervision. Laura Brown (2016) outlines an approach for translating feminist therapy constructs, such as thinking critically about dominant cultural norms and the impact of systemic hierarchies, into the supervision arena. Highlighting practices from queer, multicultural, and other critical psychologies, Brown empowers trainees and supervisors to reflect on challenging and complex questions about the presence of bias as well as the distribution of power in education, psychotherapy, and supervision contexts. In offering her reflections on supervision, one psychology trainee of color made the following observation:

> As a Black woman, I have had lifelong practice in being conscious of my sociocultural identities and how they align or misalign within various environments and social contexts. Hence, being critically minded has become a natural and necessary framework for my everyday processing and carries into my professional work as a psychologist-in-training. For this reason, I am most drawn to theoretical approaches to counseling and supervision that are culturally informed and acknowledge the impact of systemic oppression as not merely discretionary but primarily relevant to the change and training process. I firmly believe that the training environment is not exempt from systemic oppression and that issues of power and privilege are consistently present whether or not they go acknowledged. (Thomas et al., 2019, p. 168)

The feminist model of supervision entails striving toward an equalization of the power base between the supervisor and the supervisee. In fact, feminist supervisors proactively analyze power dynamics and differentials between supervisor and supervisee, model the use of power in the service of the supervisee, and vigilantly avoid abuses of power. Although the supervisory relationship cannot be entirely equal, the supervisor shares power in the relationship by creating a collaborative partnership with supervisees. Together they participate in acquiring, sharing, and reshaping knowledge. This collaborative spirit leads to an empowered relationship that is characterized by a sense of safety. This sense of trust and security forms the basis for increased risk-taking, higher levels of performance, and greater individual confidence.

Martinez, Davis, and Dahl (1999) suggested that feminist supervisors should foster a mutually agreed-upon approach to working with a client rather than using the usual supervisor-directed approach. Supervision focuses on the trainee's philosophy and practice of counseling. A supervisee's assumptions, beliefs, and values pertaining to gender, race, culture, sexual orientation, ability, and age are often the subject of discussion during supervision sessions.

Because social change is a key goal of the feminist approach, feminist supervisors advance and model the principle of advocacy and activism. Supervisors do this by guiding their supervisees into thinking about their role and power in influencing the systems in which they work. At times, they assume responsibilities for challenging sexist and racist attitudes and behaviors of their supervisees, including the negative use of stereotypes and the misuse of diagnoses. Feminist supervisors are aware of the fine balance between imposing their beliefs and being apolitical in supervision. It will come as no surprise that feminist supervisors advocate for their supervisees and clients in the educational and training settings within which they practice. Supervisors recognize that the feminist tenet of working for social change often originates in their own institution.

Solution-Oriented Model

The solution-oriented model differs from traditional psychotherapy models by eschewing the past in favor of both the present and the future. Murphy (2015) describes this as a "strength-based approach that shifts the focus from what's wrong with students [or clients] to what's right" (p. 12). This approach has implications for the supervisory relationship because it is grounded in the optimistic assumption that people are healthy, resourceful, and competent and have the ability to find solutions that can enhance their life. In solution-oriented supervision, the basic assumption is that the supervisee is the expert and has the resources to problem solve clinical situations (Thomas, 1994). According to Thomas, there are two steps in solution-oriented supervision: (1) building the conceptual map, which includes a discussion of what supervisees want from supervision, the supervisory relationship, and assumptions about solution-focused supervision; and (2) implementing solution-oriented supervision, which includes setting goals and encouraging a future orientation. Operating within the framework of a solution-oriented approach, supervisors strive to design a collaborative style in working with supervisees. Supervisees are assumed to be capable and resourceful when it comes to achieving their supervision goals.

Practitioners using a solution-oriented approach use several techniques to steer clients toward solutions. One of these techniques is the *miracle question*, which can be effective with a variety of complaints and situations (de Shazer, 1991). Miracle questions can be used as an assessment technique to determine what the client would see as a satisfactory solution to a given problem. A practitioner might ask, "If a miracle happened and the problem you have was solved overnight, how would you know it was solved, and what would be different?" Clients are then encouraged to enact "what would be different" in spite of perceived problems. Supervisors can effectively incorporate the miracle question into supervisory sessions, thereby modeling the technique. If a supervisee discloses that she struggles with feeling inadequate around certain clients who remind her of her critical father, for instance, the supervisor might ask, "If a miracle happened and you did not feel inadequate around your clients the next time you met with them, what would be different? How would your feelings affect your actions? How might your clients react to you if you felt more confident?"

Another technique involves asking *exception questions*, which direct clients to times in their life when the problem didn't exist. This exploration reminds clients that problems are not all-powerful and have not existed forever; it also provides a field of opportunity for evoking resources, engaging strengths, and positing possible solutions. Solution-oriented therapists focus on small, achievable changes that may lead to additional positive outcomes. Their language joins with the client's, using similar words, pacing, and tone, but also involves questions that presuppose change, posit multiple answers, and are goal directed and future oriented. A therapist might ask the client, "Was there a time when you weren't feeling stressed out at work? What was different about the situation and your reaction?" In the supervision context, exception questions can be quite effective in assisting supervisees in realizing that their own issues do not have to control them and that change is possible. A supervisee who is working on being less judgmental with clients may be asked to think about an occasion when he did not feel critical toward them. His supervisor might ask, "What was that like? How did that differ from times when you felt judgmental toward them?"

Solution-oriented therapists also use *scaling questions* to evaluate changes that are not easily observed, such as feelings, moods, or communication. For example, a woman reporting feelings of panic or anxiety might be asked, "On a scale of 0 to 10, with 0 being how you felt when you first came to therapy and 10 being how you feel the day after your miracle occurs and your problem is gone, how would you rate your anxiety right now?" Even if the client has only moved away from 0 to 1, she has improved. How did she do that? What does she need to do to move another number up the scale? To measure growth on any number of dimensions, a supervisor may ask a trainee scaling questions. To gain a baseline measure in the early stages of supervision, a supervisor might ask the following questions: "On a scale of 0 to 10, how would you rate your anxiety related to trying new techniques or meeting with new clients? Using this scale, how would you rate your comfort with making mistakes?" As the trainee develops competence, these questions can be revisited to assess how the trainee's views have changed over time.

There are many ways to apply the solution-oriented therapy model to an optimistic model of supervision. Such an approach has a great deal of potential for empowering supervisees. Just as clients improve their self-efficacy and self-confidence when they can connect their improvements with their own decisions and actions (Murphy, 2015), supervisees feel empowered and more confident when they can focus on their strengths and acknowledge, with their supervisor's support, what they are doing right.

Integrative Models of Supervision

Integrative models of supervision, like integrative models of counseling and psychotherapy, rely on more than one theory and technique. A variety of integrative approaches can be designed that are based on a combination of techniques, common principles, and concepts from a number of different theories. Integrative supervision is based on systematically drawing on effective methods across various theoretical models and by matching those methods to particular supervisees (Norcross & Popple, 2017). An integrative approach based on various techniques is more flexible than a single approach. Interventions can be combined to uniquely fit the supervisor's beliefs and values about change, the therapeutic process, and the client's and supervisee's needs.

Because no one theory contains all the truth, and because no single set of counseling techniques is always effective in working with diverse client populations, integrative approaches hold promise for both counseling practice and the practice of supervision. Norcross and Popple (2017) contend that "no single supervision theory or method is effective for all supervisees and situations, no matter how good it is for some" (p. 7). Norcross and Beutler (2019) describe multiple pathways to achieving integration, two of the most common being technical eclecticism and theoretical integration. *Technical eclecticism* tends to focus on differences, chooses from many approaches, and is a collection of techniques. This path calls for using techniques from different schools without necessarily subscribing to the theoretical positions that spawned them. Technical eclecticism focuses on selecting the best treatment techniques for the individual and the problem. For technical eclectics, there is no necessary connection between conceptual foundations and techniques. In contrast, *theoretical integration* refers to a conceptual or theoretical creation beyond a mere blending of techniques. This path has the goal of producing a conceptual framework that synthesizes the best of two or more theoretical approaches to produce an outcome richer than that of a single theory (Norcross & Beutler, 2019).

An integrative perspective at its best entails systematic integration of underlying principles and methods common to a range of therapeutic approaches. To develop an integrative perspective, you need to be thoroughly conversant with a number of theories, be open to the idea that these theories can be unified in some way, and be willing to continually test your hypotheses to determine how well they are working. An integrative perspective is the product of a great deal of study, clinical practice, research, and theorizing (Corey, 2019).

An integrative perspective of the supervision process is best characterized by attempts to look beyond and across the confines of single-school approaches to see what can be learned from other perspectives. Unless you have an accurate, in-depth knowledge of theories, you cannot formulate a true synthesis. Simply put, you cannot integrate what you do not know (Norcross & Beutler, 2019). Constructing an integrative orientation to the practice of supervision is a long-term venture that is refined with experience. Ideally, an integrative approach dynamically integrates concepts and techniques that fit the uniqueness of your personality and style of supervision.

There are some drawbacks to encouraging the development of an integrative model. Some practitioners are critical of an inconsistent eclectic approach that is reduced to a random borrowing of ideas and techniques. At its worst, eclecticism can be an excuse for practice that is not well thought out—a practice that lacks a systematic rationale for what you actually do in your work. If you merely pick and choose according to whims, it is likely that what you select will reflect your own biases and preconceived ideas. It is important to avoid the trap of emerging with a hodgepodge of theories thrown together hastily (Corey, 2019).

The kind of integrated model of supervision we subscribe to and suggest to you is based on common denominators across the different models. At its best, this involves identifying core concepts that different models share or concepts that can be usefully combined. It is essential to identify your key beliefs underlying the practice of supervision. Your philosophical assumptions are important because they influence which "reality" you perceive, and they direct your attention to the variables that you are "set" to see in carrying out your functions as a supervisor.

Beware of subscribing exclusively to any one view of human nature; remain open and selectively incorporate a framework for counseling that is consistent with your own personality and your belief system. When blending different theoretical frameworks, it is essential that these frameworks lend themselves to a fruitful merger. For example, you will find many commonalities of philosophy shared by person-centered and feminist models of supervision. These commonalities include minimizing power differentials, focusing on supervisees' attitudes and behaviors, and striving to build and maintain collaborative relationships. Both models focus on development of the supervisee as a person, but the feminist model also has a primary goal of social advocacy and change. Even though there are some clear differences between these two models, there is enough commonality that they lend themselves to integration.

Clinicians who use an integrative model of psychotherapy are inclined to use an integrative model of supervision as well. This approach could involve the complete integration of several theories or an integration of concepts from a number of theories fashioned into one's own model. One advantage of an integrative approach is that the supervisor can uniquely tailor the supervision methods to fit the supervisee, the client, and the setting. Norcross and Wampold (2019) maintain that no single therapy approach is effective for all clients and situations. Evidence-based practice demands a flexible and integrative perspective, which implies that different types of clients require different treatment methods and different relationship styles. As Norcross and Popple (2017) emphasize, one size and one theory do not fit all supervisees: "An individualized supervision plan can be formulated for each trainee on the basis of his or her style, stage, preferences, experience, complexity, and other considerations" (p. 80). The limitation of an integrative approach is that it requires the supervisor to have a broad understanding of the range of supervision models and techniques.

In the following sections, we briefly describe the discrimination model, the common factors discrimination model, and the TEAM-based supervision process model, all of which are integrative models of supervision.

Discrimination Model

The discrimination model, developed by Bernard (1979), is rooted in technical eclecticism. It is called the discrimination model because the supervisor's approach is determined by the individual training needs of each supervisee (Bernard & Goodyear, 2019). In this model, the supervisor focuses on three separate areas for supervision: the supervisee's intervention skills, the supervisee's conceptualization skills, and the supervisee's personalization skills or personal style in therapy. Once the current level of functioning in each of these three areas has been assessed, the supervisor chooses a role that will facilitate the supervisee's learning and growth. In this model, the three roles that the supervisor may adopt are teacher, counselor, and consultant. The discrimination model continues to be a viable and useful framework for counseling supervision (Bernard & Goodyear, 2019; Borders, 2005).

Common Factors Discrimination Model

The common factors discrimination model, developed by Crunk and Barden (2017), expands on the discrimination model by offering specific recommendations for how supervisors might use the roles of teacher, counselor, and consultant as opportunities for developing and maintaining the supervisory relationship. This model "integrates the common factors of counseling and supervision approaches with the specific factors of Bernard's discrimination model for a structured approach to common factors supervision" (p. 62). Common factors theorists and researchers emphasize that positive outcomes in therapy are linked more to factors that apply across theories—the therapeutic alliance, empathy, positive regard, and collaboration within the therapeutic relationship, for instance—than to the actual theory or interventions employed (Norcross & Lambert, 2014). Norcross and Popple (2017) note that commonalities are more important in accounting for therapy outcome than are unique factors. They state that "the common factors approach seeks to determine the core ingredients that different therapies share, with the eventual goals of creating more parsimonious and efficacious treatments based on these commonalities" (p. 7). Although the blending of common factors with the discrimination model has not yet been empirically tested as an integrated supervision approach, each approach has received substantial empirical support as a stand-alone model (Crunk & Barden, 2017).

In the Personal Perspective, Patrice Moulton explains how she developed the TEAM-based supervision process model over the course of 30 years of supervising across various clinical and educational settings and supervisory roles (Moulton, 2019b).

 ## PATRICE MOULTON'S PERSONAL PERSPECTIVE

Like many supervisors who did not receive formal supervisory training in my graduate studies, I spent many years working to understand and improve my practice of supervision through trial and error. Over the years, I actively sought guidance from mentors (Gerald Corey, Marianne Corey, Rick Myer, and Richard James) and attended trainings and workshops to strengthen my competence and confidence in supervision. I've had excellent supervision, which set a high standard for me to match, from Mary Ann Adams, Russ Youngblood, Lin Harper, Bill Montgomery, and Pat Leverett.

One key observation I made when I began to supervise second-year practicum students about to work directly with clients for the first time was that they needed, and indeed were hungry for, detailed information regarding procedures, documentation, structure, and other essential parts of the counseling process. These students were at a critical juncture in their professional development and training; they were expected to pull together and synthesize all of the theoretical knowledge they had acquired in the first year (e.g., ethics, counseling theories and techniques, diagnosis, group work, diversity) and put it into action with "real clients." Understandably, this stage of professional development was an anxiety-producing yet exciting time for many trainees. The stakes were much higher now that they were about to interact with real clients (as opposed to peers serving as mock clients) and could influence their clients' mental health and well-being, for better or worse.

Given the high stakes involved, I began to flesh out a process that would address the many areas of responsibility and liability of supervising beginning therapists. I was interested in outlining detailed steps that would allow for a strong supervisor-supervisee relationship amid the many documents, forms, and procedures required for quality care of clients. An important discovery I made while developing my supervision framework was the power of involving multiple trainees in the process and the potential for them to enrich each other's learning.

The TEAM-based supervision process model rests on the premise that numerous benefits result from individuals working together. Teamwork has a positive impact on learning and self-improvement and promotes inclusion, healthy competition, creativity, idea generation, and an enriched perspective. Although originally designed for use with second-year practicum students in a university-based clinic, this model can easily be adapted to other clinical contexts and settings. This model is currently being transitioned for use in an online environment for Zoom. The current situation with COVID-19 demands that we forge new paths in providing and receiving supervision. The TEAM approach provides the peer/social support needed for learning. The overarching goal is to facilitate the development of the counselor from novice to competent independent practitioner.

TEAM-Based Supervision Process Model

The TEAM-based supervision process model includes four sequential stages: teach, evaluate, assure, and mentor.

Teach
The first phase of the TEAM model focuses on the foundational work required to conduct counseling sessions effectively. Just as supervisors have the responsibility to prepare themselves for the supervisory role through training, self-reflection, and self-assessment, beginning counselors or trainees need to be taught content knowledge in key domains. They need to successfully complete coursework in subjects such as ethics, counseling theories and techniques, diagnosis and psychopathology, crisis intervention, group work, and diversity and social justice, just to name a few. Evidence of mastery of this knowledge might include course grades, certifications, and comprehensive exam scores.

Gatekeeping. Multiple levels of gatekeeping are necessary in the teaching stage. These include providing formative remediation at the individual course level, at the performance/participation level, and at the comprehensive exam level with summative testing and evaluation. Remediation often is provided through having trainees retake specific coursework or comprehensive exams. If students do not pass courses at a satisfactory level to progress in the program, dismissal may be one of the recommended courses of action. Counselor educators and clinical training programs are wise to explain this gatekeeping function to prospective students when they enter the program as one of their risk management practices.

Evaluate
The second phase of the TEAM model begins as counselor trainees are assigned to fieldwork (e.g., practicum, externship) and get ready to work with clients for the first time. This stage provides the transition from coursework to practice. The task is to evaluate readiness to work clinically. Assuming that the supervision team is composed of 8–10 practicum students or interns, the supervisor is responsible for evaluating the knowledge and skill level of each supervisee on the team to determine basic competency to practice under supervision and to determine readiness to begin conducting therapy. It is extremely important to take time to assess the abilities of supervisees to perform the tasks they have learned, mostly theoretically to this point, before allowing them to care for clients under supervision. This careful assessment is required to ensure quality care for the clients they will see and to address the vicarious liability involved in supervision.

The following steps are suggested for team building and evaluation of trainees' competence. Supervisors are urged to conduct sessions in workshop format.

Introduction: This step focuses on getting to know your supervisees, having them know one another, and letting them explore the supervisor-supervisee relationship. Structured intentional icebreakers that create universality, allow unique qualities to be introduced, and encourage inclusion are advisable.

Orientation: This step orients trainees to the practicum/externship course requirements, including expectations related to documentation and resources. The logistics and myriad documentation required are detailed and intense, often overwhelming supervisees. Supervisors should build in time for clarification, support, and encouragement throughout this process. Anxiety may understandably rise as the reality sets in of what practicing therapy entails and visualizing, for the first time, how all the separate components taught in their classes merge to provide care to clients. Details of the counseling and supervisory process need to be shared and discussed, and sample documentation forms provided. Avoid rushing through the support documents, and ensure supervisees understand how to use them because they form the backbone of the counseling/supervision process. Orientation should also include a trip to the therapy rooms and instructions on the use of any required technology. It is important that supervisors supply team members with documentation outlining the criteria for their evaluation.

Supervisory contract: Once supervisees have been adequately oriented, they are in a position to make informed decisions regarding a supervisory contract. Meet individually with each supervisee on the team to review the contract, confirm the process and procedure of evaluation, discuss any questions or concerns, and sign the contract as evidence of consent to begin.

Assessment/remediation: Supervisors should create an opportunity to observe each supervisee in action, even if briefly, prior to first sessions with clients. This can be accomplished by creating a team experience with the goal of assessing basic knowledge and skills. This session can be very lively and interactive, using Socratic questioning to assess team members' knowledge about ethics, theories, diversity, diagnosis, documentation, and a host of other relevant topics. Small-group activities, role plays, case studies, and technology-assisted tasks can be used to evaluate supervisees' strengths and challenges. If supervisees lack knowledge or skills at this point, the supervisor can recommend appropriate remediation.

Risk management: Supervisees should not be practicing, even under supervision, if they cannot demonstrate a sound basic understanding and application of confidentiality and emergency procedures. In this step, supervisors review HIPAA requirements with supervisees and provide specific standards regarding confidentiality beyond merely keeping clients' identities and verbal information private. Policies are needed to safeguard client files, mobility of information, and team communication. It is impossible to be too specific. If technology is used in any way, the supervisor should set policies and expectations regarding its use. Emergency procedures that include the supervisor's hours of availability and contact information as well as community resources should be clearly outlined. Supervisees must also show proof of liability insurance before they begin to see clients.

Evaluation of readiness: At this point, the supervisor should have a clearer understanding of supervisees' areas of strength and possible opportunities for improvement. In this step, the supervisor and supervisee meet individually to determine the supervisee's readiness to begin seeing clients. If deemed ready, the supervisee is paired with a peer partner for direct supervision and partner support within the team, and the client selection process begins.

Logistics of first client session: Once peer observers have been assigned and clients selected, the first sessions are scheduled. Supervisees should review the tasks/goals of the initial session and be reminded to document scheduling clients, wear appropriate attire, review and rehearse the use of required technology, and check therapy rooms for placement of furniture, clocks, tissue boxes, etcetera. Taking care of details creates confidence.

Gatekeeping. Evaluation is primarily performance-based at this point. The supervisor assesses the ability of each supervisee to provide basic skills competently. If needed, remediation will align with the specifics of the identified deficit.

Assure

The third phase of the TEAM model has two major goals: (1) assuring that supervisees provide competent services and quality care to their clients, and (2) providing supervisees with rich opportunities to facilitate their professional development in a supportive team environment. This stage incorporates all the documents needed for direct care and legal documentation, which can seem overwhelming to supervisees. The supervisor is at the center of a complex team dynamic during this stage. Responsibilities include direct supervision of supervisees, facilitation of team feedback meetings, and oversight of the quality of care provided to clients. The supervisor sets the tone, maintains a safe environment, provides support, and challenges comfort levels. Myer, James, and Moulton (2011) suggest creating an environment in which supervisees are not afraid to take risks or make mistakes as they practice techniques. This is the time to learn with the confidence of a safety net. Confidentiality, expectations, and other relevant topics should be discussed among the team to ensure appropriate professional behavior. This includes providing guidance on how to handle difficult professional or ethical issues that arise.

In this phase, the TEAM model is broken down into three steps: observing the counseling session, supervisee team staffing/case consultation, and an individual supervision session.

Observe counseling session: Each counseling session is video or audio recorded and can be reviewed and analyzed later; however, it is observed in real time (or live) behind a one-way mirror by the supervisor and the supervisee's assigned peer partner. Bug-in-the-ear or bug-in-the-eye technology may be used. Following each session, time is allotted for review of the session and for documentation to be completed.

Team staffing of client cases: The entire team meets weekly for staffing of each client contact. Every team member is responsible for their direct client contact summaries, self-assessment with video review of their sessions, and appropriate documentation. They also utilize peer observation notes to provide feedback to their assigned partner, which is presented in front of the whole team, not just the partner. Everyone is expected to participate and provide input regarding each case. As cases are staffed, the supervisor facilitates a discussion regarding the presenting problems, priorities, case conceptualization, ethical considerations, diagnosis, theoretical orientation, and treatment strategies. Team members learn from the supervisor, each other, and clients. Brainstorming is actively encouraged. Each meeting is closed with a round-robin technique in which members each state the lesson of the day that stands out most for them, a personal goal for improvement, and next steps regarding their clients.

Individual supervision session: Each supervisee meets individually with the supervisor for remediation or emergency intervention (if needed) and for the formal evaluation of progress.

Gatekeeping. Supervisees should be showing observable progress, a working knowledge of key components of counseling, competence in the process, and performance at the beginning professional level. It is imperative to address any concerns directly during formative evaluations because this is the final opportunity for gatekeeping prior to releasing supervisees into the field. Supervisors may question whether they would be comfortable hiring a supervisee when making a final determination about beginning competence. Newer, inexperienced counselors can do a magnificent job if they work from a steady foundation, know their limits, seek assistance when needed, and care deeply.

Mentor

The fourth and final phase of the TEAM model is a time for celebration! Supervisees have progressed to the point that they are able to practice as independent professionals. Rather than being seen as novice counselors-in-training, they are now regarded as new colleagues. This is an empowering phase of professional development for members of the team. The task of the supervisor is to help supervisees move on and to hold an empowering termination session emphasizing strengths while challenging their continued development. The supervisor also provides resources (including letters of recommendation) as team members step into independent practice. As a mentor, the supervisor assists in transitioning the supervisee to new positions, settings, and new supervisors.

Standard gatekeeping is not required during this phase because supervisees have met and demonstrated the requirements to take the next step in their career. However, we hope supervisees find mentors who make a significant impact personally and professionally at every step in their development. Figure 4.1 provides a visual illustration of the model.

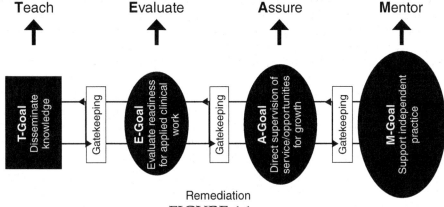

FIGURE 4.1
TEAM-Based Supervision: A Process Model

In Voices From the Field, Abigail Hunter, a student who experienced the TEAM approach to supervision, underscores the importance of peer feedback.

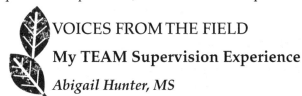 VOICES FROM THE FIELD

My TEAM Supervision Experience

Abigail Hunter, MS

In my first practicum, my supervisor followed the TEAM model of supervision. Upon reflection, I realize that I attained invaluable knowledge and insight that assisted my growth as a therapist-in-training through my participation in the TEAM model. During my first TEAM-based supervision meeting, I learned about the expectations of this practicum, including team-oriented conduct, paperwork, policy, and the step-by-step overview of the upcoming experience. Time was spent reviewing basic skills and knowledge through didactic methods that made me think about how the content I had learned separately in classes combined to create the art of therapy. My supervisor ensured that I checked the logistics of preparation for my first client and reviewed my responsibilities for the first session. I felt prepared for my first session, and I remember my supervisor radiated encouragement and support for us all. Time had been taken to be sure we were ready.

My sessions with clients were observed directly by my supervisor and team members, and my team provided insightful feedback; they also had the opportunity to learn from both my successful moments and my challenges. I reviewed my own sessions on video recordings, noting behavioral observations, raising questions, developing ideas, identifying areas to improve, and recognizing moments of success. I discussed components of my self-assessment with my team during supervision meetings. This open discussion provided valued feedback and new information from my team through Socratic questioning, a review of knowledge, and shared ideas.

After my first session with each client, case conceptualization began. My peers and I were asked to prepare our client's presenting problem, possible theoretical approaches, potential ideas and activities for treatment, and sources. This was to be completed before the next supervision meeting. A solid conceptualization was followed by feedback and guidance, including selection of well-suited theoretical approaches and creative spins on treatment techniques. For the following supervision meeting, I prepared a treatment plan derived from my case conceptualization and the team's previous discussions. This team-oriented approach to practicum provided step-by-step guidance and ideas from different perspectives, which aided my development of autonomy.

During my practicum experience, I gained a better understanding of the application of various theoretical approaches and techniques. I was encouraged to be more autonomous with my second client, and I continued to demonstrate competence and to communicate my thoughts, feelings, and ideas. I received valuable feedback from my supervisor, as well as my peers, throughout the entire practicum experience. Dr. Moulton's TEAM approach provided me with a sense of reassurance through the challenges of practicum. I thrived with the constructive feedback and the immense feeling of support from an outstanding professional model and dedicated peers. I felt prepared to move into the workforce as a therapist.

As a supervisee, I believe the facilitation of a safe, yet challenging, learning experience with very high expectations is of significant value. The structure of the TEAM sessions created confidence. I was not afraid to make reasonable mistakes and to push myself outside my comfort zone. Ultimately, my supervisor's mentorship had a significant impact on my development as a future therapist.

Developing Your Own Model of Supervision

In most of the single theory models, supervisors accept an underlying philosophy and incorporate key concepts and specific methods of supervision. If you adopt a primary model, you will need to adapt this theory to your supervisory style. Using an integrative model of supervision is a more complex task; you need to draw from several approaches and integrate these perspectives with the person you are. Even though developing a personalized approach to supervision is a complex and challenging task, we favor an integrative approach to clinical supervision and recommend it to you. This is the most flexible approach, and it can be adapted to many situations and settings.

You need to have a basic knowledge of various theoretical systems and counseling techniques to work effectively with a wide range of clients and supervisees in various clinical settings. Subscribing strictly to one theory may not provide the therapeutic flexibility you require to deal creatively with the complexities associated with clinical and supervisory practice. When you begin your work as a supervisor, think about the theoretical framework that can help you make sense of what you are doing. Certainly, your theoretical orientation to supervision will not be complete as you begin supervising trainees; it will evolve and develop with experience. Engage in reflective practice and look for a conceptual framework that will assist you in making sense of your interventions with supervisees.

When developing your approach to supervision, a good place to begin is by reflecting on the meaning of your own experiences of being supervised. What was especially helpful for you? What model of supervision enabled you to develop to the fullest extent possible? What kind of different experience might you have wanted from your supervision? How would you characterize the theory from which each of your supervisors operated, and what could you learn from each of them with respect to designing your own model of supervision?

After this personal reflection, put your efforts toward mastering a primary theory that will serve as a guide for what the supervisor and the supervisee do in the supervision process. Select a theory that comes closest to your beliefs about human nature and the change process, and deepen your knowledge of the theory to determine the aspects of it that fit best for you. Look for ways to personalize the theory or theories of your choice.

Consider how your supervision model might be modified when moving from face-to-face to technology-based supervision using videoconferencing and other online tools such as texting and emailing (Jencius & Baltrinic, 2016). In the midst of the COVID-19 pandemic, we all have had to learn creative ways to transition to online delivery of services in many aspects of life, and competence in online supervision has become a necessity. It is not realistic to ignore the influence of technology on your professional activities and the role that technology may increasingly play in communication and relationships.

Commit yourself to a reading program, and attend a variety of professional workshops. Reading is a realistic and useful way to expand your knowledge base and to find ideas on how to create, implement, and evaluate techniques. As you attend workshops, be open to ideas that seem to have particular meaning to you and that fit the context of your work. As you experiment with many different methods of supervision, strive to bring your unique stamp to your work. Personalize your techniques so they fit your style, and be open to feedback from your supervisees about how well your supervisory style is working for them.

As you practice, be open to supervision throughout your career. Westefeld (2009) notes that we "need to inculcate the idea that supervision should never stop, that long after graduate school, persons delivering psychotherapeutic services should be engaged in the supervisory process regularly," adding that "it may be even more important to supervise someone 25 years post-Ph.D. than a 3rd-year graduate student" (p. 301). Talk with other supervisors and colleagues about what you are doing, and think about alternative approaches you could take with supervisees. Remain a long-term learner, and continue to think about alternative theoretical frameworks. Be open to borrowing techniques from various theories, yet do so in a systematic way. We encourage you not to leave your personal style out of the process of developing your integrative approach in supervision. Continue reflecting on what works for you and what set of blueprints will be most useful in creating an emerging model for supervisory practice. None of these established models will fit you perfectly. Challenge yourself to tailor your unique supervisory model to fit you and each of your supervisees.

Summary

It is essential that supervisors have a clear understanding of the goals of supervision and the theoretical model they use. The models of supervision have been refined in recent years but need further clarification and validation. Some models are uneven in the topics they cover and the methods for application in supervision. A supervision model describes what supervision is and how the supervisee's learning occurs. Although there are many different supervision models, the most common ones are developmental models, psychotherapy-based models, and integrative models. Become familiar with the various models of supervision and begin to develop your own model, yet realize that doing so is a long-term process based on study, reflection, clinical experience, and experience in practicing supervision. The practice of supervision can best be viewed as an evolving and developing process that will continue to change throughout your professional career.

SUGGESTED ACTIVITIES

1. Interview one or two clinical supervisors and ask them about their model of supervision. Ask how they arrived at using that model, how it is applied with supervisees, and about its pros and cons.

2. Identify the different kinds of activities, feedback, assessment, and evaluation that can be used in supervision models. Consider these as you develop your own model.

3. Sketch out some ideas for your own model of supervision. Discuss these ideas in small groups in class, comparing your thoughts and ideas. What common themes were identified by your classmates?

4. Working in small groups, develop a hypothetical composite model that all members in the group support. Include in this model the types of activities and structures that apply. What are the basic components of a useful model? What kind of framework will help you be most effective as a supervisor? Have each group present their model to the entire class.

5. As a supervisee, how important is it for you to feel you can work within your supervisor's theoretical orientation? How much value do you place on being able to conceptualize a case from your preferred theoretical orientation? Discuss this topic in small groups.

6. As a supervisor, could you work effectively with a supervisee who has a theoretical orientation different from your own? For example, if you work within a person-centered supervision model and your supervisee's theoretical orientation is largely psychodynamic, how would you work with that supervisee? What challenges might you face? What challenges might your supervisee face?

7. Divide into teams and debate whether it is more productive to focus on the common factors in supervision or to adopt a specific theoretical model of supervision.

8. To become more informed about neuroscience concepts related to your work as a counselor or supervisor, visit credible websites such as the National Institute of Mental Health, Division of Neuroscience and Basic Behavioral Science (https://www.nimh.nih.gov/index.shtml).

CHAPTER 5

Methods of Supervision

FOCUS QUESTIONS

1. What have you learned about supervision methods from being a participant in supervision?
2. What supervision methods do you currently use, and what additional methods would you like to learn?
3. What are the pros and cons of individual versus group supervision approaches? Which do you prefer as a supervisee? As a supervisor?
4. What are some challenges of triadic supervision for supervisees and supervisors? What could you do as a supervisor to address these challenges?
5. What criteria would you use to determine supervision methods you would use with supervisees?
6. What methods do you recommend for supervisees at different levels of development?
7. How would you incorporate technology into your supervisory practice?

A "model" provides a theoretical description of a style of supervision, whereas supervision *methods* provide a general approach to supervising and may describe specific techniques. Clinical supervision is a rapidly expanding field, and methods are continually being developed, and they evolve over time. Some methods have been borrowed from psychotherapy techniques; others have been developed specifically for supervising. We refer to both the approaches and the techniques of supervision as *supervision methods.* In this chapter, we describe some of the more common supervision methods.

Professional standards (AAMFT, 2015; ACA, 2014; ACES, 2011; APA, 2017; NASW, 2017; NOHS, 2015) address supervision methods and techniques in a number of ways, but they all emphasize that supervisors are expected to have a good understanding of methods and the ability to apply them.

> Prior to offering supervision services, counselors are trained in supervision methods and techniques. Counselors who offer supervision services regularly pursue continuing education activities, including both counseling and supervision topics and skills. (ACA, 2014, F.2.a.)

Supervision requires many skills used in counseling (e.g., empathy, respect, active listening, and challenging), but supervision has a different focus and different goals. Supervisors have a gatekeeping function and are charged with monitoring and evaluating supervisees. Therapists also monitor and carefully assess a client's progress, but therapists do not have a gatekeeping function.

Some of the methods suggested in the standards of the various codes of ethics are live observation, cotherapy, live supervision, audio and video recordings, role play, interpersonal process recall, suggestions and advice, feedback, and demonstration of skills. Historically, supervisors have applied therapy skills and methods to the supervisory process. However, as mentioned in Chapter 3, the personal characteristics and style of the supervisor are just as important as the supervisor's knowledge and skill in the application of methods. The literature on clinical supervision supports the critical role of the supervisory relationship, and methods cannot be considered apart from the context of the working alliance. Norcross and Popple (2017) conclude that the success of supervision depends a great deal on the quality of the supervisory alliance: "The supervisory relationship is paramount. Explore the relationship, nurture it, and, if at all possible, enjoy it" (p. 69).

A clearly articulated model of supervision (see Chapter 4) provides the basis for the selection of supervision methods. Methods vary depending on the theoretical orientation of the supervisor, the supervisee's developmental level and needs, the client population being served, the setting in which the supervisee works, the supervisee's role in that setting, and the supervisor's competence when using those methods. Generally, supervisors should be competent in the use of a variety of supervision methods. Determine the methods best suited to a particular supervisee at the outset of supervision, reassess the supervisee's needs periodically, and adjust your methods as needed.

Supervision Formats

Supervision can be effective in a number of formats. Individual supervision is the most common form, and it is used in virtually all of the helping professions. The supervisor and the supervisee meet face-to-face, or at times in an online format, to discuss cases and a variety of topics surrounding the supervisee's personal and professional development. Individual supervision is required by many licensing and certification agencies because it lends itself to detailed personal attention to the clinical work and development of the supervisee. The frequency and duration of meetings vary depending on the situation and the supervision requirements for licensure.

Next, we introduce a new format that is becoming increasingly popular, triadic supervision. This is followed by an in-depth exploration of group supervision, the preferred method for many supervisors both because of the economy of supervising several supervisees at once and the benefits to the supervisees of group interaction and learning from one another. Finally, we discuss ways to combine individual and group supervision to maximize the strengths of both formats (Norcross & Popple, 2017).

Individual Supervision

The majority of methods described in this chapter can be applied to individual supervision. The most common format is self-report, in which the supervisee describes his or her clinical activities and case conceptualizations to the supervisor without the use of case notes, recorded information, or other forms of supporting data. However, self-reporting is not satisfactory as an exclusive method for supervision (Johnson, 2019). If self-report is the primary method used, supervisees may avoid discussing problematic situations or be cautious in bringing up difficulties they are encountering with their clients.

Direct observation methods such as cotherapy, live observation, and video recording are highly recommended for use along with self-report methods to ensure that the supervisor has a clear understanding of the supervisee's work. These direct methods give supervisors the advantage of gaining "full access to the nuanced data required to provide corrective feedback and promote skill development that is tailored for efficacy with the particular client, generate valid summative evaluations, and meet their clinical oversight obligations" (Johnson, 2019, p. 292). Another common method involves the use of process and progress notes that the supervisee has recorded for each counseling session.

Some supervisees respond best to the personal attention received in individual supervision, and they may be more comfortable disclosing information regarding their professional development in this setting than they would be in a group setting. However, individual supervision does not afford the learning that occurs from the interaction in a group supervision setting, nor does it offer the opportunity to view the supervisee's interaction with other supervisees as a parallel process of how the supervisee might interact with clients. Individual supervision is most effective when used in conjunction with group supervision methods.

Triadic Supervision

One widely adopted form of supervision, particularly in the counselor education arena, is triadic supervision. The Council for the Accreditation of Counseling and Related Educational Programs (CACREP, 2016) describes triadic supervision as "a tutorial and mentoring relationship between a member of the counseling profession and two counseling students" (p. 44). CACREP has included this form of supervision as an acceptable substitute for the weekly individual supervision requirements for accredited programs since 2001. Triadic supervision, as defined by CACREP, is different from the "triadic system" discussed in Chapter 1, which referred to supervision involving the supervisor, the supervisee, and the client.

Hein and Lawson (2008) conducted a qualitative study and interviewed doctoral students about their experiences with triadic supervision. These students were operating as supervisors of master's-level students in a counselor education program, and they used triadic supervision. Overall, triadic supervision increased the demands on the supervisor because the supervisor was interacting with two individuals simultaneously who had varying levels of skill, ability to accept feedback, and possibly differing therapeutic approaches. Balancing the dynamics of the supervisory relationship with two supervisees was a major challenge. Monitoring, responding appropriately to, maintaining engagement with, and supporting two people at the same time increased the cognitive load of the supervisor. Supervisors need to be adequately trained and experienced in this form of supervision prior to implementing it. Triadic supervision can lighten the load of the supervisor under optimal conditions, such as when there is a good fit between supervision peers (Hein & Lawson, 2008). An effective match based on developmental level may minimize difficulties in giving appropriate feedback, reframing supervisee feedback, and monitoring supervisee interactions and enable the supervisor to challenge both supervisees in a similar way. When supervisees are well matched in personality and motivation, they may be more comfortable challenging each other and more open to feedback, thereby allowing the supervisor to be more flexible and creative with interventions (p. 29). However, when the match is poor and supervisees prove to be incompatible, the negative feelings (e.g., anxiety, frustration) supervisees can experience pose a serious risk to the supervisor-supervisee relationship and to triadic supervision in general (Hein et al., 2011).

In a more recent study, Lonn and Juhnke (2017) investigated supervisees' nondisclosure within triadic supervision and concluded that supervisors facilitating this form of supervision need to purposefully foster positive relationships with each supervisee and promote positive peer relationships between peer supervisees. These findings are consistent with those of Hein and colleagues (2011), and Lonn and Juhnke (2017) illustrate how important it is "not [to] underestimate how the presence of a peer in supervision may enhance openness and the willingness to be vulnerable with disclosure, as well as possibly limiting comfort with disclosure and sharing" (p. 92). Avent and her colleagues (2015) examined the categories of peer feedback given in triadic supervision, including counseling performance skills, cognitive counseling skills, self-awareness, professional behaviors, and self-reflection. They reinforced the idea that "to capitalize on the learning outcomes of triadic supervision, supervisors must know more about the types of peer feedback exchanged and how this feedback varies across the experience level of counseling trainees" (p. 75).

Group Supervision

Group supervision provides supervisees with opportunities to share their work with peers, to take advantage of the collective wisdom of their peers, and to create a cohesive community. It also provides opportunities for reflection, clinical input, and skill enhancement. Group supervision maximizes supervisor and supervisee resources and experiences and offers peer support (Russell-Chapin & Chapin, 2020).

Supervisors who conduct group supervision should have skills in group supervision methods and experience in facilitating group process. Supervisors conducting group supervision must go beyond a focus on the content of cases and issues raised by supervisees. Supervisors need to create a safe and accepting atmosphere within the supervision group that will encourage trainees to meaningfully participate in the supervision process.

Regardless of the particular method used in group supervision, group dynamics will develop and the group will move through a number of stages (Corey, Corey, and Corey, 2018). We describe the four typical stages of group process and explain how they apply to supervision groups.

Initial Stage

During the early phase of supervision, it is essential to develop a supervision contract and make sure all supervisees in the group are aware of what is expected of them and that informed consent is given. This is a time to formulate goals, discuss how group supervision works, and prepare supervisees to actively engage in forming the agenda for each session. Supervisees should be encouraged to take active steps to create a trusting climate by sharing their thoughts and feelings pertaining to being in the group.

Transition Stage

In the transition stage, supervisees may wonder about others' acceptance or rejection of them, performance anxiety is often present, and supervisees may struggle with appearing competent. This is a time for supervisees to take risks by expressing their vulnerabilities pertaining to their training experience, disclosing their thoughts regarding issues being explored, and asking for what they want from supervision in the group setting.

Working Stage

As the group begins to feel safe and resolves conflicts and resistance, the working stage focuses on active problem solving and learning from each other and the supervisor. This is a time of increased cohesion, and a sense of community develops. Supervisees interact with one another and with the supervisor freely and directly. If conflict emerges in the group, it is dealt with directly and effectively. Participants are willing to bring their concerns to the supervision group, to give one another feedback, to ask for feedback regarding their cases, and to consider this feedback in a nondefensive manner.

Ending Stage

The ending stage is a time for each supervisee to identify what was learned from the field placement and from the supervision group itself. The group supervisor assists supervisees in developing a conceptual framework that will help them understand, integrate, consolidate, and remember what they have learned in the group.

The Value and Benefits of Group Supervision

If well designed, the group supervision format offers many training and mentoring benefits that cannot be obtained through individual supervision alone (Valentino et al., 2016). The unique characteristics and benefits of group supervision include peer feedback, having multiple listeners for the same event, social networking, observational learning, modeling, rehearsing positive and productive discussion, developing empathy, practicing public speaking and presenting, and developing professional repertoires (Valentino et al., 2016).

According to Stinchfield, Hill, and Bowers (2019), "group supervision plays a critical role in promoting counselor identity, cultivating clinical skill development, and orienting counselors-in-training to the professional expectations of counselors and supervisors while leveraging the opportunity for vicarious learning" (p. 141). The group supervision format can be a useful training tool in a variety of clinical contexts. For example, Valentino and colleagues (2016) described the benefits of offering group supervision for those training to practice applied behavior analysis (ABA). Some professionals in that field view group supervision as "one of the only forums to cultivate professional repertoires needed to be successful with certain clinical populations, such as individuals with autism" (p. 320). Group supervision was also used by Radis (2020) when facilitating a trauma-informed clinical supervision group for helping individuals and families facing homelessness. The major aim of this supervision group was to "build resilience in those doing this challenging work" (p. 46).

Group supervision lends itself to a variety of role-playing approaches that enable trainees to become aware of potential countertransference issues and to acquire alternative perspectives in working with clients they sometimes perceive as being "difficult." A supervisee can assume the role of the client by "becoming" the client while the supervisor demonstrates other approaches for dealing with the client. The supervisor can then assume the client's position as the trainee experiments with another way of dealing with the client. Supervisees also can assume various roles for one another, which often generates rich discussion material following the enactment. Many techniques of psychodrama, such as role reversal, can be fruitfully applied in supervision groups. Role-playing techniques bring concrete situations to life, and by enacting them in the here and now, rather than merely *talking about problems*, supervisees gain experience with these issues. Role playing and role reversal are discussed at greater length later in the chapter.

Three Voices From the Field follow, illustrating different approaches to group supervision. Valerie Russell explains how she combines both individual and group approaches. Erik Braun describes his mega-conceptualization in group supervision. And Marianne Schneider Corey shares the challenges involved in combining experiential and didactic ways of teaching group process with supervision for group workers.

 VOICES FROM THE FIELD

Creating a Trusting Climate in My Supervision Group

Valerie Russell, PhD

In this narrative, I reflect on my experiences conducting supervision groups at a community mental health agency. My goal was to create a safe and supportive environment in which interns felt comfortable presenting their cases in a candid manner, and I paid particular attention to their feelings of transference and countertransference. Although supervision is not therapy, I incorporated a number of therapeutic techniques to establish a trusting environment in my supervision groups. I spent a significant part of our first meeting "establishing the frame," a psychoanalytic descriptor, in which I described the parameters of the group, explained the goals of group supervision, and described my expectations of the interns. Establishing the framework contributes to a sense of safety. I emphasized collegiality among the interns and encouraged them to provide support, validation, and feedback to their colleagues. By paying particular attention to how the supervision group is shaped at the outset, and then by carefully adhering to its parameters, the interns quickly recognized the supervision group as a valuable resource and a unique learning opportunity.

At my agency, an intern supervision group had a structure similar to that of a therapy group. Ideally consisting of six to eight interns, the group met weekly for 2 hours. At the beginning and end of each group, the interns were expected to check in and check out. A check-in provided interns with the opportunity to request whether they would like time during our meeting to discuss a particular case. It also gave interns the opportunity to inform the group of any personal concerns that might affect their participation or performance in the group that day. Intern evaluations were handled by the individual supervisors, so I was not formally evaluating the interns in group supervision. This freed the students to speak more openly about their presumed "mistakes" and to more readily discuss their feelings of transference and countertransference.

Confidentiality was handled in the supervision group as it would be in a therapy group: "What is said in the group stays in the group." There was one caveat. I made it clear to the interns that I would talk with their supervisors occasionally, and I assured interns that I would be tactful in how I presented this information. If it was important for the supervisor to be informed about potentially sensitive material, I made every attempt to include the intern in the dialogue, and I encouraged interns to bring particular concerns to the attention of their supervisor directly.

I did my best to create an environment in which interns were encouraged to take risks. Interns often came from different theoretical backgrounds, which added to the creativity of the group. They suggested hypotheses based on their particular theoretical orientations and offered different intuitive hunches. I suggested that they talk about a case the same way they would approach a workout at the gym. The idea was to push themselves somewhat in order to feel a little "sore" the next morning, but not so much that they would be too sore to get out of bed! In discussing a case, the interns were challenged to demonstrate some level of vulnerability, but not to the point that they might feel uncomfortable seeing their colleagues the following day.

Group and individual supervision are both valuable, and the two formats complement each other nicely. My focus in individual supervision has always been to help each intern develop an increased understanding of the client's process and an awareness of the intern's transference and countertransference. Although in-depth exploration can be done in either format, individual supervision lends itself to deeper and longer discussion, and matters more threatening to the supervisee can be addressed more readily individually. In contrast, my goal in group supervision is to assist interns in developing confidence in presenting their own cases. They also are able to hypothesize about their colleagues' cases, drawing from their various theoretical orientations.

Group supervision is also a more viable format for practicing techniques (e.g., role playing). When I have had the opportunity to work with an intern in both individual and group supervision, I gained a broader perspective on the intern, but this sometimes evoked a variety of feelings in either the intern or his or her group supervision colleagues.

VOICES FROM THE FIELD

The Mega-Conceptualization in Group Supervision

Erik Braun, PhD

As a faculty supervisor of master's-level internship students, I hope to develop five areas in all of my supervisees by the end of a semester: clinical writing skills, clinical interviewing skills, research knowledge of client issues, case conceptualization, and self-awareness. To be sure that each area is adequately developed, each student presents a *mega-conceptualization* twice during the semester. Supervisees select a client and have the client in mind for each item: (a) the written case conceptualization, (b) the in-class case conceptualization discussion, (c) presenting a 5-minute overview of an article on a topic related to the client's issue, (d) a video presentation for feedback, and (e) sharing passages from the student's personal growth journal. Faculty supervisors of all levels (including doctoral students facilitating group supervision as part of their training) will find that this method provides structure, depth, and engagement to supervision groups while also ensuring comprehensive learning. All that is required is planning at the beginning of the semester and group facilitation skills.

The main class discussion starts with a short statement about the presenting problem. The group is then tasked with a *reverse interview*. That is, the group draws out the relevant information from the presenter by asking questions, and the presenter gives somewhat minimal answers. I have found this to be an engaging way to do case presentation because it gives the group the sense that they are solving a mystery. The reverse interview serves two purposes. Of course, the presenter learns to communicate information to her or his peers, but it also trains the rest of the group to ask the most pertinent questions—a key skill for developing insights about their own clients.

Once the group feels they have enough information, the presenter describes a particular issue (selected in advance) that is particularly challenging about the client. This could be something that is stumping the supervisee about the dynamics of interactions during session; which interventions would be best; brainstorming activities; or anything else for which the supervisee may not yet have the skills, insight, or knowledge.

The student then summarizes the article read on this issue, highlighting any notable lessons learned. Finally, the student shares an entry from the personal growth journal and comes prepared to discuss insecurities about being a new professional, fears that might be pertinent to the beginning counselor, and even issues such as conflicts with coworkers at their sites.

Using this mega-conceptualization method ensures that each student has developed in each of the important areas expected from a professional counselor. This technique can be used with master's students in discussing their clients or doctoral students in discussing their supervisees. This is applicable for all types of client issues, but best practice is to encourage students to present a client issue with which they are currently experiencing difficulties.

In that way, the mega-conceptualization becomes a working meeting, and students are able to focus on developing in the areas in which they need the most help.

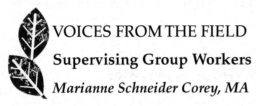

VOICES FROM THE FIELD

Supervising Group Workers

Marianne Schneider Corey, MA

My experience as a supervisor has been in the area of training and supervising group workers as they facilitate groups. I believe the best training is provided in an experiential group in which trainees function as coleaders of their group with my supervision. I have used experiential approaches to teach group counseling and supervise students interested in learning skills as a group facilitator. Trainees in these groups have opportunities to explore personal concerns as members, and they also gain supervised experience in facilitating their group. An early challenge for me was to set clear boundaries regarding the purpose and context of group training and to communicate that to the supervisees. I struggled from the beginning with not getting in the way of trainees as they facilitated the group. By recalling what it had been like when I first began, I was able to appreciate the difficulty they were experiencing as trainees. Although I wanted to be helpful, I learned the importance of not being too helpful. Trainees need to find their own voices and direction, and I must guard against them becoming dependent on me. A key issue has been to avoid taking over a group too soon.

It is a challenge to communicate direct and constructive feedback to supervisees without being perceived as being judgmental and critical. Many trainees lack confidence and sometimes feel inept. I want to offer hope and specific feedback that trainees can use to increase their self-confidence and to enhance their skills. When I first began supervising, it was essential for me to establish my own style. There is no one right way of supervising, but carving out my own identity as a supervisor took some time.

It was sometimes difficult to allow trainees to accept responsibility and trust that they would learn through a process of experimenting with supervision. When trainees do not perform adequately in leading a group, my task is to find a way to make this a teaching opportunity. My goal is to assist trainees in becoming less aware of me and instead focus on the group members. Early in supervising a training group, I encourage participants to be active. I tell them that being self-conscious and critically judging what they say or do will get in their way of learning. I emphasize that there is something to be learned no matter what happens. If a group session does not meet their expectations, they can explore specific factors that contributed to that outcome. Group members usually react to these instructions with relief and report feeling much less anxious. As their supervisor, I let them know that I understand and empathize with their difficulty in being observed by their peers and by supervisors. I typically tell trainees that allowing their fears to immobilize them is a great mistake. Trainees often find it helpful to openly share their fears in the group, and their fears appear to be lessened by simply verbally expressing them. I am very aware of the performance anxieties of most trainees, and I strive to gain their trust. My intention is to help them become more skilled clinicians, not to criticize them or put them down.

My main challenge is to create a safe and accepting group atmosphere in which they can learn new skills as a group facilitator without converting the group into a therapy forum for them. Supervising experientially presents the challenge of teaching in a personal way and dealing with personal concerns brought up by the members while maintaining appropriate boundaries so the supervision goals are not lost. For example, supervisees sometimes comment that they feel stuck with a particular client because that individual triggered them. They may even be willing to describe personal problems that surfaced for them as they attempted to focus on a client. I use this opportunity to teach the importance of handling countertransference, but I do not abdicate my role as a supervisor and become a therapist in the supervision session. Instead, I encourage them to consider exploring some of their personal issues further with a therapist.

When I am processing a group session, I ask questions that encourage self-reflection by the coleaders: "Did you have any persistent thoughts or reactions during the time you were coleading this group that you did not express? Was there a time when you wondered what to do?" I also ask coleaders to focus on specific skills such as opening a group meeting, linking members with common themes, following a member's cues as a way to deepen group interaction, and closing a group session. My emphasis is on helping group trainees become increasingly aware of what is going on in the context of here-and-now interactions within the group and assisting them in developing interventions based on statements members make during a session. I emphasize that it is not a matter of "right" or "wrong"; rather, interventions are often a function of the leader's interest in something that is occurring in the group.

Years of teaching group counseling and supervising trainees have convinced me of the value of combining didactic and experiential approaches and giving trainees opportunities to talk about personal issues in these groups. Supervising in this way can be ethical, effective, and a rich resource for learning how groups function. This approach has many benefits for trainees learning how to facilitate groups, how to work with a coleader, and how to do meaningful personal work in a group.

Peer Supervision Groups

The peer supervision group is a common format used in training programs and in agency and school settings. Campbell (2006) described peer supervision and team supervision as two forms of group supervision. *Peer supervision* involves a group of similarly trained clinicians who meet together on a regular basis to informally supervise one another, discussing cases and ethical issues and providing support and feedback about their work. Peer supervision groups are useful for counselors at all levels of experience. For trainees, peer groups offer a supportive atmosphere and help them learn that they are not alone with their concerns. For counselors and other mental health professionals in practice, they provide an opportunity for continued professional growth. For instance, Clemens (2015) describes the value of a peer consultation group for early-career psychiatrists who are invested in further developing their psychodynamic psychotherapy skills. Similarly, Thompson and colleagues (2015) provide a detailed outline of an acceptance and commitment therapy (ACT) peer consultation group created for clinicians hoping to strengthen their ACT skills, which they refer to as the Portland model. Discussion of ethical dilemmas and alternative perspectives to difficult situations can be explored in peer supervision groups. These groups are informal and typically do not include an evaluation component. In addition to the case consultation method, peer supervision frequently involves the use of training tapes, discussions of the counseling literature, licensing law updates, and other didactic methods.

Peer supervision groups are valuable for practitioners for many reasons, including ongoing consultation and support for difficult cases, networking, and combating professional isolation and potential burnout. Clinicians often recognize a renewed need for supervision at a later point in their careers because they want additional training, because of the emotional intensity of practicing therapy, or because of the stress associated with their professional work.

Team supervision is found primarily in agency settings in which a group of mental health professionals from different disciplines meet to discuss cases and other clinical issues. It is similar to the case conference but broader in the scope of topics addressed. Other forms of group supervision include grand rounds, staff meetings where clinical issues are discussed, seminars, and tutorials.

In Voices From the Field, Wendy Logan Cuellar, a school counselor, describes the evolution of a peer supervision group she started that functions as a peer consultation group and its value to those who have participated in it.

 VOICES FROM THE FIELD

Peer Supervision Groups for School Counselors

Wendy Logan Cuellar, MAEd

I wish I could say that I developed a peer supervision group out of a thirst for professional knowledge and a desire to increase my skills as a school counselor. But to be honest, the group was formed out of fear, panic, and sheer necessity. I had a new job, a new principal, and a variety of client issues I had never dealt with before. I contacted my designated "supervisor" at the school's central office for help, only to learn that she primarily handled paperwork and out-of-district students, not clinical issues. That is when fear and panic took over.

I began by inviting 12 counselors from different grade levels and school systems to attend a meeting designed to explore the potential benefits of regularly meeting as peers. The group was open to any school counselor and began primarily as a way to gather resources and get support for our stressful and sometimes emotionally overwhelming jobs. Agendas for each meeting were set based on the needs of the group. For example, one month, we might discuss how to organize and facilitate parent groups. Another month, we might discuss school politics and how to navigate the balance between counseling and all of our other tasks.

After 2 years, a deep trust within our group had developed, and our process became more like peer supervision than consultation. We identified areas for individual growth and asked for feedback in those specific areas. It was at this point we made the difficult decision to close our group to new members. There is a place for ongoing consultation and sharing of resources, but our group was ready to move away from general concepts to more specific clinical issues.

We began periodically inviting local therapists to speak to our group. A cognitive behavioral therapist spoke about using CBT with children and adolescents. We visited the office of a therapist who demonstrated how to incorporate sand tray therapy into our sessions. We invited a clinician who specialized in clients with disordered eating to speak about recognizing eating disorders and identifying when referrals were needed. This was a win-win arrangement. We received training on specific clinical issues and learned about community resources, and community practitioners were able to make personal connections with school counselors who were excellent referral sources for them.

An unanticipated benefit of our group was the opportunity to contact each other outside of our monthly meetings as needed for clinical consultations. We were able to call any group member and feel that the member had a working knowledge of our areas of strength as well as weakness and would be able to consult.

Our group continued to meet for more than 10 years. To this day, this is the only supervision that many of us every received as school counselors. As group members moved on to other fields or took jobs in other places, we would discuss asking someone else to take their spot. Several factors contributed to the group's success over such an extended period of time. First, a designated facilitator was responsible for leading the group, setting an agenda, and sending out reminders. Having one designated person in charge decreased the potential for subgroups to develop. Second, the group process belonged to the group. Although there was a facilitator, the group members set the guidelines, discussed confidentiality, and developed agendas, which promoted group ownership. A third factor contributing to the group's success was maintaining a diverse group of counselors representing different grade levels, different county school systems, and different experience levels. This way of organizing the group expanded the potential for diverse perspectives and brainstorming.

Methods Used in Supervision

Verbal exchange and direct observation are the most commonly used forms of supervision and, arguably, could be considered the two overarching categories of methods. Historically, the verbal exchange method—in which supervisor and supervisee discuss cases, ethical and legal issues, and personal development—has been the preferred form of supervision. Direct observation supervision methods—in which the supervisor observes the supervisee practicing either through live observation or video—have become increasingly popular in recent years. The verbal exchange method is more easily accomplished and can be done in person or by telephone or using computer-assisted technology in a crisis. The downside to "talking about" treatment and other issues is that much of the supervision's effectiveness depends on the degree to which the supervisee is straightforward and accurate in describing his or her activities (Johnson, 2019). Direct observation methods, although requiring more time and effort, provide a more accurate understanding of the supervisee's skills and abilities.

Because verbal exchange methods rely exclusively on the supervisee's self-report, the use of this method alone is no longer acceptable, especially for students and novice counselors. Supervisors are strongly encouraged to ensure that supervisees have adequate skills by observing their clinical work (ACES, 2011). This protects client, supervisee, and supervisor. Using both methods together combines the economy of the verbal exchange method with the accuracy of direct observation. This pairing of methods provides better risk management for the supervisor, who carries vicarious liability for all the actions of her or his supervisees.

We describe a number of commonly used supervision methods in the following pages. Consider your own experience as a supervisee or supervisor with these methods and how these methods could be applied to both individual and group supervision settings.

Case Consultation

The case consultation method involves a discussion of the supervisee's cases, and it is the most commonly used supervision method. This verbal exchange usually involves the supervisee describing to the supervisor the major issues surrounding each case. These might include the client's purpose for seeking therapy; diagnostic formulations; therapy techniques used; relationship issues; ethical, legal, and multicultural issues; and process notes regarding the case. This method is effective in individual as well as group supervision settings. Campbell (2006) claims that the case consultation approach can be used to "protect clients and promote development; explore assessment and diagnostic skills; teach case conceptualization; apply techniques and theory; process relationship issues; promote self-awareness, especially the impact of personal feelings on client care; teach ethics; explore the impact of multicultural issues on client and client care; and promote development of self-efficacy in supervisees" (p. 86). Shilkret (2012) points out that case consultation is an integral part of deepening a clinician's therapeutic skills. However, it is not theory neutral. Supervisors tend to be guided by their own particular theoretical orientation.

Case consultation focused only on the supervisee's self-report is widely used, but it is a limited method. The supervisee may say all the right things in the self-report, but when observed directly with the client, a very different picture of the supervisee's skill level is seen. The supervisee may be able to conceptualize well, but actual performance may be another matter. In addition, the supervisee's perception of what is going on may not accurately depict the reality of the counseling situation. Although the supervisee does not deliberately try to deceive, the reality is that the supervisee hopes to receive a positive evaluation from the supervisor in addition to learning from the supervisor.

Cotherapy

The cotherapy method involves the supervisor and the supervisee working together as cotherapists with a client or a group. It is essential that the two discuss the nature of the case or the group and the respective roles that the two of them will play as they work together (Campbell, 2006). Supervisors using this method must guard against taking over and doing therapy the way they think it should be done, not allowing the supervisee to struggle and learn in the process.

In cotherapy, the supervisor and supervisee typically discuss their work together in formal supervision sessions. This method offers the supervisor a firsthand view of the skills of the supervisee and provides an arena for modeling and demonstration on the part of the supervisor. Although cotherapy may provide an exciting in vivo training experience and appears to have advantages (e.g., the opportunity for the supervisor to provide the trainee with more immediate feedback), the scholarly literature "provides mixed support for the effectiveness of cotherapy over the single therapist model in terms of client outcomes" (Clark et al., 2016, p. 160). One team of investigators discovered that cotherapy supervision did not lead to better client outcomes than supervision that did not include cotherapy (Tanner et al., 2012). In other words, clients who received counseling by (solo) trainees who had experienced cotherapy supervision did not improve more than the clients counseled by trainees who had not experienced this method of supervision. However, others have noted the value of cotherapy as a supervision approach. Clark and colleagues (2016) found that participants in their study deemed the relational skills they learned as cotherapists useful when they practiced as single therapists. Moreover, the skills also generalized to other practice settings, such as coworker relationships, treatment teams, and agency relationships.

Live Observation

Live observation has advantages over delayed forms of supervision (Weck et al., 2016). The supervisor or observing team directly observes a supervisee in action either by sitting in on a counseling session or through a one-way mirror or video monitor. The focus is on the counseling session and the supervisee's therapy skills.

Written permission of the client must be given for the supervisor to sit in on the session or to observe the session from outside the room. The supervisor may sit in occasionally or on every session, and supervisor and supervisee meet beyond the observation sessions to discuss the case and the work of the supervisee. This method has a number of variations (Weck et al., 2016). The supervisor could remain silent throughout the session or could interrupt the session occasionally to discuss the supervisee's approach, either with or without the client present. Too many interruptions, however, can be distracting for both supervisee and client.

Another variation uses built-in breaks during the session for the supervisee and supervisor to discuss the supervisee's approach. The supervisor may take over the session to demonstrate how to proceed with the client, but the supervisor must be aware of the potential impact of his or her presence in the session both on the client and the supervisee. Maintaining concern for the welfare of the client and the dignity of the supervisee are of paramount importance.

Another way the supervisor can view the supervisee in action with clients is through a one-way mirror in an adjoining room. Neither the client nor the supervisee can see the supervisor in the observation room, but both are aware of the supervisor's presence. The therapy room is wired for audio, which is broadcast into the observation room. The supervisor may simply observe and provide feedback following the session, but several methods of providing feedback during the session are available as well. The bug-in-the-ear method uses an audio receiver that the supervisee wears in the ear, and the supervisor provides feedback and direction to the supervisee via a microphone. This enables the supervisee to make adjustments during the session rather than waiting to discuss the case later. It can become a distraction, however, if the supervisor does too much talking to the supervisee. Sometimes a buzzer is used to signal the supervisee that the supervisor needs to discuss the clinical work of the supervisee. The supervisee can take a break to talk to the supervisor or have a telephone available to call the supervisor. A promising form of live supervision is the bug-in-the-eye (BITE) method in which the supervisor provides instructions and cues via a visual display on a monitor that only the supervisee can see during therapy sessions. In a randomized controlled trial, Weck and colleagues (2016) showed that BITE supervision is a less invasive procedure than some methods and is more effective than delayed video-based (DVB) supervision. The "therapeutic alliance was significantly stronger among the treatments conducted under BITE supervision than those conducted under DVB supervision. Moreover, a higher level of therapeutic competence was found in the BITE condition than in the DVB condition" (p. 386).

Using a one-way mirror is an effective way to observe the work of the supervisee directly and to intervene as the work of the supervisee is in progress. It does, however, require two rooms, a one-way mirror, and audio or visual equipment for contacting the supervisee during the session. It also requires the permission and the cooperation of the client involved. In the Personal Perspective, Bob Haynes provides some further thoughts on the value of live observation supervision.

 BOB HAYNES'S PERSONAL PERSPECTIVE

I participated in the live observation method many times as a supervisee, and I found it to be an excellent learning experience for me. As a young and anxious supervisee, it gave me confidence that a supervisor would suggest what to say next via the bug-in-the-ear should I get stuck when counseling a client.

In my work as internship director, I found live observation to be effective in establishing a baseline on interviewing skills during internship training. Although live observation was anxiety producing, interns typically reported that it was one of their most valuable learning experiences. The supervisory staff found direct observation extreme-ly useful in obtaining a snapshot of the intern's abilities and deficiencies early in the training program. The clients (forensic patients) usually enjoyed being in the "spotlight" and rarely objected to participating in the observation. When they did object, they were excused from participating. Overall, the staff and I found this to be a valuable and expe-dient method of supervision.

Case Study 5.1 illustrates how effective the method of live observation can be in iden-tifying trainees' skill deficits, enabling supervisors to provide corrective feedback and develop appropriate strategies to remediate the deficiencies.

CASE STUDY 5.1: TOBY

Toby is a master's-level addictions counseling trainee who is able to describe and discuss therapy cases with ease and apparent competence. He is a bright student and has done well academically. He appears to have a clear under-standing of the diagnostic issues, treatment goals, and methods needed in counseling clients for addiction issues. One of Toby's clients is an African American male, about Toby's age, with a history of chronic depression. When observed in therapy with this client through the one-way mirror, Toby did have a clear picture of the diagnostic and treatment issues, including differ-ential dual diagnosis, but he experienced considerable difficulty identifying with the young client and using basic helping skills. He did not take time to listen to the client or to truly attempt to understand the client's perspective and what it was like to be poor, hungry, unemployed, hopeless, and suffer from alcoholism; nor did Toby understand what role cultural issues and con-structs of privilege played in his work as a White student with an African American client.

What are the main supervisory issues with Toby? What are the multicultural issues here? What supervision methods would you use to help Toby develop basic helping skills?

Due to direct observation of Toby, his supervisor was able to identify the need for work on basic helping skills and multicultural competence and sensitivity. He also rec-ognized the importance of educating Toby regarding his privilege and the responsibility that privilege carries, as well as the damage that can be done when it goes ignored. It is not uncommon for a student to intellectually understand a case but to lack the basic helping skills needed to "connect" with clients. Many supervisees-in-training are still developing and do not yet have the personal growth and insight needed to truly share compassion with others who live in worlds different from their own. Mentoring, model-ing, role playing, and more direct observation supervision methods helped Toby develop his basic counseling skills with clients.

Video and Audio Recording

Using video or audio recording, the supervisee records one or more sessions with the client or group and reviews them in supervisory sessions. There are many technological means of creating video and audio recordings for use in supervision, and this technology frequently changes and improves. Major considerations for use of this technology are the ethical and legal ramifications of making and storing these recordings. It is essential that clients are provided with full disclosure regarding the process: who will have access to the recording, how will the recording be used in supervision, where and how long will the recording be maintained, and how will confidentiality of the recording be guaranteed?

In addition, clients have the right to decline to be recorded, and they must be allowed to withdraw consent at any time during the process of making or storing the recording.

Crucial segments of the interaction can be played as many times as needed to review the interaction, and role playing of alternate methods can be conducted between the supervisee and the supervisor. Recording sessions at various stages of therapy provides a comparison of the supervisee's progress as a therapist. The major drawback to video or audio recording is the possibility of technical complications. Nevertheless, if you work out the technological details in advance, video recording can be an extremely useful supervision method.

More progressive forms of communication can incorporate telephones, email, or video conferencing in supervision. Blogs, video chats, virtual worlds, podcasts, and social networks are also being used as supervision tools. These methods have been found to be especially helpful for supervision in geographically isolated areas (Martin et al., 2018),

Interpersonal Process Recall

Interpersonal process recall (IPR) is a long-standing, effective, and widely known method using video recording in supervision, and it can be used in conjunction with many different supervision models. Kagan, Krathwohl, and Miller (1963) developed IPR to assist supervisees in processing relationship dynamics with the client and to increase self-awareness. Although developed many decades ago, this model remains viable and can be adapted to facilitate supervisees' growth, including the development of multicultural awareness (Ivers et al., 2017). In this method, supervisees are recorded on video while counseling a client and shown the recording immediately following the interaction. When the recording is reviewed right away, supervisees are able to recall thoughts and feelings they experienced during the therapy session but did not express for various reasons.

The supervisor and supervisee may stop reviewing the recording at any point for exploration and discussion. The primary task of the supervisor is to assist the supervisee in investigating his or her own internal processes, including motives, thoughts, and feelings, that were at work during the therapy session. Several supervision sessions may be needed to get through one videotaped therapy session. Bernard and Goodyear (2019, pp. 174–175) suggest that the supervisor might ask the following questions during an IPR session:

- What were your thoughts, feelings, and reactions? Did you want to express them at any time?
- What would you like to have said at this point?
- What was it like for you in your role as a counselor?
- What thoughts were you having about the other person at that time?
- Did you have any ideas about what you wanted to do with that?
- Were any pictures, images, or memories flashing through your mind then?
- How do you imagine the client was reacting to you?
- Did you sense that the client had any expectations of you at that point?
- What did you want to hear from the client?
- What message did you want to give to the client? What prevented you from doing so?

Role Play and Role Reversal

Role playing, acting out a variety of scenarios with supervisor and supervisee acting as therapist and client, can be a very effective supervision approach when used in conjunction with other methods described in this chapter. Role playing also can be used creatively in a group supervision setting with many possible variations. The real value of role playing lies in the supervisor's ability to see the supervisee in the here and now rather than talking about situations and issues.

Role reversal is a kind of role play in which the supervisee plays the role of the client and the supervisor plays the role of the therapist. This is useful to assist the supervisee in developing empathy for the client and the client's role in therapy. Another method of role reversal is for the supervisee to play the role of the supervisor while the supervisor plays the role of the supervisee. This invites the supervisee to examine the issues discussed in supervision from a different perspective, which can aid the learning process.

Modeling and Demonstration

Modeling is teaching the supervisee by means of observing the supervisor's behavior, showing how the supervisor would go about various professional tasks from ethical decision making to formulating and applying clinical methods. This form of teaching occurs throughout the course of supervision, and it conveys attitudes and beliefs and demonstrates behaviors for the supervisee. We hope that an attitude of empowerment is displayed by the supervisor to the supervisee—empowerment for the supervisee to be able to self-supervise. Demonstration involves showing the supervisee how to perform specific tasks and skills such as conducting an intake session or offering various interventions for managing an angry client. Supervisors can demonstrate skills via role play or in cotherapy by modeling how to effectively handle certain situations or by talking aloud about how they might work through a particular dilemma. It is important for supervisors to emphasize that there is no one "right way" to approach a problem situation and that they are merely illustrating one of many ways of intervening. Give supervisees a chance to demonstrate what they have learned from your demonstration, and encourage supervisees to bring their own unique style to this work.

Coaching

Coaching was originally developed in management supervision as executive coaching, and it has been developed into the specialty of life coaching. Although rarely identified as a supervision method in the literature, coaching can be readily adapted for use in certain types of supervision. Using this method, the supervisor facilitates the supervisee's learning by helping the supervisee examine various topics. The coach functions less as an authority and more as a personal adviser focusing on the supervisee's agenda.

In coaching, asking the right question is often as important as having the right answer. Coaching is similar to person-centered supervision; the job of the supervisor is to actively listen to supervisees to help them discover for themselves what they need to learn. If supervisees are encouraged to examine the issues, they will be able to arrive at their own conclusions and solutions.

This approach can be applied with novice or experienced clinicians, but it lends itself more to work with the experienced clinician and in peer supervision. Coaching is less structured and requires the supervisee to determine what is needed from supervision. This may not be the best approach when working with a supervisee who needs more structure and direction from the supervisor. Coaching is built on a relationship of trust.

Coaching can be done in brief and informal sessions or in more systematic and formal supervision sessions. This approach can be collaborative and is aimed at developing supervisee autonomy and self-direction. Coaching provides a format for supervisor and supervisee to work in a partnership to accomplish the goals of supervision.

Homework

Assigning homework might include readings, reviewing websites and blogs, and viewing videos. All of these can be an adjunct to supervision sessions. Assignments can be given on any clinical, ethical, legal, or other topic. Just as homework or out-of-session activities can be a powerful complement to psychotherapy (Muratori & Haynes, 2020), homework can enhance the supervision process. Homework is most effective when it results from a collaborative effort on the part of the supervisor and the supervisee, which is likely to increase compliance. To maximize their learning process, supervisees should regularly come to supervision prepared to discuss homework assignments. If a supervisee wants to learn more about suicide assessment and intervention, for instance, the homework could be reading selected articles and viewing a video on this topic. Time during the next supervision session could be spent talking about how the information applies to clients. Homework covering basic concepts that could easily be learned outside of supervision increases the time available in supervision to discuss cases in greater depth.

Methods Using Written Information

According to Bernard (2014), "the documentation of clinical supervision has not received a great deal of attention in the literature outside of admonitions to keep records of one's supervision for ethical reasons, for troubleshooting with challenging supervisees, or for legal protection" (pp. 199–200). She believes that supervision notes or documentation can be used as a pedagogical strategy to help supervisors-in-training develop "both an understanding and an ability to articulate their use of theory in supervision, use of a supervision model, and an ability to assess the developmental level of their supervisee" (p. 198).

Process notes are written notes outlining the supervisee's conceptualization of the counseling, including diagnosis, goals, objectives, and treatment strategies. Process notes deal with client reactions such as transference and the therapist's subjective impressions of a client. Intimate details about the client, details of dreams or fantasies, sensitive information about the client's personal life, and a therapist's thoughts, feelings, and reactions to the client might be included. Process notes are not considered a component of the client's medical record; they are the personal property of the therapist and are not kept in the medical file but in the therapist's professional files for his or her own use. *Progress notes* are more factual notes regarding what took place in counseling, including the client's statements, behavior, and demeanor. These notes are a portion of the official medical record of the client. These methods offer more detailed reviews of the counseling session than the supervisee's self-report alone. Progress notes are behavioral in nature and address what people say and do. They contain information on diagnosis, functional status, symptoms, treatment plan, consequences, alternative treatments, and client progress.

Nonlinear Methods

Bernard and Goodyear (2019) refer to nonlinear supervision interventions as methods that rely on right-brain strategies. Waalkes, DeCino, and Borders (2018) found that writing and listening to "found poetry" during group supervision not only helps supervisees think in more complex ways but also improves their listening and empathy skills and increases their tolerance for ambiguity. By combining creativity with traditional supervision approaches, supervisees are afforded opportunities to "use reason and logic at the same time they employ intuition and imagination" (p. 16).

We have described some of the commonly used supervision methods as well as some newer developments in the field of supervision. Selection of a particular method depends on many contextual factors surrounding supervision. The supervisor's model of supervision is also a factor in determining the methods used. Licensing boards and professional associations are emphasizing supervision, and we encourage supervisors to remain current with developments in the literature regarding supervision methods.

Using Technology in Supervision

The fallout from COVID-19 has created an opportunity for technology to become a normative means of providing supervision. Many supervisors are concerned about the loss of valued face-to-face interactions with supervisees and have strong opinions about the changing supervision landscape, but technology is proving to have the ability to enhance supervisory relationships and outcomes when used effectively and ethically (Belšak & Simonič, 2019). Nelson, Nichter, and Henriksen (2010) remind us that the definition and purpose of supervision never change, regardless of the method of delivery. The increasingly important role of technology in supervision can be seen in the professional ethics and best practice guidelines for counselors, supervisors, and counselor educators (e.g., American Counseling Association's *Code of Ethics* [2014]; Association for Counselor Education and Supervision's *Best Practices in Clinical Supervision* [2011]). The ACA (2014) encourages us as members to "actively attempt to understand the evolving nature of the profession with regard to distance counseling, technology, and social media . . . and strive to become knowledgeable about these resources" (sect. H, Introduction).

The use of technology in supervision is nothing new. Rousmaniere and Renfro-Michel (2016) suggest that the first wave of technology in the supervision process was primarily through mechanical devices such as live one-way mirrors, audio gear, and video cameras. The second wave of technology in supervision relies on internet-based tools such as video conferencing, webcams, iPads, virtual reality, the internet cloud, supervision software, wikis, email, and texts. When reading this list of technological resources, most of us may realize that we are more involved in using technology for supervision than we first thought. Take a minute to think about how you felt when first using some of the technological tools you now take for granted. Regardless of our proficiency in understanding and using technology, we can increase our effectiveness as supervisors by taking some risks and learning new skill sets. Here are a few terms to be familiar with when having meaningful conversations about incorporating technology into your supervisory practice (pp. 8–9).

- *Online supervision* is participating in supervision through the internet. This supervision may occur across countries or be used in emergency situations.
- *Hybrid or blended supervision* is the practice of combining face-to-face and online or distance methods. One example of hybrid supervision is the use of routine outcome measurement (ROM), which is software that records clinical outcome measures (Bernard & Goodyear, 2019, p. 171). More than 50 ROM systems are available to counselors, and clients can complete these assessments on laptops, PCs, smartphones, and the like, with the outcome data reviewed in supervisory sessions.
- *Synchronous supervision* uses technologies that permit you and your supervisees to interact at the same time. Examples include video conferencing, chats, and instant messaging. These techniques are usually called "live" events.
- *Asynchronous supervision* is the use of technologies that provide you and your supervisees the flexibility of time and space. You do not have to be in the same location or participate at the same time to have effective communication. Examples of these technologies may include discussion groups, GroupMe pages, email, social media websites, or cloud-based storage systems. These technologies allow more flexibility in the ways we can learn about the abundant resources available to us.

Feeling some degree of "technology reluctance" is a nearly universal fear response brought on by the thought of having to learn another new technology (Rousmaniere & Renfro-Michel, 2016). This anxiety can keep us from moving forward and trying new strategies, techniques, and resources. If we want to progress with the field, be relevant to this new generation of counselors, and provide the best practice of supervision, it is time to update our practices to include new technological tools and to put our plan into action. Everything doesn't have to change at once. Here are a few things to consider in making progress in your use of technology in supervision.

Supervision First

Consider your supervision process and goals first. Create a list of supervision hopes and expectations. What kind of supervision do you want to practice? What are the options for process? What would you like to accomplish? What do you believe about supervision, and what theory best suits this belief? What type of relationship do you want to have with your supervisees?

Technology Second

Identify the technology you currently use in supervision. Brainstorm the technologies available that might assist you in achieving your supervision goals and might best meet the needs of your supervisees. Assess your comfort level with each. Determine whether you have the time and budget resources to incorporate different technologies, and consider the resources your students will need to use each technology effectively. In this process, evaluate all the potential resources: time, money, equipment, internet access and reliability, internet connection requirements for needed internet speed, and the logistics of confidentiality and the environment.

Make a Plan

Make an action plan using the technologies that best fit your needs. Purposefully integrate technology into your supervision practice. Maybe a hybrid method is best at first. Rely on the technology you are most comfortable with as your foundation. Become confident in your use of this technology so you do not raise the supervisee's anxiety by expecting performance for which neither the student nor the supervisor is prepared.

Have an Emergency Plan

You may have concerns regarding glitches with technology and how to handle emergencies with technology-assisted supervision. Backup plans become prevention and good risk management procedures. Have a clear understanding of the weak links in your technology-assisted supervision, and identify areas that could create a crisis if things go wrong, for example, if a connection goes down. Clearly communicate your policies regarding steps supervisees should take to access direct supervision when concerns arise. This measure is of upmost importance when the need to breach confidentiality for the protection of a client may arise.

Supervisors can model openness to new learning, even though they may have anxiety about change. Share your struggles in learning new technological skills with supervisees. This is an opportunity for relationship building and meaningful conversations. Supervision courses and workshops should include detailed information regarding equipment and software, skills and knowledge, and the ethical and legal issues involved in using these techniques.

For further reading on using technology in supervision, we recommend *Distance Counseling and Supervision: A Guide for Mental Health Clinicians* (Williamson & Williamson, 2021), especially chapter 1, Ethical, Legal, and Risk Management Considerations, and chapter 5, Distance Supervision.

In Voices From the Field, three contributors address different aspects of using technology in clinical supervision. Marty Jencius shares his perspective on what supervisors need to consider when using technology in supervision. Michelle Wade deals with ethical considerations in providing online supervision. And Benjamin Noah shares his experience of grappling with and ultimately answering the question of whether teaching online counseling courses and doing supervision online can be effective.

VOICES FROM THE FIELD

Training Counselors to Provide Online Supervision

Marty Jencius, PhD

For more than 25 years, I have been looking at the relationship of technology to counseling training and supervision. My work has been in connecting teaching and practice, integrating the new desktop hardware for video conferencing, and developing supervision classrooms in virtual worlds. The barriers of using technology for teaching have been largely overcome, except for equal access to the internet and available hardware. Clinical supervision using technology is still new to many and has not yet developed a foothold similar to online clinical practice.

Online clinical supervision still has barriers related to supervisor qualities, available platforms, and ethical/legal standards. Supervisors considering online clinical supervision should first address their comfort with using technology for real-time communication. Supervisors should receive training in online supervision practices. A supervisor's ability to create a virtual presence— a projected experience of self—helps transcend the technology so the trainee perceives the immediacy of the supervisor. The choice of the technology platform is contingent on how (email, text message, video conferencing, or virtual world) and when (synchronous or asynchronous) supervision will take place. A safe and secure platform is essential, with every effort made to ensure security and minimize the risk of information being transmitted. Clinicians practicing in different parts of the world use different technology platforms for supervision, which are often limited to what is permitted by national guidelines. For U.S. practitioners, the platform must be Health Insurance Portability and Accountability Act (HIPAA) compliant. Supervisors must also have a backup plan should the technology fail. Ethics require online supervisors to follow the directions of their professional associations and work within the practice laws of their license. In addition, clinical supervisors need to know the licensing statutes enacted by states and governments that restrict the use of online counseling and supervision within the regional boundary.

When it is available, technology-assisted supervision and training (TAST) provide the opportunity for trainees in remote areas to receive supervision. Online supervision increases the flexibility for supervisor and trainee, enables increased peer consultation, and reduces or eliminates travel costs for supervision. In my view, many clinical supervisors, out of necessity or a desire to create flexibility in their supervision practice, began using technology for supervision, often without training, skills, or the full awareness of ethical or legal issues.

Models and methods for training online counselors have become available, but there is little about training online supervisors. In response, Eric Baltrinic and I created a six-session online training course for clinical supervision that touches on many of the components needed to perform effectively as an online supervisor. The course was developed as an online course, training directly with the tools that an online clinical supervisor will use. Sessions were designed to address the shift from traditional supervision to online platforms. A session in training covers ethical considerations and minimizing the use of identifying client information for safety and security. Sessions in the course include the process of conducting an online supervision session using case examples and "fish-bowling" the supervisor and supervisee with other class members in observation—this process allows for an online simulation of clinical supervision practice. The course also provides methods for creating online group supervision for practitioners.

I believe the next decade will bring increased use of technology platforms to provide clinical supervision. We need to prepare clinical supervisors in an ethical way that ensures they are using the best technology tools with the best practice model to provide technology-assisted supervision. To do so means we have to rely less on our technology intuition and adopt a comprehensive model of training online supervisors.

For a more complete discussion of this topic, see *Training Counselors to Provide Online Supervision* (Jencius & Baltrinic, 2016).

VOICES FROM THE FIELD

Ethical Considerations for Online Supervision

Michelle E. Wade, EdD

When I decided to provide supervision to counselors-in-training via technology, I thought I was prepared for all that it might entail. After all, I present and write about technology and counseling fairly regularly. However, a recent situation made me take a step back and reevaluate my preparedness, not necessarily from a technology standpoint but from an ethical one.

Providing supervision via technology requires supervisors to consider a number of aspects from an ethical and legal standpoint. Is it within your scope of practice? Is it allowed by your licensing board? What technology will help you meet HIPAA compliance? However, one discussion seems to be lacking depth: navigating the different look and feel of the online supervisory relationship versus a traditional face-to-face supervisory relationship.

One of my supervisees runs a specific support group, and one group member's interactions within the group led other group members to feel the need to terminate their own involvement in the group. It is not unusual for group members to make each other uncomfortable, but these interactions were clearly detrimental to the group as a whole. After processing the situation with my supervisee, we both agreed a referral for this member was in the best interest of the group. We then discussed how to make the referral and role-played best and worst case scenarios. As expected, the client contacted me to address displeasure with the referral. The client's perception was very different from that of my supervisee and raised a legitimate concern: Why I, as the supervisor, could not attend a group session to assess group dynamics. I explained that was not possible due to distance and logistics, (i.e., informed consent, lack of proper technological resources), but I understood the client's frustration with my reliance on information provided by my supervisee. However, my supervisee and I had walked through an ethical decision-making process and determined a course of action that was in the best interest of the group.

The biggest ethical dilemma in this situation was not whether I was competent to practice online supervision or whether I took precautions to protect client confidentiality. The ideas of competency, confidentiality, and nonmaleficence are ingrained in a supervisor. The ethical dilemma I faced rested on fidelity and justice. How do I honor my commitments to supervisees and treat them as fairly as supervisees I can see face-to-face? My inability to be in *physical* proximity to support my supervisee, and to step in if needed during a difficult process, bothered me the most.

Issues of competency, confidentiality, and crises are of paramount importance in online supervision. However, I imagine that most online supervisors rarely consider how different the online supervisory relationship looks when compared to a face-to-face relationship. We need to address the differnce in how the "security blanket" looks and feels when the supervisor is right down the hall versus a video conference or telephone call away. We have an ethical responsibility to our supervisees to prepare them for the fact that we are not going to be in the room when they may feel they need us there the most. Conversely, we have an ethical responsibility to help supervisees process and challenge their perceptions of the supervisory relationship within this new digital context. Online supervisees may be required to have a higher level of self-reliance and self-regulation.

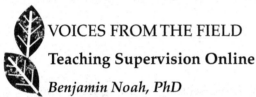 ## VOICES FROM THE FIELD

Teaching Supervision Online

Benjamin Noah, PhD

When I first moved from teaching face-to-face to online, I was concerned about the question I often heard: "How can you teach counseling online and know it is valid?" After teaching online for 16 years, I now know the answer is "yes, it is valid." That is, it is valid if the course is properly developed, has a trained instructor and motivated students, and is in an active learning environment.

Teaching supervision online involves developing an active learning environment in my class. When I think of an active learning environment, I think of Aristotle, walking with his students through the woods that formed his Lyceum and asking questions in the true Socratic method of teaching. Socratic teaching is designed to let the instructor challenge the students and expand their view of the topic—to look beyond the obvious by asking questions rather than providing answers. This style of teaching moves the instructor from being a "sage on the stage" to being a "guide on the side," becoming an integral part of the learning process. Because the interaction is based on my writing, I write like I counsel—with a touch of humor when I can get away with it. If I do it right, it draws all the students into the discussion.

For years, I've told students that there is no hiding in the back of the classroom online—everyone is in the first row. This may be the reason for their high motivation to succeed. The Socratic style also may be a factor because learning becomes a collaboration among the students and between the students and the instructor. My experience in face-to-face classes was that a percentage of the students were always involved in the discussion and a near equal percentage were not involved. In online classes, being silent is not an option—everyone must be part of the discussion process. This increased interaction is one of the strengths of the online format. I believe this interaction to be the reason one can effectively teach counseling online—at least the book knowledge. The true application of the learning takes place during the required residencies and internship.

Teaching supervision online must have two components: the academic course followed by a supervision internship. I now teach only master's-level fieldwork courses and often have a supervision intern (a two-quarter requirement). The master's students meet weekly for group supervision conducted in a web-conference format. The supervision intern interacts with the other students, and I add input as needed. I also meet weekly with the supervision intern. In the first quarter, I tend to be more clinical in my feedback and coaching. With the second-quarter student, I like to move more into the mentor role in supervision and concentrate on building a level of comfort in the supervision role. As more states allow some level of distance supervision for postgraduate counselors, having supervisors who are comfortable in a cyberenvironment can benefit the counseling profession as a whole.

What Supervisors Say to Supervisees

The statements and questions that follow are typical of the lead statements and questions supervisors use with many of the methods described earlier. In most cases, the focus is on the thoughts, feelings, and actions of the supervisee rather than suggesting what the supervisee should do. These questions and statements focus on the content of supervision:

- What would you like to accomplish during the course of our supervision together?
- Let's talk about the topics and issues you might bring to supervision to discuss.
- What ground rules do we need to establish that will help make our supervisory sessions a safe place for you as we work together?
- How can we work together to help you become a more confident and competent clinician?
- What experiences have you had in your lifetime with other cultures?
- What do you need to learn about multicultural issues in dealing with your clients?
- How do the gender differences in this case affect your work with the client?
- What do the legal, ethical, and professional standards indicate regarding this issue?
- Let's talk about how we will handle the evaluation portion of your supervision. How could it be most useful for you?
- Where are you headed with this client? What are your thoughts about the work you did with this client? How did the client affect you?

Developing Skills

Supervisors need a therapeutic skill set that supports communication with their supervisees. The communication skills that create trust, warmth, and responsiveness in clients are the same skill sets to use with supervisees. Conversations with supervisees, particularly difficult ones, are the perfect opportunity to model what to do and what not to do in communicating.

First- and second-order communication skills set the tone of conversations. First-order skills come naturally after practicing therapy for a period of time. They include basic attending, rapport building, appropriate use of open-ended and closed-ended questions, paraphrasing, reflecting, and empathic listening. Second-order skills require some practice and awareness, even for seasoned counselors and supervisors. These skills are easy to understand theoretically but may be more difficult to perform in the moment if they are not used regularly. They require purposeful intent and mindfulness as we communicate (Moulton, 2019a). Let's review a few important secondary therapeutic communication skills that can enhance supervisors' feedback and discussions with supervisees.

I Statements

Taking ownership of our reactions and emotions and asking for what we need without blaming is a simple concept, yet significant practice and coaching is needed for students to learn to use "I" statements. There is the tendency to express thoughts rather than emotions, anger or frustration rather than the underlying emotion, and blame rather than owning the vulnerability of feelings. When used in a flexible and authentic manner, I statements are a powerful life skill for supervisors, counselors, and clients. The goal of I statements is to use your voice positively and assertively and to enhance the likelihood of being heard. This skill can be very helpful when giving feedback to supervisees. It can ease the impact of constructive criticism or be used as positive reinforcement.

Validation

Validating someone's statements doesn't mean "agreement"; rather, it means understanding and acknowledging the other person's perspective, even if you do not "agree" with it. Without validation, people often feel unaccepted, unimportant, or incompetent. Our supervisees need to know we care about them and that they can feel safe sharing their experiences and emotions. When supervisees feel validated, they will talk about difficult issues and trust us not to judge them. If we are not actively practicing validation in our communication, it is easy to unintentionally act in ways that tell our supervisees we are not paying attention, that we do not have time for them, that we do not approve, that they can't be successful. These may seem like insignificant words or actions, but they can have a substantial negative impact on supervisees. They include actions such as dismissive or frustrated sighs, multitasking rather than focusing, interrupting, rushing, and bored facial expressions. Validation strengthens our relationship with supervisees, but we must also recognize ways we may unintentionally hurt our supervisees, both verbally and nonverbally, if we are not aware and skilled.

Perception Checking

Perception checking is a good way to confront words or behaviors of supervisees that are confusing, uncomfortable, or upsetting without judging their actions and words. Address confusing moments directly, but give the benefit of the doubt to the supervisee that the words or behaviors in question have a perfectly good and understandable reason. Checking your perception is a three-part process involving description, interpretation, and clarification. A supervisor might use the following format when checking a perception with a supervisee:

> *Description of behavior:* "I am aware that when I asked you about [confusing response identified], your behavior changed. You became loud, your face turned red, and you leaned toward me."
> *Possible interpretations:* "I don't know whether you are angry with me or whether you are struggling with this topic somehow."
> *Clarification:* "Can you help me understand?"

Taking the time to practice perception checking keeps the supervisory relationship clear and on the right track.

Apologizing

No matter how hard we work at our supervision relationships and skills, we are going to make mistakes. When we do, it is important to take responsibility and ownership for our mistakes. It helps to remember that we are a human first, a therapist second, and a supervisor third. Perfection is not a realistic option, and apologies are part of our responsibility when mentoring and supervising trainees.

Deliberate Practice

Deliberate practice requires intensive training of specific skills to reach a level of mastery. Professionals from a wide range of fields, from music to athletics to chess to medicine, rely on deliberate practice to achieve expert performance (Ericsson & Pool, 2016). In Voices From the Field, Tony Rousmaniere explains how deliberate practice can be used in clinical supervision.

 VOICES FROM THE FIELD

Deliberate Practice for Clinical Supervision and Training

Tony Rousmaniere, PsyD

Deliberate practice involves an intensive training process with repetitive skill-building exercises informed by expert feedback and performed throughout a professional career. Professionals from a wide range of fields rely on deliberate practice to achieve expert performance. Deliberate practice can help supervisees who understand their treatment model to be better able to apply it with their clients. Deliberate practice maximizes time spent on simulation-based behavioral rehearsal rather than time spent teaching theory or talking about skills. Unless a supervisee is practicing a skill, the learning is theoretical, not behavioral.

Deliberate practice for psychotherapy follows this procedure:

1. *Supervisee presents a case to the supervisor.* Pick a client who is stalled or at risk of deterioration or dropping out. Use video of a therapy session or role-play a challenging moment in therapy.
2. *Supervisor identifies one to three microskills.* Examples of skills are not interrupting or talking over the client, reflecting the client's experience, or inviting the client to explore thoughts or feelings.
3. *Supervisee practices.* Practice in role-play with a supervisor or by talking at your video. The supervisor might say, "Notice whenever you feel the urge to interrupt or talk over the client. Instead, press your lips together. Simultaneously, notice any complex feelings or anxiety you may have." The supervisee should be mindful of complex feelings, anxiety, and countertransference both within the supervisee and toward the supervisor.
4. *Repeat sufficient times.* The goal is for the skill to become more comfortable and to expand the supervisee's capacity for self-awareness and mindfulness while working with clients.
5. *Consolidate skills via homework.* Deliberate practice alone or with a partner is where most development happens in other fields. The supervisee should aim for 1 hour of practice per month, in 15–20 minute chunks, to practice in a role play with a colleague or to carry out deliberate practice homework exercises with the supervisee's videos.

Deliberate practice facilitates skill development and maintenance throughout an entire career, and clinicians should never stop practicing. Furthermore, deliberate practice is not mindless repetition but a constant attempt to push oneself to upset one's homeostasis. Clinicians should aim for continual improvement rather than automaticity. If it doesn't feel challenging, then the supervisees are not advancing their skills.

For more information on deliberate practice, we recommend *Deliberate Practice for Psychotherapists* (Rousmaniere, 2017), *The Cycle of Excellence* (Rousmaniere et al., 2017), and *Mastering the Inner Skills of Psychotherapy* (Rousmaniere, 2019).

Other Considerations Regarding Supervision Methods

Supervisors in the helping professions are probably most comfortable talking about therapy-related issues, but they should become equally adept at providing supervision for the broader range of topics that may be a focus of supervision. These topics might include preparation for licensing, coping with the bureaucracy of agencies, coping with burnout, and working effectively with other helping professionals. The verbal exchange method is often used in addressing these issues. However, many of the methods in this chapter could be adapted to address problems or topics that are not clinical in nature. For example, coaching could easily be adapted to address coping with burnout. Using a supportive and encouraging approach, the supervisor could assist the supervisee in exploring aspects of bureaucracy that are the most frustrating, coping methods that are effective and ineffective, and barriers that prevent the supervisee from coping effectively. From this coaching, a strategy that employs more effective skills for coping with the bureaucracy might be developed.

Supervisors must be flexible in assessing the skill level and learning abilities of supervisees and in applying methods that best match that level. Supervisors move from an unequal power base at the beginning of supervision to a more collegial one toward the end of supervision. The task is to determine where the supervisee currently is and what training model and methods are best suited to take the supervisee to where he or she would like to be. Growth is often an uneven process, and the rate at which the supervisee develops will fluctuate throughout the supervisory process. As maturity and experience are gained, the supervisee will become more self-directed, and the supervisor should respond accordingly.

Determining Which Methods to Use

A major question asked by many supervisors is, "How do I determine which methods to use with a given supervisee?" Supervisors must be familiar with the array of methods and techniques available to them. They also must be tuned in to the supervisee's strengths, deficiencies, and preferred style of learning (Campbell, 2006). Their options may be narrowed by logistics and available resources.

Novice clinicians generally require an approach that is supportive, facilitative, and structured. Careful monitoring, observation, demonstration, and teaching are required from the supervisor. As supervisees develop, they can become more actively involved in the supervisory interaction and more confident in bringing issues to supervision and exploring their own thoughts, feelings, and reactions to clients and to supervision. Toward the successful conclusion of supervision, the relationship becomes more collegial, and supervisees feel empowered to provide the direction for supervisory sessions. Supervisees develop into competent clinicians at their own unique pace; attempting to standardize the length of time supervisees spend in each developmental stage is a futile task. The supervisor and the supervisee must work collaboratively to assess the supervisee's level of development and the best methods by which the supervisee can learn.

Self-supervision is clearly not to be employed by beginning counselors or intended to take the place of drawing from the wisdom and experience of seasoned professionals. Supervisees can work toward the ultimate goal of self-supervision while they are under the umbrella of traditional supervision. Self-supervision does not imply that there is no need to seek consultation, and it is important to remember that even supervisors with many years of experience can profit from input from colleagues.

Using Methods in Context

Much like therapy methods with clients, supervision methods are much more effective when used in the context of a healthy supervisory relationship. Trust and respect are essential and should characterize this relationship. The supervisor fosters this relationship early and continuously throughout the supervision process. The use of supervision methods without the base of a healthy relationship is like psychotherapy techniques applied mechanistically without an understanding of the context of the therapist-client relationship.

Supervision methods are not a smorgasbord of techniques from which the supervisor can choose freely. The supervisor must have a clear model of supervision, a rationale for the use of any particular method, and competence in training and experience with that method. Several professional standards (AAMFT, 2015; ACA, 2014; ACES, 2011; APA, 2017; NASW, 2017; NOHS, 2015) require supervisors to demonstrate that they have the knowledge and skills to apply supervision methods. The level of competence of supervisors does not simply increase with the accumulation of clinical and supervisory experience. Supervisors also learn from courses, workshops, readings, colleagues, and supervisees. Remain open to the growth and learning that occurs from each individual you supervise.

Practical Application of Methods

For additional help in choosing appropriate supervision methods, we offer the following suggestions:

1. Ask open-ended questions of supervisees to facilitate discussion.
2. Include some direct observation of the supervisee in action with clients during supervision. It is important to "oversee" what the supervisee is doing, not just "overhear" what the supervisee is telling you.
3. Adapt your supervision methods to fit the learning style of supervisees. Invite them to give feedback regarding how those methods are working for them.
4. A major task of supervision is to help the supervisee conceptualize what is going on with the client (or other situation) and how to proceed. This is often difficult for supervisees who may want the supervisor to provide answers to their questions.
5. Remember that supervision is a collaborative process; supervision methods are most effective when applied in that spirit.
6. Some supervisors focus more on the therapy with clients than on the learning and development of the supervisee. Do periodic self-assessments to ensure that you are focusing on the supervisee's development and not solely on your interest in the therapy process.
7. Be supportive, facilitative, and structured with inexperienced clinicians. Be sensitive to the fact that supervisees are most likely anxious about their skills and abilities and want to perform well for their supervisor.

8. Challenge supervisees to explore thoughts, feelings, and reactions to clients and to supervision. As supervisees develop into more experienced clinicians, allow them to take the lead in supervisory sessions and provide their own self-supervision as you work toward empowering them.
9. Model responsibility by keeping to your scheduled supervision appointments and sticking to the primary tasks of the supervision.
10. Maintain a healthy perspective on your role as a supervisor. Learn from your supervisees and your supervisory experiences.
11. Some clients may not welcome supervisory methods such as video or audio recording or live supervision. Be sensitive to the client's needs and desires in this regard.
12. Enjoy your supervisory experiences while maintaining proper professional boundaries.

Summary

Some supervision methods are specifically designed for use in supervision, and others are adapted from psychotherapy-based approaches. The case consultation model, in which the supervisee discusses clinical cases with the supervisor, is the most common method, and direct observation methods are highly recommended to ensure that the supervisor sees the supervisee's clinical work. Group supervision is frequently used and requires special training in group dynamics and methods. In recent years, more attention has been paid to nonlinear methods in supervision, such as the sand tray or artwork, and the use of technology in supervision has accelerated. Careful study of the efficacy of the various methods is needed.

The selection of supervision methods is determined by the supervisory situation, the needs of the supervisee, the training goals, the client, and the setting in which the supervision occurs. Supervision methods are most effective in the context of a healthy and productive supervisory relationship characterized by trust and respect. Supervisees can benefit from being exposed to a variety of supervision methods.

SUGGESTED ACTIVITIES

1. Richard is a marriage and family therapist who has been in private practice for more than 20 years. He decided to further his education and training and went back to school to work toward a doctoral degree in counseling psychology. Rosa works in the counseling center at the university where Richard is a student. She received her doctorate 5 years ago and has been licensed as a psychologist for 3 years. Richard will be a student therapist in the counseling center, and Rosa will be his supervisor. Their first meeting is next week. If you were Rosa, how would you answer these questions?

   - How would you prepare for the first session with Richard?
   - What would your major focus be in supervising Richard?
   - What are your fears and concerns about working with him? What do you suppose his concerns might be about working with you as his supervisor?
   - To what degree do you feel qualified to work with Richard?
   - What supervision methods would be most applicable with Richard?
   - What will be the greatest challenge in supervising him? What will be the greatest reward?

2. Melissa is a first-year student in a social work master's degree program. She is young, bright, eager to learn, and eager to please; she graduated from college one year ago. Laura has been a licensed social worker for 5 years

and is on the staff at the county juvenile probation department. Laura has just met with Melissa in their first supervisory session. Melissa is assigned to the probation department for 9 months of internship training. Melissa expressed her eagerness to learn anything she can and is excited to begin working with the kids. If you were Laura, how would you answer these questions?

- What are your thoughts about working with Melissa?
- What would you include in your contract with Melissa?
- What supervision methods would be most applicable? Why?
- What methods would you use to evaluate Melissa's progress in the internship?

3. Select two or three supervision methods that seem most useful and have members of your group role-play how they might be applied in working with Richard or Melissa (see activities 1 and 2). Take turns role-playing and discuss what methods seemed to be most useful. Which methods were not as useful? Why?

4. What methods of supervision would be useful in the following situations? How would you go about deciding which methods to apply in each situation?

- Supervising a doctoral-level psychology intern in a community mental health center or at a state hospital.
- Supervising a social worker who is on probation with the licensing board in a private practice setting.
- Supervising a student in the master's program in guidance and counseling at a university counseling center.
- Supervising a mental health counselor who has worked in the field for years in another state and is now under your supervision until she becomes licensed in your state.
- Supervising a student who is doing volunteer work with the homeless as a requirement for a class you are teaching.

5. Which methods seem to fit best with which models? What is your understanding of how models and methods of supervision tie together? Must they always be consistent in that the methods flow from the model?

6. Identify the different types of technology options available for supervision. In small groups, discuss the benefits and challenges of using these technologies. Debate the pros and cons of live versus distance supervision.

CHAPTER 6

Becoming a Multiculturally Competent Supervisor

FOCUS QUESTIONS

1. Why is it so important to develop social justice competence in addition to multicultural competence?
2. How might you identify and examine your hidden agendas, biases, and prejudices that may result in countertransference in the supervisory relationship?
3. What primary knowledge and skills do you need to become a culturally competent supervisor? What does it mean to show cultural humility?
4. What is "culturally competent assessment," and why is this important in supervision?
5. How might you determine the level of cultural competence your supervisees possess?
6. If you lack expertise in dealing with multicultural concerns with a supervisee, what steps might you take to ensure cultural competence in supervision?
7. What does "social advocacy" mean to you, and how might it apply to your role as a supervisor? What action steps do you take to become a strong ally?
8. What steps might you take to establish a supervisory environment that is respectful, inclusive, and reciprocal?
9. In culturally competent supervision, why is it important for the supervisor and the supervisee to educate each other regarding the processes of their orientation, goals, and expectations?

The supervisory relationship and process can become highly complex when diversity and multicultural issues are taken into account. Imagine that you are a supervisor in a community setting and are scheduled to meet for individual supervision sessions with each of these three counselors-in-training:

- Charlene is a young woman of color who holds strong liberal views. She wants to refer her client—an unemployed White middle-aged man with a substance abuse problem and an unraveling marriage—to another therapist after discovering that he holds staunch conservative views and believes the U.S. population is too diverse. He has been making negative remarks about the Black Lives Matter movement in recent sessions.
- Rosa's father was deported to Central America following an Immigration and Customs Enforcement raid in 2019, and she is devastated by the separation of her family. Her thoughts are filled with wondering whether she, her mother, and her siblings will ever see her father again. She bursts into tears when discussing cases that involve grief or loss, and she admits to struggling in sessions with her clients.
- Michael is a Black male who identifies as being gay. He recently came out to his friends, but he has yet to discuss his sexual orientation with his parents, who have been judgmental of the LGBTQ+ community. He is experiencing strong counter-transference toward his older clients, who remind him of parental figures (especially those who are extremely religious), and he spends the majority of his time in supervision discussing how he gets triggered by certain types of clients. You notice that Michael spends little time and energy discussing his other cases.

What are your first thoughts as you reflect on how you might work with Charlene, Rosa, and Michael in supervision? Would you struggle with any countertransference reactions? What salient aspects of their identities (gender, race, sexual orientation, age, and political views) might interfere with their clinical work and interactions with clients? How would you address this in supervision sessions? Moreover, how might your own multiple identities affect your interactions with each of these trainees? For instance, if you are old enough to be Michael's mother or father, could your age affect the dynamics of the supervisory relationship and influence the process? How could your own biases influence your response to these supervisees and their difficulty interacting with these clients?

Some recent trends in the social fabric are extremely disturbing and distressing, such as spikes in White nationalism, racism, xenophobia, sexism, homophobia, transphobia, hate crimes, divisive politics, and tribalism (Muratori & Haynes, 2020). Helping professionals need to be equipped with the knowledge, skills, and attitudes to respond in a culturally sensitive and effective fashion to clients who have complex needs and identities. The professional associations have responded to these challenges, in part, by updating their multicultural standards. In 2015, the American Counseling Association endorsed the *Multicultural and Social Justice Counseling Competencies* (MSJCC; Ratts et al., 2015), which replaced the multicultural counseling competencies developed by Sue, Arredondo, and McDavis in 1992. Helping professionals are recognizing that social justice competencies are of paramount importance in today's polarized world, and they can expect to encounter an increasingly diverse clientele, including people from marginalized groups who are assaulted daily with microaggressions and more brazen forms of discrimination. Simply put, as the chasm between the privileged and the marginalized grows wider and deeper, helping professionals in all fields must be prepared to combat systemic oppression and injustice across this country. Sparked by outrage over the death of George Floyd in 2020 and that of many other Black Americans, protesters took to the streets in cities large and small demanding that we all confront the brutality of racism and finally act to correct racial inequality. ACA (ACA Knowledge Center, 2020) and several of its divisions issued statements making their stance against racism and racial violence abundantly clear—Black Lives Matter. To support the professional development of counselors-in-training and clinicians on the frontlines serving clients from diverse cultures and backgrounds who have complex needs and identities, supervisors must be well versed in multicultural supervision practices.

In this chapter, we highlight issues in multicultural supervision and address the guidance on multicultural and social justice competencies provided by Ratts and colleagues (2016) for supervisory practice. We explain how counselor educators and supervisors can use the multidimensional model of broaching behavior (MMBB) introduced by Day-Vines and her colleagues (2020) to help trainees effectively broach racial, ethnic, and cultural concerns with clients. Supervision of trainees from diverse backgrounds and cultures and supervision of those who plan to serve clients from backgrounds that differ from their own (e.g., clients with disabilities) are also addressed. This chapter includes an exploration of spirituality as a facet of multicultural supervision. We conclude with a discussion of how technology can enhance diversity and cultural understanding in our practice as supervisors.

Embracing Multiple Identities and Intersectionality in Supervision

Gutierrez (2018) points out that "research continues to show complexities of multicultural supervision and power within racial identity, ethnicity, gender, sexual orientation, language and educational identities" (p. 14). To explain the interaction of identities within multicultural supervision, Gutierrez begins by defining the term *intersectionality*, "the acknowledgement of differences and related systems of oppression, domination, or discrimination that stem from a position of power and privilege in society" (p. 14). Gutierrez believes multicultural supervisors are responsible for integrating cultural systems into the supervisory process, and this process entails the following:

- Supervisors' recognition of cultural systems
- Supervisors' examination of their own worldviews, privileges, and biases
- Supervisors' willingness to question their personal multicultural sensitivity
- Supervisors' awareness of cultural interactions and power
- Supervisors' commitment to aid supervisees in identifying their prejudices and augmenting the supervisee's cultural knowledge base without stereotyping
- Supervisors' commitment to maintain an open and safe space for their trainees
- Supervisors' ongoing participation in developing cross-cultural competence. (pp. 16–17)

Thomas and her colleagues (2019) describe "the unique ways that supervisors invite the multiple salient identities of trainees into the supervisory relationship and engage in a mentorship approach tailored to each trainee" (p. 167). From the personal narratives of three women of color who were psychology trainees, the following growth-promoting supervision practices emerged: (1) the critical importance of a supervisor pivoting between the roles of expert and learner; (2) the value of embracing an attitude of shared responsibility toward promoting supervisee growth; and (3) the function of cultural humility in the supervisory relationship. Thomas et al. describe an interaction between one of the psychology trainees and her supervisor that nicely captures the concept of *cultural humility*:

> It takes a supervisor with a particular lens toward self-reflection to assist supervisees to not only find their space but also to feel confident to own that space. In one of our early meetings when we were discussing potential dissertation topics, it was my supervisor who encouraged me to pursue research questions that aligned with my prior professional experiences and personal values:
>
> *Supervisor:* What are your thoughts about doing a global mental health project for your dissertation?
> *Trainee:* Is that possible? Global mental health research doesn't seem to align directly with clinical psychology.
> *Supervisor:* In what way? This will be your project and your opportunity to establish a niche area of research. I do not have experience in the area, but if you can figure out how to set this up, I will advocate for you and support you as best as I can. (pp. 169–170)

By modeling cultural humility in this instance and many others, the supervisor supported the trainee in developing her research interests in global mental health and served as an inspiration for how she wanted to practice supervision in the future. As Sue and Sue (2016) have pointed out, "cultural humility as a dispositional orientation may be equally as important as cultural competence (awareness, knowledge, and skills)" (p. 63).

In Voices From the Field, Jude Austin and Julius Austin write about the impact of their supervisor's cultural humility on their development as counselors and counselor educators.

VOICES FROM THE FIELD

Becoming a Multiculturally Skilled Supervisor

Jude T. Austin II, PhD, and Julius A. Austin, PhD

The world is becoming a more diverse place, and the supervision triad of supervisor, supervisee, and client most often includes someone of a different culture. Culture, ethnicity, race, and other issues related to diversity permeate the counseling room. These issues are then brought to supervision and reverberate within the supervisory process. Supervisor and supervisee also may have different cultural, ethnic, or racial backgrounds, putting their own cross-cultural issues in play. Supervisors need to build their awareness of how culture is influencing the supervision process.

Our graduate counselor training and doctoral studies included supervision with supervisors from cultures different from our own. We have had meaningful and less helpful experiences in cross-cultural supervision. Our most meaningful supervision came from White male supervisors who did not use their privilege to hurt us. We grew up in southern Louisiana where plenty of powerful White males wielded their power and privilege like a weapon. Navigating systems with these individuals taught us a lesson that all Black children learn: "You have to work twice as hard to get half as much."

We took that lesson into our graduate counselor training program. Our first supervisor was a White male faculty member, and our minds went straight to the lesson we had learned. Our trust and vulnerability decreased as our work ethic increased. If we worked hard enough, we thought there would be no reason to dismiss us from the program, and we would stand a better chance of success when our supervisor tried to take advantage of us or abuse his power. What made that supervision experience meaningful was the *humility* of our supervisor. He slowly built our trust in him and the process by addressing the issue of power and privilege in the supervisory relationship. He made a point of letting us take the lead in this conversation. It empowered us in supervision as well as in sessions with our clients. He provided the corrective emotional experience we needed to grow as counselors.

However, not all supervisors are created equal. We have had some cross-cultural supervision experiences that were less helpful. Those experiences included supervisors who took away our voice by dictating and micromanaging our experience. Although the supervision experience is an evaluative process with an inherent power differential, in the less helpful supervision experiences this power differential was overt. Those supervisors sent an insidious nonverbal message to us to be less like ourselves and more like them.

For cultural issues to be addressed in supervision, supervisors have to be willing to address them. This courage models for supervisees how to address these issues in session with their clients. Humility is an essential part of this process. Supervisors can humbly meet supervisees where they are and how they are, not as the expert but as a curious observer. This curiosity can spark questions in supervision that we have found helpful, such as "Tell me about your culture" or "How does your culture influence your work?" Inviting supervisees to share their culture can build safety, which increases trust and the willingness to show vulnerability in the supervision process.

For a more extensive discussion of how cultural factors influence the supervision relationship, see *Surviving and Thriving in Your Counseling Program* (Austin & Austin, 2020).

Failure to Practice Multicultural Supervision: What's at Stake?

Despite the ethical imperative to develop multicultural competence, supervisors may deny the existence of cultural variables or downplay the importance of diversity issues. Some may avoid practicing culturally competent supervision due to their own personal insecurities (Gutierrez, 2018). Gutierrez believes much is at stake when supervisors avoid practicing multicultural supervision: "[A]voidance of multiculturalism and power to utilize avoidance, can potentially become extremely harmful to supervisees" (p. 20). To illustrate this, suppose a supervisor who identifies as a White heterosexual man supervises an Asian bisexual woman yet avoids discussing intersectionality with her. This would be tantamount to avoiding the supervisee's Asian identity, gender identity, and sexual orientation— dimensions of identity that are oppressed within the larger societal context.

Day-Vines and her colleagues (2020) state that "the ability to broach the sociocultural and sociopolitical meanings clients attach to their concerns is especially important for counselors" (p. 107). Supervisors who fail to effectively model broaching behaviors (i.e., those who intentionally block efforts to discuss racial, ethnic, and cultural concerns) are doing their supervisees and their clients a disservice. By not providing a safe space for trainees to discuss and process issues that may be integrally related to their clients' presenting concerns (e.g., depression, anxiety, posttraumatic stress disorder), supervisees may not be adequately prepared to be effective helpers. Moreover, supervisees who identify with or are triggered by their clients' concerns will be deprived of an opportunity to work through their countertransference issues in supervision.

Novice counselor trainees with lower levels of multicultural competence and empathy may adopt a race-neutral counseling style and avoid discussing cultural content during sessions with their clients (Day-Vines et al., 2018), but it is surprising when we encounter this with supervisors. Unfortunately, culturally insensitive supervision occurs more often than most would imagine. According to McKinley (2019), "studies have shown that Black supervisees in cross-cultural supervision often experience microaggressions, invalidation of cultural issues, and stereotypical assumptions about their Black-ness, as well as negative interactions and evaluations from White supervisors" (p. 177). Despite the advantage of having more years of clinical training and experience, some supervisors may have an underdeveloped skill set in serving culturally diverse trainees and may avoid conversations related to race, ethnicity, or culture. Day-Vines and her colleagues (2018) emphasize the importance of helping counselor trainees get comfortable with discomfort around these topics, and those who take on the supervisory role must be willing to get comfortable with discomfort as well.

Defining Multicultural Supervision

Multicultural supervision requires acknowledging the cross-cultural dynamics between supervisors and supervisees from different cultural backgrounds. As noted by Qi and colleagues (2019), "the term 'cross-cultural' often refers to dynamics between two distinct cultures, whereas 'multicultural' indicates that more than two cultures are involved" (p. 186).

McKinley (2019) points out that all supervision is multicultural "because the supervisor and supervisee bring to supervision the sum of their intersecting identities" (p. 177). Expounding on this point, Tohidian and Quek (2017) suggest that understanding and addressing the effects of intersections of the dimensions of race, ethnicity, sexuality, gender, age, socioeconomic status, physical differences, and spirituality in supervision are vital and necessary components of ethical practice and quality supervision. Multicultural supervision encompasses other aspects of culture as well, including ability, privilege, sexual orientation, values, family characteristics and dynamics, country of origin, and language (ACES, 2011).

Practicing Multicultural Counseling and Supervision

Over the past several decades, prominent scholars in the multicultural counseling field have described multicultural competence and what is required to develop it. Sue, Sue, Neville, and Smith (2019) have long emphasized three dimensions of multicultural competence. The first dimension deals with the practitioner's attitudes and beliefs about race, culture, ethnicity, gender, and sexual orientation; the need to monitor personal biases; development of a positive view toward multiculturalism; and understanding how one's values and biases may get in the way of effective helping. The second dimension recognizes that a culturally competent practitioner is knowledgeable and understands his or her own worldview, possesses specific knowledge of the diverse groups with whom he or she works, and has a basic understanding of sociopolitical influences. The third dimension deals with skills, intervention techniques, and strategies necessary in serving diverse client groups. Part of multicultural competence entails recognizing our limitations and is manifested in our willingness to (a) seek consultation, (b) participate in continuing education, and, when appropriate, (c) make referrals to a professional who is competent to work with a particular client population.

Lee (2019a, 2019b) developed a conceptual framework for multicultural counseling competency that includes eight components organized along two dimensions. The *foundational dimension* consists of knowledge of traditional counseling theories and ethical standards. The *cross-cultural dimension* includes self-awareness, multicultural counseling theoretical knowledge, cross-cultural encounters, global literacy, cross-cultural skill development, and commitment to social justice. Lee asserts that the apex of his conceptual framework is multicultural counseling competency. He asks all practitioners to reflect on who they are as a cultural being, what they know about cultural dynamics and how they might influence a client's worldview, and how they can promote client mental health and well-being in a culturally competent manner. Lee suggests that this summarizes the essence of the evolution of multicultural competency.

For master's-level trainees, developing multicultural competence in addition to acquiring all the other skills and competencies needed to be an effective counselor within a relatively short time frame might seem overwhelming. For the supervisors training these counselors, their task initially might seem Herculean! The comforting news is that this task becomes much more manageable for supervisors when they have a framework for assisting their trainees in developing multicultural competence. Some scholars point to the utility of a model developed by Ancis and Ladany (2010) that uses a multicultural framework to assess competencies across these six dimensions.

- *Supervisor-focused personal development*, in which supervisors engage in self-examination about their own values, biases, and limitations.
- *Supervisee-focused personal development*, in which supervisors assist their supervisees in exploring the various dimensions of their identity development with the goal of raising awareness and increasing knowledge.
- *Case conceptualization*, in which supervisors use case conceptualizations of the supervisees' clients to help them understand the impact of both contextual and individual factors in shaping their clients' lives.

- *Skills/interventions*, in which supervisors promote the use of flexible strategies and psychotherapeutic interventions, including group work and nontraditional methods such as indigenous helping networks.
- *Process*, in which supervisors are aware of their power and focus on developing a positive supervisory climate characterized by open communication and respect.
- *Outcome/evaluation*, in which supervisors evaluate their supervisees on their multicultural counseling competence and, if necessary, recommend appropriate remedial training.

Crockett and Hays (2015) maintain that supervisors must have multicultural knowledge, awareness, and skills among all six dimensions to demonstrate multicultural competence. They add that competence is evident when supervisors show interest in and sensitivity to supervisees' cultural backgrounds as well as when they address cultural differences and convey warmth. Using structural equation modeling to test their mediation model, Crockett and Hays examined the relationships between supervisor multicultural competence, supervisee counseling self-efficacy, the supervisory working alliance, and supervisee satisfaction with supervision. These investigators found that "supervisor multicultural competence was related to the supervisory working alliance and that alliance, in turn, was related to supervisee satisfaction with supervision" (p. 258).

Lee (2019a) provides the following guidelines for culturally competent counseling in cross-cultural encounters. Reflect on how these guidelines could help you foster a working alliance with diverse clients.

- Consider cultural factors in all of your counseling interactions.
- Examine and critically evaluate your preconceived notions, prejudicial assumptions, and stereotypes about people who are different.
- Identify and examine your cultural privilege or marginalization.
- Think about the relevance of your theoretical orientation and your willingness to adapt your approach with clients.
- Be willing to learn from culturally diverse clients. Let them tell you their story.
- Make a commitment to advocacy and social justice.

To understand your responsibilities in guiding the development of a supervisee's multicultural competence, a logical place to start is by examining the ethics codes pertaining to multicultural supervision (Box 6.1).

The Multidimensional Model of Broaching Behavior: Implications for Supervisors and Counselor Educators

Day-Vines and her colleagues initially introduced the continuum of broaching behavior model in 2007 in an effort to describe the various orientations counselors may adopt when they discuss racial, ethnic, or cultural (REC) concerns with their clients. The continuum stretches from *avoidant, isolating, continuing/incongruent,* and *integrated/congruent* to *infusing* broaching behaviors. At the lower end of the scale are counselors who ignore REC issues and may deflect focus away from these issues during sessions and redirect clients' attention to more generic topics. As counselors progress along the continuum, they move from broaching "minimally, perfunctorily, and in an obligatory fashion" (Day-Vines et al., 2020, p. 108) to broaching in an increasingly more effective manner that is validating for the client.

The MMBB builds on the continuum of the broaching behavior model, which has received a growing body of empirical support. In addition to demonstrating cultural sensitivity, broaching the client's REC concerns provides clients with the clear message that it is safe for them to discuss their concerns openly with their counselor. As Day-Vines et al. (2020) point out:

Box 6.1
ETHICS CODES AND STANDARDS REGARDING MULTICULTURAL SUPERVISION

American Counseling Association (2014)

Code of Ethics

Counseling supervisors are aware of and address the role of multiculturalism/diversity in the supervisory relationship. (F.2.b.)

Counselor educators actively infuse multicultural/diversity competency in their training and supervision practices. They actively train students to gain awareness, knowledge, and skills in the competencies of multicultural practice. (F.11.c.)

Association for Counselor Education and Supervision (2011)

Best Practices in Clinical Supervision

The supervisor attends to ethical and cultural concerns that impact the supervisory relationship. (5.c.)

The supervisor recognizes that all supervision is multicultural supervision and infuses multicultural considerations into his/her approach to supervision. (6.a.)

The supervisor attends to the full range of cultural factors, including race, ethnicity, gender, sexual orientation, socioeconomic status, privilege, ability status, family characteristics and dynamics, country of origin, language, historical processes (e.g., history, migration), worldview, spirituality and religion, and values. (6.a.iii.)

The supervisor encourages supervisees to infuse diversity and advocacy considerations in the work of their clients. (6.b.)

Given the power dynamics that operate within the counseling relationship wherein the counselor wields the balance of power, unless asked explicitly, many clients from marginalized groups may compartmentalize their REC concerns due to apprehensions about the counselor's willingness to address such topics, fear that the counselor may withdraw emotional support, or concerns that the counselor may respond defensively. (p. 109)

An important feature of the MMBB are four fluid broaching dimensions that interact and overlap to facilitate the counselor's effort to discuss the contextual REC dimensions: intracounseling, intraindividual, intra-REC, and inter-REC.

- Counselors who broach *intracounseling* dimensions convey that they welcome discussions of REC concerns within the counseling relationship. When the counselor does not fully understand clients' REC concerns, acknowledging this fact demonstrates cultural humility and "an abiding respect and curiosity about the client's cultural frame of reference" (Day-Vines et al., 2020, p. 110).
- Counselors who broach *intraindividual* issues are interested in exploring the client's overlapping dimensions of identity (e.g., race, gender, ability, religion, social class, immigration status, linguistic diversity, physical stature, and sexual orientation) and how oppression in any or all of these domains is embedded in the client's presenting issues.
- Counselors may also broach *intra-REC* concerns; that is, they may address cultural issues that clients are experiencing with others who share a common REC

designation. As pointed out by Day-Vines et al. (2020), "clients may have beliefs, values, and behaviors that differ markedly from those held by the cultural group" (p. 113).

- Finally, counselors may broach *inter-REC* concerns; that is, cultural differences clients detect between themselves and those outside their REC group that they have difficulty navigating. Clients may be distressed by "varying forms of racism and discrimination that include but are not limited to overt and covert acts of meanness, microaggressions, and varying forms of structural inequality" (p. 114). By openly addressing the topic of systemic oppression with clients, counselors can challenge their clients to avoid blaming themselves for their experiences with racism or other forms of discrimination. Moreover, counselors who are aware of such inter-REC injustices can employ appropriate social justice advocacy interventions to combat barriers and oppressive conditions on behalf of their clients.

For a more detailed explanation of the MMBB broaching dimensions, see Day-Vines et al. (2020).

Day-Vines et al. (2018) state that supervisors who train counselors can adopt a variety of educational strategies to assist counselor trainees in developing competence and confidence in broaching REC factors during sessions with their clients. These include a combination of enhancing racial self-awareness; using multicultural case conceptualizations, case studies, films, and other media; and using role-play interviews. In Voices From the Field, Norma Day-Vines describes her approach to assisting trainees in developing competence in broaching.

 VOICES FROM THE FIELD

Training Counselors to Broach Effectively

Norma L. Day-Vines, PhD

Following development of the continuum of broaching behavior, I observed that many counselor educators, clinicians, and students assumed that broaching referred exclusively to two issues: (a) the discussion of racism and discrimination or (b) the discussion of counselor-client differences. Although these two types of broaching events are relevant when considering the contextual dimensions of race, ethnicity, and culture during the counseling process, they capture neither the breadth and depth of topics counselors can broach nor the universe of clients' concerns. Focusing only on racism and discrimination or counselor-client differences oversimplifies the very complicated and nuanced client realities that warrant more in-depth exploration.

To help counselor trainees develop broaching competence, I use clinical supervision to promote a more complex conceptualization of clients' broaching concerns. It is important to help counselor trainees understand that, first and foremost, racism and discrimination function as veritable realities that compromise the mental and physical well-being of people from marginalized groups; however, racism and discrimination do not define the totality of the client's experience or existence. That is, clients are more than the sum total of their encounters with racialized oppression and discrimination; hence the need for the MMBB. To illustrate, clients may grapple with multiple competing identities (e.g., intraindividual dimensions) such as race, gender, social class, and disability simultaneously. Reducing a broaching event to only race or gender obscures the intersectional manner in which social class positionality and disability also affect the client's experience. Likewise, clients may confront challenges from people with whom they share the same racial, ethnic, or cultural designation (e.g., intra-REC concerns) due to differences in their attitudes, beliefs, and value orientations. For instance, clients may experience challenges around issues such as colorism, wherein lighter skin tones are idealized over darker skin tones as a determinant of one's beauty, dignity, and worth. Similarly, clients may experience ostracism from members of their communities as they achieve social mobility, which places social distance and subsequent strain on existing social and familial relationships. Clients also may be accused by members of their specific REC groups of not being ethnic enough or of assimilating. It is incumbent, then, that counselor trainees recognize culture-specific concerns that affect client functioning. Foundational knowledge of clients is important, as is an openness to hearing clients' experiences. More important, clinical supervisors can help students recognize that people from marginalized groups do not constitute a monolith. There are many ways of being ethnic, and sometimes those differences contribute to intraracial strife that clients may discuss during treatment. Moreover, intra-REC concerns may result in psychological distress that parallels or even exceeds distress levels resulting from racism and discrimination.

Early on in their counseling training, as I have observed, counselor trainees often regard intra-counseling broaching dimensions as a statement of differences between counselor and client that they just check off on a counseling "to do list." In reality, intracounseling dimensions explore differences between counselor and client, but this dimension is inextricably bound to the counselor trainee's intention of communicating the acceptability of REC discussions within the counseling dyad in an effort to neutralize the power dynamic, invite the client to bring their cultural experience more prominently into the counseling environment, and strengthen the therapeutic relationship. Without explicit invitations from the counselor to explore cultural concerns, some clients may think such discussions are not desired in counseling. My observation over the past 20 years is that when the counselor trainee invites the client to discuss REC concerns and REC are important to the client, the client expresses concerns more freely and from a cultural frame of reference.

A growing body of literature has addressed cultural concealment, the prospect that clients may withhold information about cultural concerns germane to their presenting concerns (Drinane et al., 2018). Counselors have the responsibility of either initiating or responding to REC content. Without an invitation to discuss cultural content, clients may internalize the notion that REC conversations are not permissible within the counseling dyad.

As a counselor educator, I have been pleased to see the way many counselor trainees have incorporated the broaching construct into their repertoire of counseling skills, moving from apprehension about the utility of a particular broaching event to having greater depth and facility with broaching usage. Scaffolding student knowledge has been instrumental in helping students develop efficacy. For instance, the concept of broaching is introduced in the Counseling Techniques course, during which time, students engage in peer counseling sessions and are required to minimally broach intracounseling dimensions. The broaching construct is revisited again in the Multicultural Counseling course, wherein students broach with mock counseling clients and have an opportunity to address at least two broaching dimensions to develop greater facility implementing broaching skills. Finally, students have an opportunity to incorporate broaching skills again in their practicum and internship placements. I look forward to future research that connects broaching behavior to counseling outcomes.

For more detailed information on preparing counselor trainees to broach racial, ethnic, and cultural factors with clients during counseling, see Day-Vines, Booker Ammah, Steen, and Arnold (2018).

In the next section, we outline the MSJCC developed by Ratts and his colleagues (2016). It is worth noting that the MMBB is supported by guidelines prescribed within these competencies. According to Day-Vines et al. (2020), "the MMBB and the MSJCC appear conceptually linked" (p. 115).

Using the MSJCC to Guide Supervisory Practice

The American Counseling Association's endorsement of the MSJCC suggests that these competencies must be infused into all aspects of the counseling profession (Ratts et al., 2016) and should be incorporated in supervisory practice as well. We provide a brief description of the competencies as well as a visual representation of the conceptual framework. For a more detailed description, see Ratts et al. (2015, 2016).

MSJCC

The MSJCC are a framework for attending to the multiple identities clients and counselors bring to the therapeutic relationship. With the expectation that counselors address issues of power, privilege, and oppression that affect their clients in profound ways, the MSJCC requires professional counselors to view client issues through the lens of a culturally contextual framework (Figure 6.1) and recommend both individual and systems-levels interventions (Ratts et al., 2016).

> A conceptual framework of the MSJCC is provided to illustrate a visual map of the relationship between the constructs and competencies being articulated within the MSJCC. Moreover, quadrants are used to highlight the intersection of identities and the dynamics of power, privilege, and oppression that influence the counseling relationship. Developmental domains reflect the different layers that lead to multicultural and social justice competence: (1) counselor self-awareness, (2) client worldview, (3) counseling relationship, and (4) counseling and advocacy interventions. Embedded within the first three developmental domains of the MSJCC are the following aspirational competencies: attitudes and beliefs, knowledge, skills, and action (AKSA). (Ratts et al., 2015, p. 3)

Include MSJCC in the Supervisory Agreement

The supervisor is responsible for educating supervisees about how you will work together in the supervisory relationship. The initial sessions of supervision should allow ample opportunity to explore cultural similarities and differences using broaching strategies as described by Day-Vines et al. (2007, 2018, 2020). To minimize later misunderstandings, it is important to clarify everyone's expectations early in the relationship. Discussion of the supervisory contract is the ideal forum in which to introduce the expectations and requirements regarding the acquisition of the MSJCC. A 5-year review of literature in supervisory practice supported discussing multicultural issues in the early stages of supervision (Borders, 2005). Three approaches for facilitating multicultural conversations were provided: the use of semistructured questions, a reciprocal exchange regarding supervisor-supervisee differences initiated by the supervisor, and the supervisor's self-disclosure about his or her own process of becoming multiculturally aware.

As you begin the supervisory relationship, pose some of the following questions to initiate a discussion with supervisees about multicultural and social justice considerations:

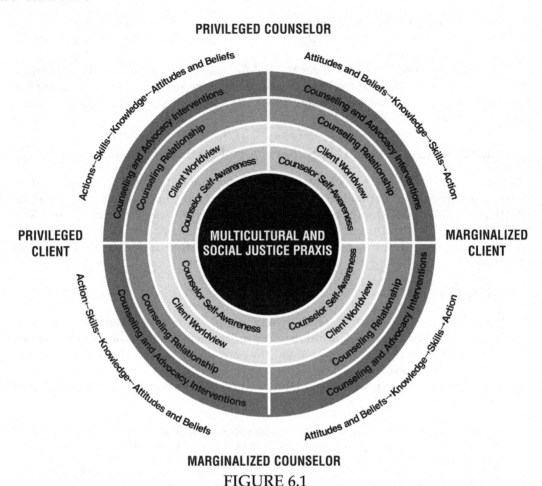

PRIVILEGED COUNSELOR

PRIVILEGED CLIENT

MARGINALIZED CLIENT

MULTICULTURAL AND SOCIAL JUSTICE PRAXIS

MARGINALIZED COUNSELOR

FIGURE 6.1
Multicultural and Social Justice Counseling Competencies

- How do you describe your cultural identity? How has this description evolved over time?
- What are the various cultural groups to which you belong? Which ones seem to take on the most importance in your life?
- How do you think your culture and your own experiences with privilege or marginalization affect the way you see your role as a therapist, your choice of theoretical orientation, and the manner in which you approach case conceptualization, diagnosis, and treatment? What parts of your counseling approach do you most strongly identify with and why?
- Can you identify, at this time, ways in which our cultural differences or similarities may affect our supervisory relationship?
- How would you rate your knowledge of and comfort with discussing cultural issues?
- If you find discussions about culture or social justice issues uncomfortable, can you identify what it is that you find awkward or threatening? Where might you have learned this fear?

- What types of academic training, professional conferences, workshops, or seminars have you completed in the area of multicultural counseling or social justice counseling?

Set the stage for an open and safe discussion regarding cultural issues both within the supervisory relationship and when client cases are reviewed and processed. It is important to develop a relationship that is respectful and reciprocal. Encourage supervisees to bring their concerns to supervision sessions at any point during their field placement when questions arise regarding cultural perspectives. In Voices From the Field, Norma Day-Vines adds her thoughts on strategies for assisting counselor trainees in developing and enhancing proficiency in broaching behavior.

VOICES FROM THE FIELD

Enhancing the Broaching Behaviors of Counselor Trainees

Norma L. Day-Vines, PhD

Recently I have been thinking about strategies for helping counselor trainees develop greater proficiency in executing their broaching behavior. Early in their training, some of my students exhibited reluctance to broach their clients' racial, ethnic, and cultural concerns. Such broaching behavior manifests as talking "around" an issue versus talking directly and explicitly "about" an issue. This ambivalence is quite understandable because novice counselors are learning skills that at first blush appear counterintuitive. The best gift we can give our clients is an honest consideration and discussion of their cultural frames of reference to help them feel deeply heard and understood. Talking about their culture-specific concerns with greater levels of transparency helps clients move forward emotionally. My aim is to help trainees become more decisive as they broach with clients.

I have introduced my students to the work of Jonathan Metzl and Helena Hansen (2014), who argue that cultural competence is a necessary albeit insufficient condition for working effectively with clients. They assert the importance of developing structural competence or the ability to name the specific systemic sources of oppression that affect clients. Accurately naming the structural barriers that undermine clients' psychological well-being serves as a foundational component of the counselor trainee's ability to broach the contextual dimensions of race, ethnicity, and culture. Moreover, naming oppressive forces in clients' lives requires a marked degree of courage, fortitude, and perspicacity on the part of the counselor trainee. When done well, this has the potential to unleash catharsis and promote psychological liberation in clients. Hanna et al. (2000) define "perspicacity" as the possession of strong perceptive abilities, the capacity of clients from oppressed groups to see beyond the surface, and the deep awareness and wisdom that allows clients to accurately interpret their environment. They argue that people from oppressed groups have refined their perceptive abilities as a means of survival. To work effectively with clients, counselor trainees must also be able to navigate the client's racial, ethnic, and cultural terrain with a marked degree of perspicacity.

I recall a supervision session in which the client was a foreign national. During her counseling session, she lamented the ostracism she experienced from a close friend in her homeland. The client's compatriot accused her of being out of touch and labeled her a "foreigner." The client disclosed her sense of hurt and woundedness by the comment and resentment toward her friend's effort to deny her connection to her homeland. The counselor trainee responded appropriately by stating that her friend's comments hurt the client's feelings. As part of the broaching effort, it is important to integrate and synthesize feeling words with broaching statements, just as the counselor trainee did in this example. The use of feeling words helps the client access her affective experience and helps her feel heard and understood. As the client continued discussing her experience, the counselor trainee reflected content by stating, "You were 'othered'." The counselor trainee was accurate in that the client was indeed othered. However, during supervision we discussed the notion that she could have been even more explicit by first using silence to organize her thoughts and frame her broaching statement.

We worked together in supervision to revise the counselor trainee's response to include the client's specific source of oppression and its intent. The revised statement was as follows: "Your friend used a microaggression to question your allegiance to your heritage and to challenge your sense of belonging to your culture of origin, and you were deeply offended." The revised broaching statement provides a more explicit and elaborated statement of what the client may be sensing and feeling and better integrates foundational counseling skills such as reflection of content, reflection of feeling, and interpretation. During supervision, we discussed the importance of using silence following the broaching statement, allowing the client to sit with and experience the feelings associated with the microaggression. Ideally, the counselor trainee and client will flesh out the counseling concern and co-construct meaning for the client in ways that contribute to alleviation of psychological distress, improved decision making, and coping behaviors.

Adopt a Growth Mind-Set as a Multicultural Supervisor and Social Justice Advocate

Unless you have studied and practiced extensively with diverse client populations, you will lack the detailed knowledge needed to work with supervisees from cultures with which you have limited familiarity. However, regardless of training and experience, it will be necessary to take the time to get to know your supervisees as individuals within the context of their cultural environment. You need to be careful about generalizing regarding specific individuals from any given culture and should seek information and clarification regarding your assumptions.

Therapists and supervisors are sometimes placed in positions requiring multicultural expertise outside their range of competence. It is not possible to be knowledgeable in all areas, and there will be times when it is appropriate and ethically responsible to seek consultation and possibly referral. If you find yourself in over your head and in need of supervision regarding multicultural or social justice issues in the supervisory relationship, seek help. Adopting a growth mind-set is a healthy way to approach your development of multicultural and social justice competence. If you are not willing to risk making mistakes, you will restrict your opportunities for learning. It is important to initiate the necessary conversations in multicultural supervision even though it may be awkward at times and you may think you are not using the "right" words. You may tell yourself you could have asked more or better questions to explore cultural issues. If supervisees are not accustomed to this type of discussion regarding their cultural identity, it is possible that you may unknowingly create discomfort or defensiveness for your supervisees. Learn how to recover after having said or done what you perceive to be the "wrong thing." Asking for help when necessary is not a failure but a sign of a competent professional willing to accept limitations and not willing to practice outside his or her scope of competence. This serves as positive role modeling for supervisees as well.

Model Social Advocacy

In line with the MSJCC, we believe it is the supervisor's responsibility to model active social advocacy and to encourage this role in supervisees. Members of certain groups have been oppressed and discriminated against, and counselors have a responsibility to act as advocates. Be willing to speak on behalf of clients who have been the target of discrimination and oppression. Supervisors must also play the role of ally to marginalized populations. Estrada, Singh, and Harper (2017) define "ally" as an individual who commits to members of a marginalized population and takes action to address and reduce injustice toward these individuals (p. 343). Being an ally is not an event but a journey. This idea came out of the controversy surrounding criticisms of allies on behalf of the LGBTQI+ communities who like to be seen as allies but do not participate in advocacy or activism on behalf of or with the LGBTQI+ community. Supervisors must be clear about their own level of competency to serve as an ally and be comfortable with the commitment made to marginalized populations, including the consequences they might face. If supervisors model this effectively, supervisees are helped on their own journey.

There are many alternatives to acting as an ally. For instance, Li and Vasquez-Nuttal (2009) suggest that school consultants need to be agents of social justice for culturally and linguistically diverse students and their families. As a social advocate, the supervisor must attend to and work toward eliminating biases, prejudices, and discriminatory practices in conducting evaluations and providing interventions, and develop sensitivity to issues of oppression, sexism, heterosexism, elitism, ageism, and racism. In your role as supervisor, we recommend that you take responsibility for educating your supervisees about the processes of psychological intervention, such as setting goals, clarifying expectations, and explaining legal rights.

Work with professional organizations and serve on committees advocating for policy changes. Encourage your supervisees to become involved in these efforts and provide education and training for other professionals regarding multiculturalism. Social advocacy has become an important responsibility of counselors and other mental health practitioners in recent years. In Voices From the Field, Kellie Kirksey describes the spiritually focused integrative approach she uses to supervise African American women and emphasizes the role of social advocacy in her work.

VOICES FROM THE FIELD

Applying a Spiritually Focused Integrative Approach in My Work as a Supervisor

Kellie Kirksey, PhD

It is not my intention to generalize but to give a personal account of my work with African American women who are in supervision for clinical or school counseling. My supervision with this population has been for the most part spiritual and integrative in nature. Discussions of advocacy and social justice are topics we cover in our supervision hour. I encourage supervisees to move beyond the counseling chair and create a presence in the community for change and well-being.

This particular group of women primarily want to know how to survive in the profession. They yearn to know how to make it through a "system" that at times characterizes passion as pathology and expressiveness as histrionics. Most of my supervisees of African descent tend to be from a Christian background and are first-generation college students. The landscape of academia is foreign to them, just as it was for me when I entered the profession.

Helping students of color deal effectively with the microaggressions they will encounter is critical. Spirituality is often the foundation of ultimate success for my supervisees. These women will be confronted at some point in their careers with racism, discrimination, sexism, sexual harassment, and ageism. This reality is discussed in supervision in terms of resiliency and determination to contribute something positive to the field. Discussing boundaries, multiple relationships, and self-advocacy are necessary conversations. We role-play these scenarios, rehearse the uncomfortable encounters, and practice healthy and proactive responses.

A critical aspect of supervision is helping students understand every aspect of the position, not just the practice of therapeutic intervention. There will be times when being present and fully engaging the client may lead to sessions ending late and the supervisee falling behind in the critical jobs of note-taking and closing charts. It is important to review ending sessions in a timely fashion and charting in the same day whenever possible. I encourage supervisees to create healthy patterns for success and work on personal and professional development. Having a healthy work-life balance is encouraged. I tell my supervisees to stay connected to themselves by doing regular personal inventories of their holistic health. Having supervisees create a plan of action for consistent attendance to their mind, body, and spirit provides a foundation of support and integrity for their personal journey as they facilitate their clients' journey to greater health and wellness.

In Case Study 6.1, Matthew, a White school counselor trainee with little experience serving marginalized students, reaches a conclusion about a student of color that does not take into account her encounters with environmental barriers and systemic oppression.

CASE STUDY 6.1: CELINE

Celine supervises school counselor trainees at a suburban middle school composed of roughly an equal number of European American and African American students. One of her trainees, Matthew, has been assigned to work with all of the students participating in the school's gifted and talented (G/T) program. A disproportionate number of the G/T program participants are of European American descent. Most of the few African American students who have participated in the G/T program over the years have dropped out. In reviewing his cases in supervision, Matthew reveals that Shae, one of the two African American students currently enrolled in the G/T program, is starting to perform poorly in class and does not seem to enjoy interacting with the other G/T students. He perceives that she has been avoiding the extracurricular activities sponsored by the G/T program, such as the after-school math club. His immediate conclusion is that Shae must be having problems at home and may be depressed, which is affecting her grades and level of involvement at school.

How would you proceed if you were supervising Matthew? What would be your responsibilities and possible liabilities with Matthew, with Shae, and with the school? How might you use the MSJCC to guide your supervision?

If Matthew was introduced to the MSJCC at the outset of supervision, Celine should ask Matthew to revisit the competencies and consider some alternative reasons why Shae may be withdrawing from the G/T program and performing poorly academically.

Celine should listen to the rationale for Matthew's conclusion and be open to the possibility that family issues are affecting Shae, but Celine could help Matthew generate some other possibilities as well. For instance, Celine and Matthew might discuss the fact that certain environmental barriers exist that prevent Shae from fully engaging in the G/T program and that Shae's behaviors and concerns might reflect responses to systemic or internalized oppression. Considering the consistently high dropout rate among other African American students in the program, it is possible that the school culture does not support African American students becoming high achievers. If Shae feels excluded by the White G/T students and is receiving the message from her African American peers that by participating in the G/T program she is acting "White," she may have little incentive to remain in the program.

Celine might encourage Matthew to advocate at the community/school level. Matthew could investigate the environmental factors that prevent African American students from being chosen and thriving in the G/T program. Celine and Matthew could contact G/T coordinators and school counselors at other local schools to develop alliances, and together they could create a step-by-step plan for change that better serves their academically talented African American students. This advocacy group would prepare themselves to deal with resistance from those at the school and in the community who are in denial about the need for change.

Matthew may not feel comfortable taking his advocacy efforts to the next level, but with Celine's support and encouragement, he could address the issues raised by Shae's case at the public/societal level. He and his supervisor could write letters to policy makers at the state level to reform gifted education practices to better serve underrepresented student populations. They might also write letters to the editors of newspapers or use a social media platform to convey their message about the underrepresentation of African American students in G/T programs and the cost society pays when the talents of able minority students are not developed. Shae may also feel empowered by Matthew to take an active role in the advocacy process and have her voice heard. Using the MSJCC in their clinical work, both Celine and Matthew will increase the number of ways in which they can intervene, and perhaps they will make a profound difference in the lives of those they serve.

Assessing Multicultural and Social Justice Counseling Competence in Supervision

With so much emphasis placed on training counselors to become multiculturally competent in serving their clients, supervisors need to develop a protocol for assessing whether counselor trainees have achieved competence. Not surprisingly, in the psychology field, in which assessment is viewed as one of the profession's foundational components, multicultural assessment supervision is now acknowledged as a specialty area within clinical supervision. In counselor education, multicultural counseling competency assessment is regarded as "a multidimensional process that involves evaluation of counselor competencies for specific cultural groups as well as awareness of power issues among groups in response to the social justice movement" (Hays, 2008, p. 100).

Even though the helping professions are making great strides in advancing multicultural assessment, especially with regard to racial and ethnic groups, much work remains to be done. Existing assessment tools need further validation and statistical support, and multicultural assessment strategies and instruments should be extended to include certain disenfranchised groups, including religious minority groups, women, lower socioeconomic groups, and gay, lesbian, and bisexual clients (Hays, 2008). Variables such as supervisor satisfaction, client satisfaction, supervisee satisfaction, accuracy of case conceptualization, cultural appropriateness of assessment, interpretive accuracy, and assessment outcomes are but a few of the possibilities suggested for further exploration in the area of multicultural assessment supervision research. For more information addressing social justice issues in supervision, see Chang, Hays, and Milliken (2009).

In Voices From the Field, Janee Both Gragg describes social justice supervision in her work with trainees in a free walk-in clinic. She shares her experience in addressing the challenge of training supervisees to fully and equally serve all groups in a society in a way that meets their needs. This example is at the heart of social advocacy.

VOICES FROM THE FIELD

A Social Justice and Advocacy Context to Clinical Supervision

Janee Both Gragg, PhD

One of the first lessons I remember from my own training to become a counselor was the importance of being able to meet clients where they are. We explored what that statement means and examined how we might go about doing that both physically and emotionally. Working with students in a free walk-in clinic is an unconventional training setting. The transdisciplinary environment challenges students from across health disciplines to identify, name, and wade through the biopsychosocial forces influencing the health of community members. Another aspect of working with students in the clinic is helping them to better understand how social justice issues influence the mental health and wellness of their clients.

As a part of the supervision process at the free clinic, students closely examine their own core beliefs about addiction, poverty, mental illness, race, gender, disease, interdisciplinary collaboration, and the medical model. Students' reactions to the training environment are as diverse as their own stories and experiences. As a supervisor, I support students as they navigate merging new textbook knowledge with these earliest supervised clinical and professional development experiences. We first explore their initial impressions, which are often marked by feeling out of place or unprepared for the observable need. Many are inspired by the large, well-orchestrated bimonthly pop-up clinic. Some reflect on the experience of giving back after sharing that their family received medical care from a free clinic when they were growing up.

Work at the clinic situates students squarely at the intersection of mental health access and service delivery injustices. They are not always easy moments, but they can be filled with lessons about the barriers and obstacles that prevent people from receiving the care they need when they need it. Students witness firsthand how limited or no insurance coverage, shortages of care providers, inadequate service delivery models, long wait lists, outdated policy, and mismatched procedures can hinder their clients' access to care. They also gain valuable insights into the approaches and strategies that can help them better meet their clients' mental health and wellness.

Integrating mental health care and counseling skills in flexible ways in nontraditional settings makes care accessible in new ways. For example, our intervention with a dental client experiencing anxiety during a routine procedure led to an ongoing counseling relationship and demonstrated a flexible application of integrated counseling skills. Students are often eager to put their skills to use, but initially they may be apprehensive about the clinic environment. They simultaneously face fears about the complexities of the clients they serve and doubts about their ability to make a difference. I encourage my supervisees to focus on each session as a stand-alone opportunity to listen fully, connect authentically, and offer something of value with the understanding that they may never see that client again or that care may be inconsistent.

In supervision sessions, we consider together how to maximize the fact that we are a transdisciplinary clinic and brainstorm a range of ways to incorporate health and wellness services that support coordinated, comprehensive, holistic care. I work with students to identify specific service gaps and co-create programming uniquely designed to meet the needs of the community, including options for supporting immigrant families and increasing mental health awareness. Overall, the free walk-in clinic has provided a depth of experiences for graduate students in training. After working with a diverse population using a short-term model with limited resources, student therapists are well prepared for their next clinical experience.

Practicing Affirmative Supervision

Supervisors must be aware of the impact their attitudes, views, and practices have on supervisees and, therefore, on each client who is served. Supervisors need to model and attend to biases both seen and felt, direct and indirect, within the supervisory relationship and between supervisees and clients (Barnett, Cornish, et al., 2007). Ginicola, Smith, and Filmore (2017) state that counselors should be able to provide affirmative and strength-based interventions, develop identity, and empower others. If our supervisees are to be able to use these skills with their clients, we must learn to be confident in these skills as supervisors. The key to culturally sensitive conversation is being able to create a warm environment, affirming another's experience, offering acceptance, and being willing to hold open discussions regarding differences. To develop a strong relationship with someone different from ourselves, we must exude acceptance and an ability to convey to the other person that we genuinely view them as valuable, strong, and resilient. Goodrich and Ginicola (2017) explored evidence-based practice in building rapport, and clients identified sensitivity, kindness, warmth, trustworthiness, openness, acceptance, attentiveness, and presence as the most important therapeutic qualities of their counselors. Allowing space for thought and reflection and providing opportunities to talk and be reassured, both verbally and nonverbally, enhances rapport. We need to respect the uniqueness of the individual as well as the cultural group membership. Too much attention placed on cultural group membership may encourage stereotyping.

Affirmative supervision is the goal in successfully and sensitively navigating a multicultural environment, and it is achieved by challenging traditional counseling theories and biases. Finnerty, Kocet, Lutes, and Yates (2017) suggest that affirmative supervisors critically question harmful assumptions, prejudices, and attitudes found in the literature. Supervisees may come from very different backgrounds, possibly from a marginalized community, and they deserve our acceptance and advocacy.

A major decision protecting the rights of LGBTQ+ people was announced June 15, 2020, when the U.S. Supreme Court ruled that sexual orientation could no longer be grounds for being fired from a job. This ruling represents a significant turning point for the civil rights of people who have been discriminated against based on their sexual orientation. This decision puts legal teeth into the nondiscrimination standard of the ACA's (2014) *Code of Ethics*:

> Counselors do not condone or engage in discrimination against prospective or current clients, students, employees, supervisees, or research participants based on age, culture, disability, ethnicity, race, religion/spirituality, gender, gender identity, sexual orientation, marital/partnership status, language preference, socioeconomic status, immigration status, or any basis proscribed by law. (C.5.)

In Voices From the Field, Logan Turner addresses having open dialogues regarding how misunderstandings of LGBTQ+ people often lead to preconceived assumptions. All of our supervisees are learning from us how to become professionals as they continue to develop their own personal identity. How we handle ourselves in multicultural conversations, regardless of how uncomfortable or difficult, is the compass that will guide their development as effective counselors.

VOICES FROM THE FIELD

Compassionate Conversations of Difference

Logan Turner, BS

Uninformed prejudice, changing societal norms, and identity recognition are major issues that can arise between supervisors and their queer supervisees. Prejudice is a significant barrier to healthy relations, and misunderstanding LGBTQ+ people has led to preconceived assumptions and discomfort that might arise in personal interactions. The queer lexicon has evolved and changed rapidly in the past decade, making open dialogue regarding similarities and differences difficult because one side no longer understands the terms and concepts used by the other side. For example, my personal identity as "queer" cannot be understood by a supervisor who does not understand the concept and is uncomfortable sharing that conversation. In addition, it can be difficult to be open and keep up with the rapid pace of societal evolution regarding culture and public opinion on LGBTQ+ people. Finally, supervisors who do not recognize the identity of their supervisees—nonbinary, gay, or bisexual, for example—are unlikely to establish a good working relationship with them in supervision. Supervisors choosing not to respect the life or pronoun preferences of their supervisees make the workplace uncomfortable, which can lead to loss of efficiency.

Educational workshops, diversity seminars, and open dialogues can help ease tensions that could arise between supervisors and their LGBTQ+ supervisees. Workshops conducted by LGBTQ+ supervisors that are dedicated to informing nonqueer supervisors how to have good relations with their queer supervisees or that inform queer supervisees how to improve troubled relations with their supervisors can be helpful. Specific strategies need to be provided. Diversity seminars for supervisors can inform supervisors about LGBTQ+ history and terminology and how these constructs influence a supervisor-supervisee relationship. An informal solution is to have an open conversation about the issues between supervisor and supervisee that is free of disrespect and prejudice where they can work toward bettering their relationship.

Some microstrategies can be immediately beneficial. Respect plays a primary role in building relationships. It takes time and patience for acceptance, particularly when ingrained stereotypes and assumptions are being addressed. Do not diminish the small steps that either you, as a supervisor, or your supervisees are making toward better understanding. Supervisor willingness, in and of itself, can have a positive impact on the relationship. Whether this is verbally stated or not, a supervisor's attempt to better the relationship can lessen the tension generated from previous negative interactions. Simple affirmations, validations, and questions go a long way toward improving interactions between a supervisor and a supervisee who have significant differences, whether LGBTQ+ or otherwise. How can I make you more comfortable? I hear you and accept you. (Or simply, "I am trying to learn.") I want to learn more about you and your community. How can I become an ally to other members of the community?

In Case Study 6.2, Sabrina and her supervisor navigate issues often associated with learning how to create an environment of cultural sensitivity when confronted with a client who is very different from the supervisee.

CASE STUDY 6.2: SABRINA

Sabrina has recently completed a master's in counseling psychology and taken a position at the local mental health center. She has limited experience beyond the required practicum and externship hours required for her degree program. She conducts an intake for a young woman approximately her age who presents with issues including anxiety, depression, and sexual identity confusion. The young woman identifies as possibly bisexual or queer. In staffing the case with her supervisor for development of case conceptualization and treatment planning, the supervisor noted that Sabrina did a reasonable job of exploring details regarding the issues of anxiety and depression, but she completely avoided the topic of sexual identity with her client. When the supervisor points this out, Sabrina states that she is not comfortable with this topic and would rather not address these issues.

If you were Sabrina's supervisor, how would you proceed? What specific strategies and techniques might you use to address the need for multicultural sensitivity and quality of care for this client? How would you support Sabrina in her development of insight, knowledge, attitudes, and skills to assist this client?

The supervisor and Sabrina might begin by reviewing the competencies and codes regarding multicultural responsibility and sensitivity. A supervisory "session" with Sabrina that demonstrates a dialogue for exploring sexual identity and personal meaning may help Sabrina understand her own sexual identification and how this can affect her ability to counsel those with same or different sexual identities. Sabrina's barriers to addressing this topic should be explored, and a shared plan of action might include having Sabrina role-play this conversation prior to meeting with her client again. Close, live supervision of the next client session may be indicated, with intervention by the supervisor, if necessary.

If too much attention is placed on the individual outside the context of his or her cultural group, the impact of the cultural environment on the individual may be neglected. It is essential to maintain a clear focus on the client's concerns rather than on those of the counselor.

In the Personal Perspective, Patrice Moulton explains her strategy for discovering gaps in her own knowledge about one cultural group.

 PATRICE MOULTON'S PERSONAL PERSPECTIVE

A number of years ago, while serving as coordinator of the family therapy program for a state substance abuse facility, I was invited to begin the first adult children of alcoholics (ACOA) group for the Seneca Nation in Salamanca, New York. I also supervised a colleague running the same type of group at a reservation in Jamestown, New York. I was proficient in substance abuse group work and family issues, but I had limited knowledge of Native American culture and little knowledge of the Seneca Nation or the reservation. I very much felt that I was in over my head and wondered if the rules that govern family systems applied in a similar enough way to build the rapport, trust, and respect necessary to provide a positive group experience for these participants.

Rather than assuming I could figure things out as I went or that group members would educate me on how their culture might affect the group dynamics, goals, and expectations, I sought help. I went to the Seneca Nation Mental Health Department and spent some time in supervision myself with one of the family counselors there. I shared with her the knowledge I had about ACOA and explained my approach to group structure and content. I made it clear that I needed her help and valued her knowledge and experience in assisting me in making appropriate changes. She helped me understand where adjustments would have to be made, and how to intertwine the cultural components into our group exercises in a way that would be meaningful to these clients.

Supervising International Trainees in Counselor Education Programs

An increasing number of international students are drawn to U.S. colleges and universities, and many graduate programs in the helping professions regularly admit international trainees. It is imperative for supervisors and faculty members interacting with these students to be sensitive to their unique experiences and challenges.

> Being an international student often means being a minority member from a certain racial/ethnic group, including speaking a native non-English language and being a foreign national. This adds extra challenges to their psychosocial adjustment on aspects such as language barriers, cultural differences, racial discrimination, and social and/or personal adjustment difficulties. (Qi et al., 2019, p. 186)

When compared to their U.S. counterparts, McKinley (2019) noted that international counselor trainees report elevated levels of academic stressors, language barriers, financial and immigration stressors, cultural adjustment issues, and discrimination by faculty members and students. Those who supervise international students must make a concerted effort to create a welcoming supervisory climate to reduce trainees' stress and to ensure they feel connected to the program. McKinley proposes adapting the model of multicultural supervision competencies formulated by Ancis and Ladany (2010) to the unique needs of international students. We have adapted the following key points to keep in mind from McKinley (2019):

- Supervisors working with international students have a responsibility to increase their knowledge about supervisees' countries of origin, language barriers, migration experiences, and other contextual factors.
- Supervisors are encouraged to use a strength-based approach rather than a cultural deficit model with international trainees.
- Supervisors should recognize international trainees as a heterogenous group and facilitate supervisees' exploration of their unique cultural background, beliefs, values, and attitudes to cultivate multicultural competencies in these students.
- Supervisors need to assist international trainees in increasing their awareness of contextual variables when working with clients, with the goal of helping them develop culturally competent case conceptualizations.
- Supervisors should encourage their international trainees to use counseling strategies in a flexible and culturally responsive manner and to incorporate their traditional therapeutic interventions in their clinical work.
- Supervisors should pay attention to the power dynamics in the supervisory relationship with international trainees.
- In addition to evaluating their supervisees, supervisors should give their international supervisees the chance to evaluate the process of supervision.
- Supervisors should select appropriate outcome and assessment measures when working with international students in supervision. The International Student Supervision Scale can be used to measure supervisory issues unique to international students.

- Supervisors should facilitate ongoing discussions with their international trainees about the transferability of the training to their countries of origin.

Cross-Cultural Supervision Abroad

Just as many international graduate students come to the United States to study, American helping professionals have traveled abroad to provide counseling services to people in need in international settings. Seponski and Jordan (2018) note that with the global expansion of certain helping professions, "it is vital to engage in culturally responsive methods of training and supervision. This is especially critical when international training involves Western-based therapy models and supervision from non-native supervisors" (p. 247). In countries (e.g., Cambodia) in which counseling and therapy training are relatively new, opportunities for supervision may be limited and tends to be conducted by visiting Western or expatriate therapists. Supervisors from the United States who practice cross-cultural supervision abroad must recognize that high rates of crisis and trauma and low mental health literacy exist in some countries, and the "need for ongoing, culturally responsive supervision is crucial to address high rates of therapist burnout, work overload and high crisis clients" (p. 249).

In the Personal Perspective, Patrice Moulton shares her challenges and rewards when supervising students in a developing country that is struggling to acknowledge mental health as a field of professional practice.

 ## PATRICE MOULTON'S PERSONAL PERSPECTIVE

For the past 10 years I have been involved in social advocacy efforts in Nepal. This began as a volunteer effort and morphed into a professional role in higher education and a Fulbright Specialist assignment to consult and train professionals, faculty, and students in the field of psychology. This training included assisting graduate students in clinical experiences. The learning curve as a supervisor was immense; almost everything I considered standard requirements and practice needed adjustment. For instance, there is no professional organization, no licensure for professionals, no protocols in place for practice or supervision, and no standard practice for supervision. In addition, the *DSM* is not used consistently for assessment.

Mental health is an emerging idea in Nepal, and the general population has little knowledge or awareness of mental health issues. Cultural and religious beliefs regarding demons and mental illness encourage those in rural areas to seek help for extreme behaviors from local religious healers. There is little access to trained professionals or treatment. In addition, a multitude of factors, including poverty, environmental crises, and social injustices, negatively affect the mental health of the population. Even though the need is immense, those training in psychology or social work have very few options for practicing professionally, applying their skills, or attaining clinical supervision. The challenge can be overwhelming. However, my joy in teaching and supervising faculty and students comes from their desire to learn, their intelligence and appreciation of any knowledge or resource provided, and their intense desire to help others.

I had to adapt to teaching and supervising in a culture that shared and received knowledge in structurally different ways. In Nepal, teachers verbally lecture and are extremely respected. They are often the only source of information because there are few other learning resources available. Students don't own textbooks, and the entire class may share only a few copies if the school provides them. Interactive teaching is not a common practice. The teacher provides information and the student receives it without question or interaction. Socratic questioning, small groups, open discussion, and experiential activities are not normal experiences for teachers or students. In the

United States, I take great pride in my interactive classes and the energy created in the learning environment, so I was completely at a loss when my "well-prepared" creative plans for class or supervision fell completely flat. It took time, patience, humility, and collaboration to establish this transition and slowly introduce not only concepts but also interactions that were reciprocal. Empowering colleagues and supervisees to use their voices has been one of my most rewarding experiences. Ten years of lecturing, listening, learning, and sharing personal and professional differences has led to rich relationships and interactions regarding the transferability of knowledge, skills, and processes. It has been a monumental challenge and also the highlight of my 30+ years in the helping professions to share our field in Nepal.

In the past few years, I (Patrice Moulton) have begun to invite my graduate students to accompany me to work in Nepal. In Voices From the Field, Rachel Alvarez shares her experience of social justice supervision from a supervisee's perspective.

VOICES FROM THE FIELD

Supervision in a Multicultural Environment

Rachel Alvarez, MS

When engaging in team supervision as a suicide prevention trainer in Nepal, our team encountered several limitations in designing a program for individuals living in a remote developing country. One of the first things the team had to consider was the lack of environmental and cultural resources available to mental health workers, their clients, and the population in general. Some villages were days or weeks away from the nearest hospital and that hospital was unlikely to provide mental health services. Training resources were often outdated, limited, or simply unavailable, and the mountains limited our travel in some rural areas of Nepal. The most available resource for someone in need was often another person from their village who could provide words of comfort.

Cultural norms also limited or negated some possible coping strategies or treatment options we might suggest. For example, a common Nepali belief is that demonic possession causes mental illness, and those affected are taken to their local shaman for treatment rather than to a professional helper. In addition, females are perceived as second class to their male counterparts, and many women are not allowed to seek professional help without a husband or father being present. In Nepal, gender significantly determines group status, especially within a family. A young married Nepali woman who is abused by her husband and in-laws has few available options because of her gender and low status in the family group.

We also needed to consider Nepal's caste system and how affiliations with certain castes affected individual resources. The differences between the highest and lowest caste were stark, from housing to how people could honor the dead, and those from lower castes were often ostracized and dehumanized. Language differences were an obvious barrier even though many of our trainees spoke English very well. We found that the heart of our message and the quality of training significantly improved when we enlisted the help of young Nepali women to provide examples of our training in their own language and translated our words when necessary. Perhaps most important, we had to check our own biases regarding our privilege and realize that the resources we so often took for granted were not necessarily available to our Nepali counterparts. By shifting our focus from ourselves and what we understood to those we sought to help, we were able to create a training program that was real and applicable to the people of Nepal.

The considerations we made in preparation for our trip to Nepal—availability of resources, sex and gender issues, language barriers, and group affiliations—can be applied to other cultures both within and outside of the United States, and these domains should be considered an integral part of training for supervisees. I was incredibly fortunate to have a supervisor who had worked with Nepali culture and had years of supervision experience. She spoke candidly about difficult subjects, challenged norms, and initiated and safely facilitated uncomfortable discussions regarding culture and privilege. When we began preparing for this trip, she made it clear that we were not there for ourselves but for those we sought to serve. She described what we would see, appropriate reactions, common courtesies, cultural norms, and much more. Supervisees and counselors cannot know all aspects of a client's culture prior to their first meeting, but we can be aware of areas of consideration, check our own biases, and strive to better understand the client on this level. Entering therapy with an open heart, an open mind, a willingness to learn, and an effort to understand another person's worldview leads to greater compassion in treatment and an increased capacity to help those in need.

Supporting Trainees Serving Clients With Disabilities

An often overlooked topic in multicultural supervision is that of training and supervising counselors who serve people with disabilities. The World Health Organization (WHO, 2016) reports that about one billion people worldwide have a disability. Most disabilities are caused by motor vehicle accidents, falls causing catastrophic injuries, acts of physical and sexual violence, and injuries sustained in war. In the United States, most people will spend the last 12 years of their life in a state of decreased medical, physical, neurocognitive, or psychological functioning due to one or more chronic illness or disability (Falvo & Holland, 2018). It is essential that clinical supervisees understand how to work competently with the psychosocial adjustment and adaptation needs of people with disabilities as well as the co-occurring mental health conditions imposed by the disability. Supervisors overseeing the professional development and training of supervisees must assist them in understanding the challenges and needs of each client. Clients' needs vary according to the nature and severity of the disability as well as other contextual factors, and supervisees must be equipped with the skills to serve their clients effectively and compassionately. For a comprehensive exploration of disability culture, we recommend *The Psychological and Social Impact of Illness and Disability* (Marini & Stebnicki, 2018).

In Voices From the Field, Mark Stebnicki, a prolific writer and expert in rehabilitation counseling, disaster mental health response, and military counseling, illustrates the importance of seeing the disability community as a diverse group that should not be treated with a one-size-fits-all approach.

 VOICES FROM THE FIELD

Working With Veterans With Disabilities

Mark A. Stebnicki, PhD

It is vital that clinical supervisees cultivate the awareness, knowledge, and skills to work competently with military and nonmilitary people who have acquired chronic illnesses and disabilities. Differentiating between the culture of veterans with and without disabilities is equally important because psychosocial adjustment, adaptation, and response to chronic illness and disability is a complex interplay of the individual's medical, physical, psychological, social, emotional, cultural, and environmental identity.

There are considerable differences to explore in the civilian versus military veteran disability community. Military service members and veterans who are survivors of extraordinarily stressful and traumatic events are in a much higher risk category for long-term chronic illnesses and disabilities. As a result of life-saving medical advances and technology, more service members and veterans are surviving longer than in previous time periods. Since the war on terrorism began in 2001, more than 970,000 veterans have filed disability claims for one or more of the following conditions: traumatic brain injury, traumatic amputation, spinal cord injury, muscular skeletal and chronic pain conditions, and other chronic health conditions (Watson Institute, 2020).

Chronic illnesses and disabilities affect veteran medical, physical, and mental health in profound ways that complicate reintegration and transition into civilian life. Consequently, veterans sustain multiple losses of mental, physical, cognitive, social, emotional, and psychological functioning. There are many other losses such as the ability to maintain jobs, careers, and educational opportunities. In addition, intimate and social relationships are affected, as well as the ability to achieve optimal independent functioning.

Considerable research in psychosocial rehabilitation discusses how counselors can assist people with illness and disability to adjust and adapt to the many challenges of limited medical, physical, psychological, social, emotional, occupational, and independent functioning. The traditional literature in counseling and psychology has been slow to explore the cultural aspects of psychosocial rehabilitation and provide guidelines for therapeutic integration. Most research in psychosocial rehabilitation is nonmilitary related, and it may be difficult for some clinical supervisees to generalize the concepts in psychosocial rehabilitation for use in the military culture.

For instance, from a developmental psychology perspective, individuals transition through critical life stages of social and emotional development, as well as other predictable and anticipated phases, throughout the life span. However, early developmental theorists did not consider the impact of chronic illness and disability on the individual's functioning throughout the life span. Moreover, developmental and psychosocial growth is hindered by negative societal attitudes and perceptions toward veterans and nonveterans with mental and physical disabilities. Consequently, individuals with disabilities have significantly higher rates of unemployment, more health disparities, less access to quality medical and mental health care, substandard housing, transportation difficulties, and restricted access to public accommodations due to accessibility issues.

Overall, it is of paramount importance for clinical supervisees to acquire training and supervision in working with veterans and nonveterans with illnesses and disabilities. Training would be beneficial in examining ones' own attitudes and perceptions toward the culture of disability; recognizing the unique abilities and within-group differences along the continuum of medical, physical, neurocognitive, and psychological functioning; exploring society's perception of what is normal and abnormal; and analyzing the unique psychosocial stressors that hinder adjustment and adaptation to illness and disability among the civilian and veteran culture.

For an in-depth understanding and information about working with veterans with disabilities, see *Clinical Military Counseling: Guidelines for Practice* (Stebnicki, 2021).

Mark Stebnicki contributed Case Study 6.3 on traumatic brain injury disability. Learning about the issues involved in working with people with a disability is a key part of becoming a diversity-competent counselor. As you review Camila's case, think about ways you would strive to create a therapeutic alliance with her.

CASE STUDY 6.3: CAMILA

Camila Chavez is a 26-year-old single, Latina who sustained a mild-moderate traumatic brain injury (TBI) from a motor vehicle accident 5 months ago. Camila has a 4-year-old daughter from a previous marriage and lives with her parents who assist in child care duties and Camila's disability of TBI.

Camila spent about 3 weeks on the critical care unit where she was medically stabilized. She was then transferred to an acute care brain injury rehabilitation unit for 5 to 6 weeks where she received speech, physical, and occupational therapy. Camila's neuropsychological evaluation indicates she has mild deficits in short-term memory and moderate deficits in expressive language (expressive or Broca's aphasia). Her receptive communication skills are considered good. Camila also reports migraine headaches on a weekly basis and has been diagnosed with a wake-sleep and substance use disorder. Her physical and occupational therapists report that she has mild deficits with ambulation, coordination, movement, and independent functioning. Her neurologist and psychiatrist concur that she has not reached maximum medical improvement. Camila is anticipated to improve and achieve 85% to 90% of residual functioning capacity if she works hard in her rehabilitation therapy.

Camila's condition places her in a high-risk category for clinically significant symptoms related to posttraumatic stress, depression, anxiety, and substance use disorders. As the counseling supervisee prepares to meet Camila for their first session, consider the following areas that should be evaluated during a comprehensive clinical assessment to develop goals for Camila's follow-up mental health counseling and related treatment.

- Discuss and identify specific multicultural issues related to Hispanics with physical and neurocognitive disabilities. How do societal attitudes and perceptions toward Latinas affect Camila's medical, physical, and mental health functioning, as well as other life areas?
- Identify specific deficits in occupational, social, emotional, psychological, psychosocial, and independent functioning that will challenge Camila in reaching her optimal mental and physical well-being.
- Appraise and list other culturally relevant natural supports and resources that would benefit Camila in cultivating increased coping and resiliency skills.

Camila's case presents a complex interplay of medical, physical, cognitive, social, emotional, cultural, and psychological challenges. Psychosocial adjustment and adaptation to disability creates a constellation of lifelong challenges for people with mild-moderate TBI. Camila will require an intensive multidisciplinary approach, particularly during the first year of her rehabilitation. She will require medical and allied health professionals as well as behavioral and mental health providers to achieve optimal healing. Consideration should be given to Camila's unique cultural identity as she perceives herself as a person with a TBI. Supervisees may need to earn the circle of trust with clients who are culturally different and identify as a person with disability to achieve an optimal working alliance.

Spirituality as a Facet of Multicultural Supervision

Only recently have we begun to explore and acknowledge the construct of spirituality as a facet of multicultural counseling and supervision. Religion and spirituality have been foundational components of recognized diversity for centuries and are central in understanding, assessing, and treating individuals from many cultural groups. Awareness of the significance of spirituality and religion in the average person's life is the driving force behind the recent integration of these constructs into multicultural counseling and supervision. Counselor training programs have increasingly supported the integration of spirituality into the practice of counseling, yet supervisors continue to face challenges in effectively incorporating spirituality into the supervisory relationship (Garner et al., 2017).

Integrating spirituality and religion into the practice of counseling and psychotherapy has received increasing attention in the literature since the 1970s. Survey data of both practicing counselors and counselor educators indicate that spiritual and religious matters are therapeutically relevant, ethically appropriate, and potentially significant topics for the practice of counseling (Francis, 2016). It is crucial that counselors approach their clients in an open, accepting, nonjudgmental, and compassionate way. In keeping with the spirit of narrative therapy, counselors do not assume the role of expert; rather, they encounter clients with genuine interest and curiosity. Cultural humility provides a framework for supervisors and therapists to approach clients with an attitude of respect, curiosity, and a desire to understand their religious and spiritual experiences (Hook et al., 2019). Young and Cashwell (2020) put this notion poignantly: "We find that the counselors who are most effective in integrating spirituality and religion into counseling begin with curiosity rather than expertise" (p. 26). If therapists are to effectively include spirituality in therapy, they must be comfortable with spiritual concerns as a topic of discussion. To effectively address spiritual or religious concerns with clients, counselors must have a clear sense of their own values and make a commitment to help their clients clarify their values.

When clients indicate they are concerned about any of their religious beliefs or spiritual concerns or practices, the therapist needs to be willing to integrate these matters into the therapeutic process. For many clients, spirituality or religion are core aspects of their sense of self, worldview, and value system. Religious or spiritual concerns may be relevant to the motivation of some clients who seek therapy, either as areas of conflict for them or as sources of strength and support that can enhance the therapy process. Both religion and spirituality can have a positive impact on physical and psychological wellness and can serve as significant coping resources during difficult life situations (Young & Cashwell, 2020). Meta-analytic studies suggest that attending to a client's religious and spiritual values and beliefs can significantly improve treatment outcome. In light of this research, it is recommended that educators and supervisors discuss religious and spiritual concerns as a part of conceptualization, intervention, treatment goals, and interpersonal processes (Hook et al., 2019).

In the course of counseling, practitioners ask many questions about a client's life, yet they sometimes omit inquiring about what gives meaning to a client's life and the beliefs that have provided support for the client in difficult times. Not all clients will express concerns about religious beliefs or spiritual practice, even when those are relevant to the issues that brought them to counseling. Assessing the salience of spirituality or religion gives a counselor an opportunity to identify possible influences that spirituality or religion may have on a client's presenting problem and can inform an effective treatment plan.

If counselors do not include questions about spiritual or religious experiences and concerns during the assessment phase, clients may be reluctant to bring up these concerns in their counseling sessions. Assessment is a process of looking at all the potential influences on a client's problem to form a holistic picture of the client's current level of functioning. The exploration of spirituality or religious influences can be just as significant as exploring family-of-origin influences. Some clients may fear that counseling is not a place where their religious or spiritual beliefs and values will be respected and honored. It is a good practice to follow the client's lead when talking about religious and spiritual beliefs and practices (Hook et al., 2019). Asking direct or explicit questions about clients' religious or spiritual beliefs and values lets clients know that counseling is a safe space to discuss their beliefs or faith traditions. For example, asking a strength-based question during an intake such as "What or who gives you hope during difficult times?" may open the door to a discussion of faith. It is not, however, appropriate to expect clients to explore religion and spirituality if they do not see these as relevant factors in their lives.

Counselors should not neglect the beliefs and concerns of people who identify as nonreligious (Sahker, 2016). Individuals experiencing spiritual or religious struggles may seek therapy when they decide to leave the religion of their family of origin. These clients often need a safe place to share and explore their distress and concerns related to internal conflicts involving nonbelief. Some who have left the religion of their family of origin experience rejection by family members, and these clients may need to express the pain they experience as a result of their choice. The assessment process is crucial in identifying any religious or spiritual concerns, both positive and negative, that clients may have.

To be of help to clients in dealing with their spiritual and religious concerns, supervisees need to acquire specific knowledge and skills. Supervision can be a place to explore and learn about competencies in this realm. The Association for Spiritual, Ethical, and Religious Values in Counseling (ASERVIC; 2009) developed "Competencies for Addressing Spiritual and Religious Issues in Counseling" and revised these competencies in May 2009. These competencies are meant to be used in conjunction with evidence-based counseling theories and in keeping with best practices in counseling. The 14 ASERVIC competencies are grouped under six categories: culture and worldview, counselor self-awareness, human and spiritual development, communication, assessment, and diagnosis and treatment. Relevant competencies for this discussion include the following numbered guidelines:

2. The professional counselor recognizes that the client's beliefs (or absence of beliefs) about spirituality and/or religion are central to his or her worldview and can influence psychosocial functioning.
3. The professional counselor actively explores his or her own attitudes, beliefs, and values about spirituality and/or religion.
4. The professional counselor continuously evaluates the influence of his or her own spiritual and/or religious beliefs and values on the client and the counseling process.
7. The professional counselor responds to client communications about spirituality and/or religion with acceptance and sensitivity.
9. The professional counselor can recognize spiritual and/or religious themes in client communication and is able to address these with the client when they are therapeutically relevant.
10. During the intake and assessment processes, the professional counselor strives to understand a client's spiritual and/or religious perspective by gathering information from the client and/or other sources.

11. When making a diagnosis, the professional counselor recognizes that the client's spiritual and/or religious perspectives can (a) enhance well-being; (b) contribute to client problems; and/or (c) exacerbate symptoms.
12. The professional counselor sets goals with the client that are consistent with the client's spiritual and/or religious perspectives.

These competencies, like the MSJCC, give a sense of various aspects of diversity that can be incorporated in training programs. If supervisees are to work effectively with various aspects of diversity, it is imperative that they possess basic competencies. These competencies can provide a basis for discussion in supervisory sessions.

Supervisors are ethically mandated to prepare students and supervisees to be culturally competent clinicians (ACA, 2014; ACES, 2011), including being able to address issues of religion and spirituality in the counseling process. Although there has been an increase in the literature that addresses spirituality and religion in counseling (Harris et al., 2016), little of it focuses on religiosity and spirituality in supervision (Garner et al., 2017). Conversations about spirituality and religion during supervision can help supervisees understand how their own beliefs may be manifested in the counseling process. Such conversations may also "facilitate transformational growth in both supervisors and supervisees, and by extension influence the individuals supervisees counsel (Ross, 2014, p. 1).

The extent to which spirituality or religion is relevant to the client's presenting problem, your ability as a supervisor to facilitate discussions about spiritual beliefs without imposing your own personal values, and your supervisee's readiness to consider alternative worldviews are factors on which to reflect. Supervisors have a specific responsibility to ensure that those who train under our guidance receive ample opportunity to understand, honor, respect, and address religious and spiritual diversity.

For a comprehensive treatment addressing spirituality and religion in both counseling and supervision, we highly recommend *Integrating Spirituality and Religion Into Counseling: A Guide to Competent Practice* (Cashwell & Young, 2020). In Voices From the Field, Scott Young and Craig Cashwell explain why addressing spirituality and religion is of paramount importance in supervision.

VOICES FROM THE FIELD

Addressing Spirituality and Religion in the Supervisory Relationship: Why It Matters

J. Scott Young, PhD, and Craig S. Cashwell, PhD

A client's spirituality and religious perspective can reveal key values that often are activated when moving through a challenging event or season of life. Questions such as "Why is this happening to me?" or "Where is God in all of this?" are not uncommon. The role of the supervisor is to support the supervisee in tactfully broaching this topic with clients and determining, if, when, and how to integrate spirituality into the counseling process. Otherwise, the supervisee is at risk of ignoring a vital aspect of the client's identity or imposing values, both of which are likely to create serious problems in the therapeutic alliance and in the counseling process.

As clinical supervisors, we have worked with supervisees who held either similar or dissimilar religious and spiritual perspectives to those of their clients. These moments present an opportunity to encourage supervisees to adopt an open-minded approach to exploring the client's spiritual and religious life without imposing values. In practice, this involves the supervisee asking open questions with real interest and sincere curiosity, followed by deep listening. We highlight the importance of supervisees being curious rather than being an expert. We recall a supervisee asking a client, "Can you help me understand your spiritual perspective and how your struggle with depression is impacted by your beliefs?" Even though the supervisee was initially quite anxious about pursuing this line of inquiry, it opened a rich discussion of how the client wondered if her depression was evidence of a loss of faith.

Grounded in our clinical work as counselors and supervisors (and supported by empirical evidence), it seems many counselors are hesitant to broach spiritual and religious issues out of a fear that they will impose their values on a client. Certainly, individual systems of belief can vary widely. Even if a client appears to interpret religious teaching in a manner that is psychologically problematic, the competent counselor is understandably and wisely hesitant to directly challenge such beliefs. It remains possible, however, that some aspect of their religious belief system is causing them unnecessary suffering. Guided by a competent supervisor, the supervisee can partner with a client to understand the client's religious and spiritual beliefs, to consider how the beliefs may support or interrupt healthy psychological functioning, and to explore whether the client sees value in modifying these beliefs in a way that facilitates greater psychological openness and freedom while still preserving the core tenets of the client's religious commitments. This approach is grounded in counselor humility, curiosity, and radical respect for client autonomy rather than expertise, a course that is supported by research and best counseling practices. It is our hope that clinical supervisors will grasp the benefits of assisting supervisees in broaching religious and spiritual material much as they would any other cultural aspects of a client's life. Religion and spirituality are meaning-making systems and are ripe for psychological exploration.

Using Technology Effectively to Create Inclusion

The use of technology in supervision is broadening cultural perceptions by including more ethnic and culturally diverse participation. We are encouraged to be progressive, relevant, and to utilize innovative tools in training and supervising to enhance diversity and cultural understanding in our practice as supervisors and therapists. However, concerns have been raised about the lack of visual contact and sensitivity to cultural norms when supervision is practiced from a distance rather than in face-to-face meetings. Rousemaniere and Renfro-Michel (2016) state that there are currently more barriers than proposed methods for achieving culturally responsive technology-assisted supervision. Thoughtfully consider the following suggestions for multicultural awareness and sensitivity when using technology in supervision.

- Share your worldview with supervisees and encourage them to do the same through early introductory and orientation assignments, and invite discussions about distance supervision.
- Get to know your supervisee through purposefully designed questions, Webex meetings, assignments, and videos. Learn about geographical norms, identity, ability, and culture before engaging in supervision based on client contact.
- Create a safe environment by providing clear boundaries and expectations in your contract with supervisees. Include clarity about the use of technology, communication standards, and boundaries as part of collaborative ground rules regarding the logistics of distance supervision.
- Encourage frequent conversations regarding culture.

- Be aware that microaggressions are common in cross-cultural interactions and are more common when communication is not face-to-face. Misinterpretation is common in technology-assisted communication.
- Misunderstandings based on race, gender, disability, and culture occur more frequently when using technology to communicate. These misunderstandings result from "invisible emotions," which allow for a lack of ownership and responsibility in online communications. It is important to examine interchanges for intent and impact.
- Purposefully practice technology-assisted models, methods, and strategies that are designed for inclusion and develop multicultural sensitivity in supervisees by modeling and setting high expectations of cultural inclusion and respect.
- Assess your supervisee's access and ability to successfully use the technology required for supervision. Poverty, lack of opportunity, deficits in educational environment, or disabilities can create unique challenges. It is the supervisor's responsibility to provide opportunities for growth and success as we incorporate technology.
- If assessment of access and ability identify the need for reasonable accommodation, ensure that requirements, activities, and technologies are purposefully chosen to allow the opportunity for equal inclusion and development.

We have opportunities to expand access for training and supervision to remote areas and across the world using technology-assisted supervision. As a supervisor, this can be a challenge with a significant learning curve. It is important to consider the needs, norms, and unique characteristics of diverse populations in your supervisory practice when designing supervision from a distance.

Summary

Before you begin your supervisory experience, it is imperative that you gain personal insight into multicultural issues, which encompass all forms of diversity, as well as the influence of power and privilege in the supervisory relationship. Multicultural supervision is a complex enterprise and must take intersectionality into account. Supervisors are strongly advised to welcome the multiple salient identities of their trainees into the supervisory relationship and to make a concerted effort to understand their own multiple identities. This personal awareness serves as the cornerstone for multicultural knowledge and skills. You have an ethical responsibility to be a competent multicultural supervisor. This means having knowledge of multicultural issues in assessment, therapy, and diagnosis and providing opportunities for your supervisees to explore and learn multicultural and social justice competencies under your supervision. This role includes teaching, modeling, mentoring, and advocating. More than anything, it requires sensitivity and openness to the diversity of the supervisees and clients for whom we are responsible.

All forms of counseling are culture centered and include diversity to some extent. It is our responsibility as supervisors to provide a safe environment for open dialogue with supervisees regarding diversity, including topics related to spirituality and religion. You do not have to know every detail about every population to be a culturally competent counselor or supervisor; however, you need to be willing to seek resources that will equip you with the tools to work effectively with diversity. A framework such as the multidimensional model of broaching behavior and the MSJCC will help guide your supervisees to greater cultural competence. These may very well be your strongest training tools in supervision.

SUGGESTED ACTIVITIES

Here are a few questions that could be explored independently or in a group.

1. Identify the cultural groups you are most likely to encounter in your work as a clinician and clinical supervisor. What assumptions and expectations do you have about people from these cultures? Which ones might be faulty or unrealistic? Which ones are realistic?

2. How does your culture (as you define it) influence others' perceptions of you? Which of these perceptions might be faulty and which are accurate? To what extent are your supervisee's assumptions about and expectations of you related to your role as supervisor? To what degree might they be related to your cultural background?

3. What values were you brought up with regarding people from different cultures? How might these values affect your ability to supervise?

4. What are five specific ways to serve as a social advocate in your community (as you define it)?

5. Identify presenting problems that you encounter in your caseload and develop case conceptualizations through the lens of various cultures. How would you deal with the issues of assessment, diagnosis, and treatment in a culturally sensitive manner?

6. List five questions you might use in initiating a discussion regarding cultural differences? Share and discuss in a small group and role-play scenarios with various cultural groups.

CHAPTER 7

Ethical Issues and Multiple Relationships in Supervision

FOCUS QUESTIONS

1. What are the most critical ethical issues in supervision?
2. What are the most important ethical responsibilities supervisors have toward their supervisees and supervisees' clients?
3. What kinds of training, coursework, and other professional experiences are essential for competent supervision?
4. If you were a supervisee, how would you like your supervisor to address multiple roles and relationships that might be a part of the supervisory process?
5. As a supervisee, how have your relationships with supervisors changed over time? What lessons can you apply from these experiences when you assume a supervisory role?
6. What kinds of activities beyond the formal supervisory relationship do you think might be appropriate for a supervisor to engage in with a supervisee?

In this chapter, we explore ethical issues frequently encountered in clinical supervision and provide guidelines for the ethical practice of supervision. Some of the topics address issues pertaining to students in training programs, but most of these principles can be applied to supervisees in many different settings. A few of these topics are responsibilities of clinical supervisors, competence of supervisors, dealing with incompetent trainees, and managing multiple roles and relationships in the supervisory process.

As discussed in Chapter 3, the relationship between the clinical supervisor and the supervisee is of critical importance in the development of competent therapists. If we take into consideration the dependent position of the trainee and the similarities between the supervisory relationship and the therapeutic relationship, the need for guidelines describing the rights of supervisees and the responsibilities of supervisors becomes obvious. Both the American Counseling Association (2014) and the Association for Counselor Education and Supervision (2011) have developed ethical guidelines for counseling supervisors that address major ethical issues in supervision such as informed consent, supervision agreements, supervisor competence, confidentiality concerns, supervisory relationships, client welfare and rights, supervisory roles, diversity considerations, due process, and multiple roles and responsibilities in supervision.

Sometimes the work of a supervisor is full of surprises regardless of how careful we are to practice in an ethical and professional manner. All of us can recall times when we were caught off guard as supervisors or as trainees, when thinking on our feet was necessary but insufficient to meet the demands of a particular situation. During those times, referring to the ethics codes and ethical decision-making models of our professional associations is of paramount importance. Many of the ethical dilemmas trainees will encounter are complex and defy simplistic solutions. It is not a matter of supervisees getting answers to ethical questions from their supervisors. These dilemmas often leave both supervisee and supervisor in a perplexed state of wondering how to proceed, as Case Study 7.1 illustrates.

CASE STUDY 7.1: FRANNIE

Frannie, a clinician in a small-town community agency, recently became a clinical supervisor and is overseeing the work of two counselor trainees who are completing their internships at that site. In a supervision session, Travis revealed that a client admitted to cheating on his partner and has had unprotected sex with this person. Travis's client is now worried that he may have contracted HIV, although he has not been tested. Frannie (who also sees her own clients) realized that Travis's client is the partner of one of her longtime clients who is unsuspecting of the betrayal and also doesn't realize that her partner is bisexual. Frannie is left wondering how to navigate the situation.

Does Frannie have an obligation to warn her own client about the betrayal and the possibility of being exposed to HIV, or would that violate the confidentiality of Travis's client? And how should she proceed in supervising Travis with his case? Will Frannie's personal reactions and biases have a negative impact on her ability to view Travis's client with compassion and fairness? If so, how would that affect the quality of her supervision and Travis's supervisory experience?

These are just a few of the questions that leave Frannie feeling perplexed and unsettled. Because the town is so small and the agency is the only mental health facility within miles, unusual ethical issues like this occasionally arise. They are both difficult to avoid and difficult to work through.

Ethical Issues in Clinical Supervision

Some critical ethical issues in supervision are balancing the rights of clients, the rights and responsibilities of supervisees, and the responsibilities of supervisors to both supervisees and their clients. Supervisors must discuss the rights of supervisees from the beginning of the supervisory relationship in much the same way the rights of clients are addressed early in the therapy process. When this is done, the supervisee is invited to express expectations, empowered to make decisions, and encouraged to become an active participant in the supervisory process.

The Supervisor's Responsibilities

Supervisors have a responsibility to provide training and supervised experiences that will enable supervisees to deliver ethical and effective services. It is essential for supervisors to be knowledgeable and skilled in the practice of clinical supervision. The topic of supervisor competence is addressed in the *ACA Code of Ethics* (ACA, 2014):

> Prior to offering clinical supervision services, counselors are trained in supervision methods and techniques. Counselors who offer clinical supervision services regularly pursue continuing education activities including both counseling and supervision topics and skills. (F.2.A.)

As we saw in Chapter 2, if supervisors do not have training in clinical supervision, it will be difficult for them to ensure that those they supervise are functioning effectively and ethically. Many practitioners who are assigned supervisory responsibilities find that on-the-job training is the standard mode of operation. Supervisors are expected to make every effort to obtain adequate education and training before assuming the supervisory role, and they should consider the ethical and legal ramifications if they are asked to take on this role prior to training.

To make optimal use of supervision, supervisees need to clearly understand what their responsibilities are, what the supervisor's responsibilities are, and how they will be assessed. Ethical supervision involves providing scheduled periodic feedback and evaluation to supervisees so they have a basis for improving their clinical skills (ACA, 2014; ACES, 2011).

Clinical supervisors have a position of influence with their supervisees. Supervisors operate in multiple roles as teacher, coach, evaluator, counselor, consultant, model, mentor, adviser, and advocate (see Chapter 2). From an ethical perspective, it is of the utmost importance that supervisors monitor their own behavior and do not misuse the inherent power in the supervisor-supervisee relationship. Supervisors are responsible for ensuring compliance with relevant legal, ethical, and professional standards for clinical practice (ACES, 2011). The main purposes of ethical standards for clinical supervision are to provide behavioral guidelines to supervisors, protect supervisees from undue harm or neglect, and ensure quality client care (Bernard & Goodyear, 2019).

Barnett, Cornish, Goodyear, and Lichtenberg (2007) claim that effective supervisors understand the importance of serving as ethical role models to their supervisees. They attend to the following areas of ethical practice in supervision: assessing their trainees' learning needs from the outset and modifying the training experience in accordance with their needs; reaching an agreement with each supervisee at the outset of supervision about the nature and course of the training process and supervisory relationship; offering supervisees timely and meaningful feedback; maintaining appropriate boundaries; maintaining clients' and supervisees' confidentiality, and when required to breach confidentiality, doing so in an appropriate manner; limiting one's clinical practice and supervision to one's areas of competence; engaging in wellness practices to ensure one remains effective; and paying attention to diversity.

Modeling Confidentiality

It is essential that supervisors teach and model ethical and professional behavior for their supervisees. One of the best ways for supervisors to model professional behavior is to deal appropriately with confidentiality issues pertaining to supervisees. Supervisors have the responsibility of keeping information obtained in the supervisory relationship confidential. As is the case in a client-therapist relationship, confidentiality in the supervisory relationship is not an absolute, it has limitations. Furthermore, supervisors are responsible for making supervisees aware of clients' rights to privacy and confidentiality in the counseling relationship.

Supervisors have an evaluative role, and at times faculty members need to be apprised of students' progress. However, personal information that supervisees share during a supervision session should generally remain confidential. At the very least, supervisees have a right to be informed about what will be revealed and what will not be shared with others on the faculty. Supervisors need to put ethics in the foreground of their supervisory practices, which can best be done by treating supervisees in a respectful, professional, and ethical manner.

Supervisors have responsibilities for their supervisees' clients, one of which is to respect the confidentiality of client communications. Supervision involves discussion of client issues and review of client materials, and supervisees must respect their clients' privacy by not talking about clients outside of the context of supervision. Supervisors have an obligation to educate trainees to become aware of the rights of the clients they see. This includes making sure that supervisees provide informed consent to their clients by letting them know that their work is being supervised and by whom, and that they are trainees and not licensed practitioners. If video or audio recording of therapy sessions is a required part of the process, supervisees must gain permission from clients prior to beginning recording. Clients should be informed that being involved in supervision means that confidential information will need to be shared with the supervisor. Supervisors must make sure that both supervisees and their clients are fully informed about the limits of confidentiality, including those situations in which supervisors have a duty to warn or protect, or to report. Supervisees need to encourage their clients to ask questions at any point during counseling process. It is a good idea that clients are introduced to the supervisor with an opportunity from them to ask any questions they may have of the supervisor or how they will be talked about during supervision. Some clients become anxious about an "unknown" person watching their counseling sessions behind the mirror or viewing video or audio recordings. This introductory meeting can reduce anxiety clients might have about the supervisory process and increase clients' trust in working with a trainee.

Teaching Supervisees How to Make Ethical Decisions

A chief responsibility of supervisors is to teach their supervisees how to think about the ethical dilemmas they are bound to encounter and to help them develop a framework for making ethical decisions. We suggest that supervisors teach supervisees the importance of involving their clients to whatever degree is possible in the process of resolving an ethical concern. Of course, supervisees would do well to bring any ethical issues they face in dealing with their clients to supervision. As supervisees learn to be open about the ethical concerns that arise, they are learning a pattern of being willing to seek consultation as they become seasoned professionals.

The American Counseling Association's (2014) *Code of Ethics* states that when counselors encounter an ethical dilemma they are expected to carefully consider an ethical decision-making process. To make sound ethical decisions, it is necessary to engage in an intentional course of ethical deliberation, consultation, and action. A number of ethical decision-making models are available, a few of which have been developed by Barnett and Johnson (2010), Corey, Corey, and Corey (2019), Herlihy and Corey (2015a), Koocher and Keith-Spiegel (2016), and Remley and Herlihy (2020). Although no one ethical decision-making model is most effective in every case, mental health professionals need to be familiar with at least one of these models (such as the one described here), or an amalgam that best fits for them.

Corey, Corey, and Corey (2019) suggest the following eight procedural steps as a way to think through ethical dilemmas. Supervisors can use this model to teach supervisees how to address ethical issues.

1. Identify the Problem or Dilemma

Gather as much information as possible that sheds light on the situation. Clarify whether the conflict is ethical, legal, professional, or moral—or a combination of any or all of these. The first step toward resolving an ethical dilemma is recognizing that a problem exists and identifying its specific nature. Because most ethical dilemmas are complex, look at the problem from many perspectives and avoid simplistic solutions. Consultation with the client and supervisee begins at this initial stage and continues throughout the process of working through an ethical problem, as does the process of documenting decisions and actions taken.

2. Identify Potential Issues Involved

After the information is collected, list and describe the critical issues and discard the irrelevant ones. Evaluate the rights, responsibilities, and welfare of all those who are affected by the situation. Consider the cultural context of the situation, including relevant cultural dimensions of the client's situation such as culture, race, socioeconomic status, and religious or spiritual background. Part of the process of making ethical decisions involves identifying competing values. Ask the supervisee for input regarding the values that must be considered. It may help to prioritize these values and principles and to think through ways in which each one can support a resolution to the dilemma.

3. Review Relevant Ethics Codes

Ask yourself whether the standards or principles of your professional organization offer a possible solution to the problem. Consider whether your own values and ethics are consistent with or in conflict with the relevant codes. Encourage your supervisee to do the same.

4. Know Applicable Laws and Regulations

Keep up-to-date on relevant state and federal laws that apply to ethical dilemmas, such as statutes of limitations. This is especially critical in matters of keeping or breaching confidentiality, reporting child or elder abuse, dealing with issues pertaining to danger to self or others, parental or guardian rights, record keeping, testing and assessment, diagnosis, licensing statutes, and the grounds for malpractice. Be sure that you discuss these issues with your supervisee as they pertain to the issue you are trying to resolve. In addition to gaining clarity about reporting incidents, you must clearly identify the reporting process and resources for immediate access when needed.

5. Obtain Consultation

At this point, it is generally helpful to consult with colleagues to obtain different perspectives on the problem. Do not limit the individuals with whom you consult to those who share your theoretical orientation. If there is a legal question, seek legal counsel. It is wise to document the nature of your consultation, including the suggestions provided by consultants. In court cases, consultation illustrates the attempt to adhere to community standards by finding out what your colleagues in the community would do in the same situation. Consultation can help you think about information or circumstances that you may have overlooked, and it can also help you gain objectivity. Doing this can protect you from legal liability. In making ethical decisions, you must justify a course of action based on sound reasoning. Include your supervisee and the client in consultation sessions when appropriate.

6. Consider Possible and Probable Courses of Action

Brainstorming is useful at this stage of ethical decision making. Consider the ethical and legal implications of the possible solutions you have identified. As you think about the many possibilities for action, discuss these options with the client, your supervisee, and with other professionals.

7. Enumerate the Consequences of Various Decisions

Ponder the implications of each course of action for the client, for others who are related to the client, for your supervisee, and for you as the supervisor. A discussion with the client about the consequences for him or her is most important, and you and your supervisee may decide to act as cotherapists when this discussion is initiated. Realize that there are likely to be multiple outcomes rather than a single desired outcome in dealing with an ethical dilemma.

8. Decide the Best Course of Action

In making the best decision, carefully consider the information you have received from various sources. The more obvious the dilemma, the clearer is the course of action; the more subtle the dilemma, the more difficult the decision will be. Once you have made what you consider to be the best decision, do what you can to evaluate your course of action. Document the outcome of your decision and include any additional actions that were taken to resolve the issue. Document any consultations you had to assist you in the decision-making process. Reflecting on your assessment of the situation and on the actions you took is essential if you are to learn from your experience. Follow up to determine the outcomes and whether any further action is needed. To obtain the most accurate picture, involve your supervisee and the client in this process.

These procedural steps should not be thought of as a simplified and linear way to reach a resolution on ethical matters. The aim of these steps is to stimulate self-reflection and to encourage discussion with the client, your supervisee, and your colleagues. Use supervisory sessions to model this process for your trainees.

Competence of Supervisors

From both an ethical and legal standpoint, supervisors must have the education and training to adequately carry out their supervisory roles. The provision of clinical supervision requires competence both in the specific areas of counseling practice supervised and in the practice of supervision. The skills used in counseling are not necessarily the same as those needed to adequately supervise trainees or to advise other helping professionals; specific training in how to supervise is needed. Many who function as supervisors have not had formal coursework and training in supervision theory and methods. If courses in supervision were not part of your program, clinicians must acquire the specific knowledge and skills, perhaps through continuing education, that will enable them to function effectively as clinical supervisors.

Becoming a competent supervisor currently involves taking coursework in theories of supervision, working with difficult supervisees, working with culturally diverse supervisees, methods of supervision, and being supervised in doing supervision, which is often referred to as *supervision-of-supervision*. The counselor licensure laws in a number of states now stipulate that licensed professional counselors who practice supervision are required to have relevant training experiences and coursework in supervision. Through this training counselors learn firsthand about the importance of mutuality in the supervision relationship and become more educated consumers of supervision. State laws or guidelines pertaining to the practice of supervision change over time; counselors and other helping professionals are advised to contact their professional associations and state licensing boards to get up-to-date information about the specific requirements they need to fulfill to practice supervision.

Supervisors not only need specialized training in methods of supervision but also need to have an in-depth knowledge of the specialty area in which they will provide supervision. It is considered unethical for supervisors to offer supervision in areas beyond the scope of their practice. The APA's (2017) position on boundaries of competence states this clearly:

Psychologists provide services, teach, and conduct research with populations and in areas only within the boundaries of their competence, based on their education, training, supervised experience, consultation, study, or professional experience. (2.01)

If supervisees are working outside the area of competence of the supervisor, it is the responsibility of the supervisor to arrange for competent clinical supervision of those cases.

To be an effective supervisor, the clinician must have acquired the following competencies:

1. Competent supervisors are *trained in supervision* and periodically *update their knowledge and skills* on supervision topics through workshops, continuing education, conferences, and reading.
2. Competent supervisors must have *effective interpersonal skills* and be able to work with a variety of groups and individuals in supervision and with counselors with a range of life and clinical experience. Examples of these interpersonal skills include the ability to listen and provide constructive feedback, the ability to challenge and confront the supervisee in a helpful manner, and the ability to set professional interpersonal boundaries with the supervisee.
3. Competent supervisors must be cognizant of the fact that *supervision is a situational process* that is dependent on interaction between the supervisor, the supervisee, the setting, and the client. Skilled supervisors will be able to modify their approach to supervision as the situation dictates.
4. Competent supervisors must be flexible and *be able to assume a variety of roles and responsibilities* in supervision. The supervisory role can change rapidly depending on the needs of the situation.
5. Competent supervisors must have a *broad knowledge of laws, ethics, and professional regulations* that may apply in a variety of situations that could arise in supervision of clinical cases.
6. Competent supervisors stay focused on the fact that a primary goal of supervision is to *monitor clinical services* so that the welfare of the client is protected.
7. Competent supervisors are willing to *serve an evaluative function* with supervisees and *provide feedback* about their performance on a regular basis.
8. Competent supervisors document *supervision activities* in a timely and accurate fashion.
9. Competent supervisors *empower supervisees.* Supervisors assist supervisees at both problem-solving current situations and developing a problem-solving approach that they can apply to nearly any clinical situation long after the supervision has ended.

You might well find yourself lacking in the competencies to be an effective supervisor, even if you are able to take a course in supervision as a part of your program. Today, there are many more workshops on supervision, books on the topic, and opportunities to obtain supervision by others as you begin practicing as a supervisor. It may be a mistake to think that your graduate program alone will adequately prepare you with experiences in supervision or with the in-depth knowledge you will need to supervise others who are working with a wide range of client populations with special problems. Part of the answer to moving toward competence is seeking quality continuing education programs dealing with special client populations and methods of supervision. Developing competence as a therapist in the areas in which you are supervising will also enhance your competence in supervision. Michelle Muratori provides a Personal Perspective on one route toward becoming a competent supervisor.

MICHELLE MURATORI'S PERSONAL PERSPECTIVE

When I decided that I wanted to be a counselor, I was not wedded to a particular special-ty area. I guess you could say that I was open-minded about the direction my career path would take. Consequently, my training experiences have been quite varied.

As part of a group leadership training program during my undergraduate education, I cofacilitated groups composed of college students from diverse cultural backgrounds. In my master's program, I was placed at a practicum site working with low-income preg-nant teenagers, followed by a second field placement at a community mental health center in an urban area, where I met with individuals, couples, families, and groups. The clients I served ranged from young children to older adults, from the worried well to the acutely psychotic. After graduating from my master's program, I worked for an agency that provided in-home counseling services to families that were at risk of losing their children to the state. Upon starting my doctoral training, I returned to community mental health and eventually took a graduate assistantship at a university center serving academically talented students. Although some might conclude that I lacked focus, the truth is that all of these educational and professional experiences combined have broad-ened my understanding of the helping process and of the problems so many encounter. I feel honored to have had the opportunity to work with individuals who have walked such different paths.

Because I have trained at different types of settings, I am used to facing a learning curve. I have always been a hard worker, so investing extra time and energy into the learning process never seemed too daunting to me. For instance, shortly after leaving my position at a community mental health center where I counseled several low-func-tioning clients, I was hired as a graduate assistant to work with highly able students who entered college early. I was excited by the challenge but admittedly concerned that I didn't have the background and skills to work effectively with them. I approached this challenge as I had approached challenges in the past. In addition to reading about gifted education, and the social/emotional issues that gifted students often experience, I was open to learning from colleagues and seeking supervision. I also attended conferences on gifted education. As my knowledge base developed, my comfort level increased, and I ended up developing a passion for counseling high-ability students and their families, which I do to this day at the Johns Hopkins Center for Talented Youth.

Later in my doctoral program I had a similar experience; however, this time I was in the supervisor's role, not the supervisee's position. As part of my supervisory training, I supervised a few master's-level trainees who specialized in rehabilitation counseling. Lacking formal training in that specialty area, I needed to learn enough about rehabilita-tion counseling to be of assistance to my supervisees and their clients, so I worked with my own supervisor to ensure that my supervisory interventions were on track.

I recognize that it is our ethical duty as counselors, counselor educators, and super-visors *not* to practice outside the scope of our competence. Realistically, none of us start out as seasoned veterans, and the only way to acquire competence is by allowing our-selves to be learners. We must be open to acquiring new information and be willing to improve our skills and modify our thinking when necessary.

Incompetent or Impaired Supervisors

There is a growing body of literature on counselor impairment, but the topic of supervisor impairment has generally been overlooked. *Supervisor impairment* is the inability to per-form the functions involved in the supervisory role because of interference by something in the supervisor's behavior or environment, with the caveat that a distinction should be made between *incompetence* and *impairment*. Some behaviors that might be indicative of supervisor impairment are engaging in exploitive or harmful dual or multiple relationships with supervisees, sexual contact with supervisees, sexual harassment, misuse of power, abusive communication, or extreme burnout. A supervisor who makes poor decisions as a result of inexperience might be considered to be incompetent. In contrast, a supervisor with a personality disorder who abuses his or her power and makes the training experiences of a supervisee negative could be considered to be impaired.

Muratori (2001) explored the implications of working with an impaired supervisor at the various levels of counselor development and discussed some of the key factors that may influence how a supervisee might deal with this problem. We must not forget that the supervisor is in an evaluative position and is expected to assess whether trainees have acquired the necessary skills and competencies to advance in the program. This fact has implications for the counselor trainee's decision when faced with an impaired supervisor. Before determining a proper course of action, the trainee must consider the precise nature and severity of the supervisor's impairment. Other factors that contribute to the complexity of the decision to either confront or endure working with an impaired supervisor include the power differential inherent in the supervisory relationship, one's level of development as a counselor trainee, and the personalities of both the supervisor and the supervisee. Trainees who have an impaired supervisor may have fewer options than a client who has an impaired counselor. Even assertive supervisees need to carefully weigh their options for action with an impaired supervisor because of the potential consequences that could be associated with this supervisor's misuse of power. In extreme cases, trainees may need to take legal action, especially if the quality of supervision is being compromised or if they believe they or their clients are being harmed by the relationship. Michelle Muratori offers a Personal Perspective on her experience dealing with an impaired supervisor.

 ## MICHELLE MURATORI'S PERSONAL PERSPECTIVE

Although I consider myself fortunate to have worked with several competent supervisors, I will share an experience I had with one who, in my view, was impaired. Early in my training, one of my fieldwork experiences was at a community mental health center where I worked with individuals, groups, families, and couples. I had been counseling a young couple who seemed to be stuck at an impasse yet wanted to work their difficulties out. This case stirred up my own countertransference because in my personal life I was having problems in my relationship with my boyfriend of many years. We, too, were stuck, and I felt inept and frustrated that I was counseling others yet couldn't resolve my own difficulties. Many questions crossed my mind that I would have liked to address with my supervisor, but I was reluctant to raise them in supervision.

Although experienced and knowledgeable, my supervisor seemed to be suffering from burnout. She seemed to have little patience for clients who were not making rapid progress. When discussing this particular case, she referred to my clients as "losers." That's right, "losers." I didn't quite know what to do with that, but my intuition told me to seek supervision elsewhere (which I did). I was afraid that if I was vulnerable with this supervisor and disclosed my countertransference, she would consider me a "loser" as well. For a number of reasons (e.g., I wanted her approval, she was evaluating me and had a gatekeeping role), I felt I could not take the risk of being open with her. The bottom line is that I did not trust what she would do with the information I gave her, so I was exceedingly careful in how I presented information, which detracted from my experience. Shortly before my training ended at the center, she retired. I finished out the year with another supervisor on staff, and I was pleased that my original supervisor knew when it was time to quit.

Incompetent Supervisees

Interacting with an impaired or incompetent supervisor is a difficult situation to navigate, but we expect such situations to be less frequent than encountering supervisees who demonstrate professionally problematic behavior. In the supervisory role, you will probably encounter some trainees with skill deficits, gaps in knowledge, personality issues, or any number of other problematic behaviors or attitudes that hinder their development of competence. What is the supervisor's responsibility when supervisees are clearly not competent to counsel others? What ethical issues must be addressed when supervisors encounter supervisees who do not meet professional competence standards? Supervisees may not have the fundamental knowledge or the basic helping skills required to carry out effective counseling, and to be sure, supervisees will be evaluated on their level of knowledge and skill development. But what about those instances in which supervisees are unable to function effectively because of personal problems or personality characteristics?

Problematic Behavioral Characteristics of Trainees

Supervisors cannot ethically avoid dealing with supervisees who are unable to competently carry out their training role because of some personal characteristics or performance problems. From both an ethical and a legal perspective, training faculty and supervisors are expected to address situations that involve trainee lack of competence due to personal and interpersonal problems.

A range of behaviors can adversely affect the ability of students and trainees to effectively carry out their clinical duties. Two severe problems are substance abuse and personality disorders. More subtle aspects of problematic trainee behaviors include interpersonal sensitivity, need for extreme control, and using one's position to meet personal needs at the client's expense.

DeLorenzi (2018b) addresses the responsibilities of supervisors in evaluating trainees' professional performance and provides a comprehensive list of behavioral misconduct. A few areas of problematic professional performance that have a negative impact on the competent delivery of services to clients by supervisees are listed here.

- Unethical behavior, which includes a failure to uphold the ethical standards of the various professional organizations
- Resistance to receiving feedback, such as being closed to supervisor feedback
- Giving priority to self needs over the client's needs
- Failure to follow the procedures and policies of a graduate program
- Failure to engage actively in training activities that promote personal and professional growth
- Inappropriate use of technology
- Failure to establish and maintain appropriate boundaries with clients and colleagues
- Displaying emotional instability
- Not giving attention to personal wellness practices
- Being resistant to examining personal reactions
- Being closed to new ideas and learning

- Lacking personal integrity
- Failure to adapt to the changing needs of the environment
- Lacking interest in self-reflection and self-exploration
- Inability to deal effectively with interpersonal conflicts
- Failure to demonstrate genuineness, empathy, and interest in the welfare of others
- Low capacity for honest self-evaluation

This list of examples of misconduct is not all-inclusive, but it provides concrete examples of problematic behaviors that call for active intervention on the part of the supervisor. The emphasis should be on prevention of problematic behaviors on the part of trainees as much as possible.

Monitoring Trainee Competence

Supervisors serve as gatekeepers for the profession by evaluating competence to practice within the mental health professions. According to Falender (2018), "supervisors are at the forefront of the process because of their roles as evaluators and gatekeepers. Supervisors engage in ongoing assessment, monitoring, evaluation, and feedback, but with the added purpose of ensuring supervisees are aware of their competence development and are planfully accruing greater competence" (p. 1244). Monitoring the competence of counslors-in-training has long been viewed as an essential component in training programs. In addition to evaluating a supervisee's academic ability, knowledge, and clinical skills, it is essential to identify and evaluate a supervisee's personal characteristics, interpersonal behaviors, and professional behaviors that are likely to influence his or her ability to effectively deliver mental health services. Given the increased awareness of possible damage caused by mental health professionals who do not possess the personal qualities necessary for effective practice, it is clear that counselor educators and supervisors have a responsibility to serve as gatekeepers for the profession (DeLorenzi, 2018a, 2018b). In addition, it is crucial that students be informed about gatekeeping policies. Students need to have clear information about the expectations of a program and professional standards. From the time students apply to a graduate program through various phases in the program and to their endorsement to licensure, students and supervisees should be notified of required standards, policies, procedures, and processes (Thanasia, 2018). Evaluating trainees on the basis of personal characteristics is often a complex and demanding task. Interpersonal behaviors of trainees have a direct bearing on their clinical effectiveness, so these factors must be taken into consideration in the evaluation process. According to Sofronoff, Helmes, and Pachana (2011), assessment of *fitness to practice* within training programs requires balancing the rights of students to pursue their career interests with the rights of their future clients.

Gaubatz and Vera (2002, 2006) contend that it is the responsibility of counselor training programs to develop formalized policies and procedures to address students' personal and interpersonal fitness for competent professional practice, as well as attending to their trainees' didactic skills. Sometimes trainees have personal characteristics or problems that interfere with their ability to function effectively, but when this is pointed out to them, they may deny the feedback they receive. In these cases, a program has an ethical responsibility to take action and not simply pass on a student with serious academic or personal problems.

Taking Action With Incompetent Supervisees

It is of the utmost importance that supervisees hear from their supervisors long before it is too late for them to take corrective measures. Supervisees have due process rights, and dismissal from a training program should be the last resort after other interventions have failed to produce needed changes in supervisees who exhibit deficiencies. Supervisors have an obligation to provide their supervisees with regular, specific, and ongoing feedback. If there are problems regarding supervisees' performance, they must be given opportunities to take remedial steps to correct these problems. A few types of remediation include increased supervision, a leave of absence, personal therapy, taking a course or workshop, repeating a practicum or internship experience, or being part of a personal growth group. We cannot overemphasize the importance of placing realistic expectations and possible consequences for deficiencies in the supervision contract and discussing these with supervisees.

The *ACA Code of Ethics* (2014) and the *Best Practices in Clinical Supervision* (ACES 2011) address matters pertaining to the gatekeeping functions of supervisors and suggest remediation measures and how to deal with dismissal from a program. The American Psychological Association's *Guidelines for Clinical Supervision in Health Service Psychology* (APA, 2015) offers guidance to supervisors in addressing professional competence problems of supervisees (see Box 7.1).

Dismissal of Students From a Program

We agree with Sampson and her colleagues (2013) that "one of the most complex and emotionally stressful situations faced by educators in clinical training programs is the dilemma of the trainee who, despite multiple corrections and ample time to improve, is not making reasonable or adequate minimal professional progress" (p. 26). In their review of the literature on the reasons for dismissal from a program, Forrest and colleagues (1999) found these common categories of incompetence: poor academic performance, poor clinical performance, poor interpersonal skills, and unethical behavior. Psychological reasons for dismissal included factors such as emotional instability, personality disorder, psychopathology, and unprofessional demeanor. Forrest and her colleagues identified some general procedural guidelines for due process that should be provided to protect both the program and the trainees:

- Written description that gives reasons for termination
- Oral and written evaluations of trainees regarding their personal and interpersonal functioning
- Written action plans for remediation specifying the expected behavioral changes, a timeline, and consequences for failing to remediate
- A notification process for dismissal
- Procedures that permit trainees to appeal a decision to dismiss

Kerl, Garcia, McCullough, and Maxwell (2002) describe the importance of designing systematic procedures for training programs to evaluate students' professional performance. When dismissal from a program is based on interpersonal or clinical incompetence, Kerl and colleagues underscore the importance of sound systematic academic evaluation and adherence to procedural and substantive due process. The evaluation of students' interpersonal and clinical skills should be part of the overall assessment of their academic performance. Courts have consistently viewed personal characteristics or behaviors as basic to academic performance, which makes this an academic issue.

When there is concern about personal characteristics or problematic behavior of supervisees, both faculty and supervisors may be hesitant in taking action to prevent supervisees from continuing a program. Forrest et al. (1999) describe some factors that get in the way of taking action: difficulties in giving clear evidence and lack of adequate procedures in place to support the decision to dismiss a student; concern about the

Box 7.1
SUPERVISORS' ETHICAL RESPONSIBILITIES
IN DEALING WITH SUPERVISEE INCOMPETENCE

American Counseling Association (2014)

Code of Ethics

Through initial and ongoing evaluation, supervisors are aware of supervisee limitations that might impede performance. Supervisors assist supervisees in securing remedial assistance when needed. They recommend dismissal from training programs, applied counseling settings, and state or voluntary professional credentialing processes when those supervisees are unable to demonstrate competent professional services to a range of diverse clients. Supervisors seek consultation and document their decisions to dismiss or refer supervisees for assistance. They ensure that supervisees are aware of options available to them to address such decisions. (F.5.b.)

Association for Counselor Education and Supervision (2011)

Best Practices in Clinical Supervision

The supervisor takes appropriate steps when remediation is necessary.

i.   The supervisor normalizes developmental challenges while also providing feedback in clear and constructive language about skills and behaviors that need to be remediated.
ii. When remediation is necessary, the supervisor notifies the supervisee promptly. The supervisor recommends specific interventions relevant to the area of deficit. The supervisor prepares a written remediation plan that includes clear objectives, requirements, a timeline, and consequences of compliance and noncompliance.
iii. If the remediation plan includes personal counseling, the supervisor avoids dual relationships and invasion of supervisee privacy. (9.d.)

American Psychological Association (2015)

Guidelines for Clinical Supervision in Health Service Psychology

- Supervisors understand and adhere both to the supervisory contract and to program, institutional, and legal policies and procedures related to performance evaluations. (F.1.)
- Supervisors strive to identify potential performance problems promptly, communicate these to the supervisee, and take steps to address these in a timely manner allowing for opportunities to effect change. (F.2.)
- Supervisors are competent in developing and implementing plans to remediate performance problems. (F.3.)
- Supervisors are mindful of their role as gatekeeper and take appropriate and ethical action in response to supervisee performance problems. (F.4.)

psychological distress for faculty and students; concern about heightened resistance and defensiveness in the trainee; the potential for receiving criticism from other faculty or supervisors who were not involved in the trainee's remediation; possible liability; genuine concern for the student's future and success in the program; and lack of administrative support. Perhaps the major deterrent to dismissing a student is the fear of legal reprisal by that student. A way to reduce the risk of liability faced by programs that determine the need to dismiss a student with problematic behavior is to standardize gatekeeping procedures and to critically evaluate and revise program policies (DeLorenzi, 2018a). Baldwin (2018) contends that it is of the utmost importance for supervisors to manage liability risk and at the same time to fulfill their supervisory responsibilities. If supervisors avoid their gatekeeping role, then problematic trainees are likely to enter the profession as incompetent clinicians.

The importance of having continuing documentation of deficiencies or difficulties, feedback provided, efforts toward remediation, and the trainee's response to that feedback and remediation cannot be emphasized enough. Even though there are many difficulties involved in dismissing students from a program for nonacademic reasons, it is critical that students not be allowed to complete a graduate program if they do not successfully remediate personal or interpersonal problems that interfere with their clinical performance. When a determination is made that a dismissal is necessary, Sampson et al. (2013) remind us that it "is important to realize that not everyone has the ability to become a competent therapist and that sometimes admissions decisions might not always result in student graduations, but the learning for that individual could be just as important. The faculty needs to remember to treat the student with dignity and respect despite the need to dismiss that person from the program" (p. 29).

It is a common occurrence for counselors to take on supervisory functions at some point in their careers, and the welfare of future supervisees and their clients might be at stake if an incompetent or impaired trainee is allowed to graduate from a training program. If a trainee is performing satisfactorily in the academic realm but has serious unresolved personal conflicts or demonstrates dysfunctional interpersonal behavior, such as Chelsea in Case Study 7.2, action needs to be taken. If remediation has not worked, dismissal is necessary. Yet this option should be a measure of last resort.

CASE STUDY 7.2: CHELSEA

Muhammad and Alonso, two master's trainees in a mental health counselor training program recently complained to the coordinator of the program that Chelsea, a 3rd-year doctoral student, has been very difficult to work with at their practicum site. Both of them say that Chelsea regularly shows up late and seems arrogant and condescending to them and other trainees at the facility. She is also perceived as manipulative. For instance, in group supervision she claimed that an idea that her coleader "supposedly came up with" was really her own idea. In truth, Chelsea takes credit for other people's ideas and becomes defensive when other trainees confront her. She also makes excuses for her tardiness and fails to take responsibility for her actions. Because Chelsea can be charming and is a straight-A student (which Chelsea makes sure everyone knows), Muhammad and Alonso believe that their site supervisor is blind to her faults and is easily manipulated by her. Moreover, although they cannot confirm this, they fear that their site supervisor may be favoring Chelsea because she is White and they are students of color. Chelsea's behavior frustrates most of the other trainees, who feel angry that their site supervisor cannot see Chelsea's true character and take control of the situation.

The program coordinator at the university is understandably troubled by this news and views this as a multifaceted problem. If the two trainees' allegations are true, he must deal with (a) a potentially personality disordered trainee who may cause great harm to her clients and who has certainly created stress for her colleagues; (b) a site supervisor who failed to do a competent job of gatekeeping and may harbor racist viewpoints and favor White trainees; and (c) faculty members in the training program who have awarded exemplary grades to a student who may be strong academically but lacks the personal qualities to be an effective counselor. Furthermore, the coordinator must make sure that the program's other trainees at that site are getting their needs met.

If you were the coordinator and were informed of this situation, what would you be inclined to do first? How might you approach Chelsea without revealing the identities of the trainees who made the complaint? What actions would you take to determine whether the allegations were true? How would you make provisions for due process for Chelsea? What might you say to Chelsea's site supervisor as well as to your colleagues on the faculty who allowed this impaired student to advance in the program? How would you broach Muhammad and Alonso's concern about the site supervisor's ostensive favoritism toward White trainees (especially without outing them and causing retribution)?

These are just a few questions that must be addressed. Given the complexity of the situation and the number of stakeholders involved, it is imperative to use an ethical decision-making model to determine the best course of action. Being mindful of your obligation to uphold ethical principles while gathering more information about the situation and examining the problem from each person's perspective should increase the likelihood that the dilemma will be resolved in a productive and fair manner.

In Voices From the Field, Jamie Bludworth describes the responsibilities involved in the gatekeeping role and in developing and implementing remediation plans for supervisees who lack professional competence.

 ## VOICES FROM THE FIELD

Remediation in Clinical Supervision

Jamie Bludworth, PhD

Over the course of my career I have had the opportunity to provide clinical supervision to trainees across a wide variety of developmental levels. Engagement with my supervisees as they learn to help their clients in systematic and culturally responsive ways has become one of the most rewarding facets of my daily professional experience. Of course, there is a counterpart to the enjoyable aspects of supervision. For me, that is the gatekeeping role and the challenges associated with development and implementation of effective remediation plans.

Determining when and how to apply a remediation plan is one of the more stressful aspects of clinical supervision. Remediation plans are developed to address skills deficits, performance deficits, or unprofessional behavior. It is important to strike a balance between fairness to one's trainee and the necessity to protect clients and our profession. This is not an easy thing to do. Too often, clinical supervisors allow students to pass through to the next level of training with underdeveloped clinical skills or professional behavior inconsistent with the standards of our profession. The hope is that the next supervisor will engage in gatekeeping and hold the student back. The further a trainee progresses, the more complex remediation issues become along the incremental developmental continuum of clinical difficulty.

To prevent such stressful, and potentially harmful, experiences for supervisees and supervisors alike, it is important to remediate significant skills deficits or behavioral issues early. The development and implementation of a formal remediation plan is the most effective way to encourage growth in our trainees who are struggling, and it also provides a pathway to counsel certain unfit trainees out of the profession. My most difficult experiences with gatekeeping have been when I have waited too long to implement a remediation plan. In my opinion, it is better to err on the side of early remediation than to allow poor performance an opportunity to establish roots.

The most effective remediation plans are written in clear language and are behaviorally anchored. I typically provide a letter notifying the student of the need for a remediation plan and in a separate document describe the steps the student must take to make appropriate progress. The opening paragraph of the letter should outline the purpose of the plan and remind students that the plan is designed to assist them to improve their performance or to modify inappropriate behavior and is not a punitive action. That being said, the opening should emphasize the seriousness of the circumstance and the likely outcomes if the student does not comply with the remediation plan. The second section of the letter should outline and describe the skill deficits or the inappropriate behavior in detail. It is important to link these descriptions to the relevant ACA ethics standards, program handbook, course syllabus, or internship handbook. This can assist the student in better understanding the importance of abiding by the remediation plan. The final paragraph of the letter should provide a description of the support the student will receive from the supervisor and the program to successfully complete the plan. Successful completion of the plan does not necessarily mean the student will be successful in modifying behavior or improving skills. Rather, the plan is intended to support the student and increase the likelihood of improvement in the identified areas. The consequences of failure to complete the plan or failure to make the necessary improvements in skills or behavior must be explicitly stated.

Challenges for Training Programs

High-quality training programs provide a supportive and challenging environment, encourage trainees to build on their life experiences and personal strengths, and provide opportunities for trainees to expand their awareness of self and others. In addition, it is essential that programs provide clear policies and direction to field supervisors regarding supervised clinical training for their trainees. Ideally, trainees will be introduced to various content areas, will acquire a range of clinical skills they can use in working with diverse clients, and will learn how to apply theory to practice through supervised fieldwork experiences.

Sometimes problems emerge as a consequence of working in a flawed system, as Janna Scarborough describes in Voices From the Field. In addition to attending to trainees' counseling skills and other areas of professional development, supervisors may have to teach supervisees how to understand, navigate through, and challenge the system when this is needed.

 VOICES FROM THE FIELD

Advocating for the Needs of Students and the School

Janna Scarborough, PhD

"Everything feels so reactive. The teachers are frustrated, and I am frustrated. I know we could be doing so much more to impact students, and I think I can help, but they only see a narrow view of what I do and, quite frankly, I'm nervous to do more than what I am doing with the students." As a school counselor educator and supervisor, I often hear statements such as this. The underlying theme of these statements is that the school counselor feels powerless to fully step into an advocacy role because of obstacles within the school's structure or policies. For example, I supervised a school counselor who worked in a school with very narrow parameters for removing students from academic time and with a limited role for the counselor with students. The counselor was aware of groups of students who were underperforming, a number of fights were breaking out routinely, and the counselor had identified students that worried the teachers. The school counselor had collected data that clearly identified certain needs, but he was not sure what to do from there.

School counselors work in complex systems with responsibilities to several constituents. School counselors often feel a bit like outsiders, given their unique role, but they understand the need to be part of the system to do their jobs effectively. The school counselor in this example had a clear grasp of the needs of the school and the students, and models and theories to guide his thinking, and was well educated in counseling theory and interventions. My focus in supervision was to help this counselor take a proactive stance working within the system to advocate for the needs of the students and the school as well as for the role of the school counselor.

With this supervisee, I facilitated a discussion regarding his frustrations. We then talked about his perceptions of the feelings and concerns of the teachers and administrators. As he spoke, he empathized with their concerns and the pressure they all felt. He also spoke of the relationships he had been working to develop, not only with the kids but with teachers and one of the assistant principals. He spoke with energy about the ideas they held in common, and he felt inspired when watching them work with students. Building on this positive base, I asked about his ideas and the impact they could have on the school. Somewhat hesitantly he spoke about gathering specific data on the students in the school and bringing in an expert to speak about adverse childhood experiences and trauma-informed care. He thought he could use some of those principles to start groups for students and perhaps also to consult with teachers about how to work with students inside this framework. If the teachers understood this framework, he felt it would not only help the students but also might help the teachers. We discussed the role of the school counselor to advocate, lead, and collaborate and identified some specific steps he could take. We spoke candidly about the challenges but also about the skills, information, and support he could develop as he moved forward.

Multiple Roles and Relationships in the Supervisory Process

The ACES (2011) *Best Practices in Clinical Supervision* document states that clinical supervisors are expected to possess the personal and professional maturity to play multiple roles. Multiple-role relationships in supervision occur when a supervisor has concurrent or consecutive professional or nonprofessional relationships with a supervisee in addition to the supervisor-supervisee relationship. Multiple roles and relationships are common in clinical supervision, they are often unavoidable, and they can be beneficial (Falender, 2017). A beneficial multiple role in supervision is that of a supervisor functioning as a mentor for a supervisee. Multiple roles are often unavoidable, they also have the potential to be problematic. It is the ethical responsibility of supervisors to carefully manage these relationships so they do not result in harm to or exploitation of supervisees. Supervisors need to clarify their roles and to distinguish between flexible and rigid boundaries. If the supervisor does not maintain objectivity, the supervisee will not be able to make maximum use of the process. Supervisors have an obligation to supervisees to openly discuss appropriate boundaries and to work with trainees to help them understand how to balance multiple roles and manage multiple relationships. It is critical for supervisors to serve as effective role models in establishing and maintaining appropriate boundaries (Austin et al., 2017).

Before entering into a multiple relationship with a supervisee, it is good practice for supervisors to consider options, alternatives, and the potential impact of doing so on their objectivity and judgment. If a multiple relationship with a supervisee may be neutral or beneficial, supervisors would do well to explore with the supervisee the pros and cons of the extra relationship before moving ahead (Barnett & Johnson, 2010).

Ethical Standards and Multiple Roles and Relationships

Ethically, supervisors need to clarify their roles and be aware of potential problems that can develop when boundaries are not well managed. Skilled supervisors are able to manage multiple roles and relationships, provide ongoing feedback, and support the supervisee's development while ensuring that the power differential is clear (Falender, 2017). Supervisors who are able to establish appropriate personal and professional boundaries are in a good position to teach supervisees by role modeling how to develop appropriate boundaries.

Supervisees may be affected by the multiple roles of their supervisors, and these blended roles may influence the supervision process. As Herlihy and Corey (2015b) point out, unless the nature of the supervisory relationship is clearly defined, both the supervisor and the supervisee may find themselves in a difficult situation at some point in their relationship. If the supervisor's objectivity becomes impaired, the supervisee will not be able to make maximum use of the process.

The codes of ethics of most professional organizations issue a caution regarding the potential problems involved in multiple relationships. Specifically, the standards caution about the risks involved in any relationships that are likely to impair the judgment or result in exploitation or harm to clients and supervisees. Box 7.2 presents principles from two codes of ethics pertaining to multiple relationships.

Managing Multiple Roles and Relationships in Clinical Supervision

Some multiple relationships may be normative in clinical supervision. Supervisors may collaborate with supervisees on research projects and on journal articles. Although multiple roles and relationships cannot always be avoided, supervisors have the responsibility to manage them in ethical and appropriate ways (Falender & Shafranske, 2017). The crux of the matter is to avoid multiple relationships that could reasonably be expected to impair the professional's objectivity, competence, effectiveness in performing duties, or have a high likelihood of being harmful to the supervisee. It is of the utmost importance that supervisors avoid multiple role relationships in the training and supervisory process that involve an abuse of power. Supervisees are in a vulnerable position because of the power differential and can be harmed by a supervisor who exploits them, misuses power, or crosses appropriate boundaries. Supervisors must not exploit supervisees or take unfair advantage of the power differential that exists in the context of training.

Corey and Corey (2021) point out that the difference between boundary crossings and boundary violations is relevant in the supervisory relationship as well as in the client-therapist relationship. A *boundary crossing* is a departure from standard practice that could potentially benefit the client or supervisee, whereas a *boundary violation* is a serious breach that causes harm to the client or supervisee. Making inappropriate comments or gestures

Box 7.2
ETHICS AND MULTIPLE RELATIONSHIPS

American Counseling Association (2014)

Code of Ethics

Counseling supervisors clearly define and maintain ethical professional, personal, and social relationships with their supervisees. Supervisors consider the risks and benefits of extending current supervisory relationships in any form beyond conventional parameters. In extending these boundaries, supervisors take appropriate professional precautions to ensure that judgment is not impaired and that no harm occurs. (F.3.a.)

Association for Counselor Education and Supervision (2011)

Best Practices in Clinical Supervision

The supervisor clearly defines the boundaries of the supervisory relationship and avoids multiple roles or dual relationships with the supervisee that may negatively influence the supervisee or the supervisory relationship. When this is not possible, the supervisor actively manages the multiplicity of roles to prevent harm to the supervisee and maintain objectivity in working with and evaluating the supervisee. (5.c.iii.)

of a sexual nature to a supervisee would constitute a clear boundary violation. Asking a supervisee to enroll in another class you teach or seeing your trainee at a social event at a professional conference that you are both attending are examples of boundary crossings.

According to Kozlowski and colleagues (2014), "an understanding of the power dynamics in supervision seems essential to maintaining appropriate supervision boundaries" (p. 110), and they add that some supervisors may be oblivious to the power they have over their supervisees. If a supervisor's actions result in harm to a supervisee, this is considered to be a boundary violation (Falender, 2018). Interpersonal boundaries are fluid; they may change over time and may be redefined as supervisors and supervisees continue to work together. As supervisors and supervisees progress in the transition toward becoming professional colleagues, boundaries often take new forms. Even though boundary crossings may not be harmful to supervisees, these crossings can lead to blurring of professional roles and can result in multiple relationships that do have a potential to be harmful. It is critical to take steps to prevent boundary crossings from becoming boundary violations.

Even well-intentioned practitioners must thoughtfully reflect on their actions to determine when crossing a boundary may result in a boundary violation. Failing to practice in accordance with prevailing community standards, as well as other variables such as the role of the client's diagnosis, history, values, and culture, can result in a well-intentioned action being perceived as a boundary violation (Barnett, Lazarus, et al., 2007).

Supervisors play a critical role in helping counselor trainees understand the dynamics of balancing multiple roles and managing multiple relationships. Supervisors have a responsibility to model appropriate boundaries in the supervisory relationship. Supervisors can bring up with their supervisees a range of topics pertaining to boundary concerns supervisees might be having with their clients, such as their reactions to their clients, appropriate boundary crossings, and exercising vigilance in avoiding boundary violations. Although students may learn about multiple relationships during their academic work, it is generally during the time they are engaged in fieldwork experiences and internships that they are required to grapple with boundary issues (Herlihy & Corey, 2015b). In addition, multiple relationships are almost unavoidable with professional peers who are seeking required supervision hours for licensure or certifications.

Prohibiting all forms of multiple relationships is not the best answer to the problem of exploitation of clients or supervisees. This matter is too complex for such a simple solution. Avoiding certain multiple relationships could be potentially harmful to some clients, and therapists should use their professional judgment to determine which multiple relationships should be avoided, which are acceptable, and which are necessary (Zur, 2017). Zur (2007) takes the position that rigid avoidance of all boundary crossings can result in a weakening of the therapeutic alliance. He adds that therapists should avoid crossing boundaries if doing so will likely harm the client or can be expected to impair the therapist's objectivity, judgment, competence, or interfere with the therapeutic effectiveness. Similarly, Kozlowski and colleagues (2014) note that "there are legitimate reasons for supervisors to be scrupulous about their boundaries with supervisees; however, supervisors who hold rigid boundaries can deprive supervisees of deeper mentoring relationships or a more authentic emotional relationship that can be valuable to supervisees learning how to provide psychotherapy" (p. 109). Both professional counselors and supervisors need to clarify their stance on a host of boundary issues they will face and develop a systematic way of making ethical decisions. In Voices From the Field, Barbara Herlihy reminds us of the importance of maintaining appropriate professional boundaries in supervision for the entire duration of the supervisory relationship.

 VOICES FROM THE FIELD

Managing Boundaries in Supervision

Barbara Herlihy, PhD

For many years, I have served as university supervisor to master's-level student interns and as field supervisor to newly minted professional counselors working toward their license. I enjoy supervision and find it rewarding to see interns and new counselors grow in skill and confidence. Occasionally, however, my experience with supervision has been unpleasant—for example, when a supervisee tried hard but failed to progress to an acceptable level or when a very competent supervisee made an egregious mistake that put a client at risk.

I will never forget Mary (a pseudonym), a master's-level supervisee who was counseling in a residential substance abuse treatment facility and working toward her license. She was a "natural" as a therapist, with incredible insights and exceptional skills. Supervising her was fun, and she felt more like a colleague than a supervisee. All was well until she fell in love with a client. He was in the intensive outpatient program, which meant that he left the facility at 5:00 p.m. each day and returned in the morning. He and Mary got together during the evenings. Although they tried to keep their relationship secret and denied that it existed, the attraction was evident to everyone at the facility. It had a negative effect on the dynamics in the treatment groups and made staff meetings uncomfortable for the counselors. After the client left treatment prematurely, Mary admitted the relationship. Knowing that her behavior was a violation of ethics, she relinquished her goal of becoming a licensed counselor and resigned her position. I had felt close to her and had been so impressed by her skills as a counselor that I felt deeply disappointed and let down on a personal level. I was painfully reminded of the importance of boundaries in the supervisory relationship.

The counseling profession's understanding of boundaries, as an ethical issue, has changed significantly over time. Early versions of the *ACA Code of Ethics* cautioned counselors to avoid dual relationships, whereas the current version (ACA, 2014) offers a more nuanced understanding of the complexities of boundary issues. It is now recognized that some forms of dual relating are inevitable and can even be beneficial to a supervisee. Examples might include socializing with a supervisee while attending a professional conference, accepting or offering a token gift to mark a milestone in supervision, or self-disclosing one's own struggles while under supervision. These kinds of "boundary crossings," which are exceptions to a general rule, are made to benefit a particular supervisee in a particular situation and generally are not problematic. "Boundary violations," in contrast, are harmful. Examples of boundary violations would be entering into a romantic or sexual relationship with a supervisee or using a session to discuss one's personal problems rather than provide supervision.

Most supervisory relationships proceed smoothly when boundaries are clearly maintained, with some flexibility. It can be tempting to ignore the boundaries of the relationship as supervisees near the end of supervision, particularly with supervisees who already hold a master's degree. After all, they are evolving into professional colleagues and soon will be peers of the supervisor. Nevertheless, it is vital to remember that a supervisory relationship is never a peer relationship; when evaluation is involved, a power differential always exists. If the boundaries have become too relaxed and the supervisor and supervisee feel personally close, any negative feedback will be difficult to give and receive. The supervisee may become reluctant to share any mistakes made for fear of disappointing the supervisor. I have found it best to maintain professional boundaries until supervision has formally ended, even when I feel quite confident that the supervisee will complete the supervision process successfully. Once the evaluative process is over, peer relationships can be established, although the perceived power differential may persist for a while.

Mentoring

A dynamic way to teach is through the mentoring process. Experienced supervisors are in a position to encourage their supervisees to envision what they might want to accomplish professionally. This role as a mentor can include many informal activities that involve meeting outside the supervision office. Mentors offer encouragement, but they also inspire supervisees to pursue their interests and offer practical suggestions of ways trainees might accomplish their goals. In many graduate programs, supervisors may invite their supervisees and students to be copresenters at a conference or convention.

Supervisors face challenges in balancing the conflicting roles that are sometimes involved in mentoring and evaluating supervisees. Different levels of responsibilities are evident, and different roles must be addressed by the supervisor in managing both mentoring and evaluative roles and functions. The person with greater power (the supervisor) initiates this discussion when suggesting collaborative projects such as copresenting at professional conferences, working together on a research project, or engaging in a collaborative writing project. A potential ethical issue lies in some supervisors not giving supervisees full credit for their participation in the project. This does not have to present a barrier and should not discourage mentoring. Instead, an ongoing process of open discussion can provide the foundation for optimum learning. From our perspective, this collaborative dialogue is far preferable to having a long list of prohibitions about multiple relationships. It is not uncommon for supervisors with lists of prohibitions to be protecting themselves in certain ways. To be a true mentor and allow a supervisee to know you outside of your authoritative role may leave you feeling somewhat vulnerable, but doing so can be beneficial for both your supervisee and you.

Boundary Considerations Between Doctoral Students and Master's Students

Counselor educators and supervisors are expected to teach students about boundary issues and multiple relationships. In counselor education programs, doctoral students often participate in roles with master's-level students in which they hold a position of authority. In their review of the literature on multiple relationships and boundary issues in counselor education programs, Scarborough, Bernard, and Morse (2006) found that little research has been done on the potential for doctoral students to inadvertently or deliberately violate boundaries with master's students. Scarborough and colleagues provided these guidelines for doctoral students who counsel, teach, or supervise master's students:

- The topic of multiple relationships and boundary considerations should be introduced and explored as a part of an orientation to doctoral study. Doctoral students should understand that multiple relationships are part of the territory in their counselor education program. However, they need a safe context in which to explore such relationships so that they do not become boundary violations.
- As a part of the orientation of doctoral students, they should receive instruction concerning the power they may have in relation to master's students in the program. Those responsible for training programs should include curricula to address multiple relationships as a professional issue.
- Multiple relationships between doctoral and master's students should not be discouraged, but ways to benefit from these relationships as well as ways to be vigilant for the potential of boundary violations should be discussed openly.

Socializing Between Supervisors and Supervisees

Supervisors may be asked to engage in some form of socialization with supervisees outside of the academic or clinical setting. For example, supervisors may be asked to attend a dinner or some kind of party that trainees are sponsoring. In the case of professional peer supervision, it may be an office gathering that all are invited to attend. Although this may not be a regular event, supervisors still need to think about the potential issues that could surface and how attending a social function might either enhance or inhibit the professional relationship.

Rather than adopt an all-or-nothing mentality with regard to this issue, we encourage supervisors to be flexible in their thinking and mindful of the ethical ramifications of these actions. The specific context and circumstances must be considered when making decisions about socializing. One may argue, for example, that an educational setting is distinctly different from a clinical setting in that it provides more room for personal and professional interactions with those we train, coach, and mentor, and for whom we serve as role models.

Reflect on your position regarding the possible benefits and risks associated with socializing with supervisees. Do you think such relationships are inevitable in supervision? If they are, what kinds of safeguards could minimize potential harm? More generally, what thoughts do you have about managing multiple roles and relationships in supervision? What have been your experiences with multiple roles as a supervisee?

Managing Boundaries in Social Media

Many agencies have policies regarding the use of social media in client-therapist interactions, but few have policies that address supervisor-supervisee relationships. The responsibility rests with the supervisor to set appropriate boundaries and to model how to carry out these boundaries with professionalism and compassion. Many of the boundary issues that emerge with the use of technology involve limiting 24/7 access and the expectation for immediacy of response that accompanies this access. It is important that supervisors consider their online presence and clearly articulate what is considered appropriate or not appropriate in the supervisory relationship regarding social media. There are few "rights" and "wrongs," but supervisors have individual preferences for technology use. For example, some supervisors may wish to address issues of formality, professionalism in writing, response time, which social media platform is acceptable and under what circumstances, and ethical and legal dimensions associated with social media. In Voices From the Field, Amanda Connell describes difficulties she faced as a supervisee when clients pushed technological boundaries and how supervisors helped her clarify her boundaries and gain a deeper understanding of the perspectives of both client and counselor.

VOICES FROM THE FIELD

Pushing Boundaries With Technology

Amanda Connell, MS

Counseling agencies handle technology policies and challenges in different ways. In my own experience as a supervisee, one of the challenging aspects of developing and maintaining healthy boundaries with clients has been managing communication via text messaging, emails, and phone calls outside of therapy sessions at unreasonable hours of the night. Of these, the most common issue I have encountered pertains to text messages. Agency policies dictate clear limitations on technological communications with clients, and a boundary is established regarding text messages during the initial intake appointment. Text messages may be used only for appointment setting or cancelling or running late. Agency policy also emphasize that client details, concerns, problems, and pictures not be shared via text message and that text messaging not be used to communicate crises, such as suicidality; more appropriate channels are used to communicate urgent and emergency matters.

Clients tend to agree to these boundaries in the beginning of therapy; unfortunately, some clients push these boundaries as time progresses. My supervisors have modeled appropriate and effective wording to address technology boundary pushing with clients, and I appreciate the many opportunities I had to practice boundary setting (and resetting) in role plays during both individual and group supervision. Some supervisors suggested increasing the level of care for clients, such as meeting twice per week instead of once, to better meet their needs. Supervisors also suggested helping clients develop alternative ways to meet their needs, such as journaling and writing letters to me throughout the week that are processed during the next session. Working with clients to expand their ability to tolerate uncomfortable feelings for longer time spans is another method I learned from my supervisors.

Rather than feeling irritated when clients do not adhere to an established boundary, my supervisors have assisted me in understanding the underlying motivations for these behaviors and how they may mirror interpersonal patterns clients engage in with others. I learned how to help clients explore possible meanings behind their need to push boundaries with me as the therapist. For example, clients who are texting information about their life instead of waiting for our session may on some level be testing my availability to them, which they may translate as how much I actually care about them.

Taking this to an even deeper level, this may translate as clients feeling un-
lovable, inadequate, or insecure, which can lead to meaningful therapeutic
interactions and deepen the therapeutic alliance.

By understanding my reactions to clients pushing boundaries, my supervisors have helped me identify countertransference issues, which has contributed to my growth personally and professionally. My supervisors have often
aided my self-exploration around the issue of clients who frequently push
boundaries, and they have guided me into transforming my own frustration
into understanding and compassion when I have needed to reset boundaries
with clients.

In Case Study 7.3, Mike confronts a common dilemma involving multiple roles and
relationships. Is this a clear boundary situation, or is it an "it depends" kind of situation?
Is Nattapong crossing the line in making the invitation?

CASE STUDY 7.3: MIKE

Mike is a marriage and family therapist and teaches in the master's-level human
services program at a state university. He is currently supervising Nattapong,
who recently relocated to the United States from Thailand to pursue his postsecondary education. Nattapong is enrolled in the human services program
and does counseling at the university's community clinic. Mike is also the instructor in one of Nattapong's classes, and they frequently see each other at
academic and social functions sponsored by the program. Nattapong respects
and admires Mike and sees him as a role model for himself. During a supervision session, Nattapong invited Mike and his wife over to his house for dinner.
Mike inquires about the purpose of the dinner and whether other students or
faculty will be present. When he learns that it is purely a social invitation and
that Mike and his wife are the only ones invited, Mike decides to politely decline. Nattapong explains how much he admires Mike and how he just wanted
to invite him over to show his appreciation for all the help he has received.
Mike realizes that Nattapong is puzzled by his decline of the invitation. To help
clear up Nattapong's confusion, Mike returns to a discussion of the parameters
of the supervisory relationship as outlined in the supervision contract.

Think about how you might explain these boundaries to a supervisee. How might the
supervisee's culture or some other aspect of diversity affect your explanation? What do
the standards and regulations say about this? Would this situation be different if the
supervisor or the supervisee had been female? Knowing that you want to maintain appropriate boundaries is the easy part; looking our supervisees in the eye and saying no
without rejecting them is more difficult.

Multiple relationships in the academic and clinical setting are common, but the respective roles of supervisee and supervisor must be clearly defined (Herlihy & Corey,
2015b), and this is best done in writing. It is the responsibility of the supervisor to define
the relationship, to discuss with the supervisee when boundaries are changing, and to
protect the welfare of the supervisee. If the situation seems unmanageable with a given
supervisee, the supervisor can either try to reduce the number of situations in which
they are together or seek another supervisor for the supervisee.

Sexual Attraction in Supervision

Ordinarily, attraction, in and of itself, is not problematic. It is what individuals do with
the attraction that determines the appropriateness or inappropriateness of these reac-

tions. The supervisor is responsible for providing a safe learning environment for supervisees. It is also a supervisor's job to train supervisees about sexual attraction in a way that encourages them to become aware of their attractions and work through them in a professional manner. Supervisees are strongly encouraged to discuss such matters in supervision, but it is largely the responsibility of the supervisor to create a safe climate that will allow supervisees to discuss matters of sexual attraction.

If you find yourself sexually attracted to your supervisees, it is important that you examine your feelings and consider that sexual harassment could be a real issue for you. If you are attracted often and to many different trainees, you cannot provide a safe place for supervisees to discuss issues of sexual attraction with clients. It is imperative that you deal with this matter in your own therapy and supervision. Consider these questions: "What is going on in my own life that may be creating this intense attraction?" "What am I missing in my personal life?" "How might I be using my professional work as a way to fulfill my personal needs?"

Sexual Intimacies Between Supervisor and Supervisee

Although multiple relationships are common in university settings, sex between students and their professors and supervisors is forbidden by ethical standards. As in the case of sexual relations between therapists and clients, sex in the supervisory relationship invariably results in a loss of objectivity and an abuse of power because of the difference in status between supervisees and supervisors. Specific standards of the various professional organizations regarding sexual intimacies in the supervisory relationship are summarized in Box 7.3.

It is the supervisor's responsibility to establish and maintain appropriate boundaries and to explore with the trainee ways to prevent potential problems associated with boundary issues. If problems do arise, the supervisor has the responsibility to take steps to resolve them in an ethical manner. Supervisors who engage in sexual behavior with supervisees are behaving inappropriately and unethically. Acting on sexual attractions with supervisees can lead to a multitude of negative outcomes for the supervisee, both personally and professionally.

The core ethical issue is the difference in power and status between supervisor and supervisee and the exploitation of that power. When supervisees first begin counseling, they are typically naive and uninformed with respect to the complexities of therapy. They frequently regard their supervisors as experts and depend on them in a way that may make it difficult for supervisees to resist sexual advances. Supervisees may disclose personal concerns and intense emotions during supervision, much as they might in a therapeutic situation. The openness of supervisees and the trust they place in their supervisors can be exploited by supervisors who choose to satisfy their own psychological or sexual needs at the expense of their supervisees.

Sexual Intimacies Between Supervisee and Client

In addition to sexual attractions or sexual intimacies between supervisors and supervisees, there is the matter of supervisees being attracted to a client or even the possibility of a supervisee becoming sexually involved with a client. It is clear that this is a matter for supervision and that the supervisor bears both ethical and legal responsibilities for the actions of his or her supervisees. Supervisees may be reluctant to admit that they are attracted to a client, or a client to them. This dilemma highlights the importance of supervisors creating a safe climate where supervisees are more likely to bring into supervision feelings they might be having toward clients. Any form of sexual intimacy between supervisees and their clients is inappropriate and unethical. However, sexual attractions may very well occur, and being able to talk about this in supervision is of the utmost importance (see Case Study 7.4).

Box 7.3
SEXUAL INTIMACIES IN
THE SUPERVISORY RELATIONSHIP

American Counseling Association (2014)

Code of Ethics

Sexual or romantic interactions or relationships with current supervisees are prohibited. This prohibition applies to both in person and electronic interactions or relationships. (F.3.b.)

Counseling supervisors do not condone or subject supervisees to sexual harassment. (F.3.c.)

American Psychological Association (2017)

Ethical Principles of Psychologists and Code of Conduct

Psychologists do not engage in sexual relationships with students or supervisees who are in their department, agency, or training center or over whom the psychologists have or are likely to have evaluative authority. (7.07.)

American Association for Marriage and Family Therapy (2015)

Code of Ethics

Marriage and family therapists do not engage in sexual intimacy with students or supervisees during the evaluative or training relationship between the therapist and student or supervisee. (4.3.)

American Mental Health Counselors Association (2015)

Code of Ethics

All forms of sexual behavior with supervisees, students, or employees are unethical. (III.A.3.)

National Association of Social Workers (2017)

Code of Ethics

(a) Social workers who function as supervisors or educators should not engage in sexual activities or contact (including verbal, written, electronic, or physical contact) with supervisees, students, trainees, or other colleagues over whom they exercise professional authority.

(b) Social workers should avoid engaging in sexual relationships with colleagues when there is potential for a conflict of interest. Social workers who become involved in, or anticipate becoming involved in, a sexual relationship with a colleague have a duty to transfer professional responsibilities, when necessary, to avoid a conflict of interest.

CASE STUDY 7.4: SHANDRA

Shandra is supervising George, a 27-year-old prelicensed social worker. George has been seeing about 15 clients per week in a group practice setting. One of his clients, Connie, is in therapy because she is dissatisfied with her current job as a cashier at a local grocery store and the dangerous conditions she has had to endure during the COVID-19 pandemic, such as inadequate access to protective gear. She is a kind woman, approximately the same age as George, and is from the same area in Georgia where George grew up. They have a number of things in common, including attending the same church. George enjoys working with Connie as a client and has compassion for her struggles. He thinks he can be a mentor in helping her decide how to proceed with changing her path and pursuing a college degree. He looks forward to seeing her every week, and he is beginning to feel sexually attracted to her. George discusses all of his cases with Shandra in supervision sessions, and he finally admits to his supervisor that he is sexually attracted to Connie.

Shandra realizes that she is responsible for the actions of her supervisee. She knows that her first responsibility is to ensure that Connie is protected from any harm that George's feelings of sexual attraction might do. In assisting George in working through this problem, Shandra wonders out loud whether it would be helpful or harmful for George to discuss his feelings of attraction with Connie. She asks George how that would affect the client and the therapeutic relationship. George realizes that telling Connie about his attraction will affect the level of trust he has with Connie and will change the therapeutic relationship forever. If George can resolve his feelings regarding Connie in supervision, he feels there is no reason to bring it up with her. If he cannot and is faced with referring Connie to another counselor, he may wish to discuss the reason for wanting to make the referral with Connie.

Shandra has established a safe and open environment in supervisory sessions, and she helps George explore and understand how and why this attraction has occurred, why it is not acceptable to act on his feelings of attraction, how to deal with this situation now, and how to handle similar situations in the future. With Shandra's help, George deals with the situation and learns from it in a way that will help him in his future professional work.

If you were in Shandra's shoes, what would you be inclined to say to George if he seemed to be in denial about his attraction to Connie? What are the potential consequences for you, George, and his client if George acts on his feelings? Consider how the social fabric has shifted with the "Me Too" movement and how the significance of your responsibility and liability for supervisees' interactions and possible attractions have increased in this climate. What actions might you have to take as George's supervisor if you suspected that he was not being forthcoming with you about the nature of his interactions with Connie? How would you feel about taking these actions?

Feelings of attraction and infatuation might well overtake reason and logic. What we typically hear from someone who has become involved with a client or a supervisee is, "I know about boundary issues, but this is different; we really do love each other, and before I realized it we were intimately involved." Somehow they think this is different and that the rules don't apply because it is love.

Supervisees need to feel safe to discuss and explore their feelings, and they need to know the consequences of what will happen if they act on their attraction to a client. Supervisees should be encouraged to learn as much as they can about their feelings and needs and what role they play in counseling. Boundary issues and sexual attraction should be a regular topic for discussion among supervisors and their supervisees and should be covered in the supervision contract.

If sex between the supervisee and the client is occurring, it is not sufficient to tell your supervisee that sex with clients is forbidden. The supervisor has a legal and ethical obligation to do everything possible to intervene immediately. Ethical standards provide guidance regarding ethical misconduct of a peer (in this instance, your supervisee). These standards include possible actions such as attempting to remedy the situation through direct discussion with the peer involved, reporting to a direct supervisor, reporting to an ethics committee, or taking administrative action such as client referral, probation, mandatory counseling, and so on. In addition, you are responsible to ensure that the client is not further damaged and is referred to another therapist to deal with the incident and to continue therapy. In all likelihood, you will be required to initiate further action with the supervisee. The specific actions you take are dependent on a number of variables, including the ethics codes that apply, licensing and other legal regulations, and the policies of your agency or institution. As a supervisor, you are legally vulnerable if you fail to take appropriate actions. (See Chapter 8 for an in-depth review of legal responsibilities.)

Combining Supervision and Counseling

The differences between supervision and providing personal counseling to supervisees are not always clear. In the literature on supervision and in professional codes, there is basic agreement that the supervision process should concentrate on the supervisee's professional development rather than on personal concerns. Supervision and counseling have different purposes; however, there is a lack of consensus and clarity regarding the degree to which supervisors can ethically deal with the personal issues of supervisees. As a part of the informed consent process in supervision, boundaries need to be discussed and clarified regarding how personal issues will be addressed in supervision. If the nature of the supervisory relationship is not clearly delineated from the beginning, both supervisor and supervisee might well find themselves in difficult positions at some later point. If supervisors overextend the boundaries of a supervisory relationship, their objectivity can become impaired, and the supervisee will then be inhibited from making full use of the supervision process.

It is expected that a supervisee's personal issues will be dealt with appropriately in supervision and that referrals will be made to a therapist when a supervisee experiences a personal problem that interferes with providing adequate care to the client. It is the supervisor's responsibility to help trainees identify how their personal dynamics are likely to influence their work with clients, but it is not the proper role of supervisors to serve as personal counselors for supervisees. Combining the roles of supervising and counseling often presents conflicts. Serving in both roles may well constitute a conflict of interest because those roles have some different and possibly contradictory goals and methods.

As personal problems or limitations of supervisees become evident, supervisors are ethically obliged to encourage and challenge supervisees to face and deal with these barriers that could inhibit their potential as therapists (Herlihy & Corey, 2015b). Sometimes the personal concerns of supervisees are part of the problem presented in supervision. At these times, supervision might well involve assisting supervisees in identifying their concerns so that the client's therapy is not negatively affected. The purpose of discussing supervisees' personal issues—which may seem like therapy—is to facilitate supervisees' ability to work successfully with clients, not to resolve their problems. With this awareness, supervisees can seek personal therapy to work through the problem rather than using supervision as a place for therapy. The best course for supervisors to follow is to make a referral to another professional. The supervisor should not offer in-depth personal therapy to the supervisee.

Good supervision is therapeutic in the sense that the supervisory process involves dealing with supervisees' personal limitations, blind spots, and impairments so clients are not harmed. Working with difficult clients tends to affect supervisees in personal ways. Certainly, it is a challenge for both trainees and experienced therapists to recognize and deal with transference in effective therapeutic ways. Countertransference issues can work either in favor of or against the establishment of effective client-therapist relationships.

We recommend that graduate students participate in personal therapy while they are in training as a way to expand their self-awareness, foster their personal and professional development, and enhance the supervisory relationship. We also believe it is appropriate for supervisors to encourage their supervisees to consider personal therapy with another professional as a route to becoming more effective both personally and professionally. Counselors-in-training can greatly profit from a self-exploration experience that opens them up to insight and teaches them about vulnerability, discipline, and freedom in their professional training.

Changing Roles and Relationships

Many of our former students and supervisees are now our valued colleagues. In fact, these former students and supervisees might be working with us in the same agency, a private practice setting, or in a department on the same faculty. It is important to have open discussions to sort out any issues that might get in the way of present collegial relationships. To illustrate how roles and relationships change over time, Jerry Corey shares his work history in this Personal Perspective.

 ## JERRY COREY'S PERSONAL PERSPECTIVE

For close to 50 years I have taught courses in an undergraduate human services program, and for 8 of those years, I served as the program coordinator in addition to teaching counseling courses. At least a dozen graduates from our program later joined the faculty in our human services program. This could have presented problems when I was the coordinator of the program because part of my administrative responsibility involved visiting the classes our faculty taught to evaluate their teaching performance. There was not a single incident, however, in which this changing relationship (from student to colleague) became problematic. Perhaps what averted conflicts was an open discussion about potential difficulties.

Of course, former students experienced an adjustment period when assuming their new role. When some of these new faculty members began, especially if they were fresh out of graduate school, their confidence in their ability to teach waffled a bit. I invited them to talk to some of the seasoned faculty members or to discuss their concerns with me. Had we not had these discussions, I am quite certain this would have interfered with their ability to teach effectively.

To illustrate how roles may change, let me cite the example of two full-time faculty members I had the responsibility of evaluating for tenure and promotion purposes. As I did with all the part-time faculty members, I visited their classes and wrote detailed letters each semester based on their teaching performance, scholarly work, contribution to the department, and professional endeavors. In both cases, these individuals eventually received tenure and, over the course of the years, progressed from assistant professor to full professor. As the program coordinator, I was required to write an evaluation letter and recommend (or not recommend) tenure status and advancement in academic rank. Fortunately, these two faculty members were of the highest caliber, which meant I could honestly write positive evaluations and could recommend tenure and promotion.

But what if their performance in the classroom had been substandard? What if they had many conflicts with their students? What if they had not produced any journal articles or done any of the research required for advancement? What if they were not contributing to the mission of the department? Certainly, it would be difficult if I were in the position of having to write negative evaluations. To avoid such awkward situations, my guiding principle has always been to initiate open and ongoing discussions about any problem areas early. Waiting until a decision time has arrived to inform faculty of their deficiencies is, in my opinion, unethical.

After many years, one of these professors assumed the role of chairperson of the program, and our formal relationship was reversed. A few years later, she became the dean of our school and my direct administrative supervisor. Changing roles and relationships cannot always be avoided, and roles and relationships do evolve over time. It is absolutely necessary that trust has been established so that everyone concerned feels free to express their desires, frustrations, concerns, wants, and complaints. No simple formula can solve all potential multiple role and relationship concerns. We need to learn how to identify potential problems and then collaborate to formulate guidelines that will result in adjusting to any changes in roles and relationships.

For further reading on changing roles and relationships and how to address them in counseling and supervision, see *Personal Reflections on Counseling* (Corey, 2020).

Summary

Supervisors must have the education and training to carry out many different roles—consultant, teacher, evaluator, mentor, role model, counselor, coach, advocate, and adviser. Continuing education in supervision is often required to fill in the gaps in one's graduate training. In this chapter, we have looked at the rights and responsibilities of supervisees, the roles and responsibilities of supervisors, the importance of informed consent in the supervisory relationship, becoming competent as a supervisor, and handling supervisees who function below an acceptable standard in academic and personal areas. We also addressed managing multiple roles and relationships in the supervision process. Challenges include establishing clear and appropriate boundaries, avoiding sexual intimacies between supervisors and supervisees, distinguishing between supervision and counseling, learning how to make supervision personal without converting supervisory sessions into therapy sessions, and understanding the changing roles and relationships from being a supervisee to becoming a colleague.

Supervisors are responsible for informing their supervisees of the relevant legal, ethical, and professional standards for clinical practice. Informed consent is a crucial part of supervision, and this process is best achieved by written documents and ongoing discussions between supervisors and supervisees. The challenge of multiple role relationships in the supervisory process is to avoid the potential for abuse of power and to learn how to effectively manage multiple roles and relationships.

SUGGESTED ACTIVITIES

1. Role-play a situation that involves a supervisor realizing that he or she does not have the competence required to help supervisees with certain client populations. Discuss how the supervisor might deal with the situation.
2. Set up a role play in which the supervisor does not provide any information about how supervision works, how the evaluation process will be handled, or what the expectations are for adequate performance. Critique what is being enacted and discuss some appropriate alternatives.

3. Investigate some of the community agencies in your area to learn what supervision they offer to interns and to newly hired practitioners. Document your reactions in a journal.

4. Interview at least one clinical supervisor to determine what he or she considers the most pressing ethical issue in the supervisory relationship. Ask questions to determine what process this supervisor uses to make decisions about ethical issues in his or her practice.

5. In small groups, formulate guidelines for handling incompetent or impaired supervisees. What kinds of remedial measures can your group suggest? If attempts at remediation fail to bring about change in problematic supervisees, what other steps can your group devise?

6. In small groups, explore the challenges involved in learning how to manage multiple roles and relationships in the supervisory relationship. Have each group pick one of the following areas and develop guidelines for practice:

   a. Socialization between supervisors and supervisee: What kind of socialization, if any, might be beneficial and appropriate in the context of supervision?

   b. Combining supervision and counseling: How can personal problems be addressed in supervision without changing supervisory sessions into therapy sessions?

   c. Helping supervisees deal with sexual attractions: What are some ways that a supervisor can offer help to supervisees who report experiencing a sexual attraction to a client? How can supervision be made safe in a manner that will allow for an open discussion of sexual attractions?

7. An eight-step ethical decision-making model is presented early in this chapter. Use this model to work through the two ethical dilemmas that follow. For each one, address the following questions:

   a. What are the potential ethical issues involved in the situation?

   b. What ethical codes and laws appear to be relevant in this case?

   c. Brainstorm possible and probable courses of action to take. What are the likely consequences of each course of action?

   d. What are the most promising and least promising courses of action? Explain your response.

   e. Ultimately, what course of action would you choose?

Dilemma 1: You work as a clinical supervisor at a high school and are supervising Derek, a school counseling trainee who seems to be doing exemplary work. He appears to be responsible, intelligent, interpersonally skilled, and well liked among the staff and students attending the school. In passing, you happen to overhear two trainees complain to each other about how inappropriate Derek has been with them. He reportedly has made sexually inappropriate comments to each of them on a number of occasions; however, neither of them has informed the staff. You must decide what to do with this information that you overheard.

Dilemma 2: You work as a clinical supervisor at a community mental health center. Harriet, who has been diagnosed with borderline personality disorder, is being counseled by one of your trainees. During a supervision session, your trainee reveals that Harriet is "up to her usual behavior again and is lashing out at people. This time she is making accusations that the staff psychiatrist seduced her." Your trainee seems to immediately dismiss the possibility that the accusation could be true. In your role as supervisor, how should you proceed?

CHAPTER 8

———————

Legal and Risk Management Issues in Supervision

FOCUS QUESTIONS

1. What are the supervisor's responsibilities with regard to legal issues?
2. Why is it important for a supervisor to have a working knowledge of both ethics codes and laws pertaining to supervision?
3. What are the major legal issues concerning clinical supervision?
4. How do ethical and legal issues pertaining to supervision differ?
5. Why is informed consent a critical aspect of clinical supervision?
6. If you drafted an informed consent document for your supervisees, what elements would you include?
7. How might supervisors use supervision as a risk management strategy?
8. What are the legal and risk management issues surrounding the use of technology in supervision?
9. What is "disciplinary supervision," and how does it differ from supervision in a training program?
10. What are some ethical and legal issues related to counseling minors? How can the professional standards provide guidance to school counselors?

Some professionals view ethical and legal aspects of clinical practice and supervision as virtually synonymous; however, this is not always the case. In addition to being well versed in ethical matters (see Chapter 7), supervisors must have a comprehensive understanding of the laws that limit their practice as supervisors and the practice of their supervisees. Ethical guidelines serve as the basis for the standard of care in supervision, but a good understanding of risk management strategies pertaining to all aspects of supervision is essential. Unethical practice often implies illegal conduct, but numerous actions that would be considered unethical are not illegal. For example, bartering and accepting gifts from clients may pose ethical problems and can lead to exploitation, but

We appreciate the following professionals who reviewed this chapter and provided suggestions for revision: Mary Hermann, JD, PhD; Theordore P. Remley Jr., JD, PhD; and Anne Marie "Nancy" Wheeler, JD.

generally these practices are not illegal. In some instances, conflicts may arise between ethics and the law, as reflected in the ethics codes of professional associations (see Box 8.1 for examples). It is important for supervisors to separate the legal aspects of supervision from ethical considerations.

In this chapter, we provide a brief legal primer for supervisors and a risk management model to address the many liabilities involved in supervisory practice. Definitions and brief discussions of legal constructs that apply to the supervisory process are provided to educate you about specific legalities directly related to the supervisor's role and responsibilities. Emphasis is placed on preventative actions you can take to protect yourself and your organization.

Legal Primer

Legal aspects of supervision may seem overwhelming at first. Most helping professionals are not versed in legal theory and practice, have little coursework in this area, and find the concept of liability quite frightening. Many mental health professionals perceive liability primarily in light of the prospect of losing their license to practice. This narrow view leaves supervisors open to legal risks.

Legal Principles That Affect Supervisory Practice

Supervisors must have a working knowledge of the basic legal principles that affect supervisory practice. Let's start by defining some basic terms fundamental to understanding legal issues in supervision. In following sections, we examine these concepts in some detail.

Box 8.1
ETHICS CODES AND STANDARDS
REGARDING LEGAL ISSUES

American Counseling Association (2014)

Code of Ethics

Counselors who engage in the use of distance counseling, technology, and social media, within their counseling practice understand that they may be subject to laws and regulations of both the counselor's practice location and the client's place of residence. Counselors ensure that their clients are aware of pertinent legal rights and limitations governing the practice counselors counseling across state lines or international boundaries. (H.1.b.)

Standards for Supervisees: Supervisors make their supervisees aware of professional and ethical standards and legal responsibilities. (F.4.c.)

American Psychological Association (2017)

Ethical Principles of Psychologists and Code of Conduct

If psychologists' ethical responsibilities conflict with law, regulations, or other governing legal authority, psychologists clarify the nature of the conflict, make known their commitment to the Ethics Code, and take reasonable steps to resolve the conflict consistent with the General Principles and Ethical Standards of the Ethics Code. Under no circumstances may this standard be used to justify or defend violating human rights. (1.02.)

Standard of care: The normative or expected practice performed in a given situation by a given group of professionals.

Statutory liability: Specific written standard with penalties imposed, written directly into the law.

Malpractice: The failure to render professional services or to exercise the degree of skill ordinarily expected of other professionals in a similar situation.

Negligence: Failure to observe (or lack of awareness of) the proper standard of care.

Negligence liability: Failure to provide an established standard of care.

Vicarious liability: Responsibility for the actions of others based on a position of authority and control.

Strict liability: Holds clinical supervisors responsible for the behavior of the supervisee without any need to establish that supervisors were negligent or careless in their supervision.

Direct liability: Responsibility for your own actions of authority and control over others.

Privileged communication: The privilege allowed an individual to have confidential communications with a professional that prevents the courts from requiring revelation of confidential communication.

Duty to warn: The obligation of the mental health professional to make a good-faith effort to contact the identified victim of a client's serious threats of harm and/or to notify law enforcement of the threat (Welfel et al., 2009).

Duty to protect: The obligation of a therapist to take action to protect a threatened third party; the therapist usually has other options besides warning that person of the risk of harm, such as hospitalizing the client or intensifying outpatient treatment (Welfel et al., 2009).

Duty to report: The obligation of a therapist to report abuse or suspected abuse of children, older persons, or as referred to in some states, vulnerable adults or vulnerable individuals, in a timely manner.

These definitions vary somewhat by state; therefore, supervisors must be aware of their respective state laws regarding these topics.

Supervisors should have a working knowledge of ethics codes and all relevant laws in their state regarding the practice of supervision. Ignorance of the law is not an acceptable excuse and certainly no defense against liability. In addition, it is important to stay abreast of the case law and theories upon which liability may attach. This type of ongoing professional development, along with supervisors' clinical expertise, is needed to provide a sound and complete risk management plan to protect clients, trainees, and supervisors.

Standard of Care

At this time, courts are defining the standard of care in supervision primarily by reviewing the licensing statutes and case law because there is neither consensus nor an explicit statement of the standard of care in psychotherapy supervision by mental health professionals. Variations in the codes of ethics and practice among disciplines make it difficult for the courts to establish liability because clear guidelines are not universal. Even specialty areas within the counseling field that share the *ACA Code of Ethics* (ACA, 2014) may have distinctly different standards of care or normative practices for some situations.

A sample scenario was provided to a group of counselors attending a state conference regarding the possible liability of the actions of a school counselor intervening with a 13-year-old student who eventually committed suicide. There was great variation in the responses to the counselor's intervention in the scenario based on the type of counselor responding. For example, the perceptions of school counselors and mental health counselors differed tremendously with regard to the actions they believed should be taken based primarily on the setting of the incident. Counselors based in schools are more likely to have a normative protocol regarding steps to be taken with a student reporting suicidal ideation. These steps are centered around assessing immediacy, reporting administratively, informing legal guardians, and making appropriate referrals for care. In clinical settings, the same layers of structure may not be present. A clinician is normatively expected to conduct a lethality assessment, use clinical judgment regarding immediacy and reporting requirements, and make a determination regarding continued monitoring and treatment. This determination may include initiating hospitalization. This is but one example of the many differences we might find in the standard of care in the helping professions.

Six underlying principles must be considered when establishing standard of care for supervisory practice (Corey et al., 2019; Kitchener, 1984):

- *Autonomy:* promote self-determination or the freedom of clients to choose their own direction; integrity; and respect for one's rights and dignity
- *Nonmaleficence:* avoid doing harm, which includes refraining from actions that risk hurting clients, either intentionally or unintentionally
- *Beneficence:* promote good for others
- *Justice:* foster fairness or a means of providing equal treatment to all people
- *Fidelity:* make honest promises and honor commitments to those served
- *Veracity:* practitioners are required to deal honestly and truthfully with clients

Together, these six principles can serve as a foundation for developing a standard of care in practice.

The various codes of ethics emphasize competence, confidentiality, informed consent, monitoring, evaluation, and feedback in the supervisory process. Beyond these themes, the professional codes have little to say about legal issues. Saccuzzo (1997) reported that these five major ethical principles were found repeatedly in statutes, case law, ethics codes, and the professional literature: (1) competence, (2) confidentiality, (3) avoidance of dual relationships, (4) welfare of the consumer, and (5) informed consent. Standard of care in mental health supervision is based on these concepts. Examples of standards of care that can be extracted through review of licensing statutes, case law, and clinical practice include supervising only within your areas of competence based on training and experience, providing a supervisory contract, providing appropriate feedback and evaluation, consistently monitoring and controlling supervisees' activities, accurately documenting supervisory activities, and providing consistent and timely supervisory sessions.

Statutory Liability

State licensing laws provide the basis for statutory liability. This type of liability is relatively clear; the standards are explicit, as are the penalties imposed if the law is broken. Statutes differ state by state, however, so supervisors must have a clear understanding of the specific statutes they must abide by in the state in which they practice and supervise. For example, state laws vary with regard to how supervisors are to monitor the performance of supervisees, whether supervisees may pay their supervisors for supervision or office space, restrictions on advertising by supervisees, and documentation required in the supervisory relationship.

Malpractice and Negligence

The word *malpractice* means "bad practice." Malpractice is the failure to render professional services or to exercise the degree of skill that is ordinarily expected of other professionals in a similar situation. Malpractice is a legal concept involving negligence that results in injury or loss to the client.

Professional *negligence* can result from unjustified departure from usual practice or from failing to exercise proper care in fulfilling one's responsibilities (Corey et al., 2019). Negligence may be found when one has failed to observe the proper standard of care in supervision. For a malpractice claim to succeed, the following four elements must be present: (a) A professional relationship with the supervisee or supervisor must have existed; (b) the supervisee or supervisor must have acted in a negligent or improper manner or have deviated from the standard of care; (c) the supervisee or client must have suffered harm or injury, which must be demonstrated; and (d) a causal relationship between the negligence or breach of duty and the damage or injury claimed by the client or supervisee must be established. The burden of proof that harm took place is the client's, or the supervisee's if the claim is filed by the supervisee against the supervisor, and the plaintiff must demonstrate that all four elements applied in his or her situation. Here is a brief discussion of each of the four elements as described in *Black's Law Dictionary* (Garner, 1999; Wheeler & Bertram, 2019).

1. *Duty.* There are two aspects of establishing a legal duty: One is the existence of a special relationship, and the other is the nature of that special relationship. A duty exists when a therapist (or supervisor) implicitly or explicitly agrees to provide professional services.
2. *Breach of duty.* Once the plaintiff proves that a professional relationship did exist, he or she must show that the duty was breached. Therapists (or supervisors) have specific responsibilities that involve using ordinary and reasonable care and diligence, applying knowledge and skill to a case, and exercising good judgment. If the therapist (or supervisor) failed to provide the appropriate standard of care, the duty was breached. In supervision, this breach of duty may involve either actions taken by the supervisee or supervisor or a failure to take certain precautions.
3. *Injury.* Plaintiffs must prove that they were harmed in some way—physically, relationally, psychologically—and that actual injuries were sustained. In supervision, injuries can occur to either the supervisees or the clients they serve. An example of such an injury is lack of due process when terminating a supervisee from a training program.
4. *Causation.* Plaintiffs must demonstrate that the therapist's (or supervisor's) breach of duty was the proximate cause of the injury suffered. The test in this case lies in proving that the harm would not have occurred if it were not for the therapist's (or supervisor's) actions or omissions.

One example of negligence in the standard of care is illustrated in Case Study 8.1.

CASE STUDY 8.1: KATHLEEN

Kathleen is a trainee providing direct services to children in an inpatient setting under the supervision of Dr. Snow. Kathleen is seeing a young boy, Jamie, with very serious acting-out behaviors and a disturbing family history. Jamie has been living with his aunt while his mom has been in a drug rehabilitation facility. Kathleen makes the decision to disclose Jamie's shared family information with his aunt to "help" with Jamie's transition at discharge. Dr. Snow is not aware of this disclosure, which is a breach of confidentiality because Jamie's aunt is not his legal guardian. Jamie's aunt uses this information in a custody hearing to help Jamie's father gain primary custody of the boy.

In this hypothetical case study, Jamie's mother might file suit against Kathleen and the inpatient clinic for breach of confidentiality. In this instance, both Kathleen and Dr. Snow would likely be in violation of both ethical and legal standards. What components of a risk management plan might help to reduce the chances of breaches of confidentiality?

Negligence Liability

Negligence liability is not as clear cut as statutory liability and is seen by many as a greater danger to supervisors. The construct of negligence liability is a process based on two components. The first step in the process of claiming negligence is establishing a standard of care. In mental health law, standard of care is derived primarily from licensing statutes, case law, and ethics codes of conduct. In fact, many state laws include specific ethics codes as part of the statute. The second step is determining negligence. One cannot be found liable without first being found negligent. Only when there is an established standard of care and one has failed to observe the proper standard of care, and therefore has been negligent, can there be a charge of liability. This charge must be proven in court; simply making claims against or accusing the supervisor is not sufficient. Supervisors need to have a working knowledge of the components of negligence liability when providing supervision (Wheeler & Bertram, 2019).

There are two main types of negligence liability: *vicarious liability*, in which the supervisor is held liable for the actions of the supervisee regardless of any fault on the part of the supervisor, and *direct liability*, in which the supervisor is held directly liable for his or her own negligent supervisory practice. Bernard and Goodyear (2019) indicate that supervisors bear both direct liability and vicarious liability. Direct liability can be incurred when the actions of supervisors are the cause for harm. For example, supervisors may give trainees inappropriate direction about treatment or give tasks to trainees that exceed their competence. Vicarious liability pertains to the responsibilities supervisors have to oversee the actions of their supervisees. Supervisors are liable for the actions of their supervisees because they have a professional relationship with supervisees. From both a legal and ethical standpoint, trainees are not expected to assume final responsibility for clients; rather, their supervisors are legally expected to carry the decision-making responsibility and liability.

Polychronis and Brown (2016) have broadened the concept of vicarious liability by applying the legal doctrine of *strict liability* to clinical supervision, which implies that clinical supervisors are fully responsible for supervisees' actions in a professional realm regardless of the supervisees' misbehavior. The doctrine of strict liability holds clinical supervisors responsible without any need to establish that they were negligent. Even if supervisors can prove that they provided exemplary supervision, they may bear legal responsibility for any wrong caused by a supervisee.

Vicarious Liability

A supervisor may be held vicariously liable under one of three separate doctrines: respondeat superior, the borrowed servant rule, or enterprise liability. Let's examine each of these doctrines.

Respondeat Superior
One who occupies a position of authority or control over another may be held legally liable for damages caused by the subordinate (Wheeler & Bertram, 2019). In terms of supervision, this means that supervisors can be held liable for the actions of supervisees. This liability pertains to whether or not the supervisor breaches a duty. Falender and Shafranske (2017) claim that ensuring competence in client care involves a fragile balance between the supervisor's competence and the level of trust in the supervisee's abil-

ity. In this balance, the supervisor must bear the responsibility for determining when a supervisee may be trusted to perform a professional duty, given the level of competence that has been assessed to conduct the activity responsibly. It appears that the doctrine of respondeat superior is inherent to the practice of supervision. Case Study 8.2 illustrates this doctrine and points out that supervisors are liable even when they lack specific knowledge about the supervisee's client.

CASE STUDY 8.2: VAIBHAV

Vaibhav is a supervisee providing therapy to a young woman in her early 20s who has met the criteria for an eating disorder diagnosis. In addition, she reports symptoms of major depression. Vaibhav is comfortable with his knowledge and ability to treat the depressive symptoms, so this is what he has focused on in treatment. The young woman's physical health is deteriorating, and an eating disorders specialist should be consulted to address the client's medical needs. Vaibhav's supervisor does not realize this, however, because he has relied exclusively on Vaibhav's self-reports during supervision sessions. Vaibhav has reported only the facts of the case pertaining to the diagnosis and treatment of depression.

In this hypothetical situation, the client is presenting symptoms outside the scope of competence for the supervisee to provide quality care. She could easily deteriorate further and become suicidal or die of complications related to her physical state. In that situation, the client's family could seek legal action against the supervisor, and the supervisor could be found liable. Consider these questions in your analysis of this situation:

- What are your thoughts about the supervisor relying exclusively on Vaibhav's self-reports during supervision sessions?
- Can you identify your areas of strength and competence pertaining to diagnosis?
- As a supervisee, how might you ask your supervisor to assist you in areas in which you decided you need close supervision?
- As a supervisor, what strategies can you put into place to keep you informed of the important aspects of your supervisee's practices?

Borrowed Servant Rule

This rule is used to determine who had control of the supervisee at the time of the negligent act. In determining whether a person is the servant of another, the essential test is whether a person is subject to another's control or right of control with regard not only to the work to be conducted but also to the manner of performing that work (Saccuzzo, 1997). This criterion regards the power to control the supervisee at the time of the negligent act. For example, in university training programs, students are often placed in hospitals or community mental health facilities to provide services. The student may then be under the supervision of the university supervisor as well as the licensed staff at the placement facility. Under these circumstances, supervisory liability may be determined under the borrowed servant rule. The critical factor in determining liability is in determining who had control of the supervisee at the time of a negligent act.

Remley and Herlihy (2020) raised the question of whether there are distinctions in types of supervising based on applied practice. For instance, it has been suggested that someone providing secondary supervision or clinical supervision may not be as likely to be held vicariously liable due to the fact that this person is not the primary, or administrative, supervisor. The distinction is that the administrative supervisor has the direct responsibility of hiring, firing, and monitoring, whereas the clinical supervisor serves more as a consultant to the supervisee and defers to the guidance of the administrative supervisor for direct service performance. This type of distinction is important for those who may choose to supervise prelicensed professionals; they can provide contracts that explicitly state the limits of services provided. Administrative supervisors generally are vicariously responsible for all actions of their supervisees.

Enterprise Liability

In this doctrine, the costs of compensating for injuries are balanced against the benefits derived by the supervisee or supervisor; damages are viewed as a part of the cost of conducting business. This theory focuses on the foreseeability of the supervisee's actions in view of the nature of the duties to be performed. If the supervisor stands to make a profit from the work conducted by a supervisee (e.g., billing for services and profiting after salary and overhead), the supervisor should be willing to bear the risk of damages to clients.

Direct Liability

To establish direct liability for negligent supervision, a clear link must be provided between the actions of the supervisor and the damages incurred. Attempts by the supervisor to negate responsibility due to not directly performing the therapy that was negligent in some manner and caused damages to the client are unlikely to succeed. The court places emphasis on proper monitoring and determining that the supervisee's competence is appropriate to the therapeutic duties assigned. Supervisors are expected to monitor and control the actions of their supervisees. The court has confronted two major issues in which direct liability has been charged because of negligent supervisory practices. First, did the supervisor have a direct duty of care arising from the supervisor-supervisee relationship? Second, did the supervision meet the standard of care for applicable service?

In addition to the possibility of clients filing suit against the supervisor for direct liability, the supervisor must be prepared for the possibility of direct liability suits filed by supervisees. The primary reason cited for these suits is based on the legal concept of due process. In this context, due process involves fairness on the part of the supervisor toward the supervisee. With regard to supervision, this means that supervisors are acting negligently if they give negative evaluations without supplying adequate feedback, remediation guidelines, and the opportunity for improvement.

Supervisors are likely to be held responsible for negligent supervisory practices, which may include any of the following:

- Allowing a supervisee to practice outside his or her scope of practice
- Not providing consistent time for supervision sessions
- Lack of emergency coverage and procedures
- Not providing a supervisory contract
- Lack of appropriate assessment of the supervisee and the clients he or she serves
- Lack of sufficient monitoring of supervisee's practice or documentation
- Lack of consistent feedback prior to evaluation
- Violation of professional boundaries in the supervisory relationship
- Failure to follow accepted practices for supervision

Privileged Communication

This brief legal primer would not be complete without a review of the legal concept of privileged communication as it relates to supervision. In *Jaffee v. Redmond* (1996), the U.S. Supreme Court ruled that communications between psychotherapists and patients are privileged in federal courts, signaling "its intention that the psychotherapist-patient privilege must be as reliable and unequivocal as possible so as to promote an atmosphere of 'confidence and trust' within the psychotherapeutic relationship"

(Mosher & Swire, 2002, p. 577). An evidentiary privilege is a law that prevents the court from requiring revelation of confidential communications. Remley and Herlihy (2020) state that "privileged communication means that a judge cannot order information that has been recognized by law as privileged to be revealed in court" (p. 107). Privilege statutes are primarily granted only to professionals who are licensed or certified.

The privilege belongs to the client and, therefore, may be waived by the client, in which case the witness (supervisor, supervisee) is obligated to testify fully. Any communication made to the supervisor by the supervisee or the client is considered privileged. However, although all privileged communications are confidential, not all confidential communications are privileged. Courts generally require a statutory or legal basis for finding a communication privileged. It is also important to remember that many states define exceptions to otherwise privileged communication.

Supervisors must be fully aware of the implications of privilege and be able to determine the duty to testify. Failure to do so may lead to breach of confidentiality when testimony is not legally mandated or to civil liability and criminal sanctions due to refusing to testify when testimony is mandated (Disney & Stephens, 1994). Supervisors are responsible for securing appropriate legal consultation when confidential information is demanded. In Voices From the Field, private practitioner Judy Van Der Wende recalls her experience supervising an intern who had to testify in a complicated child custody case.

 ## VOICES FROM THE FIELD

Dealing With Child Custody Cases

Judy Van Der Wende, PhD

In my private practice, I have had a great deal of experience with family law matters (e.g., child custody). I met the State of California qualifications as a child custody evaluator after extensive postdoctoral training. This area of practice brings the highest number of board complaints against psychologists in California. I ultimately left the child custody arena due to the incredibly high level of stress these cases entailed and my own horror when being grilled on the witness stand. It simply wasn't for me.

A few years ago, I took on an intern in my private practice. My general style as a supervisor is to offer encouragement, insight, and advice based on my experience. Typically, I allowed the intern to find her own way and her own voice as a clinician. It was important to me not to stifle her but to allow her to grow in her own manner. However, in matters of family law and child custody, I definitely had a much more directive and opinionated approach. First of all, I felt child custody issues were far above the expertise level of a generalist-practice intern. I was firm with her not to take a case like this. I was also very anxious that my own license would be in jeopardy, and the stress from this type of case bothered me greatly.

She chose to become involved in a very complicated child custody case anyway. Her insistence in taking this case created a lot of conflict in the supervision. It was difficult for both of us to balance a supervisory style that was generally supportive and encouraging with my need to maintain great control over this particular situation. With much trepidation, I coached her through testifying and was extensively involved in supervising the case.

I believe I acted ethically as a supervisor throughout this difficult case. I made sure we followed legal guidelines and documented rigorously. However, as I have grown stronger, firmer, and more assertive with experience, I would approach this situation much differently today. I would take the initiative to explore the following issues with the intern: We are engaging in a power struggle over whether or not to take a questionable case—why? What is going on in the supervision to allow this dynamic? What training needs does the intern have that she feels are not being addressed? How can we meet these needs without compromising our training relationship? For instance, should I find a cosupervisor for one case or consider transferring the intern to a different supervisor to address her training concerns? I would absolutely consult with colleagues and seek my own supervision.

Ultimately, I question whether the teaching experience for the intern was worth the anxiety we both incurred. In the future, when interviewing a prospective intern, I would explicitly explain that child custody cases are off limits for this type of practice. The intensity of time and energy involved detract too greatly from other clients. I would clearly indicate in a contract with the intern that following my supervision guidelines is mandatory. Any boundary or power conflicts would be clarified in weekly supervision. With regard to custody cases, I clearly and firmly advise that only forensic interns take on these cases in the appropriate training setting.

Duties to Warn, Protect, and Report

The specific definitions and requirements of the duties to warn, protect, and report vary across states, but the supervisor's responsibilities are relatively clear. Supervisors are responsible to be knowledgeable regarding their duties to warn, protect, and report and must ensure that supervisees have a clear understanding of their duties to warn, protect, and report. Supervisors must educate supervisees about agency policies and procedures; review legal statutes pertaining to duties to warn, protect, and report; and establish an emergency plan that includes the supervisee notifying the supervisor immediately about these concerns. Welfel, Werth, and Benjamin (2009) address some of the limitations of the duty to warn and suggest that options other than warning exist. They contend that accurate predictions of dangerousness are difficult to make. Furthermore, warning third parties of a danger from a client does not guarantee their safety. They assert that the duty to protect allows for the possibility of maintaining a client's confidentiality, whereas the duty to warn requires disclosing confidential information to the alleged victim. Although exercising a duty to warn is the most appropriate option in some cases, it is not the *only* course of action.

Wheeler and Bertram (2019) suggest risk management strategies that include informing clients of limits of confidentiality; consulting, reviewing codes of ethics; maintaining legal counsel; making appropriate referrals; conducting thorough lethality assessments; knowing institutional policy; and documenting all actions considered, rejected, and taken with justification for each. It is essential that all possible limits of confidentiality be addressed in the informed consent process and that these limits be revisited periodically over time to ensure clients know of these potential limits. Supervisors are responsible for training supervisees in appropriate assessment of violence potential, suicidality, and abuse, and supervisors should encourage trainees to treat informed consent as a process rather than a one-time event. Bernard and Goodyear (2019) state that "in the eyes of the law it is more important that reasonable evaluation be made than that the prediction be accurate" (p. 72). Supervisors are ultimately responsible for the actions carried out by their supervisees.

Risk Management in Supervision

Risk management is the practice of focusing on the identification, evaluation, and treatment of problems that may injure clients, lead to filing of an ethics complaint, or initiate a malpractice action. Informed consent, documentation, and consultation are key elements of risk management.

As you read, you may be having some reservations about taking on supervisory responsibility. Even though the responsibilities are numerous and at times the path may seem somewhat treacherous, there truly are safeguards in supervision that are reasonable to pursue. Many of the safeguards are addressed through the process of informed consent. Bernard and Goodyear (2019) suggested three levels of informed consent for supervision: (a) client consent to treatment with the supervisee; (b) client consent to having their case supervised; and (c) supervisee consent to supervision. Safeguards are also available to supervisees to minimize becoming embroiled in legal problems and to avoid potential problems with applying for licensure. In Voices From the Field, Leah Brew offers sage, practical advice she gained from sitting on the state licensure board.

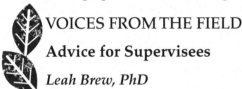

VOICES FROM THE FIELD

Advice for Supervisees

Leah Brew, PhD

When I graduated with my MEd in counseling, I thought I had a really good understanding of legal and ethical issues related to supervision. I knew about the hours I needed, how to advertise, that I needed to discuss the limits of confidentiality due to supervision with clients, and how to be an open supervisee. I thought that was enough.

Fast forward about 18 years: I became the licensed professional clinical counselor board member on the state licensure board. By sitting on the board, I learned so much more. Rather than discussing the usual topics, I am going to tell you about some issues I did not consider fully when I graduated.

Let's start with three commonly discussed issues that are worth reviewing: case notes, confidentiality, and boundaries. First, many supervisees neglect to complete their case notes immediately after the session, or at least within 24 hours. When cases from clients against supervisees have emerged, the case notes have protected the supervisee (about 90% of the time, in my estimation). If you wait too long, you are not only breaking the law but also are at risk for writing case notes that may not be detailed or accurate enough to protect you. Write those notes within 24 hours.

Second, supervisees may get too comfortable and neglect being conscientious about keeping case notes or other clinical records confidential. When transporting case notes or recordings of sessions on a laptop or your phone, you must keep them in a secure way with password protection or a lock. I have heard cases in which the supervisee running a group has the group file in the room and steps out of the room for a moment, leaving the file vulnerable for others to see. Keep all materials confidential at all times.

Third, boundaries with your supervisors are just as important as boundaries with your client. I have heard cases in which a supervisor invited supervisees over for parties and everyone drank too much alcohol. I have also heard cases in which the supervisor asks the supervisee to drop off dry cleaning or pet sit their animals. These are inappropriate behaviors and, ultimately, can hurt the supervisee. You have a responsibility to maintain boundaries even though as the supervisee you have less power.

Five other areas surprised me when I became a licensure board member. First, make sure that your supervisor's license is renewed each cycle. In our state, sometimes supervisors had a current license when they started supervision but neglected to renew their license. All of the hours earned after the supervisor's license was not renewed were lost to the supervisee. This is easily preventable if you make a note on your calendar to check your supervisor's status each renewal cycle.

Second, get signatures on your supervision hours each week; this advice is especially critical if you work in a private practice setting. Supervisees have lost hours because they did not get signatures regularly, and then their supervisor either died or was incapacitated. All of those hours without a signature will be lost unless you are at an agency where someone else can verify your hours.

Third, know the supervision laws for your state; read the statutes and regulations. Every state is different. You should know about supervision contracts and supervisee evaluations. You should be reviewing case notes with your supervisor and discussing clinical challenges as well as countertransference issues. Many supervisors can be strong in one or two areas but neglect the others, which limits what the supervisee can learn from supervision. Take ownership of YOUR supervision.

Fourth, do not write letters for your clients unless you and your supervisor have been trained to do appropriate assessments, and have your supervisor review the letter before it is sent. Clients may request general letters or letters for court cases or support animals. Supervisees want to support their clients, but they put themselves at risk without proper training or certification. Clients in our state have been known to ask for an innocuous generic letter and have used it in court (without the counselor's permission), which resulted in the counselor being disciplined.

Finally, always drive sober. In many states, the state licensure board requires supervisees to be fingerprinted so the board can review any recent arrests or convictions. Receiving a recent wet and reckless conviction or DUI conviction (or multiple convictions) can result in 3 to 5 years of probation at a cost of around $12,000 per year (in California). Even if you live in a state that does not ask for fingerprints, you may move to a state at some point in the future that will. Use rideshares or other forms of transportation when you drink; it's much cheaper in the long run.

I hope I have covered some areas that will be helpful to you. You are on a wonderful journey toward licensure, and your time as a supervisee can have a positive impact on your skills as a professional. You have probably heard this advice before, but it is worth repeating: Enjoy the process, engage in self-care now, and pay attention to the details.

In Voices From the Field, Nancy Wheeler and Burt Bertram address a range of risk management strategies for clinical supervisors from a legal perspective.

 VOICES FROM THE FIELD

Risk Management Strategies in Clinical Supervision

Anne Marie "Nancy" Wheeler, JD, and Burt Bertram, EdD

Supervisors in the mental health arena have ethical and legal obligations to their supervisees and, in turn, to clients served by their supervisees. Risk to the clinical supervisor can be based on direct liability (negligent supervision), which might occur when a supervisor tells a supervisee dealing with an imminently suicidal client that "we can discuss this after the weekend." Risk sometimes stems from vicarious liability, through the legal doctrine of respondeat superior, which maintains that the employer or supervisor is responsible as the "master" of the supervisee. Yet another form of potential risk derives from a failure to follow state laws and regulations, which could leave the supervisor vulnerable to an administrative licensure board complaint or a lawsuit based on negligence per se (strict liability). This risk underscores the critical importance of supervisors remaining current and adhering to all state laws and regulations bearing on the supervision of prelicensed mental health professionals.

Failure to follow state laws deserves particular attention as it is the source of many, if not most, legal entanglements for clinical supervisors. Most states have instituted credentialing requirements for clinical supervisors, and many states now require specific supervision continuing education units to remain current. States also frequently make significant changes to statutes and regulations related to supervision of mental health professionals in training. For example, the State of California substantially revised many of its laws pertinent to mental health practice and supervision, effective in 2019 and 2020. See the California Board of Behavioral Sciences website for more information (https://www.bbs.ca.gov/pdf/legupdate_18.pdf and https://www.bbs.ca.gov/pdf/publications/lawsregs.pdf). One recent change to the California law mandates that supervisors *ensure* the supervisee's compliance with laws and regulations governing the practice of marriage and family therapy, clinical social work, and professional clinical counseling. Although the intent is laudable, this law may pose new liability risks to supervisors because no supervisor can practically monitor the supervisee's actions on a 24/7 basis.

Here are some risk management strategies that counseling and other mental health supervisors might take in 2020 and beyond:

- Read your state's statute and regulations regarding supervision. Are you following the laws? If changes have been made to any of the laws governing your discipline, you should read them and instruct your supervisees to do the same. Continuing education may be advisable. If you believe revisions to the laws are impractical, consider working with your state professional association and legislature to amend them.
- Recognize that clinical supervision, correctly done, is time consuming and requires the supervisor to be dependably available to the supervisee for regularly scheduled supervision, complex emergent situations, and emergencies. Too often, supervisors think they can fold these responsibilities into their existing workload only to discover the impossibility of that extra work in the real world. Supervisors open themselves and their supervisees to administrative and civil liability risk when supervision is not taken seriously, such as when supervision time is not honored and supervisees are required to fend for themselves.
- Review your supervisory contracts and make changes as needed to comply with your state laws. A sample checklist to help in development of a supervisory contract is provided in *The Counselor and the Law* (Wheeler & Bertram, 2019). This book contains a more extensive treatment of legal perspectives on clinical supervision.

Disciplinary Supervision

Licensing boards may mandate supervision as part of a disciplinary order. This is referred to as *disciplinary supervison,* and it is called for after a determination has been made by a licensing board that a mental health practitioner has violated ethical or practice standards or relevant laws. Thomas (2014) states that the key objectives of supervision in such a case include protection of the supervisee's clients and the public and rehabilitation of the mental health professional. The major goals of disciplinary supervision include helping the sanctioned clinician resolve these issues.

- Develop a comprehensive formulation of both personal and professional factors that paved the way for the violations/errors to occur.
- Examine the actual and potential effects of their ethical or legal violations on clients, students, and supervisees, as well as other stakeholders.
- Transfer what they are learning in supervision to their current cases, and identify any thematic similarities to the case that led to the complaint.
- Recognize circumstances, events, or experiences indicating that they could be at risk for impaired objectivity and efficacy. (Thomas, 2014)

Completing a document review is essential for a supervisor working with a clinician who is mandated to receive supervision. As Thomas notes, "one of the first tasks of supervisors in disciplinary cases involves review of the board's order, including its findings and its requirements for the supervision. Correspondence between the licensee and the board may also be helpful in assessing the supervisee's level of insight" (p. 1106). Thomas goes on to say that "supervisees' amenability to supervision, capacity to benefit, and concurrent work performance must be assessed initially and on a continuing basis" (p. 1106). Disciplinary supervisors need to have advanced knowledge of both the legal and ethical aspects of clinical practice, not to mention "expertise in the ethical challenges associated with the supervisee's particular practice areas" (p. 1107).

Risk Management and Dealing With Multiple Tasks in the Supervisory Process

In this section, we outline the multiple tasks for which supervisors are responsible and suggest an organized approach to managing these tasks in the supervisory process. We provide an orientation checklist to assist you in your first session with a new supervisee. To address the structure of the supervisory relationship in detail with a new supervisee, we recommend that the first supervisory session be at least 2 hours. The checklist will ensure that you have reviewed the primary components included in risk management as part of supervisee orientation.

Supervision: First Session Checklist

- ❑ 1. Provide a safe and welcoming environment, and take time to get to know your supervisee. Affirm that the supervisee is not expected to know everything. The process is about development as a person and a professional.
- ❑ 2. Review the supervision contract requirements, and answer all of the supervisee's questions.
- ❑ 3. Inform the supervisee of factors that might influence the supervisee's work with the supervisor.
- ❑ 4. Initiate an open conversation on cultural differences and similarities and how they might affect the supervisory relationship.
- ❑ 5. Review the ethical issues relevant to supervision.
- ❑ 6. Review the process of supervision.
- ❑ 7. Identify specific models and methods of supervision that will be employed.
- ❑ 8. Establish that the supervisee has adequate access to resources to meet the standards and requirements of supervision.

☐   9. Review policies and procedures.
☐ 10. Review all forms.
☐ 11. Review and discuss state regulatory/legal requirements.
☐ 12. Discuss crisis management strategies, and provide a clear emergency plan.
☐ 13. Structure supervision (day, time, length).
☐ 14. Assess the supervisee's competence (including evidence-based performance).
☐ 15. Establish goals and objectives collaboratively.
☐ 16. Have the supervisee indicate acceptance and sign the supervision contract.
☐ 17. Discuss the policies and procedures regarding evaluation.

Liability is a consistent component of our field because of the nature of the work we do, whether practicing directly or supervising practice. Sound practices can minimize the risk from liabilities inherent to supervision. Take the following proactive steps to minimize your liability risks.

Don't Supervise Beyond Your Competence

Competence in supervision requires appropriate training and experience both in areas of clinical expertise and in supervision itself. In addition, effective supervision entails the ability to assess what one knows and what one doesn't know. Competence includes abilities such as being able to apply knowledge to practice, critical judgment, interpersonal skills, and ethical conduct; it also includes continued self-assessment, self-motivation, and professional development to maintain competence throughout one's career (Falender & Shafranske, 2017).

Training in supervision is essential in making sound judgments about your supervisory practices. This includes choosing an appropriate supervisory model from which to work given the setting, the level of training of supervisees, and the target population that will be served. Supervisors should not supervise cases that they are not competent to counsel independently. If a client of the supervisee has a presenting problem that is outside the supervisor's scope of training, make alternative arrangements for supervision of that client's case or make an appropriate referral for the client. This type of responsible practice requires careful screening and monitoring, not only of supervisees but also of each of the clients they serve.

Evaluate and Monitor Supervisees' Competence

Supervisors are responsible for making sure supervisees practice within their scope of competence. To appropriately assign clients and duties to supervisees, it is necessary to assess their level of knowledge and skill. Barnett and Johnson (2008) recommend that supervisors carefully assess the supervisee's level of competence and training needs from the outset. They also note the importance of providing adequate oversight of supervisees and delegating only those tasks that supervisees are competent to perform. Components of assessment may include education; licensure or certification; goals and interests; clinical practicum experience and treatment settings; supervision received; cultural diversity of experience; past criminal history and disciplinary actions; experience with assessment, diagnosis, treatment, and documentation; and ability to interface with other professionals. Remember that evaluating competence is not only a preliminary activity in supervision but also an ongoing process that requires careful monitoring through observation, work samples, feedback, and formal evaluation.

Remind yourself that you have a choice about whether to begin or continue supervision with a supervisee you believe to be incompetent for the tasks that would be assigned in your setting. Discuss the competencies required and the results of the assessment with the potential supervisee. A referral to a different setting may be the reasonable choice. If you determine incompetence after beginning the supervisory relationship, it is important to decide if the supervisee's competence might improve through your teaching, coaching, or mentoring. If not, provide alternatives for both you and your supervisee. These alternatives may include referral, shared supervision, consultation, or remediation.

Be Available for Supervision Consistently

Being available on a consistent basis to supervisees is a common struggle for supervisors who are active professionals. Competent supervision requires much more than the understood hour per week face-to-face meeting with a supervisee. A supervisor must be available to monitor, to review documentation, and to assist if a crisis arises. This also requires having competent supervisory coverage when you are, in fact, unavailable and having an emergency plan in place so that supervisees are never left without appropriate backup should they need help.

Critical incidents in mental health settings require immediate, complex decision making and action (Falvey, 2002). The safety of clients and others can be at risk. These incidents are challenging and often intimidating even for seasoned professionals; therefore, supervisees should not be left to struggle with these situations alone. If you, as the supervisor, are off-call for a specified period of time, provide emergency numbers and arrange consistent, on-site coverage for supervision of your supervisees. Many situations need to be addressed as they happen; these problems can turn into serious liability issues without timely intervention. Having an emergency plan in place provides a model for supervisees to follow, under close supervision, to learn the steps taken for primary emergencies. For instance, supervisees should know the specific steps to take when a client reports immediate danger to self (suicidality). Every setting has a slightly different process based on type of population served and resources available, but the list of actions to be taken should include primary contacts (police, emergency rooms, coroner, and physicians who assist in involuntary admits) and phone numbers. Specify when you expect to be contacted if you are not present at the time of an emergency.

Formulate a Sound Supervision Contract

The use of a contract in supervision is essential to protect the client, the agency, the supervisee, and the supervisor. The majority of governing boards either strongly recommend or require a written agreement or contract for supervision. Contracts need to be operational, and supervisors must be prepared to behaviorally support them. For example, if you require supervisees to videotape sessions, make certain that you view them and cue them for effective use in supervision. Contracts should be in writing with signatures and dates required of both supervisee and supervisor and be completed as early in the supervisory relationship as is practical. (See Appendix 2A in Chapter 2 for one sample contract.)

We have mentioned the differences in administrative and clinical supervision roles and responsibilities previously. In brief, *clinical supervision* is focused on developing the attitudes, knowledge, skills, and professionalism of the supervisee during the therapy process. *Administrative supervision* involves directions given by direct-line administrators to their employees. This form of supervision is often focused on the policies and procedures of supervision and making certain that everyone adheres to the standards and protocols. The purpose of administrative supervision is to see that counselors who are employed are doing their jobs competently. Administrative supervisors generally have direct control and authority over those whom they supervise (Remley & Herlihy, 2020). It is important to address these differences of roles and responsibilities accurately in the supervision contract. For instance, a supervisor providing outside supervision to a supervisee who is working full-time in an agency may serve as a clinical supervisor, and the agency supervisor may serve as the administrative supervisor. This may also be normative for internship settings in which responsibilities are shared between a site supervisor and an academic supervisor. However, supervisors in certain settings may cover both clinical and administrative functions. It is critical in designing a supervisory contract to understand these distinctions and to carefully word the contract to address specific expectations and responsibilities as part of a risk management plan. Suggested items for inclusion in the supervisory contract are listed here, but you can customize the contract by selecting the relevant items for your situation, or those required by state law.

- Purpose and goals of supervision
- Logistics of supervision, including frequency, duration, and structure of meetings
- Roles and responsibilities of supervisor and supervisee
- Guidelines about situations in which the supervisor expects to be consulted
- Brief description of supervisor's background, experience, and areas of expertise
- The model and methods of supervision to be used
- Documentation responsibilities of supervisor and supervisee
- Evaluation methods to be used, including schedule, structure, format, and use
- Feedback and evaluation plan, including due process
- Supervisee's commitment to follow all applicable agency policies, professional licensing statutes, and ethical standards
- Supervisee's agreement to maintain healthy boundaries with clients
- Supervisee's agreement to function within the boundaries of his or her competence
- Supervisee's commitment to provide informed consent to clients
- Reporting procedures for legal, ethical, and emergency situations
- Confidentiality policy
- A statement of responsibility regarding multicultural issues
- Financial arrangements (if applicable)

Be sure to clarify the distinction between a supervision contract and informed consent documents. A sound supervision contract provides a clear blueprint for what is to occur in supervision. The supervisor-supervisee informed consent document primarily outlines duties, training philosophy, expectations, and evaluation of the supervisee. The supervisee-client informed consent document outlines the boundaries of the counselor-client relationship, training status of the supervisee, and confidentiality. These forms and guidelines are often contained within the supervision contract along with additional materials regarding assessment.

In Voices From the Field, Ted Remley offers guidelines for limiting legal liability when developing a supervision contract for supervisees who are receiving supervision for licensure from a supervisor who does not work in the supervisee's counseling setting. His narrative is based on his strict legal definition and distinction between administrative and clinical supervision. In practice, the supervisor may serve in both clinical and administrative roles simultaneously, and in many settings the clinical supervisor is available to supervisees on an ongoing basis.

VOICES FROM THE FIELD

Designing a Supervision Contract to Limit Legal Liability

Theodore P. Remley Jr. JD, PhD

I am both a lawyer and a counselor, and I have a more legalistic perspective on supervision contracts. Perhaps the most common supervision contract I see today is a document that defines the relationship between counseling supervisors and supervisees with their master's degree who are receiving supervision required for state licensure. This discussion refers only to this type of supervision contract.

In this type of supervision contract, clinical supervisors should include language that could limit their vicarious liability should a supervisee engage in unethical behavior or commit malpractice. Although it is impossible to avoid any vicarious liability for the acts of a supervisee, a carefully crafted contract could be used as evidence that clinical supervisors do not have control or authority over the supervisee in these types of supervision relationships.

In my opinion, the first item clinical supervisors should address is to clearly outline the nature of the supervision they will provide. In this instance, supervisors should clearly state that they will be meeting weekly with the supervisee for the purpose of helping the supervisee develop his or her skills as a counselor. Clinical supervisors should describe themselves as mentors, teachers, or consultants.

The contract should indicate that clinical supervisors will be providing input regarding their opinion of the supervisee's development as a counselor to the licensure board periodically and at the end of the supervision relationship but that the supervisors assume no responsibility for the supervisee's daily activities as a counselor. When the supervisee must make decisions related to clients, the contract should make it clear that the supervisee must consult with his or her administrative supervisor at the work site and must follow that administrative supervisor's directives.

The contract should state that the supervisee agrees to act professionally and ethically at all times and to bring to the supervisor's attention any incident that occurs in the supervisee's counseling practice that might be considered unethical or unprofessional. The contract should also state that, during the time of the supervisory relationship, contact outside the supervision sessions will be limited to interactions at professional meetings and will not include socializing together.

Clinical supervisors in arrangements such as these should make contact with the supervisee's administrative supervisor at work and get permission to provide clinical supervision for the supervisee, but clinical supervisors should not interfere with the work duties of the supervisee such as reviewing case notes created at the work site, directing the supervisee on how proceed in particular types of cases, or doing anything in a different way than the supervisee has been directed by his or her administrative supervisor. In the event clinical supervisors suspect that a supervisee is working in an agency that is engaged in unethical or illegal conduct, the contract should state that clinical supervision cannot continue to be provided if the counselor continues to work at that agency.

If clinical supervisors determine that a supervisee is resistant to supervision or is not progressing developmentally in acquiring counseling skills, supervisors should give the supervisee adequate notice and end the supervision relationship, and that process should be outlined in the supervision contract.

Following these contract suggestions will not ensure that clinical supervisors will not be held liable for ethical or illegal behavior by a supervisee employed at an agency and under direct control of an administrative supervisor, but the contract will demonstrate the relationship of the clinical supervisor and the supervisee and will be evidence that clinical supervisors do not have control and authority over their supervisees.

Maintain Written Policies

Many of the policies supervisors need to provide for supervisees already exist (professional standards and guidelines). It is a supervisor's responsibility to review these documents with supervisees. The types of written documents needed may include but certainly are not limited to the following: state legal statutes and regulations, codes of ethics, informed consent, emergency procedures, supervisee-client rights, and agency policies and procedures.

Document All Supervisory Activities

Supervisors are responsible for keeping records regarding all of their supervisory activities and contacts. Supervisors are sometimes responsible for reviewing and cosigning all client documentation written by supervisees. This signature is intended to ensure that supervisors have reviewed the information. It serves as protection for the supervisees, supervisors, and agencies. Some examples of supervisee documentation include client information sheets, intake reports, psychological evaluations, treatment plans, progress notes, and termination summaries.

Supervisory documentation consists of three primary components: (a) supervisory agreements and contracts (previously discussed), (b) supervision notes, and (c) feedback and evaluation materials. It should be clearly stated and understood exactly who, including the supervisee, has access to the different types of documentation.

Supervision notes for each supervisory session need to minimally include a summary of cases reviewed, concerns, recommendations made, actions taken, and justification for decisions regarding high-risk situations. In addition, if supervisees fail to follow the supervisor's directions, this should be noted. Thomas (2007) suggests that supervisors clearly delineate situations in which they expect to be consulted, and this document should be signed and kept on file as part of the supervision documentation. This list might include disputes with clients, impasses in therapy, allegations of unethical behavior, threats of complaint or lawsuit, mental health emergencies, high-risk situations, exceptions to general rules, suspected or known clinical or ethical errors, contact with clients outside the context of treatment, and legal issues. This may lessen culpability for the supervisor if a lawsuit or board complaint is filed. Clearly state what you will be responsible for supervising, whether that is all activity or a limited scope of activity, and document it accordingly.

The third component of supervisory documentation consists of forms, such as progress notes, completed by the supervisee in clinical practice. These documents can be used in supervisory sessions to provide feedback and evaluation for supervisees.

Consult With Appropriate Professionals

Maintaining consultative relationships with other supervisors, attorneys, and physicians is imperative. These relationships provide a forum for discussion of roles, responsibilities, and concerns regarding supervision. It is an appropriate place to ask for feedback about issues such as vicarious liability, confidentiality, dual relationships, dealing with difficult counseling situations, and power differential situations. It is essential for the supervisor to share concerns and limitations along with knowledge and success to get the most from consultation. A certain level of trust and vulnerability are required for maximum benefit. Consultation is not just for trainees and graduate students; it is good practice to use consultation at various times throughout your career.

Consultation is particularly critical when supervisees are working with at-risk youth. Remley (2009) had some advice for school counselors who do not possess competency in identifying and managing students who may be suicidal. If supervisees are working with this population, they need careful supervision, consultation, and direction from counselors who possess such expertise. Although school counselors are not expected to predict all suicide gestures or attempts, Remley states that they are expected to use sound judgment in making clinical decisions, and their reasoning should be document-ed in their notes. When school counselors make an assessment that a student is at risk for suicide, it is imperative to notify the student's parents or guardians that such an assessment took place. Of course, if an intern is working in a school, the intern needs to make the supervisor aware of any potential risks posed by minors. Parents or guardians also have a legal right to know when their child may be in danger.

Maintain Working Knowledge of Ethics Codes, Legal Statutes, and Licensing Regulations

Having a working knowledge of ethics codes and legal statutes as well as an awareness of current trends in the field is essential for the protection of both supervisor and supervisee, as well as for the client's welfare. It is important to integrate relevant ethical and legal issues into all aspects of supervision and to make this a topic of discussion. Thomas (2007) suggests assigning supervisees homework to review and prepare for discussions related to ethical and legal situations. A review and evaluation of the supervisee's ability to implement the steps in ethical decision making is sound practice. It is also considered good practice to require supervisees to sign a statement verifying their review of documents, policies, ethics, and procedures to limit liability should an ethical violation occur. For example, an area of increasing concern in the counseling field is appropriately handling acts or threats of violence. These situations are a challenge for both supervisors and supervisees, and the frequency of these acts seems to be increasing. Case Study 8.3 illustrates the need to be aware of ethical and legal statutes regarding reporting and intervening in acts of violence.

CASE STUDY 8.3: LUCIA

Lucia is a student in a marriage and family counseling program and is doing her internship at the local community mental health center. She is seeing Dena, who is married, has two children, and wants to return to school to get a degree in secondary education. Dena reports that her husband was laid off from his factory job recently and has blamed the "elites" for "making too big of a deal" over the coronavirus response and causing him financial hardship. Dena says he has slapped her on the face on two occasions. Dena hasn't expressed major concerns about her safety or that of her children, but she has reported that he seems to be increasingly upset when she talks of returning to school. Lucia is unsure of the degree of threat Dena and her children are experiencing and doesn't know what to do about it.

Lucia takes her dilemma to her supervisor, and together they talk through the steps of the ethical decision-making model (Corey et al., 2019) to determine what is in the best interest of Dena (and her children). As part of this discussion, they consider actions that have the highest probability of assuring confidentiality and safety. The supervisor suggests that Lucia obtain more specific information from Dena regarding her husband's agitation. When does it occur? Was it evident prior to the COVID-19 crisis and his layoff from work? How does he act? What does he say? How is it resolved? In addition, the supervisor suggests that Lucia assess the appropriateness of having Dena invite her husband to a session. Taking into account that Dena could be a victim of domestic violence, the supervisor needs to be cautious when making these recommendations.

What are your thoughts about the degree of risk of violence in this case? As Lucia's supervisor, what additional assessment would you suggest? What are your responsibilities as a supervisor? Would your actions be any different if you were handling the case yourself?

The supervisor must be familiar with the legal and ethical requirements pertaining to reporting and intervening with threats and acts of violence and abuse. The supervisee also must be aware of these requirements and is required to bring these topics to supervision for discussion as outlined in the supervision contract. The supervisor can help the supervisee assess the situation, determine if there is an imminent risk, decide whether reporting to the authorities is required legally or is necessary for the protection of those involved even if there is no requirement for reporting, and devise a plan for how to proceed.

There are many ramifications of reporting (or taking action) and of not reporting (or not taking action). Taking action may aggravate a domestic abuse situation, and the client may not return for counseling. However, taking no action could result in the threats of violence being carried out. The possible outcomes should be discussed in a way that will enable the supervisee to problem solve these kinds of situations after supervision has concluded. Supervisors are responsible for the actions of their supervisees, and this situation is no exception. The supervision you provide and the suggested direction you give to your supervisee is your responsibility legally and ethically.

Use Multiple Methods of Supervision

Relying on self-report as the sole method of supervision is no longer acceptable. Supervision standards state that "reasonable steps" should be taken to ensure appropriate client care by supervisees. However, "reasonableness" is not clearly defined and often is not debated until after damage has occurred. Monitoring supervisees' practice should be based on level of education, training, and experience. This developmental perspective of monitoring begins with direct supervision, video recording, close review of all documentation, and ongoing assessment. As experience and skill are gained, supervision may transition to an increased use of video and audio recording, self-report methods, and selected therapy notes and less use of direct observation. Many forms of technology and distance supervision are now available to match the needs of the supervisee with supervision methods.

Implement a Feedback and Evaluation Plan

Supervisors are typically expected to evaluate supervisees' progress over a specified period of time and to render judgment regarding supervisees' competence to practice independently. Supervisees have a right to be given regular feedback, and they should be provided with opportunities to remediate any deficiencies. It is essential to consistently follow an evaluation process and to inform all supervisees of this process as they begin supervision. Remember that there is a direct relationship between the constructs of competence, fairness, and due process. A professional disclosure statement is strongly encouraged that informs supervisees of (a) how they will be evaluated, (b) what standard evaluation will take place, (c) how and when feedback will be provided, (d) how information will be shared, and (e) how often supervision will occur and in what manner (individual or group). Feedback should be provided in both written and verbal forms throughout supervision. It is essential that supervisees have the opportunity to implement feedback from the supervisor. Providing information about specific areas and skills that need improvement and providing appropriate time and attention for remediation prior to a negative summative evaluation is the essence of due process. If personal counseling is required at the supervisor's recommendation as part of the supervisory process, supervisees must be made aware of this practice. Evaluation is discussed in greater depth in Chapter 10.

Provide Complaint Procedures

Supervisees may experience dissatisfaction at some time during the supervisory process, and open communication to discuss both strengths and weaknesses supervisees perceive in the supervisory process should occur early in the supervisory relationship. Due process procedures should be described in the consent form or provided in a policy and procedure handbook for the supervisee (Bernard & Goodyear, 2019). Generally, resolutions should first be sought directly between supervisor and supervisee. If opportunities for these discussions are not provided, if the discussions do not bring about resolution, or if the situation is not appropriate to address with the supervisor directly (e.g., sexual harassment by a supervisor), alternatives for discussion and resolution should be spelled out in policy and procedure statements and ample opportunity provided for due process. In extreme circumstances, reporting to the administrative level of supervision or to professional ethics committees may be necessary. If it is not an unsafe or extreme circumstance, it is best to settle supervisory issues through open and direct communication in which both share responsibility for finding options for resolution.

Clearly Address the Endorsement Process

Supervisors are often looked to for endorsement through letters of recommendation for licensure, certification, and employment. Supervisors may wish to spell out the manner in which concerns will be addressed in the supervisory contract. Some of these concerns include letting supervisees know what the schedule of feedback will be, how concerns will be shared as they arise throughout the process, and what will happen if the supervisor becomes concerned about the supervisee's professional ability to function appropriately. Supervisors may wish to verify hours and participation as part of normal supervision practices, but if concerns about competence persist, these concerns will be shared in an endorsement as well. Thomas (2007) maintains that informing supervisees about the importance of gatekeeping minimizes related misunderstandings. Supervisory relationships may be terminated prior to the planned duration due to unforeseen circumstances beyond anyone's control or as a result of specific supervisee behaviors. Supervisors may wish to clearly identify the types of behaviors that may lead to early discontinuation. These may be different for various supervisors, but examples provided by Thomas include noncompliance with supervisory directive, concealment or misrepresentation of relevant information, violations of ethical standards or laws, frequent tardiness or absences, and inability to practice with reasonable skill and safety.

Purchase and Verify Professional Liability Insurance Coverage

Professional liability insurance is a must for both supervisors and supervisees. Check with the company that holds the malpractice policy, prior to purchase, to confirm coverage for damages incurred outside of direct service or due to negligent supervision. In addition, confirm that coverage applies to supervisees' level of education or training. It is a good idea for supervisors to get a copy of the statement of coverage (not necessarily the policy itself) to include in the supervisee's record as part of the documentation. When it comes to legal matters, it is wise to have all proceedings and agreements in writing.

Evaluate and Screen All Clients Under the Supervisee's Care

Supervisors have a responsibility to evaluate both the client and the supervisee. It is essential that supervisors carefully assess each client who receives services from the supervisee. This assessment is for the dual purpose of making certain the case is within the supervisor's area of competence and for referring the case to the appropriate supervisee based on training, skill, and experience. It is a good practice for supervisors to meet with each of their supervisee's clients and to continue assessing each client under the care of the supervisee throughout the duration of supervision. From a legal perspective, it is expected that supervisors will have adequate knowledge of each of their supervisee's clients.

Establish a Policy for Ensuring Confidentiality

Establish a process to ensure confidentiality. Have a written agreement with supervisees that includes the right of the supervisor to have consultative discussions with appropriate colleagues regarding the supervisory relationship and duties. Have supervisees use appropriate disclosure statements for clients describing the supervision process, clearly identifying the supervisee as "in training," and the limits of confidentiality and privilege. Review the ethics codes regarding confidentiality as part of the orientation to supervision and discuss these principles with supervisees.

Never take for granted that a supervisee is prepared to handle difficult situations where confidentiality is concerned. Check this out first by providing situations and requesting a course of action by the supervisee to determine his or her working knowledge of confidentiality. As a supervisor, model appropriate confidential behavior regarding discussion of both your supervisees and the clients they serve. Make expectations regarding confidentiality very clear. For example, if clients are only to be discussed within the confines of a therapy room or your office, state this clearly. If you expect your supervisee to communicate his or her status in training before the first formal counseling session, state this expectation clearly. Explain the consequences of breaches of confidentiality.

Supervisors are not expected to have all the answers regarding confidentiality, and you may wish to share instances when you needed guidance in this area. Make it clear that supervisees are expected to raise questions and seek guidance whenever there is a concern. Acknowledge that self-report is not sufficient to monitor most instances in which confidentiality may be breached. Observation is often required to assess and prevent these situations. Breaches of confidentiality are less likely to be reported in supervision due to the supervisee's lack of awareness. These breaches often occur with good intent, but they are breaches nonetheless. Audio, video, or other methods of direct observation are encouraged to monitor these issues.

Establish a procedure that can be shared with clients regarding the process of supervision of cases. This process should include with whom the case information will be shared and how the information will be managed following either ending of supervision or termination of treatment.

In addition, describe the circumstances under which supervisory information may be shared. Supervisees should understand who will have access to information about them. If multiple supervisors are involved, coordination of services is needed to minimize confusion. Agreement to this coordination of service and communication should be established as a condition of supervision. Disclosures beyond those outlined in the initial informed consent require the agreement of the supervisee. Supervisors should also communicate circumstances that require breach of supervisees' confidentiality, such as reporting unethical behavior. The *Ethical Principles of Psychologists and Code of Conduct* (APA, 2017) requires that supervisees be informed about who will have information about their performance, personal disclosures, and assessments.

Incorporate Informed Consent Into Practice

Proper informed consent procedures protect both supervisees and the clients they serve. In fact, "under the Health Insurance Portability and Accountability Act (HIPAA), supervisors are required to inform all clients of a supervisee's status and the potential impact of this fact on the client's care and confidentiality of client information" (Campbell, 2006, p. 130). In much the same way that therapists provide their clients with a professional disclosure statement, supervisors need to inform supervisees about the relevant aspects of the supervision process. To comply with HIPAA, supervisors must also inform their supervisees' clients about the purpose of supervision and the procedures that will be used to carry out supervision and maintain the confidentiality of clients' disclosures (Campbell, 2006). Visit the HIPAA website for more information (https://www.hhs.gov/hipaa/index.html).

Ethical and Legal Perspectives on Counseling Minors

From an ethical perspective, supervisees who work with children and adolescents have the responsibility to provide information that will help minor clients become active participants in their treatment. Barnett and Johnson (2010) note that state laws vary regarding the definition of a minor. Consistent with the increasing concern over the rights of children in general, more attention is being paid to the minor's right of informed consent. Barnett and Johnson maintain that therapists should clearly discuss the limits of confidentiality with minors as part of the informed consent process, even in those cases when a parent or guardian consents to treatment. If children lack the background to evaluate the risks and benefits and if they cannot give complete informed consent, the trainee should still attempt to provide some understanding of the counseling process to them. Even though minors usually cannot legally give informed consent for treatment, they can give their *assent* to counseling. Assent to treatment implies that supervisees involve minors in decisions about their own care.

Counseling minors in schools presents numerous legal and ethical challenges. The American School Counselor Association (ASCA) has multiple documents to guide school counselors and supervisors as they navigate their ethical responsibilities, including the *Ethical Standards for School Counselors* (ASCA, 2016), *Ethical Standards for School Counselor Education Faculty* (ASCA, 2018b), and various ASCA position statements. These documents can inform the practice of school counselors and their supervisors, although only ASCA members are obligated to practice in a manner consistent with these ethical standards.

Observing the legal and ethical rights of students and parents can be difficult, especially in situations related to confidentiality. School counselors have an ethical obligation to safeguard the confidentiality of minors to the extent that it is possible. Counselors are ethically obliged to respect the privacy of minor clients and maintain confidentiality, but this obligation may be in conflict with laws regarding parental rights to be informed about the progress of treatment and to decide what is in the best interests of their children. School counselors have an ethical responsibility to ask for client permission to release information, and they should clearly inform students of the limitations of confidentiality and how and when confidential information may be shared. When school counselors are required to provide information to parents and school personnel, they must do so in a manner that will minimize intrusion into the child's or adolescent's privacy. To the degree possible, school counselors aim to establish collaborative relationships with parents and school personnel. A sample of ethical standards for school counselors is presented in Box 8.2.

In Voices From the Field, Mary Hermann, a counselor educator and an attorney, provides sound advice for practicing ethically and legally for supervisees and supervisors who work with minors in a school setting.

Box 8.2
ETHICAL STANDARDS ON COUNSELING MINORS

American School Counselor Association (2016)

Ethical Standards for School Counselors

The ASCA addresses the matter of the school counselor's responsibilities to parents:

> School counselors recognize that providing services to minors in a school setting requires school counselors to collaborate with students' parents/guardians as appropriate. (B.1.a.)

The ASCA provides the following standards on confidentiality and privacy in school settings:

School counselors inform students of the purposes, goals, techniques and rules of procedure under which they may receive counseling. Disclosure includes informed consent and clarification of the limits of confidentiality. Informed consent requires competence, voluntariness and knowledge on the part of students to understand the limits of confidentiality and, therefore, can be difficult to obtain from students of certain developmental levels, English-language learners and special-needs populations. If the student is able to give assent/consent before school counselors share confidential information, school counselors attempt to gain the student's assent/consent. (A.2.b.)

School counselors recognize their primary ethical obligation for confidentiality is to the student but balance that obligation with an understanding of the parents'/guardians' legal and inherent rights to be the guiding voice in their children's lives. (A.2.f.)

The school counselor informs parents/guardians of the counselor's role to include the confidential nature of the school counseling relationship between the school counselor and student. (B.1.f.)

VOICES FROM THE FIELD

Challenges in Supervising School Counselor Interns

Mary Hermann, JD, PhD

I have been a counselor educator for almost 20 years, and one of the most challenging experiences I encounter is supervising school counselor interns when they are dealing with issues related to confidentiality. As an attorney, I am particularly cognizant of my legal responsibilities. And as a former member of ACA and ASCA ethics committees and ethical revision task forces, I am acutely aware of my ethical obligations. When working with minors in schools, legal and ethical guidelines related to confidentiality often conflict. From an ethical stance, I want my supervisees to do what is in the best interest of the students with whom they are working. Supervisees also have to balance the students' ethical rights to confidentiality with the legal rights of parents. Ensuring that interns understand they need to consult with their supervisors in these situations is critical.

In addition to the legal and ethical dimensions of these cases, supervisees often experience emotional conflict when they realize they have to disclose a student's private information to parents. When I was a school counselor intern, I worked with a student with suicidal ideation as well as with a student who was frightened that she might pose a danger to others. Both cases were terrifying new experiences for me, and I knew I needed to help both students and keep them and other students safe. These situations always seemed to happen around 2 p.m. on Friday, creating a short timeline for action. In both cases, I quickly realized that contacting parents was in the best interests of the students and was supported by legal as well as ethical guidelines. I was able to help both students understand that keeping them safe involved contacting their parents.

In addition to helping supervisees determine when to contact parents, it is important to talk to supervisees about how the circumstances dictate what the conversation might look like. For example, one of my interns had a 3rd-grade student tell her that she was going to go to her father's unlocked gun case when she got home and she was going to kill herself with one of the guns in the case. In that situation, the parents and the intern needed to communicate immediately and discuss how to keep the student safe. Conversely, a case in which a student casually says "I just blew the math test. I could just shoot myself for not preparing more" requires a different conversation. I advise supervisees to express to the student and parents that they have concerns any time they hear a student use suicidal language, even if the student is just using a figure of speech.

I dealt with a gray area as an intern when students engaged in potentially dangerous activities. My school counseling experience was in a community in which underage drinking was somewhat culturally condoned at the time, and many high school students went to bars on the weekends. If I contacted parents every time I heard that a student had gone to a bar, I may not have been able to develop trusting relationships with students, and as a result I may not have had many students to counsel. I had to make tough decisions about how to best keep students safe. Some of the best school counselors I know take some legal risks to do what is in the best interest of the students, and I realize that my supervisees will make informed choices about the legal risks they are willing to take when they are in practice. However, I tell my supervisees that while they are under my supervision they must consult with their supervisor about the best course of action in these situations.

Summary

Legal responsibility and accountability are strongly shaping the evolving role of the supervisor. The legal issues of negligence and liability, specifically vicarious liability, can be somewhat daunting, and it is important to remember that there are clear guidelines for risk management. This chapter has provided a brief legal primer for understanding liability and its implications for the practice of supervision.

We have also provided you with guidelines for risk management that, if practiced, can minimize the risk of liability for you and your supervisees. Know your own limits and scope of practice, and practice within your limits. Remember that you have a choice about whom you supervise and which cases you directly supervise. When you do take on supervisees, be available to them and closely monitor their competence. Of course, the process should begin with a thorough supervisory contract and sound orientation so that expectations are clear from the outset of supervision. Be certain to make distinctions between administrative and clinical supervisory roles and responsibilities. As a responsible professional, use multiple methods of supervision, document all supervisory activities, and provide supervisees with clear emergency policies. In addition, never assume that supervisees have an adequate working knowledge of ethics. Be honest and constructive in your feedback to supervisees and document your evaluations of their work. Identify appropriate professionals to consult with, and always carry liability insurance.

SUGGESTED ACTIVITIES

As you consider the following activities, look for opportunities to consider how you might answer the same or differently depending on whether you were serving as a clinical supervisor or an administrative supervisor.

1. Form small groups and have each group develop a detailed case scenario (from problem presentation through sanctions, if any) of liable supervisory practice. Then have groups exchange scenarios and answer the following questions:
   - Was the supervisor competent to supervise in this situation?
   - Was the supervisee competent to treat this patient given the level of supervision?
   - How was the supervisee monitored?
   - How was this monitoring process documented?
   - Did the supervisor follow accepted ethical principles, such as providing timely and periodic evaluations of the supervisee?
   - Was there a dual relationship of any kind?
   - Was the client fully informed of the training status of the supervisee, the role of the supervisor, the limits of confidentiality, and other relevant factors pertinent to the relationship?

The ability to answer these questions in a positive light at any given time during supervisory practice has become essential.

2. Read this case example and discuss it in small groups. Then reconvene in a large group and share your answers.

CASE STUDY EXAMPLE

A supervisee has been working with a teenage girl in a private family clinic, and Bianca says she has taken some drugs in the past. The counselor gets a call late one night from Bianca from her home, and she says she just needs to talk. In the conversation, the supervisee learns that Bianca has taken some drugs, and she is not feeling well. The supervisee insists that she put her mom on the telephone, and the supervisee tells the mom what has happened and that Bianca should be taken to the hospital. Bianca survives, but her parents threaten a malpractice case against the supervisee for not having told the parents of her past drug use. If they had known about the previous situation, they believe they could have prevented the current one from happening. The supervisee calls his supervisor first thing the next morning to report what has transpired. This call is the first knowledge that the supervisor has of the details of the case.

- What are the ethical, legal, and clinical issues in this case?
- What kinds of questions would you raise with your supervisee regarding this situation?
- What would you most want to say to your supervisee?
- How would you guide your supervisee in thinking through this situation, including the ethical, legal, and clinical issues?
- How would you help your supervisee formulate a plan of action and think through the consequences of the various courses of action?
- If a malpractice suit is filed, is the supervisor alone responsible or is the supervisee also responsible?

3. As you read each of the examples that follows, answer these questions: Is this an example of vicarious or direct liability? What risk management steps could have been taken to prevent the situation?

- The supervisor or agency provides an intake form to be used by the trainee, but it omits relevant questions (homicidal tendencies, suicidal tendencies, previous therapy). The client receives improper treatment and injures himself or others.
- The trainee takes relevant notes during therapy; however, the supervisor does not study these notes and does not realize that the notes describe a therapy method that is not standard practice with this type of client situation.
- Even with the supervisor's help, the trainee is incapable of offering proper therapy. There is a need to refer to a more competent professional.
- A medical problem, which would have been discovered by a person with more training, is not discovered by the trainee. A physician is not consulted, and treatment continues even though the psychological problem is caused by a hearing loss, a vitamin deficiency, or other physical imbalance.
- Psychological tests are conducted, and diagnosis and a treatment plan are based on the test results. The diagnosis is improper due to inappropriate norms of the test and lack of supervision regarding test selection and multicultural case conceptualization.
- The diagnosis is improper, the prognosis is faulty, or the treatment plan ineffective. The supervisor does not discover the error in any of the three areas or the interrelationship of one to the other, and therapy continues inappropriately.
- Written progress notes are inadequate or do not support the treatment plan.
- The trainee and client (or trainee and supervisor) have a conflict of personalities, yet the treatment continues.
- The trainee becomes socially involved with the client but cleverly hides the involvement from the supervisor. The supervisor would have known if more complete supervisory sessions had included live observation.
- The trainee goes on vacation, and there is no adequately prepared relief therapist for her clients.
- The client consents to treatment but does not know it will be provided by a trainee. He assumes it will be provided by a qualified professional.
- The trainee is subpoenaed to testify in court and is improperly prepared by training or experience for courtroom testimony.
- A student trainee is released from a graduate training program based on unsatisfactory performance in a practicum experience. There is minimal documentation of supervision, no documentation of direct observation, no procedure for formal feedback, and no due process prior to termination.

CHAPTER 9
Crisis Management in Supervision

FOCUS QUESTIONS

1. What is important to include in an emergency plan for your supervisees?
2. How would you assess the readiness of your supervisees to address critical incidents in a competent manner?
3. How could you be of most help to a supervisee whose client has attempted suicide or ended his or her life by suicide?
4. How could you be of most help to a supervisee whose client has committed an act of violence?
5. Should you intervene with a supervisee to help him or her through a personal crisis? How would you assist the supervisee? When would you refer the supervisee for personal counseling?
6. How would you help a supervisee cope with an incident of school violence?
7. What do you think supervisees need most from supervisors in crisis situations?
8. How would you help a supervisee handle a critical incident (such as a shooting or a threat of violence) that occurs in the clinical setting?
9. How will the challenges that climate change poses affect the demands on counselors and those who supervise them?
10. What would be your main focus with a supervisee who is working via distance counseling with the spouse of a COVID-19 patient?

A doctoral student in a counseling psychology program began his first practicum at a community mental health center. During his second week there, the trainee was assigned the case of a client with psychosis who brought a chainsaw to the session. The client informed the student counselor that he intended to use the chainsaw (which fortunately was still in its box) to harm a particular person. To encounter such a client so early in training may seem like one's worst nightmare, but this was a straightforward matter. Little guesswork was involved. The client articulated his intent, plan, weapon, and victim. The trainee had the presence of mind to remain calm and contacted the center's director for assistance. Navigating through this crisis was clearly beyond the scope of the trainee's competence, and he welcomed the director's intervention. This scenario seems unlikely, but it is a true story. Life can indeed be stranger than fiction.

Many tragic events have captured national and international attention since the unspeakable acts of terror committed in the United States on September 11, 2001. The COVID-19 pandemic is the most recent example of a global tragedy that has spread at an alarming rate and has led to an unthinkable number of deaths throughout the world. Of course, we have all been inundated with tragic news over the past 20 years. "Breaking News" stories of mass shootings in schools and other public settings have become all too common in the United States. In addition to these human-caused mass tragedies, we have witnessed natural disasters ranging from catastrophic hurricanes (e.g., Harvey, Maria, and Dorian) to devastating fires. The 2018 Camp Fire in northern California destroyed more than 18,000 structures, caused 82 deaths, and left an estimated 100,000 people traumatized. According to independent analyses by the National Oceanic and Atmospheric Administration (NOAA) and NASA (2020), in 2019 Earth's average global surface temperature was the second warmest since 1880, when modern record-keeping began. We must anticipate and prepare for an increase in crises brought on by climate change. Muratori and Haynes (2020) describe the rapid increase in both natural and human-caused disasters as the "new normal," and these experiences are leading to extreme trauma among Americans. The increase in hate crimes, human rights abuses, sexual misconduct crimes, gun violence, divisiveness, tribalism, racism, xenophobia, homophobia, transphobia, cyberbullying, and cybercrimes is more than enough reason for people to experience a kind of "global anxiety." Add pandemic viral emergencies and the far-reaching adverse effects of climate change to that already daunting list of stressors, and it is no wonder that living in today's world is so stressful.

Being reminded of the challenges facing our society and the world may leave you feeling overwhelmed by the task ahead of us as clinical supervisors and helping professionals. We urge you to take a deep breath and remember these words of John F. Kennedy: "The Chinese use two brush strokes to write the word 'crisis.' One brush stroke stands for danger; the other for opportunity. In a crisis, be aware of the danger—but recognize the opportunity." Crisis counseling is becoming part of every helper's portfolio, and the counseling profession is poised to make a positive and substantive difference in the management of crisis situations. We can use our skills, knowledge, and training to help clients and supervisees weather these crises with support and skillful interventions.

One of our colleagues stated that she has seen a sharp increase in the number of clients seeking support during the COVID-19 pandemic. She saw this crisis as an opportunity to help her clients tap into their own creativity and resourcefulness to connect with others in a safe and healthy way. Clients who were inclined to act selfishly or with little regard for others were suddenly challenged to think of the greater good and public health. And, as Adlerians would attest, showing signs of "social interest" or "community feeling" is a step in the direction of mental health and well-being. For creative exercises and techniques designed for both clients and counselors as they navigate these difficult times, we recommend *Coping Skills for a Stressful World: A Workbook for Counselors and Clients* (Muratori & Haynes, 2020).

Tarvydas, Levers, and Teahen (2017) believe that "the counseling profession has both the opportunity and obligation to improve the capabilities of counselors to provide effective and ethical trauma counseling in both individual and mass trauma circumstances" (p. 266). We can safely say that every counselor in the mental health profession can expect to either directly experience or have their clients experience a serious crisis situation at some point in their lives. We must prepare our supervisees to work with clients in this new era, and we must have emergency plans in place to manage these situations.

This chapter is designed to better equip supervisors and supervisees with the specific tools and knowledge needed to effectively intervene in crisis situations of all magnitudes. Topics include the supervisor's roles and responsibilites in a crisis, becoming an effective crisis supervisor, a framework for crisis management, handling selected crisis situations, and self-care for the counselor. It is imperative that supervisors, faculty, and training programs emphasize crisis management to prepare the next generation of counselors for the roles they will be expected to play in crisis prevention, intervention, and recovery. The conceptual framework we provide for the use of supervisors in assisting their supervisees in making timely and appropriate client interventions makes crisis work more manageable and reduces anxiety for all those involved.

Crisis Defined

In this chapter, we are restricting our discussion of "crises" to events clients bring to therapy that may be beyond the supervisee's competence and require assistance from the supervisor. Among the crises clients may bring to counselors are suicides or suicide attempts; experiencing acts of terror or violence in schools, places of worship, or other public spaces; experiencing natural or human-caused disasters such as tornadoes, earthquakes, or plane crashes; experiencing public health crises or pandemics; and personal crises such as death, divorce, illness, or termination from one's job. We focus on a number of situations and discuss how supervisors can work effectively with supervisees to assist their clients. In each instance, it is the job of the supervisor to help supervisees examine the situation, act in the best interest of the client, do what is legally and ethically appropriate, and learn from the situation so supervisees are able to problem solve independently in the future. We provide the foundational knowledge to help you prepare for and respond to crisis situations as a supervisor. In addition, we hope you will be inspired to learn about resources in your own community and beyond that you can draw upon should the need arise during an emergency.

The Supervisor's Roles and Responsibilities in Crisis Situations

In our work as supervisors, we have experienced many crisis situations, and each of these situations posed a new challenge. Supervisors need to have a clear idea of what to expect from supervisees and a framework for how to approach these problems. For example, being threatened by a client or witnessing a violent act can be very disturbing for a supervisee. The supervisor should first allow the supervisee to talk about the incident and express any reactions and concerns before you both move on to problem solving. Supervisees often react strongly to a crisis and feel compelled to proceed without thoroughly examining the situation and the ramifications of their actions. Although we do not want to curb our supervisees' inclination to initiate action, it is the obligation of the supervisor to help the supervisee proceed using sound, objective assessment and problem-solving strategies that address the clinical situation.

Supervisors may experience their own anxiety when providing supervision in a crisis situation because of limited experience as a supervisor or lack of training and experience with the crisis at hand, or both. New supervisors may act too quickly to solve the problem and simply instruct the supervisee on how to proceed, but these events offer fertile ground for the supervisee's learning. Great patience and reserve are required on the part of the supervisor to allow the supervisee to process the information, examine courses of action, and determine the best intervention for the situation. Sometimes quick action on the supervisor's part is necessary to save a life or to protect a victim. In those situations, you must intervene as quickly as possible. However, in many crisis situations, the supervisor has time to help the supervisee do the major portion of the problem solving and subsequent intervention. Allowing the supervisee to process the issue is preferred and will foster long-term growth for the supervisee.

Supervisors must be aware of the limits of their own competency and know when to seek outside consultation or supervision. It is effective modeling, as well as ethical practice, for a supervisor to share with the supervisee the limits of the supervisor's knowledge and competence and to work with the supervisee in devising a plan for obtaining the needed assistance. Minimally, supervisors faced with crisis management should be knowledgeable about and competent in the practice of lethality assessment; current organizational crisis policy and procedures; basic models of and strategies for crisis intervention; and critical incident assessment skills. Supervisors who are ill-prepared in any of these areas may find it useful to attend a crisis management workshop as part of their professional development.

Some of the professional standards specifically address crisis situations in supervision, and most of the standards address topics related to handling these situations (see Box 9.1).

Becoming an Effective Crisis Supervisor

When done well, crisis intervention is much more than the sum of knowledge and techniques. A true master at crisis intervention supervision possesses a wealth of technical skill, theoretical knowledge, and the following attributes: life experience supported with thorough training, knowledge, and supervision; poise; creativity and flexibility; energy and resiliency; and quick mental reflexes (James & Gilliland, 2017). Other characteristics that have been observed in effective crisis intervention workers include tenacity, the ability to delay gratification, courage, optimism, reality orientation, objectivity, a strong and positive self-concept, and an abiding faith that human beings are capable of overcoming seemingly insurmountable odds. In research by Dupre and colleagues (2014), counselors "characterized the ideal crisis supervisor as one who is accessible and affirming, insightful and aware of how counselors may have been 'getting caught up' in client dynamics, optimistic and calm under fire, and culturally competent" (p. 90).

Effective crisis supervisors also possess strong communication skills and appropriate interpersonal boundaries. Under dire circumstances, supervisors need to be able to be fully present for their supervisees. This entails being able to differentiate between empathy, sympathy, and distancing. Empathy is the ability to accurately sense and articulate the inner feelings of the supervisee's experience in a meaningful way. Sympathy involves accepting the supervisee's problems and feelings associated with the issue. Distancing, or becoming emotionally removed, occurs when we are overwhelmed and feel the need to say something meaningful but don't know where to start. James and Gilliland (2017) called this "funeral home counseling," and it may include statements like "Everything happens for a reason," "It could have been worse," or "Try to get your mind off it." Although a supervisor may have the best of intentions when making these statements, distancing communication is generally not helpful and can hinder intervention. It might say more about the supervisor's state of discomfort than the supervisee's. The same is true for supervisees working with clients in crisis who attempt to comfort the client with these hollow phrases, which can further upset the client. Supervisors who seem to absorb their supervisees' feelings or, conversely, keep them at bay may benefit from examining their own boundaries to decrease the likelihood that they will communicate ineffectively at a critical time in their supervisees' training and professional development.

In moments of crisis, many supervisors feel tremendous pressure to convey wisdom and all of the right answers to their supervisees, who may be in a state of panic. We need to remind ourselves and our supervisees that there is no single best way to accomplish a task, and multiple pathways may lead to resolving a dilemma. In crisis situations, we use our knowledge and skills to willingly step up to difficult situations, to care about the

Box 9.1

ETHICS CODES AND STANDARDS REGARDING MANAGING CRISIS SITUATIONS IN SUPERVISION

Association for Counselor Education and Supervision (2011)

Best Practices in Clinical Supervision

The supervisor provides the supervisee with his/her emergency contact information, parameters for contacting the supervisor in emergency situations, and specific instructions for emergency protocols. (1.b.vi.)

American Counseling Association (2014)

Code of Ethics

Supervisors establish and communicate to supervisees procedures for contacting supervisors or, in their absence, alternative on-call supervisors to assist in handling crises. (F.4.b.)

American School Counseling Association (2016)

Ethical Standard for School Counselors

Implement procedures for students to follow in both emergency and nonemergency situations when the school counselor is not available. (A.15.c.)

American Psychological Association (2017)

Ethical Principles of Psychologists and Code of Conduct

In emergencies, when psychologists provide services to individuals for whom other mental health services are not available and for which psychologists have not obtained the necessary training, psychologists may provide such services in order to ensure that services are not denied. The services are discontinued as soon as the emergency has ended or appropriate services are available. (2.02.)

American Mental Health Counselors Association (2016)

Standards for the Practice of Clinical Mental Health Counseling

The treatment of trauma and chronic traumatic distress is essential for the practice of clinical mental health. Many clients/patients seeking counseling deal with symptoms associated with traumatic experiences. Patients who suffer from the aftereffects of traumatic events or related chronic distress can develop a variety of related disorders and often form negative core self-beliefs. The U.S. Department of Health and Human Services, Substance Abuse and Mental Health Services Administration (SAMHSA), has addressed trauma in the publication, *Concept of Trauma and Guidance for a Trauma-Informed Approach.* All competent clinical mental health counselors possess the knowledge and skills necessary to offer trauma assessment, diagnosis, and effective treatment while utilizing techniques that emerge from evidence-based practices and best practices.

human beings involved in the situation, and to try to make a difference while searching for safe and reasonable solutions. Because of the stressful nature of a crisis, we will see our supervisees struggle to thrive. Even those seasoned in this area will admit to occasionally feeling perplexed, frustrated, angry, afraid, threatened, incompetent, foolish, and otherwise unequal to the task. Crisis supervision requires patience, practice, practice, and more patience.

Crisis work is often associated with high levels of stress and burnout. Abassary and Goodrich (2014) state "that professional counselors who are exposed to crisis-, trauma-, and disaster-based clinical situations can have a variety of reactions including stress, anxiety, and trauma. If the work is ongoing, this could lead to burnout for the professional counselor" (p. 66). Although you may not choose a career as a full-time crisis worker, most of us will, in fact, be "crisis workers" at some point in our counseling careers. As a clinical supervisor, you will need to develop a variety of ways to work with a supervisee who encounters a crisis situation. There is opportunity for growth, development, and research in the supervision field to prepare supervisees for this challenging work. Although known as some of the toughest work, crisis work is also regarded as some of the most rewarding work. Certain counselors even describe an addictive quality to the work tied to the feelings of accomplishment one has following the successful resolution of a critical incident.

In Voices From the Field, crisis intervention expert Rick Myer offers advice to supervisors on how to proceed when their supervisees encounter client crises.

 ## VOICES FROM THE FIELD

Acquiring Crisis Intervention Skills

Rick Myer, PhD

A little over 25 years ago I was working in a general hospital doing crisis intervention. My first weekend on call was in many ways baptism by fire. I was called upon to help a family in which a tragic death occurred as well as respond to several other crisis situations in the emergency room. I had received the appropriate induction with respect to procedures, policies, and general do's and don'ts, but I recall wondering if I had the knowledge and experience to be doing crisis intervention.

Since that fateful beginning, I have spent much of my professional career conducting research, writing about, and teaching crisis intervention. I have found that the most important issue for beginning professional counselors to understand is that crisis intervention is a specialty. Although we use the same basic counseling skills used for individual therapy, these skills are applied in a very different manner. Using the same approach as you do in individual therapy is at best inefficient, and at worst ineffective. And when a client is in crisis, being ineffective can lead to disastrous results such as the death of the client or others. Supervisors must understand this issue and assist supervisees in recognizing when a shift to using crisis intervention skills is warranted. The focus of supervision should be on helping supervisees assess the severity of the crisis and learn to shift to crisis intervention strategies as needed. Supervision must involve helping supervisees recognize when they need to use a more directive approach.

One mistake supervisors should avoid is to insist that supervisees maintain the same therapeutic relationship with clients in crisis as in traditional therapy. The standard of preserving a professional boundary of autonomy may need to bend in times of crisis, and the supervisee may need to learn ways to enter into the life of the client. The reason for dropping the boundary is that clients experiencing a crisis may become so vulnerable or incapable that they are not able to care for themselves. However, when supervisees and professional counselors choose to drop those boundaries, I have learned that efforts to reestablish them should begin as soon as possible. This process may take minutes or hours, depending on the severity of the client's reaction to the crisis.

Although there is no cookbook approach to addressing crisis concerns, we provide a framework for crisis management in the next section. It is important to develop your own plan well in advance of entering into a supervisory relationship.

A Framework for Crisis Management: What Every Supervisor Needs to Know

Counselors and others in the helping professions need to prepare themselves to handle crises and emergency situations that appear to be happening all too frequently these days. Supervisors play a critical role in guiding their supervisees in helping clients navigate these complex situations. The absence of such support and oversight can have a lasting adverse impact on the counselor's professional development and personal well-being. In addition to increasing the likelihood of difficult countertransference reactions, limiting the availability of supervisory support can increase "empathic strain, burnout, and compassion fatigue" (Dupre et al., 2014, p. 84).

Later in the chapter, we present a model of supervision that was designed specifically for crisis situations, followed by guidelines for counselors dealing with mass trauma, and a description of psychological first aid. But first we present our basic framework for crisis management.

Crisis Preparation

Supervisors should have emergency procedures in place and communicate those to the supervisee at the outset of supervision (Barnett & Molzon, 2014, p. 1059). Supervisees should have your contact information on hand as well as detailed instructions about procedures and best practices to use in case of emergencies. Information regarding crisis preparation should be written into the supervision contract and discussed as needed throughout the supervisory and training process. To help supervisees avoid being blindsided by client crises, make provisions for them to acquire the knowledge, skills, and awareness to work effectively and efficiently in crisis situations *before* the situations occur (Barnett & Molzon, 2014). A wealth of information about emergency preparedness can be found on the website of the Centers for Disease Control and Prevention (https://www.cdc.gov/). Your agency's policies and procedures can be tailored to reflect the unique needs and challenges of the population you serve and the type of crises that you are more likely to encounter, but these policies must be guided by credible information from the CDC and crisis management experts.

Crisis Response

When a crisis occurs, assess the situation and identify the various components, including the clinical, legal, ethical, personal, and client safety issues involved. It is important to make the distinction between a *primary trauma*, which affects the individual client, and a *shared communal trauma*, in which a larger group or community is involved (Del Vecchio-Scully & Glaser, 2018; Muratori & Haynes, 2020), and interventions will vary accordingly. Trauma-informed care and treatment should be provided for an individual or a community. Supervisees have client welfare as their first priority, but supervisors should ensure that the rights, welfare, and safety of the supervisee are protected as well. Federal and state laws are the first point of reference. Where laws are not clear, however, the good judgment of the supervisor is guided by relevant ethical standards, client welfare, supervisee welfare, supervisor welfare, and program or agency needs. This is a sound framework for decision making for any of the helping professions.

In the event of serious client crises, guide the supervisee to effectively and efficiently expedite de-escalation and safe resolution. This may entail having the supervisee shift counseling priorities from long-term goals to the crisis at hand; encourage the supervisee to be flexible while simultaneously attempting to follow the predetermined crisis response protocol (McAdams & Keener, 2008). To further refine your plan for crisis management, address the principles of risk management presented in Chapter 8.

As a supervisor, you will discover that parallel processes occur that create the opportunity for a rich learning experience to unfold for supervisees. Your modeling during a crisis situation has the potential to have a powerful and enduring impact on the trainee's professional development. In their phenomenological study, Dupre and colleagues (2014) discovered that even licensed professional counselors who are well beyond the training phase may need support during crisis situations. Consider the following ways in which the steps you take as a supervisor mirror the steps that your supervisee must take in responding to a client crisis:

- Both you and your supervisee must gather as much information about the crisis as possible. You will be drawing on the observations of and discussions with your supervisee, whereas your supervisee will be gathering information directly from the client.
- Both you and your supervisee are required to assess the clinical, legal, ethical, personal, and client safety issues involved.
- You must review all possible courses of action and their potential consequences with your supervisee and ultimately assist your supervisee in deciding which path to take. The supervisee experiences a similar process with the client to determine the course of action that best suits the client's needs.
- As a supervisor, you must decide how best to meet the needs of your supervisee as he or she works through the crisis situation, which may be frightening and places the supervisee in uncharted territory. Your supervisee experiences a similar process with the client, who also may be frightened.

Supervisors strongly encourage trainees to seek supervision when they need guidance. Supervisors should heed that advice as well and seek consultation and provide referrals when necessary. To safeguard yourself as the supervisor, consider the clinical, legal, and ethical ramifications for *any* action you suggest, and rely on supervision contracts and ground rules already established with your supervisee.

Crisis Recovery

You have a responsibility to offer guidance to your supervisee as he or she facilitates the client's crisis recovery, which McAdams and Keener (2008) describe as a four-phase process. The supervisee should begin with triage immediately after the crisis ends, then help the client deal with losses incurred, convince the client to reinvest in the counseling process, and finally, help the client integrate what has been learned into future thought and action.

Just as your supervisee must help the client recover from the crisis, you have a responsibility to assist your supervisee with this parallel process. Here are a few tips:

- Have a plan in mind for reentry of the supervisee into the work setting following a crisis situation.
- Be prepared to assist the supervisee in dealing with fallout from the crisis situation and evaluating how well the supervisee's intervention worked. On a similar note, you will learn a great deal about your supervisory skills if you honestly evaluate the effectiveness of your supervisory intervention.
- If the supervisee seems sufficiently traumatized by the crisis to warrant personal counseling, provide a referral.
- Investigate how far-reaching the crisis may be, and consider the effect the situation might have on other supervisees and staff as well as clients. Take appropriate steps to ameliorate these effects, if possible.
- Encourage your supervisees to take the needed time to process their experience with a crisis.

Finally, in a supervisory session, discuss the decision-making process, the learning that occurred, better interventions for handling similar situations, and ways to use the problem-solving process to resolve similar client crises in the future.

The CARE Model of Crisis-Based Clinical Supervision

Aware of the growing need for crisis-based supervision to support counselors working with clients in crisis across settings (e.g., schools and mental health clinics), Abassary and Goodrich (2014) developed the context, action, response, and empathy (CARE) supervision model. They were motivated, in part, by the fact that professional counselors who interact with clients in crisis over long stretches of time tend to be susceptible to developing fatigue syndromes and vicarious trauma. If left unaddressed, these conditions can erode a counselor's ability to empathize with clients and lead to serious negative psychological consequences. Abassary and Goodrich also note that the opposite can occur: "The counselor may feel some sense of personal meaning after working with those experiencing difficult life events, including heightened sensitivity, compassion, insight, tolerance, and empathy" (pp. 68–69). Based on these insights, they suggest that "vicarious posttraumatic growth can be incorporated into the supervision relationship; basically, the positive outcome of safeguarding against vicarious trauma is added in the form of providing empathy and emphasizing self-care" (p. 69).

The CARE supervision model explores the unique needs specific to crisis-, trauma-, and disaster-based counseling contexts. Each of the four components of the model address areas that require explicit attention in crisis scenarios (Abassary & Goodrich, 2014).

- *Context:* Time, place, and logistics are all important considerations, and the following questions should be asked by supervisors: "What is the specific situation, and how is it impacted by time and place? Are the client and supervisee safe in their current environment? Is the supervisee adequately trained and prepared to face such a situation (on his or her own, or conjointly with others)? What resources are available to supervisor/supervisee/client; what is lacking in providing adequate care?" (p. 72). Understanding contextual factors is as critical to assessing success as identifying challenges that these clients might continue to face in their recovery process.
- *Action:* In this component of the CARE model, "the supervisor covers all immediate needs and addresses concerns of the supervisee as well as the client in providing for care" (p. 73). The supervisor regularly checks in with the supervisee to inquire about the effectiveness of the supervisee's interventions. The supervisor wants to know what worked well and, conversely, what was not as effective.

- *Response:* Once the crisis situation has passed, a review of the crisis and treatment strategies are undertaken. This often overlooked step is vital to ensure adequate care and follow-up. At this time, an assessment can be made regarding protocols that may need to be updated, as well as missing pieces of the care process for all parties involved—client, supervisee, and supervisor.
- *Empathy:* A compassionate and caring response is a necessary ingredient in this supervisory approach. In Abassary and Goodrich's own words, "empathy may be related to posttraumatic growth for the therapist working with trauma victims, and this may be the most important component of the supervisor intervention process" (p. 74).

Abassary and Goodrich believe that their CARE model can be integrated with the discrimination model developed by Bernard (1979), which was presented in Chapter 4. Essentially, in crisis situations, supervisors determine which aspects of the CARE model are of primary importance for the case and then decide which role and focus from the discrimination model are most appropriate for their supervisee.

At the time of this writing, the world is in the midst of a pandemic. In Voices From the Field, Mark Stebnicki, who has written a great deal on the topic of disaster mental health, addresses the challenges both supervisors and supervisees are facing in coping with this pandemic.

 ### VOICES FROM THE FIELD

Managing Crisis During a Pandemic: At War With an Unseen Enemy

Mark A. Stebnicki, PhD

Today we are in the midst of a paradigm shift in the counseling and psychology profession when providing disaster mental health and crisis response for individuals and groups affected by pandemic disasters such as COVID-19. For many, planet Earth does not appear to be a safe place. Clinical counseling supervisees cannot rely solely on older models of disaster mental health and crisis response to deal with pandemic viruses. Newer models have been developed based on Ebola, HIV/AIDS, and other global pandemics.

Each disaster and crisis (school and church shootings, floods, hurricanes, mass gun violence) has unique characteristics and requires helping skills that deal with the mental, behavioral, and psychosocial health response of survivors. A new type of fear and anxiety is associated with a world at war with an unseen enemy combatant, and it is essential for clinical counseling supervisees to understand the biopsychosocial dynamics of vulnerable populations during pandemic viruses. Individuals with preexisting posttraumatic stress and co-occurring mental health conditions may be at risk of increased medical, physical, and mental health stresses that hinder their coping and resiliency. Acute and chronic health problems may be exacerbated when disaster scenarios are replayed on the nightly news, by television specials, in Hollywood-style disaster movies, and in the print and electronic media. This negative reinforcement is compounded when viewers watch this crisis unfold in real time each day.

Clinical counseling supervisees who become energized by helping clients cultivate coping and resiliency strategies during a pandemic can find a renewed sense of meaning and purpose in their chosen career path. Facilitating approaches that help clients mend their mind, body, and spirit and come out of the darkness and into the light can potentiate an attitudinal shift for clients from surviving to thriving in the face of adversity.

As a mental health and rehabilitation counselor, counselor educator and supervisor, and researcher in disaster mental health and trauma counseling, I have become aware that pandemic disasters require new crisis response models. I have lived and provided disaster and crisis response service in communities that have been at the epicenter of school shootings, workplace violence, hurricanes, floods, and tornadoes. Crisis and disaster response require our complete and full attention as helping professionals. It appears that many clinical supervisees and professional counselors now are in a constant state of disaster preparedness. As a result of their profession and training, helping professionals are called to provide psychological first aid and mental health disaster response to clients affected by critical events. However, there is a cost to helping others at the epicenter who have experienced pain, suffering, loss, and trauma. Consequently, many professionals may be at risk for the emotional, social, physical, spiritual, and occupational exhaustion I refer to as *empathy fatigue*.

Clinical counseling supervisees entering the counseling profession who serve clients in crisis and disaster should be open to the idea that all experiences have potential to create opportunities for personal and professional growth. The search for personal meaning in one's traumatic experiences is an existential or spiritual pursuit. Clinical supervisees who want to work in a dynamic therapeutic environment need to know how to cultivate coping and resiliency resources with clients by integrating the mind, body, and spirit during critical events such as pandemics.

Mass Trauma Counseling Guidelines

In 2008, McAdams and Keener noted that "the frequency of serious client crises confronting human service professionals has escalated to such proportions that crises have been referred to as an 'occupational hazard' in the professional literature" (p. 388). Unequivocally, matters have only gotten worse since then. McAdams and Keener were struck then by the "curious absence in counselor preparation, certification, supervision, and ethical practice standards of a consistent or comprehensive guideline for crisis prevention/intervention and postcrisis recovery" (p. 388). Noting the absence of such guidelines, Tarvydas and her colleagues (2017) recently developed mass trauma counseling guidelines, and they emphasize the importance of adhering to professional codes of ethics in these complex situations. As they point out, "counselors . . . should understand that advanced ethical knowledge and skill must be cultivated to meet the unpredictable and often highly complex ethical challenges represented in trauma work" (p. 263). They remind counselors to be cognizant of the core ethics principles of autonomy, beneficence, nonmaleficence, justice, fidelity, and veracity, and to "apply a specific, credible ethical decision-making model to the process of selecting an ethical course of action when responding to mass trauma situations" (p. 263). We cannot provide the guidelines in their entirety, but we have summarized many of their key points. Many helping professionals may encounter people suffering from trauma, and clinical supervisors should prepare their supervisees to work in disaster situations by making them aware of these guidelines and reinforcing them.

- Refrain from providing a diagnosis prematurely, and avoid pathologizing normal reactions to severely abnormal circumstances.
- Use a strength-based and evidence-based approach that emphasizes resilient trauma responses.

- At a minimum, honor the need for as much confidentiality and consent as possible under the chaotic circumstances.
- Avoid taking unnecessary responsibility for clients' decisions, and honor their self-determination even though they may be in a vulnerable state and feel out of control. Deepening or prolonging clients' feelings of dependency and vulnerability can cause long-term harm.
- Help clients reestablish a sense of control by supporting their decision-making processes.
- Be cautious about interacting with media and other public figures in a way that could sensationalize a situation that is already emotionally charged because this could have negative consequences for survivors.
- Offer accurate information to survivors and family members regarding the scope, duration, and nature of the care that will be provided. When providing short-term crisis services, counselors should help link clients to long-term supports and services, if needed.
- Work within the scope of your practice and seek predeployment/preservice education, training, and supervised experience in disaster mental health counseling or mass trauma work if you plan to function in this role.
- Provide emergency care if no other care is available until the incident is over or until a more skilled provider arrives on the scene. In such instances, "counselors will work to the utmost capacity of their applicable skills and training, seek consultation from more experienced responders where available, and take care to do no harm" (p. 265).
- Actively consult with and involve people from the local community to guide interventions. To be strong advocates for vulnerable client-survivors, counselors must be willing to learn about culturally appropriate resources.
- Recognize the potential for clients to be retraumatized or injured if they are deprived of much needed resources or conditions due to the actions (or inactions) of people in the response environment. This can be especially challenging in mass trauma situations in which resources and services are scarce and need to be allocated fairly among others who are also in need.
- Be mindful of the physical and emotional toll of mass trauma work and the potential for it to adversely impact your own well-being.

For further reading on the topic of disaster mental health counseling, we recommend *Introduction to Crisis and Trauma Counseling* (Duffey & Haberstroh, 2020), *Disaster Mental Health Counseling: A Guide to Preparing and Responding* (Webber & Mascari, 2018), and *Disaster Mental Health Counseling: Responding to Trauma in a Multicultural Context* (Stebnicki, 2017).

Psychological First Aid

One of the most widely accepted and practiced approaches for intervening with a range of individuals including adults, adolescents, and children in a crisis is psychological first aid (PFA). PFA is "an evidence-informed modular approach to help children, adolescents, adults, and families in the immediate aftermath of disaster and terrorism (National Child Traumatic Stress Network, 2006). PFA is designed to reduce the initial distress caused by traumatic events and to foster short- and long-term adaptive functioning and coping" (Brymer et al., 2006).

PFA is an evidence-based concrete crisis response system that can be taught and practiced with supervisees and trainees and can be applied in any number and types of emergency and crisis situations. The eight core actions in PFA are:

- Contact and engagement
- Safety and comfort
- Stabilization
- Information gathering on current needs and concerns
- Practical assistance
- Connection with social supports
- Information on coping
- Linkage with collaborative services

The goal of crisis intervention is to increase an individual's functioning to a normal or higher level, which is done by assisting the individual in perceiving events differently and by acquiring coping skills (Kanel, 2018). Crisis workers create support through their attitudes and behaviors. One of the most powerful tools they have is to offer is their gift of presence. This is the capacity to be emotionally available for individuals in crisis as they tell their story and seek human connection to guide them to some sense of stability amid the temporary chaos they are experiencing.

Understanding Specific Crisis Situations

Suicide and Suicide Attempts

Forty-seven thousand people committed suicide in the United States in 2017, and the rate has increased every year since 2014 (Bacon, 2018). According to Whisenhunt and colleagues (2017), "most counselors regularly have contact with clients who are, or may be, at risk for suicide" (p. 452). Perhaps that is not surprising. Suicide rates have been on the rise on college campuses (David, 2019), and suicide is now the second leading cause of death for persons age 15–24 (Hedegaard et al., 2018). A team of scholars point out that the vast majority of those who complete suicide have a diagnosable mental disorder, but they note that "data regarding the frequency of client suicide while under the care of a counselor are limited" (Whisenhunt et al. 2017, p. 452).

Without question, an increasing concern for schools and communities throughout the United States is suicidal preoccupation and behavior of adolescents. Professional associations such as the American School Counselor Association (ASCA, 2018a) have responded by developing best practices and resources such as the *After a Suicide* toolkit to help guide school counselors through the ordeal of student suicide. Many helping professionals can easily recite the list of suicidal risk indicators (e.g., writing about death and dying, lacking a sense of purpose or reason for living, hopelessness, dramatic mood changes). But memorizing a list as an intellectual exercise is completely different from the experience of assessing a client for lethality and actually losing a client to suicide. For further reading on the topic of suicide assessment and treatment, we highly recommend *Suicide Assessment and Treatment Planning for Counselors: A Strengths-Based Approach* (Sommers-Flanagan & Sommers-Flanagan, 2021).

In Voices From the Field, psychologist David Shepard discusses his experience as a trainee with his supervisor when David encountered a suicidal client.

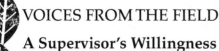 VOICES FROM THE FIELD

A Supervisor's Willingness to Be Vulnerable

David Shepard, PhD

Supervisors need not be so-called master therapists; rather, effective supervisors model what it means to accept the unique vulnerabilities that all counselors truly feel. These supervisors have the courage to share their own vulnerability, and in so doing, they forge a bond with supervisees that extends beyond the time frame of their trainees' tenure. The ideal supervisor is someone who, like the ideal teacher, inspires. Their supervisees leave the supervisory experience with the expectation that anxiety and uncertainty are necessary experiences on their journey of growth, with respect for the limits of their knowledge, and with a clear-eyed anticipation of continued learning.

I will never forget an experience I had when I was a trainee that taught me not only how to deal with a suicidal client but also how a supervisor's courage to share her own vulnerability inspired me to strive for similar courage in my own work (and life.) One night, I received a call from the agency's late-night receptionist that I needed to immediately phone a client (Aaron) who was threatening suicide. It was my first experience with suicide away from the safer confines of the agency. In my panic, I first called (and woke up) my supervisor, Hannah, who said, "I'm going to stay on the line with you the whole time. Put me on hold and get back to me." I called my client and listened to him rant about how no one really cares about him, and he'd prove it by killing himself. Aaron was a hulking 40-year-old, and his voice was loud and filled with terrifying rage. I said to Aaron, "I hear you, Aaron. I'm really listening. Would you mind if I spoke to my supervisor for just 60 seconds." So I put him on hold, switched back to Hannah, updated her, and she told me how to calm him down. I then immediately went back to Aaron. In retrospect, the whole experience was surreal: "Aaron, can I have a moment?" "Hannah, here's what he just said." "Aaron, OK, I'm back now—let's both take a deep breath." "Hannah? He's a little calmer." "Aaron? Let's keep talking."

This back-and-forth went on for 2 hours until we both felt that Aaron did not need immediate hospitalization. What happened after that is the "inspiring" part. I was emotionally drained and desperately needed to process this experience with Hannah. I expected her to tell me to get some sleep and we'd talk tomorrow. Instead, Hannah said, "I need to process just as much as you do. I've been a therapist for 20 years, but this kind of thing still leaves me terrified. Let's just you and I talk." And so we did—just two people sharing their anxieties, engaged in a real relationship, one that felt more like a conversation with a peer than with an authority figure. Hannah's realness, her normalization of the scariest part of our profession, and the close connection we experienced in that processing discussion have stayed with me my whole career. I learned as much about being a human being who allows himself to be vulnerable as I did about handling suicide. And when I think about it, what could be a more inspiring lesson from a supervisor than that?

Suicide and suicide attempts on the part of a client can be devastating for a helping professional, and especially for a supervisee (Rudd et al., 2008; Whisenhunt et al., 2017). After a client suicide, a supervisee typically experiences feelings of shock, grief, loss, guilt, depression, and responsibility. "Client suicide is a significant loss and, as such, supervisees may experience profound grief" (Whisenhunt et al., 2017, p. 453). This event and the feelings it evokes may shake the confidence of a novice clinician. Although supervisees may be trained to work with a range of disorders and emotions in clients, they are rarely prepared for the personal and professional toll suicide can take. Case Study 9.1 details the experiences of one supervisee upon the suicide of a client.

CASE STUDY 9.1: CARLOS

Carlos, a prelicensed counseling psychologist, was recently hired at the university counseling center and is under the supervision of a licensed counseling psychologist at the center. Carlos had seen Kayden for five sessions to help him work on improving his relationship skills. Kayden was in the midst of a rocky relationship with his girlfriend when he came in for counseling, and he wanted help on what he could do to make things better. He would keep his feelings to himself and did not communicate well with his girlfriend. Carlos thought they were making good progress on these issues in the counseling sessions. At their last counseling session, Kayden reported that his girlfriend wanted to break up with him. He was upset and confused, and Carlos worked with him to sort things out and develop a plan for how he would deal with the imminent breakup. It seemed that Kayden was feeling better by the end of the session. A day before their next scheduled session, Carlos got word from the campus police that Kayden had been found dead in his garage: The car was running and the garage door was closed; he had asphyxiated himself. Carlos was shocked and dismayed; he immediately went to his supervisor to tell him what had happened.

It is common for helping professionals to assume an inordinate degree of responsibility when a client chooses suicide. We must do everything we can to help our clients, but we have to be able to identify when we cannot—and not allow it to immobilize us. If you were Carlos's supervisor, how would you respond to this news?

- What would you most want to say to Carlos, and how would you help him process this event?
- How would you guide Carlos in thinking through the ethical, legal, and clinical issues following this event?
- How would you expect the agency administrators to react to this situation?
- How might you work with Carlos if he kept telling himself that he must have missed something and was partially responsible for Kayden's death?
- How should you have addressed the possibility that a client would present with suicide potential?

The supervisor will help Carlos fulfill his agency responsibilities and will work with Carlos to process his reactions. A common reaction of helping professionals is to doubt themselves and believe that had they done or said something different or recognized some signs and symptoms the client would not have committed suicide. Perhaps the point at which Kayden was upset and confused should have alerted Carlos to do a more careful assessment of depression and suicide ideation. In most cases of suicide, there are warning signs, but Kayden appears to have given little indication of suicide risk. It is important to be cognizant of suicide potential and warning signs, but helpers cannot predict what individuals will do or how they will react to their situation. It is the task of the supervisor to help Carlos adopt a balanced attitude between caring and maintaining an objective perspective.

While Carlos is dealing with his own feelings of grief, loss, and responsibility, the supervisor must assess what other immediate actions are necessary. This might include carefully documenting the events of the last few sessions and conducting a psychological case review to see what can be learned from the case. Agency regulations often require an immediate review of the incident, and administrators may seek accountability and want answers about how this could have happened while a client is under the care of a counselor. The supervisor would be liable, however, only if it was determined that the supervisee's treatment of the client was substandard and that this treatment was a factor in the client's death.

It is important that supervisors attend to the personal feelings and reactions of the supervisee as well as to the regulatory needs of the agency. Carlos may never be quite the same as a result of a client suicide, and he will need to examine how this incident may affect his clinical attitude and work. He may become overly cautious and begin to detect suicide potential in many clients he will see in the future. Carlos may benefit from an increased frequency of supervision, and the supervisor should also review standard suicide assessment and intervention procedures with Carlos so he is better prepared to respond to clients' concerns.

This case illustrates the role of the supervisor in suicide risk management. Whenever suicide risk is suspected by the supervisee, this topic should be explored in supervision sessions. Suicidal ideation or behavior is the most frequently encountered emergency situation in mental health settings and may trigger intense feelings of anxiety in supervisees, so the clinical supervision process should routinely include thorough coverage of this topic. Supervisees must know the risk factors and warning signs of suicide, and every client should be assessed for suicidal risk. The supervisor needs to have a working knowledge of all the supervisee's clients so that risk assessment is not left solely to the supervisee.

Further information on suicide is available on the websites of the National Institute of Mental Health (https://www.nimh.nih.gov/health/statistics/suicide.shtml) and the National Suicide Prevention Lifeline (https://suicidepreventionlifeline.org/).The following publications also provide in-depth discussion of therapeutic techniques for counselors and supervisors: *Brief Cognitive-Behavioral Therapy for Suicide Prevention* (Bryan & Rudd, 2018), *Crisis Assessment, Intervention, and Prevention* (Jackson-Cherry & Erford, 2018), *PROTECT: Relational Safety-Based Suicide Prevention Training Frameworks* (Kar Ray et al., 2019), and *Supporting Counselors After a Client Suicide: Creative Supervision Techniques* (Whisenhunt et al., 2017).

Supervisees will encounter many clients who will challenge their skills, and effective supervision can prepare trainees to meet these challenges. Two discussions follow that illuminate crises students may face and the importance of the counselor's role.

In Voices From the Field, Matt Gragg, director of a university counseling center, describes the increase in mental health concerns and in symptom severity among the college student population over the past 20 years.

VOICES FROM THE FIELD

The College Experience

Matt Gragg, MS

For more than 15 years, I counseled male adolescents on probation who were mandated to therapy. In 2001, I was offered the opportunity to work part-time in the evenings at a small private university counseling center. In contrast to my mandated clients, college students actually wanted my help and treated me with respect. It was refreshing to be able to apply the clinical skills I learned in my MFT program, and most students responded well to treatment. I worked with students who were homesick, depressed, anxious, or had relationship difficulties. It was an excellent fit for me and a positive change from my previous position.

Fast forward to 2020. I am now the full-time director of the same university counseling center. College mental health has transformed significantly since 2001. I have observed a significant increase in symptom severity among students who seek help at the center, including students with severe diagnoses and more hospitalizations for suicidality. Some trainees are not expecting college students to present with complex issues such as disordered eating, significant trauma history, psychotic symptoms, and personality disorders. Thinking back to college mental health in 2001, I can relate to the expectations practicum students have for the client population. It is definitely more challenging to meet clients where they are today.

Due to the high demand, we have had to shift to a short-term therapy model, which means supervisees have less time to make an impact on clients. This can be frustrating for supervisees, and I help them focus on only a few goals with a client to increase the productivity of the sessions. I use the analogy of planting the seed and watering it as their role in therapy and emphasize that they may not see the plant grow to its potential. We try to give the client a good experience in therapy in preparation for a possible transition to a long-term therapist in the community.

Many of the students we see have already been in therapy, some for multiple years with different therapists. These students are more likely to challenge a novice therapist's lack of experience, signaling verbally or nonverbally that they are too complex for the therapist. For a supervisee who already feels like an imposter, this could enhance feelings of inadequacy. In addition, many new therapists are most comfortable with cognitive behavior theapy (CBT) interventions. However, some university students have already been exposed to CBT and want something different. This also makes the new therapist feel vulnerable and unprepared. I find it helpful to normalize these feelings and focus on the strengths of supervisees to help them build their confidence. In addition, creating dyadic trainings on short-term treatment options and interventions helps to expand their toolbox and increase their competence.

The mental health needs of college students have changed significantly in the past two decades, and this has created a change in supervision. After a year at a university counseling center, practicum graduate students are better prepared to diagnose, create a treatment plan, manage their countertransference, and remain calm in crisis situations within a short-term treatment model. I feel privileged to be able to mentor supervisees who help college students manage their mental health needs during such a crucial time in their development.

In Voices From the Field, Gretchen McLain describes the challenges she faced in not being adequately prepared to deal with the demands of being a school counselor when a student died and other students struggled with depression and suicidal ideation.

 VOICES FROM THE FIELD

Carving Out a School Counselor's Role

Gretchen McLain, MA

After teaching for 5 years, I became the school counselor at a small rural school. I was responsible for individual counseling, guidance, special education, scheduling, computing grade point averages, and state testing for grades 7–12. My degree was not yet complete, so this small school served as my practicum and internship site. My university program was accredited by CACREP; however, I did not feel adequately prepared to advocate for myself. With only one other school counselor in the district, I did not have access to a mentor who could advocate for me or help me learn my role, so I had to carve out my own role.

The demands of the school counseling office can be extreme. During the fall of my first year as a school counselor, one evening the football field was struck by lightning as the team was practicing. All 40 football players and coaches suffered the effects of that lightning strike, and one student, Robert, died the next day. Robert was popular among the teachers and students, and the community's outpouring of support was overwhelming. However, several students struggled with depression and suicidal ideation, and I found myself in over my head. One day, I had five students report that they wanted to commit suicide. On that day, I requested that the elementary school counselor provide assistance.

My induction into the role of school counselor is not unique. Novice school counselors have been expected to sink or swim for many years. There is ample literature regarding teacher and administrator induction, but little research explains the induction processes for school counselors. Novice school counselors often have few resources available with regard to counselor duties such as classroom guidance and group counseling. With a lack of formal induction activities, school counselors are more prone to experience burnout and compassion fatigue.

The expectation in the education community is that school counselors perform on their first day as if they have been serving in that capacity for years. In larger schools, a counseling team may be available for novice school counselors to lean on for support. Unfortunately, that is not the case in most small schools. New school counselors can profit from reaching out to experienced school counselors for guidance and mentorship. A mentor can help the new school counselor feel affirmed while learning this new role. With the support offered by a mentor, new school counselors are less likely to experience burnout and will be better able to serve their students.

This situation is an example of what happens when counselors are placed in positions in which the roles and responsibilities are unclear. A supervisor's job is to help supervisees examine how to go about preparing themselves for emergency situations.

- If you were the school counselor in this situation, what would you have done?
- If you were the supervisor of this school counselor, how would you help the supervisee prepare for future crises?

Personal Threats by Clients

Threats of violence or actual assaults by clients are rare, but they do occur. The supervisor should be prepared for any situation that might arise with the supervisee and have a plan in place for how to proceed. Threats of violence or actual assaults can affect a supervisee both physically and emotionally and may shake the very core of the individual's confidence as a helping professional. Concern for the safety of both supervisee and client is paramount. The supervisor can work with the supervisee to find ways to continue to work with the client while managing these heightened emotional reactions. Case Study 9.2 describes a supervisee's personal reaction to a client who threatened her life.

CASE STUDY 9.2: KENDRA

Kendra has worked as a group counselor in a prison setting for 15 years. She is well trained and experienced in working with inmates. Several of her colleagues meet weekly in a peer supervision group for support and to problem solve clinical cases. Yesterday, an inmate who has participated in her group wrote a note to Kendra, threatening her life if she did not give him a positive evaluation to assist with his release. Kendra met with the peer supervision group today and talked about the fact that this has affected her dramatically. She is truly frightened and is considering resigning from her position at the prison.

This situation should be reported to Kendra's superiors so the prison system can address the inmate's behavior within the institution's rules of conduct. However, many questions remain as Kendra assesses her feelings and tries to resolve her concerns about continuing to work in this environment.

- What are the ethical, legal, and clinical issues in this case?
- What kinds of questions would you raise as a peer supervisor regarding this situation?
- What would you most want to say to Kendra about this situation?
- Do you think Kendra should resign from her position? If not, how would you help her proceed?
- Have you ever been threatened? What was it like for you? What did you learn that you could use in working with Kendra?
- Do you think the peer supervision group can handle this, or should someone else in authority in the prison address it?

The peer group members can help Kendra sort through what has happened, what brought it about, and what it is about this particular threat that has been so upsetting. (She has probably experienced others in her 15 years there.) The peer supervision group could discuss what action is necessary in notifying the prison authorities and prison police to ensure the safety of Kendra and any other staff who may be involved. The ethics codes of the American Psychological Association (2017) and some other professions address the fact that the counselor may terminate therapy when threatened or otherwise endangered by the client. Kendra might consider a legal consult if there is any uncertainty about how to proceed. The peer supervision group can also help Kendra develop a plan for how to deal with this situation and how she will handle these kinds of events in the future. Kendra might benefit from some time off from the job. Her documentation of this event is essential.

Once Kendra has recovered from the fear and shock of the threat, the supervision group could help her review the case and the options she has for talking with this individual in the future. A role play could assist Kendra in exploring ways for her to talk with the inmate. Members of the group might take turns playing the inmate and the therapist to try out different ways of responding. Then Kendra might role-play talking with the inmate.

The interventions discussed here would be equally applicable had Kendra been a supervisee rather than a member of the peer supervision group. The supervisor, however, would have greater responsibility and liability than does the peer group.

Violence in Schools and on College Campuses

Although crime in the nation's schools and colleges has declined overall in the past two decades, the reports of opioid use, active-shooter incidents, and bullying are on the increase. "From 2000 to 2017, there were 37 active shooter incidents at elementary and secondary schools and 15 active shooter incidents at postsecondary institutions" (National Center for Education Statistics, 2019). CNN (2019) examined 10 years of shootings on K–12 campuses and found two sobering truths: School shootings are increasing, and no type of community is spared.

Counselors who work in schools and college counseling centers and their supervisors increasingly have to deal with violence, which presents both legal and ethical issues. When counselors are called to the scene of a violent act, their work affects them personally, and they frequently require debriefing and personal counseling. Those who supervise school or college counselors who deal with the aftermath of a violent incident will need the skills to effectively work with their supervisees' personal reactions.

Furthermore, both supervisees and their supervisors have some responsibility to take action if they become aware of a potential problem in the making. Trainees, counselors, and supervisors need to be vigilant in monitoring and reporting students who have threatened to commit violent acts or who have been part of previous violent activity. School counselors may also need to act on student reports of their peers who intend violence. The basic standard of care for school counselors and their supervisors is that school personnel have a duty to protect students from foreseeable harm. Schools are now developing crisis management plans.

Sometimes students make veiled threats, as Jake did in Case Study 9.3. When threats do not seem clear cut, helping professionals are ethically obligated to obtain the information they need to make proper assessments of the potential for violence.

CASE STUDY 9.3: JAKE

Jake is a high school student who has been seeing Myra, a school psychology intern. Jake was referred by a teacher because he has been disruptive in class and his academic performance is rapidly declining. After the first counseling session, Myra sees that Jake is depressed, anxious, and currently quite agitated. He is upset at the teacher for referring him to counseling, and Jake says that he has "ways to take care of teachers like that." After some further discussion, Myra excuses herself for a moment from the counseling session and immediately calls her supervisor to discuss what has transpired and seek direction about how to proceed.

School counselors and their supervisors must take every threat of violence seriously. They must be prepared to assess whether or not a potentially violent student has a plan and the ability to act on his or her threats.

- What are the ethical, legal, and clinical issues in this situation?
- As Myra's supervisor, what additional information would you like to hear from her?
- What would you instruct Myra to do with regard to the immediate situation?
- What are the immediate issues to address with Myra? What will you want to discuss in her next supervision session?

The first task is to find out more from Myra about Jake's statement that he has ways to take care of teachers like this. Did she ask Jake exactly what he meant? If not, she should discuss that with Jake to obtain more detailed information. Other questions might focus on Jake's history of other incidents, problems at home, whether he is having problems only in one class or in others as well, his access to weapons, and his use of drugs or alcohol. Because Myra is an intern and this situation could rapidly become a crisis, her supervisor may want to assist Myra as a cotherapist with Jake. This can be a significant learning experience for Myra as she discusses this cotherapy in supervisory sessions.

School personnel may be held accountable if a student's writing assignments contain evidence of premeditated violence. Preventing students from harming other students is an implicit duty of school personnel. Both counselors and their supervisors may find themselves legally responsible for preventing students from harming others. Acting on any evidence indicating that a student may be violent and warning others of threats of violence made against them can protect others in the school from harm.

Witnessing Disasters and Violent Events

Those of us who have experienced some kind of disaster—fire, flood, hurricane, accident, war—know the strong emotional impact such events have on each of us. Although the helping professions have recognized these emotional effects for years, only in the last few decades has a response been developed and organized to systematically help victims of a disaster cope with their emotional reactions and head off the posttraumatic stress response. We are seeing violence and its emotional toll on a grand scale in today's world, and counselors and supervisors must be trained and prepared to work with clients, communities, and supervisees. Supervisors need to be able to deal with their own as well as their family members' existential anxiety about the uncertainty of our times. In addition, supervisors need to be trained and ready to assist their supervisees and clients in dealing with the anxiety and fear that result from terrorist violence.

Those in the helping professions who provide disaster mental health services are also subject to disasters and subsequent emotional reactions. It is within the scope of supervision to identify when supervisees need help to cope with their own reactions as well as those of their clients. Consider the supervisor's role in helping Devin in Case Study 9.4.

CASE STUDY 9.4: DEVIN

Devin has a doctorate in psychology and is completing his postdoctoral training for licensure in a community mental health center. He has 3 years of clinical experience in a variety of settings and has been at the community mental health center for 6 months. This morning a client came in with a gun and threatened to shoot one of the mental health workers. Devin did not see it happen but heard the commotion and ran into the hallway to see the gunman pointing the gun at the worker. As the gunman turned his sights on Devin, some of the agency staff wrestled the gunman to the floor and subdued him.

Devin will see his supervisor this afternoon in an unscheduled meeting to talk about what transpired this morning. If you were Devin, what do you think you would most need from your supervisor?

- What are the ethical, legal, and clinical issues in this case?
- What kinds of questions would you raise with Devin regarding this situation?
- How would you guide Devin in thinking through this situation?
- How would you help Devin decide what to do now?
- What kind of reactions would you expect from Devin?
- How might this situation affect the supervisory relationship?
- What kind of interventions will Devin need to help cope with this situation?

Before we discuss the case of Devin, let's review two more cases in which a supervisee benefited from the knowledge, skills, and support of a supervisor: one involving repercussions from our wars in the Middle East (Case Study 9.5: Isabelle) and another case involving a natural disaster (Case Study 9.6: Jody).

CASE STUDY 9.5: ISABELLE

Isabelle is completing her internship at a community mental health center. Two weeks after her husband left for a year-long tour of duty in the Middle East, Isabelle met with Todd, a new client. Shortly after the session began, Todd explained that he had served in Iraq, and although some time has passed since he returned home, he is traumatized by the horrific events that he witnessed, including the deaths of three men in his unit. Todd appears to be suffering from posttraumatic stress disorder, and he revealed that upon returning home he began provoking fights with his wife and drinking heavily. Worried about the safety of her own husband and the emotional toll his experiences in the war zone will have on their marriage, Isabelle seems to be distancing herself from Todd when he is in dire need of professional help.

Isabelle's need for ongoing support while her husband is serving in the Middle East has triggered significant personal issues, and she may benefit from personal counseling. Isabelle's supervisor needs to be sensitive to the stressful situation that her supervisee is currently experiencing and be careful to avoid assigning her cases that may trigger strong countertransference reactions.

- What are the ethical, legal, and clinical issues in this case?
- If you were supervising Isabelle and noticed her distancing behavior, what might you say to her?
- At what point would you recommend that Isabelle seek personal counseling to address her reactions?
- How would you help Isabelle proceed in this case? Would you recommend that the client be transferred to a different counselor, or would you encourage Isabelle to remain assigned to the case?
- Would you consider serving as Isabelle's counselor for a brief time to help her separate her personal concerns from her ability to provide effective counseling?

CASE STUDY 9.6: JODY

In September 2017, Hurricane Maria became the worst natural disaster in recorded history to affect the islands of Dominica, St Croix, and Puerto Rico. Jody, a recent college graduate, was visiting a friend in Puerto Rico when Maria struck. Jody was terrified, not only by the sheer force of the hurricane and threats to her and others' safety but also by the devastating humanitarian crisis that followed. When she returned home, Jody continued to ruminate about the situation and felt guilt about leaving her friend's family behind in such dismal conditions. Several years have passed, and Jody is now completing her master's degree in counseling. She is doing her practicum at a community mental health center, where she is supervised by a licensed clinical social worker who has worked there for 12 years. They have just received the warning that a Level 5 hurricane is heading toward their region, and it is a near certainty that the city will experience major devastation when the hurricane strikes in approximately 10 hours.

The staff is preparing to provide counseling for the next several weeks to victims of the hurricane. Jody's supervisor needs to decide whether Jody is able to help during this disaster. If her previous trauma experience has not been resolved, Jody may need to evacuate before the hurricane arrives.

- What are the ethical, legal, and clinical issues in this case?
- What kinds of questions would you raise with Jody regarding this situation?
- How might Jody's traumatic experience surviving Hurricane Maria affect her ability to provide crisis counseling to other hurricane victims?
- How would you guide Jody in thinking through this situation in which she may be both a victim of the impending disaster and the provider of services to other victims?
- What is your role as the supervisor in this case? What interventions are you likely to use with Jody?
- Do you think Jody should be counseling other victims of the hurricane? Why or why not?

The three events described are all disasters, and any kind of a disaster can take its toll on the victims and on those caring for them. Supervisees Devin, Isabelle, and Jody will need special attention and monitoring by their supervisors in the coming weeks. Helping professionals must be properly prepared to work with disaster victims, and supervisors must be competent to prepare their supervisees for this work. The message we want to convey to victims is twofold: They should expect some kind of emotional reaction, and they can expect to recover (normalize) in time. It is essential that helping professionals who will provide services and supervision in disaster mental health receive formal training on this topic. Disaster counseling has become a specialized field in recent years, with research available on assessment and intervention strategies. Supervisees who will be providing disaster mental health services must receive formal training as well.

Devin's supervisor may schedule a meeting the morning after the incident to assess whether debriefing would be an appropriate strategy in his case. If Devin seems eager to discuss the crisis and needs to vent, ask him what he saw and what it was like for him, what his thoughts have been in the last 24 hours, and how he is currently coping with the situation. Remind Devin that he has control over how much detail he provides. Offer support and reassurance that his reactions are normal, and talk with him about possible reactions he can expect over the next days and weeks to come.

Devin should be encouraged to attend counseling if his reaction warrants an in-depth follow-up. He could resume counseling clients, but his supervisor will need to carefully monitor his caseload and refer cases to other counselors that might pose particular difficulty for Devin. This can be an excellent opportunity for Devin to learn from his own experience, his subsequent reaction, and from the debriefing process in his supervision, which modeled managing a critical incident in a way that will lead to normalization.

Isabelle's reaction to Todd suggests that she is having great difficulty separating her own circumstances from his experiences and issues. Isabelle appears to be experiencing a constellation of feelings that prevents her from fulfilling her responsibilities as his counselor. The first obligation is to protect the welfare of clients, so Isabelle and her supervisor will need to discuss how best to talk to Todd about referral to another counselor.

Jody is a hurricane survivor and is likely to be a victim of a second major hurricane. Her supervisor needs to assess whether Jody should be called upon to counsel other hurricane victims. Jody's supervisor should meet with all of the supervisees before the disaster strikes to review the center's emergency protocols and crisis management plan. Because the hurricane is a few hours away, Jody and her supervisor may have time to talk about any posttraumatic reactions related to Hurricane Maria that are being triggered before sending Jody home to pack her belongings and evacuate. Jody and her supervisor will need to meet after the hurricane passes, not only to discuss her current level of adjustment as a victim of the disaster but also to determine how ready she is to counsel clients who have been affected by the hurricane.

If Jody has strong reactions to the event she experienced, she should not work with victims at this time. If she is handling the reaction in a positive way and is making a good adjustment, counseling victims could be very productive. She knows what it was like for them and what they are experiencing. Jody should probably not do any grief counseling with those who have lost family and friends in the hurricane. The intensity of that process may be more than she is ready to handle. Nonetheless, with sound supervision, Jody can provide helpful counseling to other victims and learn from this entire experience in a way that increases her sense of empowerment to self-supervise in the future.

Coping With Personal Crises

Personal crises such as divorce, relationship problems, family difficulties, death, or financial problems can have a profound effect on the work and training of mental health professionals. Supervisees experiencing such crises often are ill equipped to continue to work and train effectively. Supervisors must decide how to help supervisees deal with a personal crisis while continuing to provide clinical services. What is your role as a supervisor to assist the supervisee in dealing with the crisis? Should you routinely address the potential effect that personal crises might have on supervisees' clinical work? To what extent, if at all, do you offer limited counseling to your supervisee? Case Study 9.7 illustrates this situation.

CASE STUDY 9.7: TREVOR

Trevor is a student in a master's-level social work program. Before enrolling in the program, he had been a probation officer for 5 years. He is enthusiastic about his training program and demonstrates strong clinical knowledge and skills. At the last supervisory session, Trevor reluctantly talked about the fact that he and his wife recently separated and that he is experiencing a great deal of difficulty dealing with the situation. He is depressed and having trouble concentrating on his coursework and on his clients in the counseling center.

As supervisors, we have to constantly assess how we can be helpful and therapeutic for our supervisees without becoming their personal therapists. It is essential to learn when to refer the supervisee to someone who can provide support and counseling who is removed from the supervisory relationship.

- What are the ethical, legal, and clinical issues in this case?
- What kinds of questions would you raise with Trevor regarding this situation?
- What would you most want to say to Trevor about this situation?
- How would you help Trevor decide how to proceed from here?
- Do you think a supervisor should address supervisees' personal issues in the supervisory relationship? How might that be relevant to supervision?
- Would you allow yourself to do counseling with Trevor under any conditions?
- What restrictions on Trevor's counseling work might be appropriate?

It is within the bounds of supervision to provide support and help Trevor gain perspective on what is occurring and how he thinks the crisis might be affecting his work. Allowing Trevor to talk through the situation and explore how it is affecting him is a powerful intervention. The focus of the discussion should be on how the personal situation affects his work with clients. Avoid the temptation to become Trevor's therapist even though you think you could be of considerable help. Be aware that the boundaries can become unclear very quickly, and encourage Trevor to seek a personal therapist to focus on his feelings about the separation. If you believe Trevor is impaired in his work with clients, you have an obligation to take action and have him refer his clients to other clinicians. At the very least, it would be best if Trevor does not work with clients who are going through a divorce or having other relationship problems until his personal situation is having less of an impact on him.

Caring for the Caregiver

No mental health professional, including supervisors and supervisees, can completely eliminate the possibility of encountering highly stressful situations at work. We are in the business of providing a precious commodity—compassion and care— to the people we serve. Mental health professionals are vulnerable to empathy or compassion fatigue (e.g., Muratori & Haynes, 2020; Stebnicki, 2016) and vicarious traumatization. With years of training and experience, professionals can develop effective strategies to cope with the stressful demands that accompany this work, but no one is 100% immune from stress.

Self-Care Is an Ethical Mandate

Self-care is an ethical imperative for counselors, trainees, and supervisors; it protects us from burnout, empathy fatigue, impairment, and other conditions that can detract from our effectiveness. Caring for self is just as important as any of the skills or strategies we have introduced in this book. One of our most potent tools for supervision is modeling, and we have an obligation to model self-care for our supervisees. If we are not taking care of ourselves, it will not be possible for us to give care to others, either in our personal or professional life. At the end of the day, we must live with ourselves. If we are to practice what we preach, we must take care of our "self" so that we can continue to help others.

Self-Care as a Way to Prevent Burnout

Supervisors and supervisees who are working in crisis situations are especially vulnerable to burnout, the physical, emotional, and mental exhaustion that results from constant or repeated pressure associated with an intense, long-term involvement with people with intense needs. Burnout is also associated with a sense of helplessness, a negative view of self, and negative attitudes toward work, life, and other people. Burnout begins slowly and progresses through several stages. It typically results in personal feelings of depression, loss of morale, feelings of isolation, depersonalization, and reduced productivity.

Self-care is best viewed as an ongoing preventive activity that can help you cope successfully with the stress of crisis counseling. It is of paramount importance that you become attuned to the warning signals that you are being depleted and that you take seriously your own need for nurturing and sustaining yourself. If you pay attention to the early warning signs and develop practical strategies for keeping burnout at bay, you will be better able to respond effectively to the challenges your work presents. By proactively engaging in self-care, you increase the odds of preventing burnout.

For further reading on self-care, we recommend *Leaving It at the Office: A Guide to Psychotherapist Self-Care* (Norcross & VandenBos, 2018), *Counselor Self-Care* (Corey, Muratori, et al., 2018), and *Personal Reflections on Counseling* (Corey, 2020).

In the Personal Perspective, Patrice Moulton shares her early experience in crisis work and her desire to assist supervisees in developing habits and boundaries that allow them to remain balanced while helping others.

 ## PATRICE MOULTON'S PERSONAL PERSPECTIVE

Early in my career, when I worked in private practice, my caseload was composed largely of dual-diagnosed clients suffering from addiction and depression; many of them were at high risk of attempting suicide. Much of my day was spent conducting lethality assessments and determining at what point hospitalization was necessary for the client's safety. I look back at those days and wonder how I survived them! But I also remember an intense sense of reward at the end of each day. This sense of reward was combined with constant anxiety about making very difficult decisions while exercising "clinical judgment" that we are all supposed to have after completing our clinical training. The upside of that work was the intense sense of meaning in my professional life. The downside was that there never seemed to be a stopping point. Crises don't occur conveniently during regular working hours, and every critical incident requires immediate attention. This meant that my personal life often had to take a temporary back seat.

Looking back, I appreciate that my husband was so supportive of my work and the hours I kept. Having a stable home life was my foundation. The feelings I experienced at that time (e.g., responsibility, anxiety, confidence, and being honored to help people during their worst times) have accompanied me throughout my career, and they now assist me when supervising. I spend considerable time with graduate students discussing topics such as the need to have a personal life that is separate from work, the need to have their own lives as stable as possible before attempting to assist others, the need to practice self-care, the need for balance, and the importance of establishing and maintaining very clear boundaries. We are caregivers and have a tendency to care for others before ourselves. Self-care is vital to renew our energy and compassion to meet the challenges of walking daily with our clients through painful experiences.

Summary

In today's world, we are experiencing a rapid increase in both natural and human-caused disasters as well as public health crises leading to extreme trauma among Americans. Supervisors must be prepared to support their trainees as they encounter client crises of varying magnitudes. Any number of crises can and will occur in supervision. It is of paramount importance that supervisors have a general plan for approaching these situations; be current on the professional, ethical, and legal standards that apply; and have a variety of supervision methods to use depending on the nature of the situation. Supervisors should remain abreast of resources that can offer guidance to their supervisees as well as supervision frameworks that can guide their practice. It is recommended that supervisors develop written emergency procedures for the variety of crisis situations that can occur and address those procedures in the supervision contract. Supervisors should review these emergency procedures with their supervisees.

Supervisees need to know which situations must be brought to the attention of the supervisor and in what time frame. For example, suicide threats should be reported immediately to the supervisor. Supervisees should have phone numbers for the supervisor and the alternate supervisor if the supervisor is not reachable. Supervisors must be familiar with all of their supervisees' clients and receive regular updates on all cases, with special attention to those that involve some level of risk. Supervisors are expected to train their supervisees in handling crisis situations. They should discuss these in supervision and refer supervisees to literature and workshops if they feel they need more training. Supervisors need to have up-to-date knowledge on assessment and intervention in these situations and the related ethical and legal issues.

At some point in your career, many of you will assume the role of a supervisor. We suggest that you reflect on what you would find helpful in your work in crisis situations if you were a supervisee. We end this chapter with some recommendations for working with your supervisees in crisis management supervision.

Take time to listen to what your supervisees have to say about a situation. Ask open-ended questions that will provide a more complete understanding of the situation. Supervisees often present only the information they think you want to hear. Exercise care in assigning clients who appear to have a high degree of risk to supervisees unless there is assurance that your supervisee has the clinical competence and judgment necessary to work with such clients.

In every case, strive to make the crisis situation a learning experience for supervisees. If the situation permits, help them think through the facts, issues, possible courses of action, and their consequences. The goal for supervisees is to learn to handle situations like these on their own. If an immediate intervention is required, discuss the situation in detail after the intervention has been made. Let supervisees know how you thought through the situation and how you arrived at your chosen course of action.

The importance of modeling and of having supervisees practice through role playing to increase their competence in crisis intervention cannot be stressed enough. Crisis preparation is an important part of supervision and training, and it may help to circumvent the mishandling of a crisis should one occur. Despite the liabilities associated with crisis intervention supervision, the most rewarding moments in supervision occur when you witness your supervisee gaining the knowledge, skill, and confidence to practice competently in difficult situations.

SUGGESTED ACTIVITIES

1. Interview at least two supervisors and ask them what crisis situations they have encountered as supervisors. Find out what it was like for them and how they intervened in the situation.

2. In small groups, identify a crisis situation in supervision and role-play the scenario. Have different members in the group take turns role-playing interventions with the supervisee. Then discuss what seemed to work best with this situation.

3. Brainstorm a list of all the possible crisis situations that might occur in supervision. Identify the ones that would be the most difficult to handle, and brainstorm possible interventions for those.

4. Invite an experienced supervisor to come to class and discuss his or her experience handling crisis situations in supervision. Ask what he or she has learned from those experiences.

5. In small groups, have each member discuss which crisis situations would be most difficult and which would be easiest to handle. Identify commonalities and have a spokesperson from each group share those themes with the class.

6. In small groups, brainstorm all the possible elements to be included in a risk management plan as it relates to crisis management. Work collaboratively to develop a risk management workshop that includes visuals for training.

7. In small groups, discuss the impact of violence and human-caused disasters in our culture, their connection to mental health, and their effects on supervisory roles and responsibilities.

CHAPTER 10
Evaluation in Supervision

FOCUS QUESTIONS

1. What do you think of when you hear the term "evaluation" as it relates to supervision? What is the value of evaluation? Must it always be a part of supervision? Explain.
2. What were some of your experiences when you were evaluated by a supervisor? Generally, was the evaluation experience helpful or not? What did you learn from those experiences that will influence your role as an evaluator in supervision?
3. What methods of evaluation did your supervisor use? What were the pros and cons of these methods?
4. What could you do to decrease the anxiety many supervisees experience surrounding the evaluation process?
5. If you could design the perfect evaluation plan, what elements and methods would you include?
6. What are the most challenging aspects for supervisors when evaluating supervisees? What action steps could assist the supervisor in addressing these difficult aspects of evaluation?

Evaluation is a critical component of ethical supervision and is the element that sets supervision apart from counseling and psychotherapy. Supervision is evaluative by its very definition—overseeing the supervisee's training and clinical work. Supervisors should be cognizant of two considerations in evaluating supervisees: (a) Increasing liability concerns have led to more objective and scientific development and use of supervision evaluation tools (Bernard & Goodyear, 2019), and (b) all evaluation tools do not fit all supervisees. Supervisors should choose instruments, assignments, activities, and technology "based on an assessment of the supervisee's developmental level, confidence, self-efficacy, and learning style; the clinical and supervision contexts; and the needs of the client" (ACES, 2011, 4.c.iii.).

Evaluation is an essential component for accomplishing these four goals of supervision:

1. Promoting development and teaching the supervisee. Evaluation measures the degree to which learning is taking place.
2. Protecting the welfare of the client. Evaluation ensures that the supervisee is measuring up to established standards of clinical and ethical competence.
3. Serving the gatekeeping function for the profession. Monitoring supervisee performance is a cornerstone in providing information about the supervisee's professional, ethical, and clinical competence as well as his or her suitability for the profession.
4. Fostering the empowerment of the supervisee to work as an independent professional. The evaluation process serves as a model for the supervisee to learn how to self-evaluate and continue to learn and grow throughout his or her career as a helping professional.

Evaluation is a process that begins with establishing goals at the beginning of supervision and provides ongoing feedback in periodic formal feedback sessions. Falender and Shafranske (2017) describe the need for *competency-based clinical supervision* in which professional competence is developed by providing the structures and processes necessary to achieve this objective. They recommend that assessment and evaluation be "anchored in behavioral terms and be specific to knowledge, skills, and attitudes." (p 41). Holt and colleagues (2015) promote the use of evidence-based supervision and endorse the idea of tracking client outcomes, which enables supervisors to provide objective feedback to counselor trainees about treatment progress. When used to guide treatment decisions, client outcome data have consistently been shown to improve the effectiveness of subsequent interventions. Holt and colleagues add, "as clinical psychology moves toward integrating science and practice, the need to teach students evidence-based principles of therapeutic change and how to use outcome measures to enhance progress is paramount" (p. 185).

In this chapter, we focus on the gatekeeping function of evaluation, essential features of evaluation, guidelines for conducting evaluations, methods of evaluation, and concerns of both supervisors and supervisees regarding the evaluation process. In addition, we discuss the importance of empowering supervisees to conduct self-evaluations as part of their career-long professional development. Several evaluation tools are provided in appendixes at the end of this chapter. Competent supervisors will develop a position on the standards, objectives, and methods of supervision and be willing to continue to learn how they can best use evaluation to help supervisees learn, grow, and develop confidence as professionals.

Codes of Ethics and Evaluation

Evaluation of supervisees is required by most of the professional and licensing standards. Although these standards may vary in details among the professions, all agree that regular feedback and evaluation are an expected part of supervision. Supervisors are obligated, both ethically and legally, to provide timely, accurate, and relevant feedback and evaluation to supervisees regarding their clinical performance. Evaluations have a legal aspect in that some degree of liability attaches to the responsibility for evaluating the supervisee's performance accurately for the supervisee, professional associations, licensing boards, and employers. An inaccurate evaluation can have serious implications for the supervisee as well as for the supervisor, clients, employers, and the field. Box 10.1 lists some of the professional standards relevant to evaluation in supervision.

Gatekeeping and Evaluation

Gatekeeping in the mental health professions continues to grow in importance for licensing bodies, academic programs, licensed clinicians, and for the clients and consumers of mental health services. "Gatekeepers are the persons responsible for ethically

Box 10.1
ETHICS CODES AND STANDARDS
REGARDING EVALUATION IN SUPERVISION

American Counseling Association (2014)

Code of Ethics

Supervisors document and provide supervisees with ongoing feedback regarding their performance and schedule periodic formal evaluative sessions throughout the supervisory relationship. (F.6.a.)

Counselor educators clearly state to students, prior to and throughout the training program, the levels of competency expected, appraisal methods, and timing of evaluations for both didactic and clinical competencies. Counselor educators provide students with ongoing feedback regarding their performance throughout the training program. (F.9.a.)

National Association of Social Workers (2017)

Code of Ethics

Social workers who provide supervision should evaluate supervisees' performance in a manner that is fair and respectful. (3.01.d.)

American Psychological Association (2017)

Ethical Principles of Psychologists and Code of Conduct

In academic and supervisory relationships, psychologists establish a timely and specific process for providing feedback to students and supervisees. Information regarding the process is provided to the student at the beginning of supervision. (7.06.a.)

Psychologists evaluate students and supervisees on the basis of their actual performance on relevant and established program requirements. (7.06.b.)

Association for Counselor Education and Supervision (2011)

Best Practices in Clinical Supervision

The supervisor understands that evaluation is fundamental to supervision and accepts his/her evaluation responsibilities. (9.a.)

The supervisor provides both formative and summative evaluations on a regular basis. (9.a.i.)

The supervisor clearly communicates the evaluation plan to the supervisee. (9.b.)

The supervisor encourages ongoing supervisee self-evaluation. (9.c.)

The supervisor takes appropriate steps when remediation is necessary. (9.d.)

monitoring trainees' progression through gatekeeping checkpoints prior to endorsing them for independent professional practice" (Homrich, 2018, p. 2). Essential to gatekeeping is clear, scheduled, documented, and systematic evaluation of supervisee performance, ethical practice, and clinical judgment. Gatekeepers are the quality control agents for the mental health professions who protect current and future clients as well as the integrity of the professions they represent. Dufrene (2018, p. 143) refers to *gateslip-*

ping as the practice of allowing impaired or incompetent trainees and other prelicensed practitioners into professional practice, which has a negative impact on the clinical professions and, more important, on the welfare of the client community. Dufrene recommends a systematic and collaborative approach to gatekeeping, along with consistency of policies and procedures, to ensure effective gatekeeping practices.

Gatekeeping may be a professional practice guided by ethics codes, legal mandates, and professional standards, but it is also an emotional journey for both the gatekeeper/supervisor and the student/supervisee. Alicia Homrich shares highlights of her journey in gatekeeping in Voices From the Field.

 VOICES FROM THE FIELD

My Introduction to and Experience of Gatekeeping in Supervision

Alicia M. Homrich, PhD

Effective supervision involves much more than monitoring clinical activities. Supervision encompasses establishing a working relationship of trust and supporting the supervisee's growth processes and identity development as a counselor. Also important are encouraging and expanding trainees' ability to conduct themselves professionally, navigate interpersonal interactions in counseling and collegial relationships effectively, and identify and successfully manage their internal intrapersonal processes, such as anxiety. These latter aspects of supervisory oversight are less tangible than measuring clinical skill performance, but they are just as vital in trainee development, particularly when cosidering the obligations of gatekeeping.

As a new supervisor, it was easy for me to support supervisees who were emotionally mature, acted professionally, and appropriately managed their internal reactions to new experiences. Challenges lay with the supervisee who did not easily possess the necessary interpersonal, intrapersonal, and professional conduct or behavior expected of a developing professional counselor.

My first encounters with gatekeeping were as a junior member of a faculty team. I observed, listened, and gradually participated in the process. I was fortunate to work with faculty colleagues who valued gatekeeping as an ethical and professional responsibility. I witnessed excellent modeling of challenging and supporting students in their developmental journey. However, as a department chair responsible for decision making and enforcement, I was overwhelmed by the depth and detail required of effective gatekeeping, as well as my own reactions to the process.

When I first encountered gatekeeping, the professional literature provided little guidance and lacked standards for trainee behavior. But the literature recognized and promoted the need to address supervisees' problematic behaviors through feedback, remediation, and possibly dismissal, particularly when the unremedied behavior posed a potential threat to future clients. While attending conference workshops, I also learned that gatekeeping processes were poorly understood and inconsistently applied across training programs. In the reports of colleagues, I found an exasperating deficit of guidance and a lack of acknowledgment of the emotional challenges encountered by gatekeepers, which I found frustrating and discouraging.

Personally, I have had strong affective reactions to the gatekeeping process. I have been upset and angry about being in the position of reprimanding a supervisee who displayed emotional immaturity or poor professional judgment. I have felt sad and downhearted for the supervisee whose dreams of becoming a professional helper were dashed because of an inability to demonstrate requisite skills, consistently engage in ethical decision making, or act professionally, regardless of supportive efforts. And I have felt dispirited when hearing about problematic student conduct that was minimized by other faculty members or administrators. As educators and supervisors who endeavor to savor our roles as effective mentors and professional nurturers to counselors-in-training, the position of disciplinarian is contradictory and uncomfortable. These conflicting values and roles can result in complex, emotionally stressful, and even painful feelings for us as gatekeepers.

It was incongruous to me that counselor educators and supervisors had to figure out how to handle gatekeeping situations without support from our professional organizations while simultaneously being ethically mandated to do so. The effort and energy to "reinvent the wheel" in individual situations and settings without guidance seemed risky and unnecessary. Fortunately, this situation has improved somewhat in recent years as more counselor educators and supervisors have sought clarification and shared successful processes and experiences in the literature and at workshops. In addition, more training programs are educating doctoral students about gatekeeping as an essential aspect of their future roles as faculty members.

Gatekeepers need support to fulfill their mandated roles, and the act of gatekeeping needs strengthening through acknowledgment of the complexity of the experience and adoption of trainee standards for the profession. The journey of consistent, effective, and ethical enforcement of standards for trainees' professional conduct, interpersonal and intrapersonal behavior, and the development of the art of gatekeeping continues.

For further reading on various aspects of gatekeeping, see *Gatekeeping in the Mental Health Professions* (Homrich & Henderson, 2018).

Diversity and Evaluation

All supervision practices must be cognizant of the individual, cultural, and ethnic differences among supervisors, supervisees, and the clients served and proficient in providing multiculturally competent services to supervisees and their clients (see Chapter 6). This applies as well to the process of evaluation in supervision and the specific tools we use when conducting evaluations. Many of these evaluation instruments have been around for some time, and little or no consideration was given to multicultural issues regarding the validity and reliability of such instruments with supervisees of a different culture, race, or sexual orientation. We have a greater awareness of the importance of multicultural considerations in the evaluation process today, and supervisors must be aware of these individual and cultural differences when evaluating supervisees both formally and informally. An Association for Counselor Education and Supervision (ACES; 2011) standard describes supervisors' responsibility in doing evaluations:

> The supervisor attends to the full range of cultural factors, including race, ethnicity, gender, sexual orientation, socioeconomic status, privilege, ability status, family characteristics and dynamics, country of origin, language, historical processes (e.g., history, migration), worldview, spirituality and religion, and values. (6.a.iii.)

This standard applies to all supervision, including both formal and informal evaluation.

Essential Features of Evaluation

Objective Versus Subjective Evaluation

In our experience, most supervisor evaluations have been largely subjective rather than objective. Few standardized methods for evaluating supervisees have existed, and supervisors developed their own systems to evaluate performance and professional be-havior. Evaluating supervisees is one of the most challenging tasks for supervisors. Professional standards exist regarding evaluation, but few standards address specific tools, procedures, and frequency of the evaluation process. For example, Lewis, Scott, and Hendricks (2014, p. 171) highlight key domains of supervision outcomes and present examples of psychometrically validated measures that have been developed. They present a model for cognitive behavior therapy supervision outcome assessment. In addition, the rapid increase in the use of technology in supervision requires that new standardized evaluation measures of those supervision practices be developed.

Kaslow and colleagues (Kaslow, Rubin, Bebeau, et al., 2007; Kaslow, Rubin, Forrest, et al., 2007) suggest that evaluation falls into two major categories: formative and summative. *Formative evaluation* is a developmentally informed process that provides useful feedback during one's training and throughout one's professional career. *Summative evaluation* is an end point evaluation typically completed at the end of an academic requirement, a professional program, or when applying for licensure status. Together, these evaluations address an individual practitioner's strengths and provide useful information for developing remedial education plans, if needed, for the person whose competence is being evaluated.

The integration of formative and summative evaluation addresses an individual trainee's strengths and areas of competence deficiencies. This kind of evaluation can be a useful basis for developing remedial plans, if needed. Johnson and colleagues (2008) state that those who are responsible for the education and training of mental health professionals are ethically and professionally obligated to balance their roles as advocate and mentor of trainees with their gatekeeping role. One of their recommendations for managing these sometimes conflicting roles is to thoroughly and accurately provide routine formative and summative evaluation for trainees, carefully document these evaluations, and ensure that multiple professionals give independent evaluations of each trainee in a program.

Standardization of Methods

Supervisors are more likely to fully invest in the evaluation process when standardized procedures and evaluation forms are in place. Many agencies, schools, and field training sites have developed rating forms and other tools for evaluation of supervisees and supervisors. Many of these forms are thorough and objective, although few have undertaken the rigors of reliability and validity testing that should be conducted on these measures. Homrich and Henderson (2018, pp. 213–216) outline a variety of specific assessment and evaluation tools frequently used by supervisors to assess supervisee readiness to enter the counseling profession as an independent practitioner.

Criteria for Evaluation

It is extremely helpful when supervisors have specific and clear criteria for evaluation and include them in the supervision contract. The supervision contract then becomes the basis for measuring the supervisee's accomplishments over the course of supervision. Having established criteria gives the supervisor standards by which to measure the performance and conduct of the supervisee. Professional associations and licensing bodies, as well as doctoral programs and training sites, have attempted to determine the criteria for measuring competence.

Ongoing evaluation of trainees is crucial to confirm that trainees are making satisfactory progress in all areas of the training program. In graduate training programs, students have a right to be informed that their knowledge and skills, clinical performance, and interpersonal behaviors will be evaluated at different times during the program. Academic programs have a responsibility to provide written policies to applicants regarding how and when they will be evaluated prior to admission. Regarding evaluations of students in a program, the 2016 CACREP standard states the following:

The counselor education program faculty systematically assesses each student's progress throughout the program by examining student learning in relation to a combination of knowledge and skills. (4.F.).

The counselor education program faculty has a systematic process in place for the use of individual student assessment data in relation to retention, remediation, and dismissal. (4.H.)

Supervisors must distinguish between performance and personality. It is possible for supervisees to perform adequately yet receive a negative evaluation from their supervisors based largely on personality factors. The difficulty, then, is in learning to separate out and measure those personal characteristics that are essential to clinical competence. As discussed in Chapter 7, the personal characteristics of supervisees play a major role in their clinical abilities. For trainees, satisfactory academic performance is essential, but it is not enough. Trainees' personal qualities, ability to relate effectively with others, and awareness of what constitutes ethical practice are key factors to consider in the development of effective therapists. In addition to assessing knowledge and skills of trainees, Orlinsky, Geller, and Norcross (2005) contend that it is essential to assess personal and interpersonal competencies, such as the capacity for self-awareness and self-reflection. They identify personal qualities of the therapist as being critical, including emotional resonance and responsiveness, social perceptiveness, compassion, desire to help, self-understanding, and self-discipline.

In summary, there is still much to be learned about the specific dimensions for measuring competence in the helping professions. Nonetheless, supervisors can use criteria and measures that have been developed rather than relying exclusively on subjective impressions when evaluating clinical competence. Competent supervisors will continue to look for better ways to accomplish the goals of supervision to base their evaluation on clearly defined measures.

Organization of Evaluation

The evaluation process is most effective when it is planned, organized, and discussed with the supervisee at the beginning of the supervisory relationship. Evaluation procedures, methods, and time frames should be clearly spelled out in the supervision contract. This encourages the supervisor to have a well-developed plan about the role and methods of evaluation rather than having to develop something at the 11th hour before the evaluation is scheduled to occur.

Evaluation should occur throughout the course of supervision on a regular and systematic basis. Supervisees have a right to know when to expect evaluations as well as to be familiar with the forms, methods, and processes used for evaluation. It is crucial that evaluation be conducted early enough in the clinical experience of the supervisee so that he or she has adequate time to correct any deficits identified by the supervisor. The supervision contract should include information regarding how the process will proceed when deficiencies are identified and what recourse the supervisee has to challenge or remediate the deficiencies. Informed consent on the part of students enrolling in graduate training programs requires clear statements about what constitutes grounds for concerns, including the reasons students may be terminated from a program.

Due Process

Due process is a means of providing supervisees with clear expectations for performance and a procedure for handling adverse actions when those performance expectations are not met (see Chapter 8). The supervisor is obligated ethically to provide due process regarding evaluation of supervisees. Supervisees have a right to be informed in writing of the procedures for evaluation, which include how and when it will occur, what the consequences of a serious negative evaluation might be, what recourse supervisees will have to correct any deficiencies identified, what they can do if they would like to challenge the evaluation results, and what the course of appeal is in the case of an extremely negative evaluation with which they do not agree. Johnson and colleagues (2008) suggest that information about due process be available in program descriptions (e.g., websites, marketing materials, and student handbooks) to reduce distress for faculty and students in the event that professional development issues arise. In the Personal Perspective, Bob Haynes describes the longevity of supervisee evaluations and the importance of assuring fair, accurate, and objective evaluation.

 ## BOB HAYNES'S PERSONAL PERSPECTIVE

Supervisee evaluations often have significant long-term effects on the careers of helping professionals. Once evaluations are completed, they become a permanent part of the supervisee's record and become the basis for making recommendations for employment, licensing, and professional association membership. As an internship director, I received many requests each year to verify supervisees' performance during internship, in some cases going back more than 25 years. Evaluation results become a part of the supervisee's record for many, many years. It would be helpful for both supervisors and supervisees to consider these far-reaching effects when participating in the evaluation process. If supervisees disagree with their evaluation, it is essential that they contest the evaluation before it becomes a part of their permanent record. Supervisors are obligated ethically and legally to ensure that the evaluation is objective and fair and provides due process for the supervisee.

Empowering the Supervisee to Conduct Self-Evaluation

A key goal of supervision is to assist supervisees to eventually be able to *self-supervise* throughout their professional career. A major part of this self-supervision includes the ability to self-evaluate. The ability to assess one's own strengths and deficits, to know the limits of one's competence, to seek supervision and consultation when necessary, and to continue to learn through reading and continuing education is the hallmark of a competent helping professional (Falender & Shafranske, 2017). Self-supervision does not imply that practitioners no longer need supervision or consultation at times; rather, it implies a level of development that enables the independent practitioner to function effectively without formal and regular supervision.

Supervisors in all of the helping professions can foster the development of self-evaluation in their supervisees by modeling this behavior and demonstrating their openness to learn and grow, accepting feedback about their performance as a supervisor, and providing the tools and skills necessary for self-supervision (Falender & Shafranske, 2017). Self-supervision should be seen as a long-term goal for clinicians rather than being used as a primary evaluation tool in supervision.

Evaluation of the Supervisor

Supervision is very often a one-way street in which the supervisor evaluates the performance of the supervisee. However, the evaluation of supervisor competence is rapidly becoming a standard part of the evaluation process. A comprehensive evaluation includes an assessment of the performance of the supervisor by the supervisee and by the agency, department, or the supervisor's supervisor, where appropriate. Some supervisors are simply not open to this idea, but those who are can use this feedback as an opportunity for growth and learning. The supervisor and supervisee could review the feedback from the supervisee and discuss actions to be taken to improve the supervisory process. This requires a supervisor who is well grounded, confident, and open to improvement. Here are some of the qualities on which supervisors can be evaluated:

- Availability
- Communication skills
- Cultural competence
- Ethical and legal knowledge
- Clinical and professional knowledge
- Professionalism
- Provision of useful feedback and evaluation
- Punctuality
- Responsiveness to supervisee's needs and ideas
- Resolution of issues/conflicts promptly and professionally
- Effective modeling for the supervisee
- Supervision of psychotherapy
- Supportiveness
- Use of supervision interventions

We encourage supervisors to seek feedback from their supervisees about their performance as a supervisor. Supervisees are more likely to be forthcoming with both positive and negative feedback when the evaluation is in writing and is conducted at the conclusion of the supervisory relationship. We are not discouraging ongoing evaluation and discussion, but the true feelings of a supervisee are more likely to be voiced at the conclusion of supervision and after the final evaluation. Supervisees know that supervisors will be asked to provide a grade or write letters of recommendation for many years to come, which may increase the reluctance of supervisees to provide feedback that is too critical or negative. Candor in providing honest feedback to the supervisor is directly related to the level of mutual trust and respect that developed in the course of the supervisory relationship.

Appendix 10A at the end of the chapter provides one example of an evaluation form that could be given to supervisees to assess their supervision experience.

Guidelines for Conducting Evaluations

Evaluations can be a positive and valuable experience for both the supervisee and the supervisor. Those positive experiences occur when evaluation is taken seriously as an important part of supervision and when careful planning and development have gone into the evaluation process. It is essential that supervisors have a clear picture of the evaluation objectives, criteria, and process and make sure the supervisee is informed of these early in the supervisory relationship and in the supervision contract. Let's look at some of the guidelines for developing the evaluation process and conducting evaluation sessions.

- Evaluation is most effective as a continuous process. Formal evaluation should occur several times over the course of supervision, and informal evaluation should be conducted on a regular basis. It is good practice to present a balanced evaluation, highlighting both the supervisee's strengths and deficiencies. Some supervisors tend to focus more heavily on the deficiencies.
- Provide feedback using specific examples and descriptions of the behaviors, skills, or attitudes being addressed. Generic feedback does not assist supervisees in improvement and is likely to increase the anxiety and often lower the performance of supervisees as they guess at what the supervisor might be asking them to accomplish.

- When the supervisee is not open to feedback and evaluation, help the supervisee become aware of and explore that aspect of ongoing learning. That could be done by helping the supervisee look at the feedback provided from various sources and discuss how the supervisee has processed that information. Conduct evaluations frequently enough to keep the supervisee apprised of progress and any need for improvement, and give the supervisee ample time to remedy deficiencies. The frequency of evaluations depends on the needs of the situation and the length of time over which the supervision will occur.
- Understand the administrative policy for evaluation and who else needs to be involved. Many agencies have their own evaluation procedures and tools. Determine how the clinical evaluation fits into the agency evaluation process, and whether it is compatible with employment practices. Does this evaluation process satisfy the needs of the graduate training program or licensing board?
- Try to involve all those who have had significant contact or supervision with the supervisee in the evaluation process. If they cannot attend the evaluation meeting, call them or send them a form to complete to give input into the progress of the supervisee.
- Involve the supervisee in the evaluation process. If feedback is given routinely, there should be no surprises for the supervisee when the formal evaluation session occurs. Encourage supervisees to evaluate their own progress and discuss how their evaluation may differ from yours.
- In conducting the evaluation conference, be sure the supervisee knows when and where it will occur and what to expect in the session. Try to meet in a room or office that is private and free of interruptions. Be as clear as possible in evaluating the supervisee's performance. Ask supervisees to evaluate their training, including the value of their supervision and what could be improved in the supervisory relationship.
- Clearly explain any remediation necessary to correct problems and include time frames, behavioral expectations, how progress will be assessed, and who will conduct the assessment. Document the session and maintain accurate records of the supervisee's performance and conduct. Ongoing documentation of the supervisory sessions and critical incidents will provide a basis for the periodic formal evaluations and serve as a record regarding the supervisee's performance under your supervision to employers, licensing boards, and professional associations.
- The issue of openness to supervision should be a major topic of any evaluation— this is a key component of the supervisee's ability to grow and learn. As a supervisor, model openness to feedback. Try to evaluate performance and behavior and not personality styles, but address personal and interpersonal characteristics that affect the supervisee's clinical work as a part of the evaluation process.

The following list provides some specific areas to include in evaluation of a supervisee:

- Intervention knowledge and skills
- Assessment knowledge and skills
- Relationships with staff and clients
- Responsiveness to supervision
- Awareness of limitations and knowing when to seek outside help
- Communication skills
- Ethical and legal practice
- Multicultural awareness and competence
- Professionalism, judgment, integrity, and maturity
- Openness to personal development
- Compliance with agency policies and procedures

Concerns of Supervisors

For some supervisors, training as a counselor may not translate well to being an evaluator. The training in many programs emphasizes that a good counselor does not form judgments about clients. Counselors strive not to judge or evaluate the client, and they are discouraged from giving advice. There is a tendency to foster that same approach in the supervisory relationship, which many supervisors liken to the counseling relationship.

Supervisors may struggle with whether they are evaluating the performance or the personality characteristics of the supervisee and what role each plays in clinical competence. Sometimes a supervisor does not enjoy working with a particular supervisee. In those instances, evaluation of the supervisee may become more difficult as the supervisor tries to sort out subjective feelings about the supervisee from the objective evaluation of the supervisee's performance.

The supervisor may determine that the supervisee can do the basic clinical work but that he or she does not seem well suited for the profession. This may be due to the personal characteristics of the supervisee, idiosyncrasies of the supervisor, personality differences between supervisee and supervisor, or some other reason. Johnson et al. (2008) point out that "graduate program training directors express concern about the moral character and psychological fitness of their students" (p. 590). If the supervisor truly believes the supervisee is not appropriate for the profession, he or she must determine how to objectively define and document the problematic behaviors and present specific feedback to the supervisee in a timely way that allows for the possibility of remediation.

Supervisors must realize that one letter to a licensing board stating that the supervisee is unfit for the profession could be sufficient to ruin a career; thus, it is critical that due process be provided to the supervisee. We suggest a developmental approach to conversations regarding the mental health of supervisees. These supportive discussions focus on the struggles supervisees may be experiencing as they attempt to meet the emotional requirements of helping others while fighting a personal mental health battle. Supervisors can refer supervisees and encourage them to obtain the assessment and help they need to be better equipped to care for themselves and others.

Some supervisors do not like to put their observations and evaluative statements on paper. Many issues supervisors have with evaluation are based on a desire to avoid the evaluation process altogether, but supervisors must be able to substantiate their observations and their evaluation of the supervisee. By developing a system of evaluation using established criteria and measures, supervisors can find their role as evaluators tolerable and productive for both the supervisor and the supervisee.

Concerns of Supervisees

Supervisees have many concerns about the evaluation of their performance and conduct as well. They have a lot on the line, including years of schooling, success in their new career, future income, and the understandable concern of wanting to perform well as a new counselor with acceptance into the profession. Most trainees and professionals experience anxiety and defensiveness about being evaluated. Concerns about performing well, being liked, and having the basic skills are common to those in the helping professions. It is reassuring to hear from a respected supervisor and professional in the field that one is progressing, performing well, and has what it takes to contribute as a helping professional.

Supervisees have a tendency to present overly positive descriptions of their clinical work when self-reporting to supervisors. This is a major problem because supervisees will not receive accurate feedback unless they are honest in providing information about their clinical work to their supervisor. Supervisors need to develop a supportive and trusting atmosphere with supervisees that fosters forthrightness. Supervisees suffer from not knowing what to expect from supervision, from the clinical experience, and from the evaluation process and will expend a considerable amount of their training energy trying to determine what is expected of them and how they will be evaluated.

Some supervisors are unwilling to balance negative feedback with comments about a supervisee's strengths. This supervisee faces a dilemma in deciding how to respond to a critical supervisor: "Do I challenge the supervisor? Do I keep quiet and try to get through the experience? Do I seek out another supervisor? What will be the consequences of these actions? Will I make the supervisor feel bad if I challenge him or her?" Supervisees are often at a loss as to what recourse is available if they receive an evaluation with which they disagree. Can they challenge it? Should they? How do they proceed if they want to challenge it? Supervisees have the right to challenge an evaluation and should be informed of the process for doing so early in supervision.

Supervisees are not always told who has access to information from supervisory sessions. This can leave supervisees with many questions: Is the information that is shared between supervisor and supervisee confidential? Can the supervisor share it with others? If so, with whom? And with whom, if anyone, can the supervisee share this information? Can information from evaluations jeopardize a supervisee's career? The supervisor has the responsibility to inform trainees of the parameters of confidentiality regarding the supervisory relationship at the outset.

In Voices From the Field, Jeffrey Barnett addresses the delicate balance between the obligation to evaluate supervisees and a supervisor's desire to create a safe environment in which supervisees can learn and grow professionally.

VOICES FROM THE FIELD

Effective Supervision and Achieving the Delicate Balance

Jeffrey E. Barnett, PsyD, ABPP

Clinical supervisors take on significant responsibilities to promote each supervisee's professional growth and development, influence the formation of the supervisee's professional identity as an aspiring clinician, promote the developing clinical competence of the supervisee, prepare the supervisee for the next stage of professional development and training, and ensure that the supervisee's clients receive an appropriate quality of care.

Supervisors also have an evaluative role in which feedback is provided both to supervisees and to their training program on an ongoing basis. The evaluative nature of the supervision relationship can have a negative impact on the supervisee. Fear of negative evaluations and their potential impact on the supervisee's ability to proceed through the graduate program and to licensure can severely limit the supervisee's functioning, both with clients and with the supervisor. Supervisees may lack the confidence to venture outside their comfort zone to experiment with new treatment techniques and strategies. Furthermore, a fear of negative evaluation may limit supervisees' willingness to share openly with their supervisors. Supervisees who share more about perceived successes with clients than what may be perceived as failures limit their opportunity for learning and professional development.

Striking a balance between the obligation to evaluate supervisees and our desire to create an environment in which supervisees have the best chance of learning and growing professionally can be quite challenging. The supervision relationship must be perceived as sufficiently safe for the supervisee to feel comfortable sharing openly and honestly with the supervisor. In essence, as much emphasis should be placed on relationship as on evaluation. By creating a warm, supportive, encouraging, respectful, and accepting relationship in supervision, supervisors help to create a safe and trusting environment in which supervisees are more likely to venture outside their comfort zone to try new treatment strategies and techniques as well as to share more openly and honestly in supervision sessions, obtaining greater benefit from the supervision.

Recommendations for promoting this delicate balance between evaluation and support include the following:

- Begin the supervision relationship with a discussion of the goals of the supervision process and relationship, setting the tone for a respectful and collaborative relationship and process.
- Openly discuss feedback and evaluation, integrating them positively into the supervision process. Constructive feedback should be provided on an ongoing basis, with a greater emphasis on professional growth and learning than on evaluation and grading. "What can you learn from that?" is a much better question to ask than "Why did you do that?"
- Evaluate supervisees on their openness to learning and willingness to experiment and venture outside their comfort zone, not on client "successes."
- Supervisees should be encouraged to provide feedback on an ongoing basis, and supervisors should demonstrate an openness to this feedback process.
- Supervisors are professional role models for supervisees, and the qualities necessary for an effective psychotherapy relationship can play a role in the supervisory relationship as well.
- When difficulties are observed with supervisees, supervisors should address them right away, providing encouragement and support when possible and offering opportunities for remediation when appropriate.

Initial Assessment of Supervisees

One type of evaluation is the initial assessment of a new supervisee. This first task in supervision is to assess the needs and goals of the supervision, the setting, the client, and your own areas of expertise as a supervisor. Take time before the first supervision session to jot down ideas regarding assessment and provide an agenda for discussion in the first supervision session. Here are some areas to consider as you formulate a supervision plan:

- What are the goals of supervision for this group or individual?
- What are the main supervisory roles I will fill for the supervisee?
- What are the licensing and agency policies pertinent to this supervision?
- Which group or individual supervision model provides the most effective and economical approach?
- Which supervision methods will serve the goals of this supervision best?
- What methods of evaluation will I use, and will there be requirements for documentation or reporting on the supervisee's performance?
- Where, when, and how often will we meet?
- Can I anticipate any legal or ethical concerns that might arise?
- What are the particular issues about the individual or group that I will be supervising? Are there multicultural considerations?
- If there are identified inherent dual roles, how will I handle them and what are the expectations?
- What are the procedures for managing emergency situations, and how will I make myself available to supervisees in those situations?

Considering these issues prior to the first session should assist in the development of a clear plan for supervision.

Evaluation Methods

Supervisors evaluate trainees in a variety of ways. The most common method is providing evaluative feedback one-on-one with the supervisee. This can be done at any time in supervision as well as at predetermined sessions for formal evaluation. Another form of evaluation commonly used is for a group of professionals who have worked with the supervisee to arrange a meeting with the supervisee to provide evaluative feedback. The advantage of the group method is that common themes can be identified by those working with the supervisee. It also provides an opportunity for the group to discuss the training objectives of the supervisee for the next period.

Team Supervision

Supervision evaluation models are also combining methods to provide increased opportunity and depth of feedback and learning. When a student sees a client, video and audio recordings with one-way mirror and bug-in-the-ear technologies allow simultaneous live supervision by the supervisor and peer observers. Documentation for multiple levels of insight and learning may include progress notes, peer observation feedback sheets, video review sheets for self-evaluation, and supervisor feedback sheets. Following the session and time for review and documentation, the supervisor facilitates a conversation with the student counselor and this team of peer supervisees. Supervisors can process the team meeting interactively in many ways:

- Inquire regarding counselor strengths observed during the session.
- Explore case conceptualization.
- Note challenges for the supervisee/counselor during the session.
- Specify areas of opportunity for intervention.
- Examine ethical considerations.
- Employ Socratic questioning.
- Apply theoretical approaches to client presenting issues.
- Consider additional assessment options if needed.
- Role-play scenarios to allow practice.
- Review best practices for application to a specific case.
- Brainstorm treatment options.
- Demonstrate techniques.
- Analyze documentation.
- Share resources for further knowledge.

This team meeting of peer supervisors encourages discussion of the students' working knowledge of counseling. Students will discuss and question different theories, diagnoses, strategies, resources, ethics, and emergency procedures together after each client session. Team feedback sessions are structured like professional staffing with the team of peers in training supporting one another as they develop skills. Team feedback is a unique teaching and mentoring experience with ample potential for insight and growth; it is designed for active engagement, practicing professionalism, and developing skills (Valentino et al., 2016). Students are encouraged to consider each session they observe as if the client were their own and play an active role in applying their knowledge to the discussion. They share ideas, attitudes, and resources toward enhancing the quality of care for the client. This multiple-layer approach to methods of supervision enables students to learn not only from their own experience but also from the experiences of team members.

Direct observation of supervisees' work is necessary to ensure an accurate picture of supervisees' clinical abilities, whether through direct observation or the use of computer-related technologies. Evaluation following direct observation can be very effective because it is based on current observation of performance. Observational learning plays a significant role in this team process. Students see various skills and behaviors modeled in sessions by their peers. Many students report this to be the most powerful aspect of team feedback and evaluation. Demonstrations of therapy are limited in most training models and settings. Students need to see therapy in action rather than guessing what it may look like as they focus mainly on theoretical learning. At the end of each team feedback session, the student counselors are encouraged to note lessons learned from the information they have processed with peers. They also need to be prepared to identify the next steps for a client. The supervisor can add to this list with suggestions, guidance, homework, and expectations. Ultimately, a supportive environment and the evaluative component of progress toward identified supervision goals remain the responsibility of the supervisor.

In some instances, the supervisor completes a written evaluation form and discusses the results with the supervisee. This can serve as the basis for the individual or group evaluation session and can provide some structure for that meeting. Some forms have a place for the supervisee to sign and indicate whether the supervisee agrees with the ratings on the evaluation. Most formal academic and clinical training sites use written evaluation forms. More often than not, the program or site has developed its own evaluation form. Few standardized evaluation tools have been available, and each program or site has its own specific evaluation needs. Two sample forms are provided in appendixes at the end of the chapter: Practicum Evaluation Form (Appendix 10B) and Supervisee Performance Evaluation (Appendix 10C). These evaluation tools are used in university and internship training settings, but they are not empirically derived, and neither may suit your particular needs entirely. Nevertheless, you can begin to see what topics are addressed by examining these evaluation tools.

Test Your Evaluation Skills

Three case examples follow to test your evaluation skills. Read the case description and answer the questions before you read our commentary on each case.

CASE STUDY 10.1: SUSAN

Susan is a bright, energetic, and motivated student in a school counseling program. Maggie is her supervisor and has worked with hundreds of trainees. Maggie likes Susan and is optimistic about her future as a school counselor but observes that Susan has little experience or working knowledge of clinical issues. The first formal evaluation session with Maggie and Susan is rapidly approaching, and Maggie is unsure about what to say to Susan. She does not want to hurt her feelings or dampen her enthusiasm or motivation, but she wants to be candid about what she has observed.

This is a common scenario for supervisors when working with students. Most are enthusiastic and motivated and at the same time inexperienced and sometimes naïve about the work. Consider these questions.

- What do you think this evaluation will be like for Maggie? For Susan?
- Can you identify with the ambivalence Maggie feels about being candid with Susan? What difficulties would you face if you were the supervisor?
- What advice would you give to Maggie?
- How would you handle the feedback session with Susan?

The supervisor's goal is to assist Susan in acquiring the experience and knowledge she needs to succeed in the profession. To do otherwise would be a disservice to Susan. It all begins with a clear contract about what is expected and a supervisory relationship built on trust and respect. If Maggie has been honest with Susan, the information she will present at the evaluation session should not come as a surprise. Maggie might assume the role of mentor and teacher with Susan, use live observation and cotherapy with her, and insist that Susan spend a fair amount of time shadowing Maggie to observe what is involved in the role of the school counselor and how Maggie carries out that role. If Maggie began the evaluation process during the first supervisory contact and continued this discussion throughout, the formal evaluation sessions should provide a summary of feedback that Susan has already heard.

CASE STUDY 10.2: PAUL

Paul has been your supervisee for the past year. He is knowledgeable of the various therapeutic approaches and how to apply them. However, he is some-what insensitive to the feelings of others, and you can see this in his work with clients. For example, one client expressed anxiety related to reentering the workforce after the COVID-19 restrictions were lifted for fear of becoming infected, and Paul minimized her feelings. He is abrasive and has a sarcastic side that can really put people off. His clinical skills are barely adequate, and his people skills leave a lot to be desired. Paul has some awareness of how he comes across to people, but he has not shown much progress in changing this.

It is likely that Paul can increase his awareness of how he affects others if given proper structure and direction. Consider these questions.

- How would you supervise Paul, and what interventions would you use?
- What methods might you use to help Paul alter his behavior and improve his people skills?
- What feedback would you provide so Paul understands exactly what he needs to do to improve?
- How do you think Paul will respond to the evaluative feedback?
- What is your plan for providing regular and systematic evaluation for Paul?
- If a licensing board asked whether Paul is qualified for licensure, what would you say?

Paul is a novice using basic counseling skills, and you can best help Paul develop empathy, respect, and active listening using a developmental model. You will need to provide structure and direction along with a great deal of constructive feedback. Your role would be more of a teacher, and live observation and role playing are good ways to give Paul direct feedback regarding the development of helping skills. Focus on behavioral observations, and avoid making value judgments about his deficiencies. At Paul's current level of functioning, it would be difficult to give a favorable recommendation to the licensing board. However, with support, feedback, and his desire for growth and learning, Paul could show considerable improvement. It is essential to report your observations of his performance to the licensing board regarding the manner in which he accepted the feedback and progressed while under supervision.

CASE STUDY 10.3: MALIK

Malik is the most capable student you have worked with as a supervisor. In addition to his current work in the doctoral counseling program, he has worked in the field as a mental health counselor for more than 20 years. He has experience, knowledge, clinical skills, good judgment, and the personal characteristics that make working with him a true pleasure. You find yourself wondering if you are providing any supervisory help to Malik. Your supervisory sessions seem more like consultations than supervision, and often you learn more from Malik than he does from you.

With supervisees like Malik, who have years of experience and are enjoyable to work with, the tendency of supervisors is to not supervise very carefully. Consider these questions.

- How do you work with someone who has more knowledge than you do? What can he learn from you?
- What are the potential problems in working with a supervisee like Malik? What are the benefits?
- Would you feel defensive if Malik challenged something you said? How would you set appropriate boundaries, respect his knowledge, and be open to feedback as a supervisor?
- What evaluation methods would be most appropriate?
- What preconceived expectations might you have that could influence the evaluation process?

It would be best to supervise Malik very carefully in the beginning, using live observation and assessing his clinical abilities. Develop the supervision contract and implement the usual evaluation procedures as you would with any supervisee. You are ultimately responsible for Malik's work with clients, and you need to be sure that all the bases are covered. Having years of experience in the field and being an enjoyable person are not guarantees that Malik's knowledge and skills, as well as his judgment, are sufficient for him to function independently in this new role.

Writing Letters of Recommendation

A natural result of evaluation in supervision is the subsequent letter of recommendation that supervisees request be sent to prospective employers, licensing boards, and professional associations. These letters are commonly based on information resulting from the evaluation of the supervisee and should provide an accurate and objective picture. Writing objective letters of reference is an ethical obligation of the supervisor as gatekeeper for the profession. Writing letters that are accurate and useful is a time-consuming and taxing process. Useful letters are personable and describe the supervisor's experience of the supervisee and whether he or she would hire this individual. These letters often include examples of things the trainee did well or out of the ordinary. To ensure that letters are descriptive and accurate, we offer these tips for writing letters of recommendation:

- Letters of recommendation are typically requested when the supervisee is applying for a job, a license, or a professional association membership. Complete the letter in a timely fashion, usually within a few weeks.
- Check to be sure you have the name and address of the person to whom you are sending the letter (misspellings of names can irritate the reader and have a negative impact on how that person views the letter). Also, try to learn something about the setting so your letter can emphasize topics that would be of most interest and relevance to them.
- Keep in mind that many readers look for summary paragraphs and may only read the first and last paragraphs. Give a good, clear summary of how you have experienced the individual in one or both of those paragraphs.
- Be brief and to the point—longer is not better.
- Be sure you are familiar enough with the supervisee's work to write an accurate letter. If you do not know the individual well but are obligated to write the letter, rely on evaluations from others and cite or quote their comments regarding the individual.

- Provide a realistic picture of the strengths and weaknesses of the individual. To over-state or understate strengths and deficiencies could be an ethical and a liability issue.
- Describe some areas of personal and professional growth that the supervisee should work toward accomplishing.
- When writing a letter that includes a description of serious deficiencies, inform the supervisee, if possible, of the information you plan to include in the letter.
- Be careful to use objective, behavioral terms when describing deficits, and include examples to illustrate your point. Rather than saying, "He is not a very good cli-nician," you might say, "His knowledge of cognitive behavioral interventions is sound, but he tries to use techniques without first building a relationship based on empathy, trust, and respect."
- Describe what the supervisee has done to remediate deficiencies and how open to feedback and supervision the supervisee was. There are so few negatives in most letters that the reader will consider these comments very carefully and may attempt to "read between the lines" in determining what you are really trying to say.
- Provide a release of information. When you receive requests for letters, you should also receive a release from the individual. Do not write a letter (or, for that matter, talk to an employer or professional association) about the supervisee unless you have written or verbal (note the date) consent to release the information.
- Keep a copy for your file, and send a copy to the supervisee if appropriate.

An alternative to letters of recommendation is to develop and use a standardized form when asked to write a letter. The rating form could conclude with a narrative summary evaluation of the individual. Another option that experienced supervisors have chosen is to develop several templates for letters. A template could be developed for each of the several types of letters that supervisors write: employment, licensing applications, postdoctoral fellowships, professional association memberships, and so forth. It is then a matter of filling in the blanks with the names and key evaluative information for the particular individual. When working from a template, you can be sure you are including all of the necessary information.

Ask your supervisees to help you write the best and most accurate letter you can write. You may want to ask that supervisees provide you with the following information in writing: name and address of person receiving the letter, purpose of the letter, and two to three highlights or facts that they would like to have included. The purpose of this information is not to have the supervisee write for you but to have the supervisee active-ly participate in providing pertinent information. If possible, provide supervisees with the opportunity to review letters of recommendation prior to mailing. Use the checklist below to be sure you have included all relevant information.

Letter of Recommendation Checklist

When you write a letter of recommendation for a supervisee, check this list to be sure you have included these relevant items.

- Your position, now and when you supervised the supervisee, and how familiar you are with the supervisee's work
- How long you have been in your position
- Position and function of the supervisee
- Dates the supervisee was under your supervision
- The supervisee's duties and responsibilities and how he or she performed
- Specific examples of training activities the supervisee participated in that illus-trate your observations; for example, "She took the initiative to seek additional

training experiences on her own by working as a coleader in the stress management group and the parenting education group, and she sat as an observer on the ethics committee for the entire year."

- Level of clinical knowledge and skills
- Was supervisee open to supervision, growing, and learning?
- Did supervisee work well with individuals and groups? Is supervisee a team player? (Many employers look very carefully at this item because so many positions involve working with a team.)
- Does supervisee have good common sense?
- Does supervisee demonstrate good judgment?
- Does supervisee demonstrate an awareness of and an ability to work with multicultural issues?
- Was supervisee enjoyable to work with?
- Was supervisee familiar with legal and ethical standards? Did supervisee demonstrate in practice that he or she can manage these well?
- How have you experienced the supervisee, and is this someone you would hire?

A Final Thought on Accurate Evaluations

Written evaluations and letters of recommendation that are inaccurately positive or negative can have serious consequences. Supervisors should avoid the tendency to minimize or omit any negative information or to give inaccurately positive evaluations. A supervisee could sue a supervisor who provides an exceedingly negative evaluation that hampers the supervisee's ability to seek employment, licensure, and professional association membership. The burden is on supervisors to provide accurate and fair evaluations based on objective information that supports their findings.

Summary

Supervisors are tasked with serving as gatekeepers of the mental health professions to ensure that clients, both current and future, are protected and receive quality care. Evaluation is an essential function of supervision and of gatekeeping, and it should be described in the supervision contract. Evaluation helps us assess the progress the supervisee has made in developing the necessary clinical skills as well as ethical and multicultural competence to function independently. It is of the utmost importance that evaluation be planned, organized, systematic, and objective. With advancements in technology and multiple methods used to enhance supervision, the evaluation process provides trainees with a much richer opportunity for learning and feedback than ever before.

Supervisees are typically anxious about being evaluated, and a supportive and trusting atmosphere, whether in an individual or a team-based format, can go a long way toward reducing that anxiety. Evaluation needs to be scheduled regularly throughout supervision, and the criteria for evaluation need to be clearly specified. The effective supervisor will find that this evaluation process is a communication tool that helps the supervisee receive honest, fair feedback toward becoming an independent professional capable of conducting self-evaluation.

SUGGESTED ACTIVITIES

1. Role-play an evaluation of a supervisee using these different scenarios:
    - When the supervisee is performing quite well
    - When serious deficiencies have been identified
    - When the supervisor informs the supervisee that he or she must be terminated from the clinical experience

2. Interview at least two practicing supervisors to learn how they view the evaluation of supervisees and what methods of evaluation they employ. Ask how often they conduct formal evaluations of supervisees, how the feedback is communicated to the supervisees, whether they use any formal mechanism for obtaining feedback from their supervisees, and how they have changed their supervision practices as a result of feedback from supervisees.

3. Write a hypothetical letter of recommendation that is complete, objective, and balanced and incorporates most of the items from the letter of recommendation checklist. Invent different scenarios to write about, such as a letter regarding a supervisee who has marginal skills and will require considerable improvement before successfully completing the supervised experience. In class, this could be done as a group exercise. Share these letters with the whole class.

4. In small groups, have class members discuss their own experiences with being evaluated as supervisees, and brainstorm how you might improve the evaluation process as supervisors. Discuss how the evaluation process can be most beneficial to the supervisee and how the evaluative feedback can be communicated in the most constructive manner.

5. What is the optimal frequency of feedback and evaluation for supervisees? Think about formal and informal evaluation procedures and how often each should occur. What obstacles might get in the way of maintaining the optimal frequency of evaluation? How could a supervisor overcome those obstacles? This exercise can be done in class in small groups for discussion or can be done through journaling.

Appendix 10A

SUPERVISEE EVALUATION OF SUPERVISION

Please rate your supervisor/supervision experience on a scale from 1 to 5, with 1 being strongly disagree and 5 being strongly agree, for each of the following supervision tasks.

Orientation

___ The environment was warm and inviting.

___ My supervisor took the time to learn about me.

___ I felt well informed about expectations including preparation for supervision sessions, communication, methods of supervision, use of technology, feedback, and evaluation.

___ I was informed about the structure and nature of future supervisory sessions.

___ My supervisor assessed my access to resources needed to be successful.

___ My supervisor assessed my knowledge and ability to practice basic skills and meet basic requirements to be successful.

___ I was provided ample opportunity to ask questions and received supportive answers and resources in response.

___ My supervisor and I collaboratively set goals for supervision both professionally and personally.

___ My supervisor reviewed the Code of Ethics.

___ My supervisor provided me with clear instruction regarding the security of client information, confidentiality, client files, and all materials utilized for documentation.

___ My supervisor reviewed informed consent and emphasized the importance of confidentiality, identifying myself as a "counselor-in-training," and written consent for technology use.

___ My supervisor clearly reviewed an emergency plan for our supervisory time with specific steps and resources available to me in case of emergency situations to take care of myself and my clients.

___ I was provided with copies of all materials reviewed and all materials needed to successfully complete the supervision process.

___ My supervisor told me I had rights and how to proceed if I felt those rights were violated and provided resources.

___ I was provided with a supervisory contract and signed that I understood the expectations and requirements of supervision.

Supervisory Relationship

___ My supervisor was accessible to me.

___ My supervisor clearly delineated boundaries in a way that was protective for both of us.

___ I feel safe with my supervisor to openly discuss topics and concerns without fear of judgment.

___ My supervisor was open and initiated conversations regarding similarities and differences, multicultural issues, and diversity.

___ My supervisor listened to me and was willing to make adjustments when needed.

___ I felt comfortable discussing strengths and weaknesses of my knowledge, skills, and attitudes.

___ My supervisor cared about my development as a person and a professional.

___ My supervisor did not act as my counselor but would refer me for counseling if needed.

___ My supervisor made my client and me a priority in times of emergency.

___ I was empowered to meet challenges to grow, take risks, and develop during supervision.

(Continued)

Appendix 10A *(Continued)*

Knowledge, Skills, and Attitudes

___ My supervisor was willing to demonstrate, role play, and assist in my learning process.

___ My supervisor reviewed materials with me in ways that were applied and meaningful.

___ There were conversations regarding beliefs, values, and attitudes that directly affected my counseling.

___ I was encouraged to explore my own theoretical orientation and to understand the application of theory in practice.

___ Case conceptualization was an integral part of the process prior to diagnosis or treatment.

___ I feel more knowledgeable and confident after supervision.

___ Conversations included generalizing material to other situations and environments for expanded learning.

___ I was expected to bring ideas, thoughts, opinions and questions to supervision sessions.

___ My supervisor shared his/her theoretical models for both therapy and supervision.

___ I felt that my supervisor cared for my clients and their well-being.

Evaluation

___ During orientation, I clearly understood by what means I would be evaluated and the structure of evaluation; I was provided with copies of evaluation forms.

___ I was given timely feedback regarding my performance and whether I was meeting expectations.

___ If there was an area of weakness identified, remedial resources were suggested with supportive and reasonable steps regarding expectations for improvement.

___ Verbal feedback was provided throughout my supervision.

___ I was given the opportunity to play an active role in my own supervision, evaluation, and development.

___ Evaluation caused me to feel more confident in my competence as a counselor.

___ I received both written and verbal formal evaluations during my supervision.

___ I felt comfortable discussing areas in need of improvement.

___ I valued my supervisor's feedback and knowledge in difficult situations.

___ My supervisor initiated helpful conversations about my performance as a counselor and ways to improve.

___ My overall evaluation of my supervision experience was positive.

Source: Adapted from Northwestern State University, Natchitoches, LA, Department of Psychology, and designed by Patrice Moulton, 2020. Reprinted with permission.

Appendix 10B

PRACTICUM EVALUATION FORM

Northwestern State University
Department of Psychology
Evaluation of Practicum Student

Graduate Student: _____ Date: _____

Faculty Supervisor: _____ Date: _____

Check one: ❏ Mid-Term Evaluation   ❏ Final Evaluation

Instructions: Please use the following scale to evaluate the student.

Not Applicable	*Poor*	*Below Average*	*Average*	*Above Average*	*Excellent*
0	1	2	3	4	5

I. *Initial Sessions*

A. Establishes Rapport   ❏ 0 ❏ 1 ❏ 2 ❏ 3 ❏ 4 ❏ 5
Responds to client's initial discomfort;
uses small talk appropriately to help relax client

B. Presents Self Professionally   ❏ 0 ❏ 1 ❏ 2 ❏ 3 ❏ 4 ❏ 5
Prepared; presents self as a competent professional; prompt

C. Structures Therapeutic Relationship   ❏ 0 ❏ 1 ❏ 2 ❏ 3 ❏ 4 ❏ 5
Verbalizes role and function of therapist and client;
explains the therapist's status and supervisory relationship;
explains limits of confidentiality; explains and obtains
informed consent and assent

D. Performs Initial Structuring Tasks   ❏ 0 ❏ 1 ❏ 2 ❏ 3 ❏ 4 ❏ 5
Orients client to process; uses forms/materials and
scheduling information; answers client's questions;
gets permission to audio/videotape

II. *Facilitative Conditions*

A. Conveys Empathic Understanding   ❏ 0 ❏ 1 ❏ 2 ❏ 3 ❏ 4 ❏ 5
Reflects client's affect; reflects client's content;
responds beyond client's words; orients client

B. Conveys Genuineness   ❏ 0 ❏ 1 ❏ 2 ❏ 3 ❏ 4 ❏ 5
Interacts with spontaneity; responds to client's emotions;
expresses congruent words/feelings;
uses self-disclosure appropriately

C. Conveys Unconditional Positive Regard   ❏ 0 ❏ 1 ❏ 2 ❏ 3 ❏ 4 ❏ 5
Facial expression/words are not judgmental;
normalizes client's concerns appropriately

D. Conveys Effective Listening   ❏ 0 ❏ 1 ❏ 2 ❏ 3 ❏ 4 ❏ 5
Appears attentive; appropriate posture and
eye contact; makes physical contact appropriately;
listens to understand

(Continued)

Appendix 10B *(Continued)*

E. Therapist Use of Confrontation ☐0 ☐1 ☐2 ☐3 ☐4 ☐5
*Identifies client discrepancies/distortions in
content/affect and between verbal and nonverbal behavior;
provides appropriate observations; confronts with purpose
and in a supportive manner; directs client to deal with
confronted content/affect; follows confrontation with
active listening/empathy; neither ignores nor blames*

F. Focuses on Therapeutic Relationship ☐0 ☐1 ☐2 ☐3 ☐4 ☐5
*Deals with relationship issues as necessary;
responds to client's expressed concerns with the therapy process;
puts client's welfare first; creates a respectful and safe environment*

III.   *Appropriate Movement Through Stages of Therapy Process*

A. Stage 1: Clarification of the Problem ☐0 ☐1 ☐2 ☐3 ☐4 ☐5
*Obtains present behaviors, feelings, symptoms associated
with the presenting problem; obtains relevant background
information; solid client conceptualization*

B. Stage 2: Understanding and Goal Setting ☐0 ☐1 ☐2 ☐3 ☐4 ☐5
*Identifies client issues by tying prior events to present;
restructures treatment strategy to meet client needs;
listens to understand with client; uses interpretation appropriately;
offers useful/objective feedback; provides information and feedback;
identifies specific goals*

C. Stage 3: Facilitating Action ☐0 ☐1 ☐2 ☐3 ☐4 ☐5
*Utilizes techniques/theory; develops action strategies
with theoretical basis; facilitates action; evaluates outcomes;
offers feedback; models desired behaviors*

IV.   *Closing of Session*

A. Structures Appropriately ☐0 ☐1 ☐2 ☐3 ☐4 ☐5
*Alerts client to time; uses summary statements
at end of session; provides client the opportunity
for closure; reviews "homework" assignment;
assesses mood at closing*

V.   *Termination of Therapeutic Relationship*

A. Structures Appropriately ☐0 ☐1 ☐2 ☐3 ☐4 ☐5
*Alerts client of termination throughout
the relationship; encourages independence;
summarizes goals and outcomes; plans for future;
addresses closure of therapeutic relationship;
describes nature of appropriate future contacts;
provides resources*

VI.   *General Competencies*

A. Time management ☐0 ☐1 ☐2 ☐3 ☐4 ☐5

B. Uses silence appropriately ☐0 ☐1 ☐2 ☐3 ☐4 ☐5

(Continued)

Appendix 10B *(Continued)*

		0	1	2	3	4	5
C.	Develops case conceptualization	❏ 0	❏ 1	❏ 2	❏ 3	❏ 4	❏ 5
D.	Demonstrates self-awareness	❏ 0	❏ 1	❏ 2	❏ 3	❏ 4	❏ 5
E.	Promotes positive work climate	❏ 0	❏ 1	❏ 2	❏ 3	❏ 4	❏ 5
F.	Interacts effectively with peers	❏ 0	❏ 1	❏ 2	❏ 3	❏ 4	❏ 5
G.	Interacts effectively with supervisors	❏ 0	❏ 1	❏ 2	❏ 3	❏ 4	❏ 5
H.	Demonstrates professional writing skills	❏ 0	❏ 1	❏ 2	❏ 3	❏ 4	❏ 5
I.	Demonstrates case management skills	❏ 0	❏ 1	❏ 2	❏ 3	❏ 4	❏ 5
J.	Demonstrates professional behavior	❏ 0	❏ 1	❏ 2	❏ 3	❏ 4	❏ 5
K.	Demonstrates ethical behavior	❏ 0	❏ 1	❏ 2	❏ 3	❏ 4	❏ 5
L.	Demonstrates cultural awareness and sensitivity	❏ 0	❏ 1	❏ 2	❏ 3	❏ 4	❏ 5
M.	Demonstrates use of good judgment	❏ 0	❏ 1	❏ 2	❏ 3	❏ 4	❏ 5
N.	Provides appropriate referrals	❏ 0	❏ 1	❏ 2	❏ 3	❏ 4	❏ 5
O.	Accepts and learns from feedback	❏ 0	❏ 1	❏ 2	❏ 3	❏ 4	❏ 5
P.	Demonstrates appropriate crisis management knowledge	❏ 0	❏ 1	❏ 2	❏ 3	❏ 4	❏ 5
Q.	Manages the use of technology effectively	❏ 0	❏ 1	❏ 2	❏ 3	❏ 4	❏ 5
R.	Shows working knowledge of emergency plan	❏ 0	❏ 1	❏ 2	❏ 3	❏ 4	❏ 5
S.	Demonstrates a working knowledge and application of theory in practice	❏ 0	❏ 1	❏ 2	❏ 3	❏ 4	❏ 5

Summary: Please provide a written evaluation of the student's performance highlights and indicate what actions you are recommending with remediation for those areas of concern.

Overall skills: _____

_____

_____

Overall process: _____

_____

_____

Actions taken: _____

_____

_____

_____	_____
Therapist	*Date*
_____	_____
Faculty Supervisor	*Date*

Source: Adapted from Northwestern State University, Natchitoches, LA, Department of Psychology, and designed by Patrice Moulton, 2020. Reprinted with permission.

Appendix 10C

SUPERVISEE PERFORMANCE EVALUATION

Supervisee: _____   Date: _____

Supervisor: _____   Date: _____

Period Rated: _____

Instructions: Please rate the supervisee's performance for the period indicated, using the scale listed below. Rate the supervisee in comparison with the average supervisee at the same level of training. Include comments at the bottom when assigning Below or Well below standard ratings. Review this evaluation with the supervisee and have the supervisee sign at bottom.

Well below *standard* 1	*Below* *standard* 2	*Standard* 3	*Above* *standard* 4	*Well above* *standard* 5	*Not* *applicable* NA

Professional Practice

A.	Attendance/punctuality	❑1 ❑2 ❑3 ❑4 ❑5 ❑NA	
B.	Responsiveness to supervision	❑1 ❑2 ❑3 ❑4 ❑5 ❑NA	
C.	Relations with staff	❑1 ❑2 ❑3 ❑4 ❑5 ❑NA	
D.	Relationships with clients	❑1 ❑2 ❑3 ❑4 ❑5 ❑NA	
E.	Ethical practice	❑1 ❑2 ❑3 ❑4 ❑5 ❑NA	
F.	Verbal communication	❑1 ❑2 ❑3 ❑4 ❑5 ❑NA	
G.	Written communication	❑1 ❑2 ❑3 ❑4 ❑5 ❑NA	
H.	Treatment team participation	❑1 ❑2 ❑3 ❑4 ❑5 ❑NA	
I.	Understanding of multicultural issues/ individual differences	❑1 ❑2 ❑3 ❑4 ❑5 ❑NA	
J.	Seeks supervision when needed	❑1 ❑2 ❑3 ❑4 ❑5 ❑NA	
K.	Seeks consultation when needed	❑1 ❑2 ❑3 ❑4 ❑5 ❑NA	
L.	Initiative/independence	❑1 ❑2 ❑3 ❑4 ❑5 ❑NA	
M.	Judgment/maturity	❑1 ❑2 ❑3 ❑4 ❑5 ❑NA	
N.	Open to personal development	❑1 ❑2 ❑3 ❑4 ❑5 ❑NA	

Assessment Skills

A.	Knowledge of instruments and methods	❑1 ❑2 ❑3 ❑4 ❑5 ❑NA	
B.	Formulation of referral questions	❑1 ❑2 ❑3 ❑4 ❑5 ❑NA	
C.	Test administration		
	Intellectual	❑1 ❑2 ❑3 ❑4 ❑5 ❑NA	
	Neuropsychology	❑1 ❑2 ❑3 ❑4 ❑5 ❑NA	
	Personality	❑1 ❑2 ❑3 ❑4 ❑5 ❑NA	
	Projective Instruments	❑1 ❑2 ❑3 ❑4 ❑5 ❑NA	
D.	Test interpretation		
	Intellectual	❑1 ❑2 ❑3 ❑4 ❑5 ❑NA	
	Neuropsychology	❑1 ❑2 ❑3 ❑4 ❑5 ❑NA	
	Personality	❑1 ❑2 ❑3 ❑4 ❑5 ❑NA	
	Projective Instruments	❑1 ❑2 ❑3 ❑4 ❑5 ❑NA	

(Continued)

Appendix 10C *(Continued)*

E.	Rapport with clients	❏ 1	❏ 2	❏ 3	❏ 4	❏ 5 ❏ NA
F.	Report writing	❏ 1	❏ 2	❏ 3	❏ 4	❏ 5 ❏ NA
G.	Provides feedback to client	❏ 1	❏ 2	❏ 3	❏ 4	❏ 5 ❏ NA

Intervention Skills

A.	Individual therapy skills	❏ 1	❏ 2	❏ 3	❏ 4	❏ 5 ❏ NA
B.	Group therapy skills	❏ 1	❏ 2	❏ 3	❏ 4	❏ 5 ❏ NA
C.	Rapport/empathy in therapy	❏ 1	❏ 2	❏ 3	❏ 4	❏ 5 ❏ NA
D.	Developing a clear treatment plan	❏ 1	❏ 2	❏ 3	❏ 4	❏ 5 ❏ NA
E.	Intervention based on theory/research	❏ 1	❏ 2	❏ 3	❏ 4	❏ 5 ❏ NA
F.	Intervention based on client needs	❏ 1	❏ 2	❏ 3	❏ 4	❏ 5 ❏ NA
G.	Evaluates progress regularly	❏ 1	❏ 2	❏ 3	❏ 4	❏ 5 ❏ NA
H.	Addresses termination issues	❏ 1	❏ 2	❏ 3	❏ 4	❏ 5 ❏ NA

Other

A.	Use of technology	❏ 1	❏ 2	❏ 3	❏ 4	❏ 5 ❏ NA
B.	File confidentiality/management	❏ 1	❏ 2	❏ 3	❏ 4	❏ 5 ❏ NA
C.	Knowledge of emergency plan	❏ 1	❏ 2	❏ 3	❏ 4	❏ 5 ❏ NA

Overall Performance   ❏ 1   ❏ 2   ❏ 3   ❏ 4   ❏ 5   ❏ NA

Comments: _____

_____

_____

_____   _____

Supervisor Signature   *Date*

This evaluation has been reviewed with me.

I ❏ agree   ❏ disagree   with the evaluation.

_____   _____

Supervisee Signature   *Date*

Source: Adapted from Northwestern State University, Natchitoches, LA, Department of Psychology, and designed by Cynthia Lindsey and Patrice Moulton, 2020. Reprinted with permission.

CHAPTER 11

Becoming an Effective Supervisor

FOCUS QUESTIONS

1. Which supervisors have you had that you would describe as being effective? What are the key characteristics of those individuals?
2. What is the relative importance of a supervisor's knowledge and skills versus the interpersonal skills of that individual?
3. What struggles do you anticipate when you first start to supervise? What resources will you use to deal with these challenges?
4. What five action steps are you willing to take toward becoming a competent supervisor?

Now that you have a clear understanding of what supervision is about and how it works, what approach would you take in fulfilling the many responsibilities of supervision? What actions will move you in this direction? Be patient with yourself. Becoming a competent and confident supervisor takes time, experience, and deliberate practice. This process can be a dynamic, professionally stimulating, and meaningful experience.

In this chapter, we showcase the characteristics of effective supervisors and ask some contributors to share their perspectives on both the "ideal" and the effective supervisor. We all strive for the *ideal* in our journey toward being *effective* supervisors. We also discuss the struggles of new supervisors. We conclude the chapter with some thoughts on finding your own style as a supervisor and developing a plan for how to proceed beyond this book in becoming an effective supervisor.

Qualities of an Effective Supervisor

We asked a clinical director of training who is in charge of practicum and internship placements in agencies what qualities she looks for in selecting effective supervisors. In Voices From the Field, Mary Read writes about the qualities of an effective clinical supervisor.

VOICES FROM THE FIELD

What Makes for an Effective Clinical Supervisor?

Mary M. Read, PhD

Drawing from over 30 years of teaching graduate students in counseling at California State University, Fullerton, I have developed some thoughts about the characteristics of effective clinical supervisors. When I interface with an agency in my role as director of clinical training for the department, I love having conversations with the clinical supervisors who will be working with our practicum students. I'm looking in part for their theory of supervision. I'm partial to a developmental view because mentoring a brand new student trainee with zero counseling experience is necessarily different from finishing supervision with someone approaching 3,000-plus experience hours for licensure. The newbies need more coaching on clinical skills, paperwork, and policies and procedures, and the seasoned folks need more consultation and mentoring into what comes next in their careers as licensed professionals.

I'm also looking for a supervisor's sense of appropriate boundaries, interpersonally and clinically, and their confidence in the process of both therapy and supervision. As we interact, I ask them what they love about supervising as well as what they might fear. By the time individuals take on the tasks of clinical supervision, I want to assure myself that they have a clear sense of what the mentoring, training, and monitoring of new professionals involves. I draw on the actions of my helpful supervisors and recognize the things my not-so-helpful supervisors contributed in this assessment. I use my own background in training and mentoring supervisors to help them feel more comfortable and competent as we work together to ensure our shared students' success. Helping supervisors develop professionally in their roles helps our counseling program and the profession as well.

Many of the processes in supervision mirror the flow of therapy, with relationship as the primary factor. That said, effective supervisors have the ability to analyze their relationship with the supervisee on multiple levels simultaneously: in therapy, in supervision, and in each supervisee's own world. A sound theory of supervision can help guide the process, just like a clinical theory helps the supervisee navigate work with a client. Good, safe, ethical boundaries are primary in both supervision and therapy, of course. Some aspects of supervision may feel a bit like therapy to the supervisee because the supervisory relationship includes a certain amount of "people gardening" for the sake of the supervisee's personal and professional growth.

Supervisors help their supervisees recognize where they are in their professional development process, including fostering a professional identity. They also recommend more support when supervisees' issues are hindering their clinical work. Sorting out what may be arising from countertransference, monitoring when a supervisee's own triggers are affecting the client's process, and even potentially reporting the deficits of a supervisee through relevant channels all fall on the supervisor's shoulders. This is in line with protecting the supervisee's clients, and potentially the counseling field, from supervisees who may be causing unintended harm. That's not the "fun stuff" of supervision, but the capacity to do that hard work when it's needed is something I check for when affiliating with a clinical supervisor.

The Supervisory Relationship as Central in Effective Supervision

"Components of effective supervision . . . include development of a supervisory relationship or alliance, a vehicle through which a trusting and collaborative process occurs that fosters reflective self-assessment" (Falender, 2018, p. 1243). Ramos-Sánchez and colleagues (2002) investigated the relationship between supervisee developmental level, working alliance, attachment, and negative experiences in supervision through a national survey of randomly selected psychology internship directors and psychology doctoral program training directors. Ramos-Sánchez and colleagues affirmed that the supervisory relationship is central in effective supervision. It is within the supervisory relationship that the supervisor trains and guides the supervisee's development in becoming a skilled therapist. They concluded that effective supervision cannot occur without a solid supervisory relationship. This conclusion aligns with our earlier discussion of the supervisory relationship (see Chapter 3).

As clinical and case conceptualization skills are developed, supervisees and their supervisor are more likely to agree on the tasks and goals of supervision, and the supervisory relationship becomes less didactic and more collegial. Supervisees at more advanced stages of development reported having a better working relationship with their supervisor and a higher level of trust, leading to a greater opportunity for development of the supervisor-supervisee relationship. Ramos-Sánchez and colleagues' (2002) survey resulted in several recommendations for effective supervision:

- Be aware that harsh criticism and judgmental attitudes by supervisors can result in serious consequences for supervisee development.
- Supervisors are encouraged to build trust, to support and advocate for supervisees, and to be open to feedback from supervisees.
- Supervisor evaluation by the supervisee should be implemented to improve the supervisor's performance.
- Supervisors are encouraged to explore the supervisee's goals for supervision and to be clear about their own expectations for the supervisee's performance.

In another study of effective supervision, Martino (2001) described the information obtained from graduate students regarding their experiences with both effective and ineffective supervision. This study rated the top 10 factors contributing to "best" supervisor (descending order):

- Demonstrates clinical knowledge and expertise
- Demonstrates flexibility and openness to new ideas and approaches to cases
- Exudes warmth and is supportive
- Provides useful feedback and constructive criticism
- Is dedicated to student's training
- Possesses good clinical insight
- Is empathic
- Examines countertransference
- Adheres to ethical practices
- Provides challenge

The top 10 factors contributing to "worst" supervisor were also rated (descending order):

- Shows a lack of interest in student's training and professional development
- Proves to be unavailable
- Is inflexible to new ideas and approaches to cases
- Has limited clinical knowledge and experience

- Proves to be unreliable
- Provides unhelpful, inconsistent feedback
- Comes across as punitive and critical
- Is not empathic
- Lacks structure
- Lacks a sense of ethics

Think about the qualities you would want in a supervisor. How is your view of an effective supervisor similar to or different from the characteristics identified in these two lists? As you read the contributors' accounts in Voices From the Field in the following sections, what themes stand out for you? Think about each individual's description of the effective supervisor and identify attributes that fit with your own picture of an effective supervisor.

A New Professional's View of Effective Supervision

In Voices From the Field, Amanda Connell, a relatively new professional in the process of applying for licensure, describes some of the qualities of outstanding supervisors she worked with as a trainee. We get a glimpse of how quality supervision is a two-way exchange between supervisor and supervisee. She sends the message that the supervisee must assume an active role in the supervisory relationship to receive effective supervision.

 VOICES FROM THE FIELD

My Experience With Effective Supervision

Amanda Connell, MS

My experiences with supervision have been fantastic. I have had several outstanding supervisors who contributed substantially to my growth and development as a therapist. Several factors coalesce to create amazing supervision experiences: the high quality of supervisors and their agencies, the diversity of clients, and my own participation.

There are multiple components of high-quality, effective supervision, and it begins with the qualities of the supervisors themselves. Excellent supervisors are empathic, intelligent, balanced, intuitive, supportive, creative, ethical, encouraging, and dedicated. They possess excellent communication and problem-solving skills. Flexibility, openness, congruence, and confidence are also important characteristics. These supervisors take a collaborative stance while also serving as guides, mentors, and facilitators. Great supervisors practice and teach strong boundaries and good self-care. This contributes to healthy interactions and models these behaviors for the supervisee.

Supervisors with a wide range of experiences to draw from are very beneficial to the process. Personally, I appreciate supervisors who provide ample opportunities to explore different techniques, theories, and modalities in my work with clients. It is also helpful to feel valued by supervisors during times of both success and failure. A part of the growth process is learning more effective ways of working with client challenges, so it is crucial to have a safe environment to freely express missteps, doubts, stuck points, and concerns. I also prefer supervisors who challenge me to take appropriate risks to expand my experience and improve my skills. The ability to offer multiple perspectives and encouragement to think outside the box are also invigorating aspects of high-quality supervision.

Obtaining high-quality supervision was a purposeful process of research and proactive behaviors. I took charge of my future by consulting with peers about their supervision experiences, and I created clear goals about what I wanted in a supervisor. Another avenue was researching internship site reference books in the fieldwork office. When hired at an agency with the supervisor I wanted to work with, I specifically requested to be placed with my choice of supervisor rather than passively waiting for one to be assigned to me. I took these steps due to early recognition that the quality of supervision makes a huge difference in both professional development and overall work satisfaction.

Effective supervision is not a one-way relationship. Supervisees will benefit most if they do their part too. One of my responsibilities in receiving excellent supervision included exercising strong communication skills. I welcomed and even requested constructive feedback. I pushed myself to ask for help and guidance, and I worked to suspend my perfectionistic tendencies so I could receive the assistance I needed. I also frequently volunteered to engage in role plays in group supervision to practice my skills and receive important feedback.

Supervision relationships work best when they are built on mutual trust and respect. I demonstrated respect and cultivated trust with supervisors. One way my supervisors trusted me to practice in an ethical and lawful manner was that I sought consultation when encountering client crises and risky situations, being mindful that it was not only my associate registration on the line but also my supervisor's license.

I am enormously grateful for the supervisors I have had the honor to work with over the years. They all encouraged me to develop my own style, but I have also incorporated aspects of each one into my practice. I often smile as I catch myself using a favorite phrase or gesture of one of my previous supervisors. In comparing the supervisor-supervisee to the client-therapist relationship, one of my supervisors stated that "there has been an energy exchange, and I am forever a part of you, and you are forever a part of me." This statement speaks to the power and significance of the supervisory relationship, which is at the heart of effective supervision.

A Recent Graduate Student's Perspective of Effective Supervision

In Voices From the Field, a recent graduate in social work explains how her supervisor created both a trusting and a challenging atmosphere that enabled her to flourish.

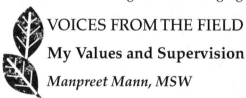

VOICES FROM THE FIELD

My Values and Supervision

Manpreet Mann, MSW

I recently graduated with a master's of social work from the University of Nevada, Reno. I have worked in the field of aging for 5 years with an emphasis on improving quality of life and promoting healthy aging within the community. Having an effective supervisor at a practicum placement was crucial to this experience reaching its full potential. My foundation year preceptor was able to do this using a variety of techniques that were chosen based on what I needed during different parts of the semester. My preceptor cultivated a relationship of trust and nonjudgment, taking time to get to know me, using initial sessions to explore tasks I had done in the past, and trying to understand what I truly was hoping to achieve from this placement. His openness to share his own experiences provided me with the opportunity to create a list of tasks and skills I would like to build within myself. The time taken out to work with me in this initial stage laid the framework for me, as a student, to feel comfortable about being honest when I was unsure or was feeling uncertain.

Effectively creating an open and honest relationship helped me identify my areas of bias and understand the implications of this in working with clients. In one instance, I was doing home assessments of clients for enrollment in our transportation program, which provided rides to medical appointments, personal errands, and socialization activities. As the social work intern for the program, I completed all of the home assessments as a way to help me better understand how the various aspects of the lives of my clients can affect their eligibility for different programs. I was feeling uncomfortable about doing an assessment at a mobile home park on the outskirts of town. I shared with my preceptor my discomfort and my guilt about having these feelings. By asking the right questions and breaking down what "guilt" and "uncomfortable" truly meant for me, my preceptor was able to help me understand that my feelings about this assessment were connected to the bias my parents had taught me about people who live in mobile home parks. I felt comfortable enough with my supervisor to share my thoughts about how these feelings had started and how they contributed to what I was experiencing. My immigrant parents had tried to protect us from anyone they thought would distract us from the path of success. My siblings and I were told to stay away from mobile home parks and those who lived there. Unknowingly, I had carried the biases my parents had into my own life. Many would think that becoming aware of this bias would be the only important thing I learned from this experience. But my preceptor knew that to be a good social worker I would need to learn how to effectively work through that bias, and he began helping me in that next step.

Our next step in supervision sessions was working through process recordings. A process recording is a form of indirect supervision that can help both preceptor and supervisee reflect on a situation and understand what may have gone right or wrong. Process recordings identify the following: what was said during the assessment, skills I used as a social worker, my internal gut reaction, an analysis of the experience and what worked and what did not, and feedback from my preceptor. These process recording sessions allowed me to reflect on the assessment and to realize that my bias could have played out and shifted the client's experience. The process recordings also allowed my preceptor to "shadow" the assessment and determine whether my bias did sway or change the outcome of the assessment. We explored effective ways for me to work through my biases, allowing me to accept that it's OK to have the thought as long as it does not change how I work with the client. Cultivation of a safe, trusting, and learning environment during my practicum placement enabled me to become a better professional.

Supervisor Perspectives on an Ideal Supervisor

In Voices From the Field, Mark Stebnicki develops the message that empathy plays a key role in facilitating clients' search for meaning in their chronic illness, disability, trauma, loss, and other major life stressors that challenge them daily. He also describes how empathy is a central factor in effective supervision and how an empathy lab shaped his theoretical orientation.

VOICES FROM THE FIELD

Clinical Supervision in Rehabilitation Counseling

Mark A. Stebnicki, PhD

During my master's and doctoral programs, I had the opportunity to be mentored by one of the most skillful, empathetic, and insightful people I have ever encountered in the counseling profession—the late Dr. Harry Allen, professor emeritus, Southern Illinois University (SIU), Carbondale. Dr. Allen, who preferred to be called "Harry," was a highly creative and visionary counselor educator, clinical supervisor, extraordinary psychotherapist, and active researcher. Harry developed a graduate-level counseling course at SIU that he titled the "Empathy Lab." Here the foundational skills of empathy were taught along with how to enter the private world of another person with deep respect and reverence. Harry facilitated multiple unique and creative experiential activities that prepared students to respond to real client issues during their practicum and internship experiences.

Harry began each new semester by telling students, "I only want you to learn three things in this course: show-up, pay attention, and be open to the outcomes." There was little explanation beyond this intention. However, as the semester pushed forward, I began to explore and process the elegance, complexity, and simplicity of this mantra. To truly understand Harry's mission, vision, and intention, we had to immerse ourselves in the process (*show up*); walk with Harry, being mindful of what he had to teach (*pay attention*); and be *open to the outcomes* by discovering and transforming our feelings, cognitions, behaviors, and experiences for optimal mental health and well-being of self and others whom we serve.

The Empathy Lab helped shape my clinical supervision theoretical orientation, style, roles, strategies, and techniques. Clinical supervision in rehabilitation counseling requires supervisees to show up, pay attention, and be open to the outcomes. *Showing up* is a dynamic process whereby supervisees increase their awareness, knowledge, and skills for working with people with chronic illnesses, disabilities, and co-occurring mental health conditions. This requires a recognition of the complex interactions that exist between the person and the environment. For instance, many people with disabilities suggest that negative societal attitudes, perceptions, inaccessibility, and architectural barriers are more disabling than the disability itself.

The process of *paying attention* requires supervisees to identify key constructs related to models of psychosocial adjustment and adaptation to chronic illness and disability. This assists supervisees in recognizing the unique cultural differences between persons with and without disabilities. When the supervisee pays attention, opportunities to earn the circle of trust, develop a strong working alliance, and integrate therapeutic strategies into the helping process increase.

The process of *being open to the outcomes* requires supervisees to become genuinely interested and honest about seeking feedback concerning their client-counselor sessions. Feedback within the supervisee-supervisor relationship that is ongoing, timely, specific, and valuable for implementation into the therapeutic process cultivates counselor competence.

Overall, effective clinical supervisors assist supervisees to facilitate their clients' search for meaning in their chronic illness, disability, trauma, loss, and other major life stressors that challenge them daily. Indeed, empathy is at the foundation of the helping profession, and it informs counselor competence and ethical practices.

In Voices From the Field, Elie Axelroth characterizes the ideal supervisor in an internship setting by describing the ideal trainee, the training environment, the client, and the relationship between all of them.

VOICES FROM THE FIELD

Supervision as a Collaborative Relationship

Elie Axelroth, PsyD

An ideal supervisor understands that new interns arrive at their setting in a vulnerable state, in need of reassurance, direction, and compassion. This vulnerability must drive much of the initial work of orientation and relationship building. Interns come to the setting filled with hopes for engaging in challenging work, and they bring with them a set of skills and enormous anxiety about their capacity to perform. The ideal supervisor assesses the training needs, is tuned in to the developmental stages of the interns, and is willing to adjust the training program to the skills and needs of the interns.

In the first weeks of internship, the ideal supervisor spends time orienting new interns by touring the setting and introducing them to staff and referral sources; reviewing crisis procedures, basic issues of confidentiality, and reporting guidelines; walking them through the paperwork and note-taking guidelines; and reviewing risk management issues such as assessment of violence and lethality. This orientation not only provides the groundwork for solid clinical work but also helps allay interns' anxiety by establishing clear expectations. Interns need to be oriented to the informal norms of the setting as well as to the more formal policies. It is often the informal norms that create the most anxiety and uncertainty.

Ideal supervisors are knowledgeable, well versed in ethics and the law, and are able to articulate a framework for making difficult ethical decisions. They can communicate a theoretical framework in terms that are accessible to their interns. They listen to the intern, are not too quick to make assessments about the client, and respect the intern's right to disagree.

A talented clinician, one with a flair for the work, is not necessarily the ideal supervisor. The ideal supervisor is willing to highlight the strengths of the intern and not his or her own glowing achievements. This person is a seasoned clinician as well as an experienced supervisor and is able to tailor a variety of interventions that meet the needs of the intern and the therapeutic goals of the client. There are times when didactic instruction is needed to help interns move beyond their knowledge set. As the intern matures and builds confidence and skill, the ideal supervisor helps the intern develop more abstract interventions through interpretation and insight. The supervisor, like any skilled clinician, is able to use these strategies intentionally.

Supervision is a dialogue, and the ideal supervisor recognizes that good supervision opens the supervisor as well as the intern to new insights, new learning, and excitement about the work. Like good teachers or mentors who are attuned to their students, supervisors learn something new from teaching others. Supervision at its best is a mutual collaborative relationship in which curiosity, excitement, and new insights are opened up to both supervisor and intern.

In Voices From the Field, Marianne Schneider Corey reminds us that it is important for supervisors to help trainees develop their own style. She reflects on her own experience working with effective supervisors.

VOICES FROM THE FIELD

What My Effective Supervisors Had in Common

Marianne Schneider Corey, MA

I had three different supervisors during my training. Although each of them had a distinct style of supervision, they were all warm and personable individuals, and they provided a good balance between demonstrating caring and being willing to challenge me. When I was discouraged, they provided encouragement. They encouraged me to stretch my limits rather than surrender to my fears. They seemed to believe in my potential to become an effective counselor at a time when I had my doubts. When I thought I couldn't meet a challenge, they provided me with a sense that I could do more than I was giving myself credit for being able to do. They provided a safety net by being available for consultation.

A key lesson they all taught was how vital the role of the counselor as a person is to the outcomes of counseling, and they encouraged me to recognize the part of me that brought me to pursue my education as a counselor. I recall wondering if I could continue my work as a counselor because I felt triggered by so much of the pain my clients expressed. One supervisor let me know that he would be worried if I didn't have concerns in this area, yet he also helped me see the value in identifying and exploring my own personal issues when they were getting in the way of being helpful to my clients. When I was concerned I would make a mistake that harmed a client, one supervisor reminded me that I did not have that much power, nor would my clients be likely to give me that kind of power. All of these supervisors had good boundaries and were able to blend therapeutic work with supervision, yet they did not take over as my therapist. They kept the focus on how my own struggles might influence my interventions with clients.

When I began counseling clients, I was tempted to pattern my therapeutic style after my supervisors. All of them encouraged me to learn from what they had to offer but stressed the importance of finding my own way as a counseling practitioner rather than becoming a carbon copy of them.

How could you encourage your supervisees to "stretch their limits rather than surrender to their fears"? If you are affected by the pain your clients express, how might you help your supervisees cope with the pain their clients will express? What might you say to a supervisee who tells you, "I am afraid I will make a mistake and that it will harm my client forever"? Take a few minutes now to write down your own description of an ideal supervisor. Doing this will help you to understand how you view the process of supervision.

Characteristics of an Effective Supervisor

We can use the descriptions of the ideal supervisor to formulate a composite picture of the supervisor we would each like to be or a supervisor we would like to have. Some of our colleagues and the contributors to this book described the attributes of effective supervisors, and we have summarized the common themes in this list. Effective supervisors:

- Understand clinical, administrative, legal, and ethical issues
- Possess strong clinical skills
- Demonstrate empathy, respect, genuineness, and listening
- Establish an accepting supervisory climate

- Create a supervisory relationship characterized by trust and respect
- Determine the developmental level and use methods that will best serve the training needs of supervisees
- Possess a sense of humor
- Develop clear boundaries
- Encourage appropriate risk-taking by supervisees
- Support a collaborative supervisory process
- Respect the knowledge supervisees bring to the supervisory relationship
- Appreciate individual differences and differing opinions about theoretical viewpoints that supervisees bring
- Are open, approachable, and supportive
- Are interested in the supervisee as a person
- Have a keen interest in training and supervision
- Show sensitivity to the anxieties and vulnerabilities of supervisees
- Value supervision sessions as "protected" time
- Provide honest, constructive feedback
- Are flexible, calm, and understanding
- Share experience, wisdom, and skills by modeling relationship skills
- Respect supervisees' right to disagree
- Provide balance between providing direction and allowing supervisees to develop independently

Struggles of Beginning Supervisors

When you begin working as a supervisor, you can expect to experience fears, doubts, and uncertainty about your role and the goals of supervision. This is a common experience for clinicians making the initial transition from supervisee to supervisor. With experience, knowledge, and learning from readings, courses, and workshops on the topic of supervision, you will be able to develop into the supervisor you would like to be. We identify some common concerns and struggles of beginning supervisors here and encourage you in your struggle to become an effective supervisor.

- Developing one's identity as a supervisor
- Setting priorities for what is important in supervision
- Dealing with self-doubt
- Setting appropriate boundaries and maintaining objectivity
- Learning what supervisors do instead of just giving answers
- Juggling the various goals and roles of supervision
- Providing feedback to supervisees in a constructive manner
- Discovering how to let supervisees come up with their own answers
- Realizing there is no one right way to supervise
- Helping supervisees accept responsibility for and have trust in the supervision process
- Creating a safe and accepting atmosphere
- Avoiding becoming the supervisee's therapist
- Making the transition to supervisor and not overidentifying with the supervisee
- Lacking self-confidence to know what to do as a supervisor
- Knowing how to handle serious clinical mistakes by supervisees
- Hesitating to play the role of expert
- Conforming supervision to the developmental stage of supervisees' professional life
- Determining the style of supervision that best fits with your skills and personality

Our Thoughts on Becoming an Effective Supervisor

We believe supervisors must be therapeutic persons. This is especially important in forming a working relationship with supervisees. Effective supervisors maintain healthy personal and professional boundaries and model them for their supervisees. They have a sincere interest in the welfare of others, and their concern is based on respect, care, and trust. They are mindful and purposeful and are present with others.

Effective supervisors are secure in the choices they have made that influenced the direction of their life. They are aware of early decisions they made about themselves, others, and the world and are willing to revise them when necessary. They feel alive, and their choices are life-oriented. They are committed to living fully rather than settling for mere existence. They are authentic, sincere, and honest and do not hide behind masks, defenses, roles, or facades.

Effective supervisors have a sense of humor. They are able to put the events of life in perspective. They have not forgotten how to laugh, especially at their own foibles and contradictions. They make mistakes and are willing to admit them, and even learn from them.

Effective supervisors appreciate the influence of culture. They are aware of the ways in which their own culture affects them, and they respect the diversity of values espoused by other cultures. They are also sensitive to the unique differences arising out of social class, race, sexual orientation, and gender.

These characteristics of effective supervisors might seem unrealistic and unattainable, but think of them as existing on a continuum. A given trait may be highly characteristic of someone at one extreme, or it may be very uncharacteristic of someone else at the other extreme. These traits and characteristics can be translated into specific behaviors that can be assessed in the development of a supervisor. Supervisors who possess many of these characteristics are in a good position to develop their own style of effective supervision.

Finding Your Own Style as a Supervisor

Some trainees limit their development by trying too hard to copy the style of a supervisor or a teacher. When you observe supervisors you respect, you may try to imitate their methods, but you will get the most from your supervision by being open to learning from peers and supervisors and from your negative experiences as well. Try on different styles, but continually evaluate what works for you and what does not. Ask yourself: "What fits my personality and belief system? Do I have any conflicts between the theory or application of my supervisor's way and my own?" If you pay too much attention to another person, you are not likely to discover your own uniqueness. Acknowledge what is good about your supervisors and teachers, but avoid being a clone. If you learn to listen to your inner voice and respect your inner promptings, you will eventually have less need to look to outside authorities.

People are not "naturally born" counselors, supervisors, or supervisees. The skills associated with each of these roles are learned, practiced, and refined. Perhaps the best way to learn how to become an effective supervisor is to reflect on lessons you are learning as a supervisee. We hope this chapter has given you a better idea of the kind of supervisor you are striving to become. You may feel somewhat intimidated by all of the variables you are expected to pay attention to in your training, but as is the case with learning any new skill or craft, it takes time and practice to become accomplished.

When you began your counselor training program, you may have made the mistake of being so focused on anything your clients said and did that you forgot to pay attention to your reactions. By trying too hard to catch every gesture and to understand every sentence, you can easily distract yourself from being present with clients. One supervisor gave a student sound advice when she said, "If you miss something with a client, the person will no doubt bring it up again later." In a similar manner, learning how to feel comfortable as a supervisor will also take time and practice.

When you eventually begin to supervise others, it is not essential that you know all the right things to say in every situation. Learning any role is an ongoing process rather than a state that is achieved once and for all. You need not be perfect, and it is important to give yourself the latitude to learn from the mistakes you might make. Giving yourself permission to be less than perfect applies equally to becoming a counselor, a supervisee, or a supervisor.

Where Can You Go From Here?

We have emphasized our belief that who the supervisor is as a person is the central aspect in being able to become an effective supervisor. It follows, then, that whatever you can do to enhance your personal development will pay dividends in your professional role. Here are some ways to enhance your development as a supervisor.

Read articles on the theory and practice of supervision in professional journals as well as books on supervision. Join a professional organization that has some linkage with supervision. For example, if you join the American Counseling Association, you can also join the Association for Counselor Education and Supervision, which is the major professional organization for supervisors and counselor educators. You may learn a great deal through networking with others, in person and online, who are experiencing similar challenges as supervisors.

At various points in your career, consider taking a course or a continuing education workshop on clinical supervision to explore new ideas that you can translate into your supervision practice. Look for ways to supervise with a colleague. For example, if you do group supervision as part of a course in a university program, invite a colleague to join you for some sessions so both of you can provide supervisees with feedback. In addition, consider peer supervision as a learning tool. In some way, seek supervision of your supervision and consult with experienced colleagues regarding your supervision practices.

If at all possible, ask a colleague or a professional with considerable experience to supervise your supervision. This supervision can go a long way toward giving you a sense of what your supervisees experience in their supervision. Be willing to share feelings of vulnerability, including your feelings about your limitations as a supervisor. Don't feel like you have to have it all together before you can begin to supervise. Realize that you will learn a great deal about supervision as you engage in this work.

Ask your supervisees for feedback. Just as instructors ask students for anonymous feedback in student evaluations at the end of a school term, you can create an avenue for your supervisees to provide input regarding the value of the supervision they received from you. Keep notes or a personal journal, and record your thoughts about being a supervisor. Write about struggles you may have and how your professional work as a supervisor is affecting you personally. A journal is an excellent way of keeping track of patterns that you can build upon or change.

Over the years, we have learned that becoming an effective supervisor entails the willingness to continue engaging in self-reflection. Rather than reaching a final goal of competence, effective supervisors, much like skilled therapists or competent teachers, are continually rethinking what they do and how they might do things more creatively. Effective supervisors are willing to participate in a process rather than remain in a steady state.

Summary

As you learn more about supervision and gain experience as a supervisee and a supervisor, your picture of an effective supervisor is likely to change. We have all experienced doubts and difficulties in becoming supervisors. That is a normal part of learning a new role and the associated new skills. Make sure that you gain the knowledge necessary to become a competent supervisor and that you give yourself time to adjust to the role. Be open to continual learning, and do not be afraid to seek additional supervision and consultation when needed.

One way to become an effective supervisor is by being an effective supervisee. Be open to learning and examining your counseling skills through self-reflection. Learn as much as you can about supervision from supervisors, both the effective ones and the ineffective ones. If you are currently a supervisor, seek supervision from colleagues for your supervisory work. Effective supervisors continually seek to learn new skills and new roles and grow with each supervision experience. We hope the material in this book, along with the perspectives of a variety of supervisors and supervisees, has provided a path forward for self-exploration and study as you work toward becoming an effective supervisor.

SUGGESTED ACTIVITIES

1. Imagine that you are going to begin supervising very soon. What are you preparing to do, and what would you need to accomplish your goals? Develop a list of tasks and support materials needed in the process of effective supervision.

2. In pairs, have class members share with their partner whether they have been supervised by someone who closely approximates the effective supervisor, and what that experience was like. What was the most outstanding characteristic of that supervisor? How did that experience influence your idea of how you would like to work as a supervisor?

3. Interview two or three individuals who are currently supervisors. Ask them what their struggles were when they first became supervisors and how they dealt with them. Bring the results back for discussion in your class or in small groups.

4. In small groups, discuss what you think will be the major struggles you are likely to encounter in becoming a supervisor. Then discuss ways you can deal with those struggles. Small groups could then share their major findings with the large group, and a master list of ways to deal with the struggles could be developed.

REFERENCES

Abassary, C., & Goodrich, K. M. (2014). Attending to crisis-based supervision for counselors: The CARE model of crisis-based supervision. *The Clinical Supervisor, 33*(1), 63–81. https://doi.org/10.1080/07325223.2014.918006

Acuff, C., Bennett, B. E., Bricklin, P. M., Canter, M. B., Knapp, S. J., Moldawsky, S., & Phelps, R. (1999). Considerations for ethical practice of managed care. *Professional Psychology: Research and Practice, 30*(6), 563–575.

American Association for Marriage and Family Therapy. (2015). *Code of ethics.*

American Counseling Association. (2014). *ACA code of ethics.*

American Counseling Association Knowledge Center. (2020). *Racism Statments.* https://www.counseling.org/knowledge-center/mental-health-resources/racism

American Mental Health Counselors Association. (2015). *Code of ethics of the American Mental Health Counselors Association.*

American Mental Health Counselors Association. (2016). *AMHCA standards for the practice of clinical mental health counseling.*

American Psychological Association. (2015). Guidelines for clinical supervision in health service psychology. *American Psychologist, 70*(1), 33–46.

American Psychological Association. (2017). *Ethical principles of psychologists and code of conduct.* http://www.apa.org/ethics/code/ethics-code-2017.pdf

American School Counselor Association. (2016). *Ethical standards for school counselors.*

American School Counselor Association. (2018a). *After a suicide: A toolkit for schools* (2nd ed.). *https://www.sprc.org/sites/default/files/resource-program/AfteraSuicideToolkitforSchools.pdf*

American School Counselor Association (2018b). *Ethical standards for school counselor education faculty.* https://www.schoolcounselor.org/asca/media/asca/Ethics/SCEEthicalStandards.pdf

Ancis, J. R., & Ladany, N. (2010). A multicultural framework for counselor supervision. In N. Ladany & L. J. Bradley (Eds.), *Counselor supervision* (4th ed., pp. 53–96). Routledge.

Association for Counselor Education and Supervision. (2011). *Best practices in clinical supervision.* www.acesonline.net/wp-content/uploads/2011/10/ACES-Best-Practices-in-clinical-supervision-document-FINAL.pdf

Association for Spiritual, Ethical, and Religious Values in Counseling. (2009). *Competencies for addressing spiritual and religious issues in counseling.* https://www.counseling.org/docs/default-source/competencies/competencies-for-addressing-spiritual-and-religious-issues-in-counseling.pdf?sfvrsn=aad7c2c_8

Austin, J. A., & Austin, J. T. (2020). *Surviving and thriving in your counseling program.* American Counseling Association.

Austin, J., Austin, J., Muratori, M., & Corey, G. (2017). Multiple relationships and multiple roles in higher education: Maintaining multiple roles and relationships in counselor education. In O. Zur (Ed.), *Multiple relationships in psychotherapy and counseling: Unavoidable, common, and mandatory dual relations in therapy* (pp. 165–173). Routledge, Taylor & Francis.

Avent, J. R., Wahesh, E., Purgason, L. L., Borders, L. D., & Mobley, A. K. (2015). A content analysis of peer feedback in triadic supervision. *Counselor Education and Supervision, 54*(1), 68–80. https://doi.org/10.1002/j.1556-6978.2015.00071.x

Bacon, J. (2018, November 30). Suicide, overdoses rise in US. *Reno Gazette Journal,* p. B2.

Baldwin, K. D. (2018). Faculty and supervisor roles in gatekeeping. In A. M. Homrich & K. L. Henderson (Eds.). *Gatekeeping in the mental health professions* (pp. 99–125). American Counseling Association.

Barnett, J. E., Cornish, J. A. E., Goodyear, R. K., & Lichtenberg, J. W. (2007). Commentaries on the ethical and effective practice of clinical supervision. *Professional Psychology: Research and Practice, 38*(3), 268–275.

Barnett, J. E., & Johnson, W. B. (2008). *Ethics desk reference for psychologists.* American Psychological Association.

Barnett, J. E., & Johnson, W. B. (2010). *Ethics desk reference for counselors.* American Counseling Association.

Barnett, J. E., Lazarus, A. A., Vasquez, M. J. T., Moorehead-Slaughter, O., & Johnson, W. B. (2007). Boundary issues and multiple relationships: Fantasy and reality. *Professional Psychology: Research and Practice, 38*(4), 401–410. https://doi.org/10.1037/0735-7028.38.4.401

Barnett, J. E., & Molzon, C. H. (2014). Clinical supervision of psychotherapy: Essential ethics issues for supervisors and supervisees. *Journal of Clinical Psychology: In Session, 70*(11), 1051–1061. https://doi.org/ 10.1002/jclp.22126

Belšak, K., & Simonič, A. (2019). Ethical issues in the use of technology in clinical supervision. *Psihoterapija, 33*(2), 233–246.

Bernard, J. M. (1979). Supervisor training: A discrimination model. *Counselor Education and Supervision, 19*(1), 60–68.

Bernard, J. (2014). The use of supervision notes as a targeted training strategy. *American Journal of Psychotherapy, 68*(2), 195–212. https://doi.org/10.1176/appi.psychotherapy.2014.68.2.195

Bernard, J. M., & Goodyear, R. K. (2019). *Fundamentals of clinical supervision* (6th ed.). Pearson.

Bitter, J. R. (2021). *Theory and practice of couples and family counseling* (3rd ed.). American Counseling Association.

Boie, I., & Lopez, A. (2011). Supervision of counselors working with eating disorders: Utilizing the integrated developmental model. *The Clinical Supervisor, 30*(2), 215–234. https://doi.org/10.1080/07325223.2011.607744

Borders, L. D. (2005). Snapshot of clinical supervision in counseling and counselor education: A five-year review. *The Clinical Supervisor, 24*(1–2), 69–113.

Borders, L. D., & Brown, L. L. (2005). *The new handbook of counseling supervision.* Erlbaum.

Borders, L. D., Glosoff, H. L., Welfare, L. E., Hays, D. G., DeKruyf, L., Fernando, D. M., & Page, B. (2014) Best practices in clinical supervision: Evolution of a counseling specialty, *The Clinical Supervisor, 33*(1), 26–44. https://doi.org/ 10.1080/07325223.2014.905225

Brown, L. (2016). *Supervision essentials for the feminist psychotherapy model of supervision.* American Psychological Association. https://doi.org/ 10.1037/14878-000

Bryan, C. J., & Rudd, M. D. (2018) *Brief cognitive-behavioral therapy for suicide prevention.* Guilford Press.

Brymer, M., Jacobs, A., Layne, C., Pynoos, R., Ruzek, J., Steinberg, A., Vernberg, E., & Watson, P. (2006). *Psychological first aid: Field operations guide* (2nd ed.). National Child Traumatic Stress Network and National Center for PTSD. SAMSHA.

Campbell, J. M. (2006). *Essentials of clinical supervision.* Wiley.

Cashwell, C. S., & Young, J. S. (Eds.). (2020). *Integrating spirituality and religion into counseling: A guide to competent practice* (3rd ed.). American Counseling Association.

Chang, C. Y., Hays, D. G., & Milliken, T. F. (2009). Addressing social justice issues in supervision: A call for client and professional advocacy. *The Clinical Supervisor, 28*(1), 20–35.

Clark, P., Hinton, W. J., & Grames, H. A. (2016). Therapists' perspectives of the cotherapy experience in a training setting. *Contemporary Family Therapy, 38,* 159–171. https://doi. org/ 10.1007/s10591-015-9358-2

Clemens, N. A. (2015). A video-conferencing peer consultation group for psychotherapy by early-career psychiatrists. *Journal of Psychiatric Practice, 21*(4), 304–305. https://doi. org/10.1097/PRA.0000000000000088

Clevinger, K., Albert, E., & Raiche, E. (2019). Supervisor self-disclosure: Supervisees' perceptions of positive supervision experiences. *Training and Education in Professional Psychology, 13*(3), 222–226. https://doi.org/10.1037/tep0000236

CNN. (2019). *10 years. 180 school shootings. 356 victims.* https://www.cnn.com/interactive/2019/07/ us/ten-years-of-school-shootings-trnd/

Cooper, C. C., & Gottlieb, M. C. (2000). Ethical issues with managed care: Challenges facing counseling psychology. *The Counseling Psychologist, 28*(2), 179–236.

Corey, G. (2019). *The art of integrative counseling.* American Counseling Association.

Corey, G. (2020). *Personal reflections on counseling.* American Counseling Association.

Corey, G., Corey, M., & Corey, C. (2019). *Issues and ethics in the helping professions* (10th ed.). Cengage Learning.

Corey, G., Muratori, M., Austin, J., & Austin, J. (2018). *Counselor self-care.* American Counseling Association.

Corey, M., & Corey, G. (2021). *Becoming a helper* (8th ed.). Cengage Learning.

Corey, M., Corey, G., & Corey, C. (2018). *Groups: Process and practice* (10th ed.). Cengage Learning.

Council for Accreditation of Counseling Related Educational Programs. (2016). *CACREP standards.*

Crockett, S., & Hays, D. G. (2015). The influence of supervisor multicultural competence on the supervisory working alliance, supervisee counseling self-efficacy, and supervisee satisfaction with supervision: A mediation model. *Counselor Education and Supervision, 54*(4), 258–273. https://doi.org/ 10.1002/ceas.12025

Crunk, A. E., & Barden, S. M. (2017). The common factors discrimination model: An integrated approach to counselor supervision. *The Professional Counselor, 7*(1), 62–75.

Cummings, J. A., Ballantyne, E. C., & Scallion, L. M. (2015). Essential processes for cognitive behavioral clinical supervision: Agenda setting, problem-solving, and formative feedback. *Psychotherapy, 52*(2), 158–163. https://doi.org//10.1037/a0038712

David, E. (2019, October 9). *Rising suicide rates at college campuses prompt concerns over mental health care.* ABC News. https://abcnews.go.com/Health/rising-suicide-rates-college-campuses-prompt-concerns-mental/story?id=66126446&cid=clicksource_26_null_bsq_hed

Davis, S. R., & Meier, S. T. (2001). *The elements of managed care: A guide for helping professionals.* Brooks/Cole, Cengage Learning.

Day-Vines, N. L., Booker Ammah, B., Steen, S., & Arnold, K. M. (2018). Getting comfortable with discomfort: Preparing counselor trainees to broach racial, ethnic, and cultural factors with clients during counseling. *International Journal for the Advancement of Counselling, 40,* 89–104. https://doi.org/10.1007/s10447- 017-9308-9

Day-Vines, N. L., Cluxton-Keller, F., Agorsor, C., Gubara, S., & Otabil, N. A. A. (2020). The multidimensional model of broaching behavior. *Journal of Counseling & Development, 98*(1), 107–118. https://doi.org/10.1002/jcad.12304

Day-Vines, N. L., Wood, S., Grothaus, T., Craigen, L., Holman, A., Dotson-Blake, K., & Douglass, M. (2007). Broaching the subjects of race, ethnicity, and culture during the counseling process. *Journal of Counseling & Development, 85*(4), 401–409.

DeLorenzi, L. D. (2018a). Challenges and strategies in addressing problematic trainees. In A. M. Homrich & K. L. Henderson (Eds.), *Gatekeeping in the mental health professions* (pp. 53–65). American Counseling Association.

DeLorenzi, L. D. (2018b). Evaluating trainee professional performance. In A. M. Homrich & K. L. Henderson (Eds.), *Gatekeeping in the mental health professions* (pp. 193–220). American Counseling Association.

Del Vecchio-Scully, D., & Glaser, M. (2018). Disaster recovery in Newtown: The intermediate phase. In J. Webber & J. B. Mascari (Eds.), *Disaster mental health counseling: A guide to preparing and responding* (4th ed., pp. 233–248). American Counseling Association.

de Shazer, S. (1991). *Putting difference to work.* Norton.

Disney, M. J., & Stephens, A. J. (1994). Legal issues in clinical supervision. In T. P. Remley Jr. (Ed.), *The ACA legal series* (Vol. 10). American Counseling Association.

Drinane, J. M., Owen, J., & Tao, K. W. (2018). Cultural concealment and therapy outcomes. *Journal of Counseling Psychology, 65*, 239–246. https://doi.org/10.1037/cou0000246

Duffey, T., & Haberstroh, S. (Eds.). (2020). *Introduction to crisis and trauma counseling.* American Counseling Association.

Dufrene, R. L. (2018). Collaboration during gatekeeping. In A. M Homrich & K. L. Henderson (Eds.),. *Gatekeeping in the mental health professions* (pp. 127–146). American Counseling Association.

Dupre, M., Echterling, L. G., Meixner, C., Anderson, R., & Kielty, M. (2014). Supervision experiences of professional counselors providing crisis counseling. *Counselor Education and Supervision, 53*(2), 82–96. https://doi.org/10.1002/j.1556-6978.2014.00050.x

Ericsson, K. A., & Pool, R. (2016). *Peak: Secrets from the new science of expertise.* Houghton Mifflin Harcourt.

Estrada, D., Singh, A. A., & Harper, A. J. (2017). Becoming an ally: Personal, clinical, and school-based social justice interventions. In M. M. Ginicola, C. Smith, & J. M. Filmore (Eds.), *Affirmative counseling with LGBTQI+ people* (pp. 343–358). American Counseling Association. https://doi.org/10.1002/9781119375517.ch25

Falender, C. A. (2017). Multiple relationships and clinical supervision. In O. Zur (Ed.), *Multiple relationships in psychotherapy and counseling: Unavoidable, common, and mandatory dual relations in therapy* (pp. 209–220). Routledge, Taylor & Francis.

Falender, C. (2018). Clinical supervision—The missing ingredient. *American Psychologist, 73*(9), 1240–1250. https://doi.org//10.1037/amp0000385

Falender, C., & Shafranske, E. (2017). *Supervision essentials for the practice of competency-based supervision.* American Psychological Association.

Falvey, J. E. (2002). *Managing clinical supervision: Ethical practice and legal risk management.* Brooks/Cole, Cengage Learning.

Falvo, D. R., & Holland, B. E. (2018). *Medical and psychosocial aspects of chronic illness and disability* (6th ed.). Jones & Bartlett Learning.

Finnerty, P., Kocet, M. M., Lutes, J., & Yates, C. (2017). Affirmative strengths-based counseling with LGBTQI+ people. In M. M. Ginicola, C. Smith, & J. M. Filmore (Eds.), *Affirmative counseling with LGBTQI+ people* (pp. 109–125). American Counseling Association.

Forrest, L., Elman, N., Gizara, S., & Vacha-Haase, T. (1999). Trainee impairment: A review of identification, remediation, dismissal, and legal issues. *The Counseling Psychologist, 27*(5), 627–686.

Francis, P. C. (2016). Religion and spirituality in counseling. In I. Marini & M. A. Stebnicki (Eds.), *The professional counselor's desk reference* (2nd ed., pp. 559–564). Springer.

Gallo, L. L. (2013). The need for developmental models in supervising school counselors. *Journal of School Counseling, 11*(19), 1–15. https://eric.ed.gov/contentdelivery/servlet/ERICServlet?accno=EJ1034741

Garner, B. A. (Ed.). (1999). *Black's law dictionary* (7th ed.). The West Group.

Garner, C. M., Webb, L. K., Chaffin, C., & Byars, A. (2017). The soul of supervision: Counselor spirituality. *Counseling and Values, 62*(1), 24–26.

Gaubatz, M. D., & Vera, E. M. (2002). Do formalized gatekeeping procedures increase programs' follow-up with deficient trainees? *Counselor Education and Supervision, 41*(4), 294–305.

Gaubatz, M. D., & Vera, E. M. (2006). Trainee competence in master's level counseling programs: A comparison of counselor educators' and students' views. *Counselor Education and Supervision, 46*(1), 32–43.

Ginicola, M. M., Smith, C., & Filmore, J. M. (Eds.). (2017). *Affirmative counseling with LGBTQI+ people*. American Counseling Association.

Goodrich, K. M., & Ginicola, M. M. (2017). Evidence-based practice for counseling the LGBTQI+ population. In M. M. Ginicola, C. Smith, & J. M. Filmore (Eds.), *Affirmative counseling with LGBTQI+ people* (pp. 97–107). American Counseling Association.

Gutierrez, D. (2018). The role of intersectionality in marriage and family therapy multicultural supervision. *American Journal of Family Therapy, 46*(1), 14–26. https://doi.org/10.1080/01926187.2018.1437573

Hanna, F. J., Talley, W. B., & Guindon, M. H. (2000). The power of perception: Toward a model of cultural oppression and liberation. *Journal of Counseling & Development, 78*(4), 430–441.

Harris, K. A., Randolph, B. E., & Gordon, E. (2016). What do clients want? Assessing spiritual needs in counseling: A literature review. *Spirituality in Clinical Practice, 3,* 250–275.

Hayes, J. A., Gelso, C. J., Kivlighan, D. M., & Goldberg, S. B. (2019). Managing countertransference. In J. C. Norcross & M. J. Lambert (Eds.), *Psychotherapy relationships that work* (3rd ed., pp. 532–548). Oxford University Press.

Hays, D. G. (2008). Assessing multicultural competence in counselor trainees: A review of instrumentation and future directions. *Journal of Counseling & Development, 86*(1), 95–101.

Hedegaard, H., Curtin, S. C., & Warner, M. (2018, November). *Suicide mortality in the United States, 1999–2017* (Data Brief No. 330). National Center for Health Statistics. https://www.cdc.gov/nchs/products/databriefs/db330.htm

Hein, S., & Lawson, G. (2008). Triadic supervision and its impact on the role of the supervisor: A qualitative examination of supervisors' perspectives. *Counselor Education and Supervision, 48*(1), 16–31.

Hein, S. F., Lawson, G., & Rodriguez, C. P. (2011). Supervisee incompatibility and its influence on triadic supervision: An examination of doctoral student supervisors' perspectives. *Counselor Education and Supervision, 50*(6), 422–436. https://doi.org/10.1002/j.1556-6978.2011.tb01925.x

Herlihy, B., & Corey, G. (2015a). *ACA ethical standards casebook* (7th ed.). American Counseling Association.

Herlihy, B., & Corey, G. (2015b). *Boundary issues in counseling: Multiple roles and responsibilities* (3rd ed.). American Counseling Association.

Hill, C. E., Knox, S., & Pinto-Coelho, K. G. (2019). Self-disclosure and immediacy. In J. C. Norcross & M. J. Lambert (Eds.), *Psychotherapy relationships that work: Evidence-based therapist contributions* (3rd ed., Vol. 1, pp. 379–420). Oxford University Press.

Holloway, E. L. (1995). *Clinical supervision: A systems approach.* Sage.

Holloway, E. L. (1999). A framework for supervision training. In E. Holloway & M. Carroll (Eds.), *Training counseling supervisors* (pp. 8–43). Sage.

Holt, H., Beutler, L. E., Kimpara, S., Macias, S., Haug, N. A., Shiloff, N., Goldblum, P., Temkin, R. S., & Stein, M. (2015). Evidence-based supervision: Tracking outcome and teaching principles of change in clinical supervision to bring science to integrative practice. *Psychotherapy, 52*(2), 185–189. https://doi.org/10.1037/a0038732

Homrich, A. M. (2018). Introduction to gatekeeping. In A. M. Homrich & K. L. Henderson (Eds.), *Gatekeeping in the mental health professions* (pp. 1–24). American Counseling Association.

Homrich, A. M., & Henderson, K. L. (Eds.). (2018). *Gatekeeping in the mental health professions*. American Counseling Association.

Hook, J. N., Captari, L. E., Hoyt, W., Davis, D. E., McElroy, S. E., & Worthington, E. L. (2019). Religion and spirituality. In J. C. Norcross, & B. E. Wampold (Eds.), *Psychotherapy relationships that work: Evidence-based therapist responsiveness* (3rd ed., Vol. 2, pp. 212–263). Oxford University Press.

Hutman, H., & Ellis, M. V. (2019, September 19). Supervisee nondisclosure in clinical supervision: Cultural and relational considerations. *Training and Education in Professional Psychology*. APA PsycNet. Advance online publication. https://doi.org/10.1037/tep0000290

Ivers, N. N., Rogers, J. L., Borders, L. D., & Turner, A. (2017). Using interpersonal process recall in clinical supervision to enhance supervisees' multicultural awareness. *The Clinical Supervisor, 36*(2), 282–303. https://doi.org/10.1080/07325223.2017.1320253

Jackson-Cherry, L., & Erford, B. T. (Eds.). (2018). *Crisis assessment, intervention, and prevention* (3rd ed.). Pearson Education.

Jaffee v. Redmond, WL 315 841(U.S. 1996).

James, R. K., & Gilliland, B. E. (2017). *Crisis intervention strategies* (8th ed.). Cengage Learning.

James, I. A., Milne, D., & Morse, R. (2008). Microskills of clinical supervision: Scaffolding skills. *Journal of Cognitive Psychotherapy: An International Quarterly, 22*(1), 29–36.

Jencius, M., & Baltrinic, E. R. (2016). Training counselors to provide online supervision. In T. Rousmaniere & E. Renfro-Michel (Eds.), *Using technology to enhance clinical supervision* (pp. 251–268). American Counseling Association.

Johnson, E. A. (2019). Recommendations to enhance psychotherapy supervision in psychology. *Canadian Psychology, 60*(4), 290–301. https://doi.org/10.1037/cap0000188

Johnson, W. B., Elman, N. S., Forrest, L., Robiner, W. N., Rodolfa, E., & Schaffer, J. B. (2008). Addressing professional competence problems in trainees: Some ethical considerations. *Professional Psychology: Research and Practice, 39*(6), 589–599.

Johnson, W. B., & Ridley, C. R. (2018). *The elements of mentoring* (3rd ed.). St. Martin's Press.

Kagan, N., Krathwohl, D. R., & Miller, R. (1963). Stimulated recall in therapy using videotape—A case study. *Journal of Counseling Psychology, 10,* 237–243.

Kanel, K. (2018). *A guide to crisis intervention* (6th ed.). Cengage Learning.

Kar Ray, M., Wyder, M., Crompton, D., Kousoulis, A. A., Arensman, E., Hafizi, S., Van Bortel, T., & Lombardo, C. (2019). PROTECT: Relational safety-based suicide prevention training frameworks. *International Journal of Mental Health Nursing, 29*(3), 533–543. https://doi.org/10.1111/inm.12685

Kaslow, N. J., Rubin, N. J., Bebeau, M. J., Leigh, I. W., Lichtenberg, J. W., Nelson, P. D., et al. (2007). Guiding principles and recommendations for the assessment of competence. *Professional Psychology: Research and Practice, 38*(5), 441–451.

Kaslow, N. J., Rubin, N. J., Forrest, L., Elman, N. S., Van Horne, B. A., Jacobs, S. C., et al. (2007). Recognizing, assessing, and intervening with problems of professional competence. *Professional Psychology: Research and Practice, 38*(5), 479–492.

Kerl, S. B., Garcia, J. L., McCullough, C. S., & Maxwell, M. E. (2002). Systemic evaluation of professional performance: Legally supported procedure and process. *Counselor Education and Supervision, 41*(4), 321–332.

Kitchener, K. S. (1984). Intuition, critical evaluation and ethical principles: The foundation for ethical decisions in counseling psychology. *The Counseling Psychologist, 12*(3), 43–55.

Kocet, M. M., & Herlihy, B. J. (2014). Addressing values-based conflicts within the counseling relationship: A decision-making model. *Journal of Counseling & Development, 92*(2), 180–186.

Koocher, G. P., & Keith-Spiegel, P. (2016). *Ethics in psychology and the mental health professions: Standards and cases* (4th ed). Oxford University Press.

Kozlowski, J. M., Pruitt, N. T., DeWalt, T. A., & Knox, S. (2014) Can boundary crossings in clinical supervision be beneficial? *Counselling Psychology Quarterly, 27*(2), 109–126. https://doi.org/10.1080/09515070.2013.870123

Lee, C. C. (Ed.). (2018). *Counseling for social justice* (3rd ed.). American Counseling Association Foundation.

Lee, C. C. (2019a). Multicultural competency: A conceptual framework for counseling across cultures. In C. C. Lee (Ed.), *Multicultural issues in counseling: New approaches to diversity* (5th ed., pp. 3–13). American Counseling Association.

Lee, C. C. (Ed.). (2019b). *Multicultural issues in counseling: New approaches to diversity* (5th ed.). American Counseling Association.

Lee, C. C., Baldwin, R., Mamara, S. M., & Quesenberry, L. (2018). Counselors as agents of social justice. In C. C. Lee (Ed.), *Counseling for social justice* (3rd ed., pp. 3–20). American Counseling Association Foundation.

Lee, C. C., & Zalkalne, E. (2019). The culturally competent counselor as an agent of social justice. In C. C. Lee (Ed.), *Multicultural issues in counseling: New approaches to diversity* (5th ed., pp. 273–276). American Counseling Association.

Lewis, C. C., Scott, K. E., & Hendricks, K. E. (2014). A model and guide for evaluating supervision outcomes in cognitive behavioral therapy-focused training programs. *Training and Education in Professional Psychology, 8*(3), 165–173. https://doi.org/10.1037/tep0000029

Li, C., & Vasquez-Nuttal, E. (2009). School consultants as agents of social justice for multicultural children and families. *Journal of Educational and Psychological Consultation, 19*(1), 26–44.

Liese, B. S., & Beck, J. S. (1997). Cognitive therapy supervision. In C. E. Watkins Jr. (Ed.), *Handbook of psychotherapy supervision* (pp. 114–133). Wiley.

Lonn, M. R., & Juhnke, G. (2017). Nondisclosure in triadic supervision: A phenomenological study of counseling students. *Counselor Education and Supervision, 56*(2), 82–97. https://doi.org/10.1002/ceas.12064

Lowry, J. L. (2001, August). Successful supervision: Supervisor and supervisee characteristics. In J. Barnett (Chair), *The secrets of successful supervision* (Symposium). American Psychological Association, San Francisco, CA.

MacKay, L., & Brown, J. (2014). Collaborative approaches to family systems supervision: Differentiation of self. *Australian and New Zealand Journal of Family Therapy, 34*, 325–337. https://doi.org/10.1002/anzf.1036

Marini, I., & Stebnicki, M.A. (Eds.). (2018). *The psychological and social impact of illness and disability* (7th ed.). Springer Publishing.

Martin P., Lizarondo L., & Kumar S. (2018). A systematic review of the factors that influence the quality and effectiveness of telesupervision for health professionals. *Journal of Telemedicine Telecare, 24*(4), 271–281. https://doi.org/10.1177/1357633X17698868

Martinez, L. J., Davis, K. C., & Dahl, B. (1999). Feminist ethical challenges in supervision: A trainee perspective. *Women and Therapy, 22*(4), 35–54.

Martino, C. (2001). *Secrets of successful supervision: Graduate student's preferences and experiences with effective and ineffective supervision* (Symposium). American Psychological Association, San Francisco, CA.

McAdams, C. R., III, & Keener, H. J. (2008). Preparation, action, recovery: A conceptual framework for counselor preparation and response in client crises. *Journal of Counseling & Development, 86*(4), 388–398.

McKinley, M. T. (2019). Supervising the sojourner: Multicultural supervision of international students. *Training and Education in Professional Psychology, 13*(3), 174–179. https://doi.org/10.1037/tep0000269

McNeill, B. W., & Stoltenberg, C. D. (2016). *Supervision essentials for the integrative developmental model.* American Psychological Association.

Metzl, J. M., & Hansen, H. (2014). Structural competency: Theorizing a new medical engagement with stigma and inequality. *Social Science & Medicine, 103,* 126–133.

Mosher, P. W., & Swire, P. P. (2002). The ethical and legal implications of *Jafee v Redmond* and the HIPAA medical privacy rule for psychotherapy and general psychiatry. *Psychiatric Clinics of North America, 25,* 575–584.

Moulton, P. (2019a). *Helping others.* Ekta Publishing.

Moulton, P. (2019b). *Team-based supervision: A process model* [Unpublished manuscript]. Department of Psychology, Northwestern State University.

Muratori, M. C. (2001, September). Examining supervisor impairment from the counselor trainee's perspective. *Counselor Education and Supervision, 41*(1), 41–56.

Muratori, M., & Haynes, R. (2020). *Coping skills for a stressful world: A workbook for counselors and clients.* American Counseling Association.

Murphy, J. J. (2015). *Solution-focused counseling in schools* (3rd ed.). American Counseling Association.

Myer, R. A., James, R. K., & Moulton P. (2011). *This is not a fire drill: Crisis intervention and prevention on college campuses.* John Wiley & Sons.

National Aeronautics and Space Administration. (2020, January 15). *NASA, NOAA analyses reveal 2019 second warmest year on record.* https://climate.nasa.gov/news/2945/nasa-noaa-analyses-reveal-2019-second-warmest-year-on-record/

National Association of Social Workers. (1994). *Guidelines for clinical social work supervision.*

National Association of Social Workers. (2017). *Code of ethics.*

National Board for Certified Counselors. (1999). *Standards for the ethical practice of supervision.*

National Board for Certified Counselors. (2016). *National Board for Certified Counselors (NBCC) code of ethics.* http://www.nbcc.org/assets/ethics,/nbcc-codeofethics.pdf

National Center for Education Statistics. (2019, April 17). New report on crime and safety in schools and college campuses (Blog). https://nces.ed.gov/blogs/nces/post/New-Report-on-Crime-and-Safety-in-Schools-and-College-Campuses

National Child Traumatic Stress Network. (2006). *Psychological first aid operations guide* (2nd ed.). https://www.nctsn.org/sites/default/files/resources//pfa_field_operations_guide.pdf

National Organization for Human Services. (2015). *Ethical standards for human services professionals.*

Nelson, J. A., Nichter, M., & Henriksen, R. (2010). *On-line supervision and face-to-face supervision in the counseling internship: An exploratory study of similarities and differences.* http://counselingoutfitters.com/ vistas/vistas10/Article_46.pdf.

Norberg, J., Axelsson, H., Barkman, N., Hamrin, M., & Carlsson, J. (2016) What psychodynamic supervisors say about supervision: Freedom within limits, *The Clinical Supervisor, 35*(2), 268–286. https://doi.org/10.1080/07325223.2016.1219896

Norcross, J. C., & Beutler, L. E. (2019). Integrative psychotherapies. In D. Wedding, & R. J. Corsini (Eds.), *Current psychotherapies* (11th ed., pp. 527–560). Cengage Learning.

Norcross, J. C., & Lambert, M. J. (2014). Relationship science and practice in psychotherapy: Closing commentary. *Psychotherapy, 51,* 398–403. doi:10.1037/a0037418

Norcross, J. C., & Lambert, M. J. (Eds.). (2019). *Psychotherapy relationships that work: Evidence-based therapist contributions* (3rd ed., Vol. 1). Oxford University Press.

Norcross, J. C., & Popple, L. M. (2017). *Supervision essentials for integrative psychotherapy.* American Psychological Association.

Norcross, J. C., & VandenBos, G. R. (2018). *Leaving it at the office: A guide to psychotherapist self-care* (2nd ed.). Guilford Press.

Norcross, J. C., & Wampold, B. E. (Eds.). (2019). *Psychotherapy relationships that work: Evidence-based responsiveness* (3rd ed., Vol. 2). Oxford University Press.

Orlinsky, D. E., Geller, J. D., & Norcross, J. C. (2005). Epilogue: The patient psychotherapist, the psychotherapist's psychotherapist, and the therapist as a person. In J. D. Geller, J. C. Norcross, & D. E. Orlinsky (Eds.), *The psychotherapist's own psychotherapy: Patient and clinician perspectives* (pp. 405–415). Oxford University Press.

Polychronis, P. D., & Brown, S. G. (2016). The strict liability standard and clinical supervision. *Professional Psychology: Research and Practice, 47*(2), 139–146.

Purswell, K. E., Willis, B. T., & Lara, A. C. (2019). Counselor development across the lifespan: A Q methodology study. *Journal of Counselor Leadership and Advocacy, 6*(2), 129–143. https://doi.org/10.1080/2326716X.2019.1628674

Qi, W., Wang, Z., Wu, L. Z., & Luo, X. (2019). Multicultural supervision with Chinese international trainees. *Training and Education in Professional Psychology, 13*(3), 185–193. https://doi.org/10.1037/tep0000254

Radis, B. (2020). Reflections on facilitating a trauma-informed clinical supervision group with housing first staff. *Social Work with Groups, 43*(1–2), 46–51. https://doi.org/10.1080/01609513.2019.1638654

Ramos-Sánchez, L., Esnil, G., Goodwin, A., Riggs, S., Touster, L. O., Wright, L. K., et al. (2002). Negative supervisory events: Effects on supervision satisfaction and supervisory alliance. *Professional Psychology: Research and Practice, 33*(2), 197–202.

Ratts, M. J., Singh, A. A., Nassar-McMillan, S., Butler, S. K., & McCullough, J. R. (2015). *Multicultural and social justice counseling competencies.* American Counseling Association. http://www.counseling.org/docs/default-source/competencies/multicultural-and-social-justice-counseling-competencies.pdf?sfvrsn=20

Ratts, M. J., Singh, A. A., Nassar-McMillan, S., Butler, S. K., & McCullough, J. R. (2016). Multicultural and social justice counseling competencies: Guidance for the counseling profession. *Journal of Multicultural Counseling and Development, 44*(1), 28–48. https://doi.org/10.1002/jmcd.12035

Remley, T. P. (2009). Legal challenges in counseling suicidal students. In D. Capuzzi (Ed.), *Suicide prevention in the schools: Guidelines for middle and high school settings* (2nd ed., pp. 71–83). American Counseling Association.

Remley, T. P., & Herlihy, B. (2020). *Ethical, legal, and professional issues in counseling* (6th ed.). Pearson.

Ross, D. (2014). *Spirituality in supervision: A phenomenological study* [Doctoral dissertation, Georgia State University]. ScholarWorks@Georgia State University. http://scholarworks.gsu.edu/cps_diss/96

Rousmaniere, T. G. (2017). *Deliberate practice for psychotherapists: A guide to improving clinical effectiveness.* Routledge.

Rousmaniere, T. G. (2019). *Mastering the inner skills of psychotherapy: A deliberate practice handbook.* Gold Lantern Press.

Rousmaniere, T., Goodyear, R. K., Miller, S. D., & Wampold, B. E. (Eds.). (2017). *The cycle of excellence: Using deliberate practice to improve supervision and training.* Wiley.

Rousmaniere, T., & Renfro-Michel, E. (Eds.). (2016). *Using technology to enhance clinical supervision.* American Counseling Association. https://doi.org/10.1002/9781119268499.ch02

Rudd, M. D., Cukrowicz, K. C., & Bryan, C. J. (2008). Core competencies in suicide risk assessment and management: Implications for supervision. *Training and Education in Professional Psychology, 2*(4), 219–228.

Russell-Chapin, L. A. (2016). Integrating neurocounseling into the counseling profession: An introduction. *Journal of Mental Health Counseling, 38*(2), 93–102. https://doi.org/:l0.17744/mehc.38.2.0l

Russell-Chapin, L. A., & Chapin T. J. (2020). *Integrating neurocounseling in clinical supervision: Strategies for success.* Routledge.

Saccuzzo, D. (1997). Law and psychology. *California Law Review, 34*(115), 1–37.

Sahker, E. (2016). Therapy with the nonreligious: Ethical and clinical considerations. *Professional Psychology: Research and Practice, 47*(4), 295–302.

Sampson, J. M., Kelly-Trombley, H. M., Zubatsky, J. M., & Harris, S. M. (2013). Breaking up is hard to do: Dismissing students from MFT training programs. *The American Journal of Family Therapy, 41*, 26–33. https://doi.org/10.1080/01926187.2011.628205

Scarborough, J. L., Bernard, J. M., & Morse, R. M. (2006). Boundary considerations between doctoral students and master's students. *Counseling and Values, 51*(1), 53–65.

Seponski, D. M., & Jordan, L. S. (2018). Cross-cultural supervision in international settings: Experiences of foreign supervisors and native supervisees in Cambodia. *Journal of Family Therapy, 40*(2), 247–264. https://doi.org/10.1111/1467-6427.12157

Shilkret, C. J. (2012). A control-mastery view of case consultation. *Smith College Studies in Social Work, 82*(2–3), 161–170. https://doi.org/10.1080/00377317.2012.693014

Skovholt, T. M., & Rønnestad, M. H. (1992). Themes in therapist and counselor development. *Journal of Counseling & Development, 70*(4), 505–515. https://doi.org/10.1002/j.1556-6676.1992.tb01646.x

Skovholt, T. M., & Rønnestad, M. H. (1995). The evolving professional self: Stages and themes in therapist and counselor development. *Journal of Career Development, 30*(1), 5–44.

Skovholt, T. M., & Rønnestad, M. H. (2012). Path toward mastery: Phases and themes of development. In T. M. Skovholt (Ed.), *Becoming a therapist: On the path to mastery* (pp. 181–202). Wiley.

Sofronoff, K., Helmes, E., & Pachana, N. (2011). Fitness to practice in the profession of psychology: Should we assess this during clinical training? *Australian Psychologist, 46*, 126–132.

Sommers-Flanagan, J., & Sommers-Flanagan, R. (2021). *Suicide assessment and treatment planning for counselors: A strengths-based approach.* American Counseling Association.

Stebnicki, M. A. (2008). *Empathy fatigue: Healing the mind, body, and spirit of professional counselors.* Springer.

Stebnicki, M. A. (2016). From empathy fatigue to empathy resiliency. In I. Marini & M. A. Stebnicki (Eds.), *The professional counselor's desk reference* (2nd ed., pp. 533–545). Springer.

Stebnicki, M. A. (2017). *Disaster mental health counseling: Responding to trauma in a multicultural context.* Springer.

Stebnicki, M. A. (2021). *Clinical military counseling: Guidelines for practice.* American Counseling Association.

Stinchfield, T. A., Hill, N. R., & Bowers, R. (2019). Integrative reflective model of group supervision: Practicum students' experiences. *Counselor Education and Supervision, 58*(2), 141–157. https://doi.org/10.1002/ceas.12137

Stoltenberg, C. D., & McNeill, B. W. (2010). *IDM supervision: An integrative developmental model for supervising counselors and therapists* (3rd ed.). Routledge.

Stoltenberg, C. D., McNeill, B., & Delworth, U. (1998). *IDM supervision: An integrated developmental model for supervising counselors and therapists.* Jossey-Bass.

Sue, D. W., Arredondo, P., & McDavis, R. J. (1992). Multicultural counseling competencies and standards: A call to the profession. *Journal of Counseling & Development, 70*, 477–486.

Sue, D. W., & Sue, D. (2016). *Counseling the culturally diverse: Theory and practice* (7th ed.). Wiley.

Sue, D. W., Sue, D., Neville, H. A., & Smith, L. (2019). *Counseling the culturally diverse: Theory and practice* (8th ed.). Wiley.

Tanner, M. A., Gray, J. J., & Haaga, D. A. F. (2012). Association of cotherapy supervision with client outcomes, attrition, and trainee effectiveness in a psychotherapy training clinic. *Journal of Clinical Psychology, 68*(12), 1241–1252. https://doi.org/10.1002/jclp.21902

Tarvydas, V. M., Levers, L. L., & Teahen, P. R. (2017). Ethical guidelines for mass trauma and complex humanitarian emergencies. *Journal of Counseling & Development, 95*(3), 260–268. https://doi.org/10.1002/jcad.12140

Taylor, R. J., & Gonzales, F. (2005). Communication flow and change theory within a family therapy supervision model. *Contemporary Family Therapy, 27*(2), 163–176.

Thanasia, P. I. (2018). Informing trainees about gatekeeping policies. In A. M. Homrich & K. L. Henderson (Eds.), *Gatekeeping in the mental health professions* (pp. 147–170). American Counseling Association.

Thomas, F. C., Bowie, J-A., Hill, L., & Taknint, J. T. (2019). Growth-promoting supervision: Reflections from women of color psychology trainees. *Training and Education in Professional Psychology, 13*(3), 167–173. https://doi.org/10.1037/tep0000244

Thomas, F. N. (1994). Solution-oriented supervision: The coaxing of expertise. *The Family Journal: Counseling and Therapy for Couples and Families, 2*(1), 11–18.

Thomas, J. T. (2007). Informed consent through contracting for supervision: Minimizing risks, enhancing benefits. *Professional Psychology: Research and Practice, 38*(3), 221–231.

Thomas, J. T. (2014). Disciplinary supervision following ethics complaints: Goals, tasks, and ethical dimensions. *Journal of Clinical Psychology, 70*(11), 1104–1114. https://doi.org/10.1002/jclp.22131

Thompson, B. L., Luoma, J. B., Terry, C. M., LeJeune, J. T., Guinther, P. M., & Robb, H. (2015). Creating a peer-led acceptance and commitment therapy consultation group: The Portland model. *Journal of Contextual Behavioral Science, 4*(3), 144–150.

Tohidian, N. B., & Quek, K. M.-T. (2017). Processes that inform multicultural supervision: A qualitative meta-analysis. *Journal of Marital and Family Therapy, 43*(4), 573–590. https://doi.org/10.1111/jmft.12219

Tromski-Klingshirn, D. M., & Davis, T. E. (2007). Supervisees' perceptions of their clinical supervision: A study of the dual role of clinical and administrative supervisor. *Counselor Education and Supervision, 46*(4), 294–304.

Valentino, A. L., LeBlanc, L. A., & Sellers, T. P. (2016). The benefits of group supervision and a recommended structure for implementation. *Behavior Analysis in Practice, 9*(4), 320–328. https://doi.org/10.1007/s40617-016-0138-8

Waalkes, P. L., DeCino, D. A., & Borders, L. D. (2018). The found poet: A new role for the structured peer group supervision model. *Journal of Poetry Therapy, 31*(1), 15–25. https://doi.org/10.1080/08893675.2018.1396727

Wahesh, E. (2016). Utilizing motivational interviewing to address resistant behaviors in clinical supervision. *Counselor Education and Supervision, 55*(1), 46–59. https://doi.org/10.1002/ceas.12032

Watson Institute. (2020). *Cost of war: U.S. veterans & military families.* https://watson.brown.edu/costsofwar/costs/human/veterans

Webber, J. M., & Mascari, J. B. (Eds.). (2018). *Disaster mental health counseling: A guide to preparing and responding* (4th ed.). American Counseling Association Foundation.

Weck, F., Jakob, M., Neng, J. M. B., Höfling, V., Grikscheit, F., & Bohus, M. (2016). The effects of bug-in-the-eye supervision on therapeutic alliance and therapist competence in cognitive-behavioural therapy: A randomized controlled trial. *Clinical Psychology and Psychotherapy, 23*, 386–396. https://doi.org/10.1002/cpp.1968

Welfel, E. R., Werth, J. L., Jr., & Benjamin, G. A. H. (2009). Introduction to the duty to protect. In J. L. Werth Jr., E. R. Welfel, & G. A. H. Benjamin (Eds.), *The duty to protect: Ethical, legal, and professional considerations for mental health professionals* (pp. 3–8). American Psychological Association.

Westefeld, J. S. (2009). Supervision in psychotherapy: Models, issues, and recommendations. *The Counseling Psychologist, 37*(2), 296–316.

Wheeler, A. M., & Bertram, B. (2019). *The counselor and the law: A guide to legal and ethical practice* (8th ed.). American Counseling Association.

Whisenhunt, J. L., DuFresne, R. M., Stargell, N. A., Rovnak, A., Zoldan, C. A., & Kress, V. E. (2017). Supporting counselors after a client suicide: Creative supervision techniques. *Journal of Creativity in Mental Health, 12*(4), 451–467. https://doi.org/10.1080/15401383. 2017.1281184

Williamson, J., & Williamson, D. (Eds.). (2021). *Distance counseling and supervision: A guide for mental health clinicians.* American Counseling Association.

World Health Organization. (2016). *Injury-related disability and rehabilitation.* http://www. who.int/violence_injury_prevention/disability/en/

Wubbolding, R. E. (2017). *Reality therapy and self-evaluation: The key to client change.* American Counseling Association.

Yee, T. (2018). Supervising East Asian international students: Incorporating culturally responsive supervision into the integrated developmental model. *The Clinical Supervisor, 37*(2), 298–312. https://doi.org/10.1080/07325223.2018.1449156

Young, J. S., & Cashwell, C. S. (2020). Integrating spirituality and religion into counseling: An introduction. In C. S. Cashwell & J. S. Young (Eds.), *Integrating spirituality and religion into counseling* (3rd ed., pp. 3–29). American Counseling Association.

Younggren, J. N. (2000). Is managed care really just another unethical Model T? *The Counseling Psychologist, 28*(2), 253–262. https://doi.org/10.1177/001000000282004

Zhou, X., Zhu, P., & Miao, I. Y. (2019). Incorporating an acculturation perspective into the integrative developmental model (IDM) in supervising international trainees. *Training and Education in Professional Psychology.* Advance online publication. https://doi.org/10.1037/tep0000278

Zur, O. (2007). *Boundaries in psychotherapy: Ethical and clinical explorations.* American Psychological Association.

Zur, O. (Ed.). (2017). *Multiple relationships in psychotherapy and counseling: Unavoidable, common, and mandatory dual relations in therapy.* Routledge, Taylor & Francis.

SUBJECT INDEX

Boxes and figures are indicated by "b" and "f" following the page numbers, respectively.
A separate Name Index follows the Subject Index.

A

(continued)

(continued)

(continued)

NAME INDEX